50th Anniversary
WHAT'S COOKIN'?

Tennessee Farmers' Cooperative
Cookbook

This cookbook is a collection of our favorite recipes,
which are not necessarily original recipes.

Published by:
TENNESSEE FARMERS COOPERATIVE
200 Waldron Road
P. O. Box 3003
LaVergne, Tennessee 37086

Library of Congress Number: 95-60115
ISBN 0-87197-422-3

Edited, Designed and Manufactured in the United States of America by:
Favorite Recipes® Press
P. O. Box 305142
Nashville, Tennessee 37230
1-800-358-0560

First Printing: 1995   12,500

Contents

Acknowledgement

We would like to thank each and every one of the dedicated cooks who have kept the "What's Cookin'?" column supplied with mouth-watering recipes through the years. The recipes found within this book represent only a portion of those that have appeared in the "What's Cookin'?" column. To our dismay, the cookbook just wasn't big enough to include the overwhelming number of recipes we've collected since the column's inception in June 1978.

We appreciate our faithful readers and ask that you keep those delicious recipes coming.

50 Years of Service

"We couldn't get along without the Co-op!"

That's the statement you hear more and more from folks all across Tennessee who have come to rely on Co-op for the products and services they need for their farms, homes, lawns, vehicles, livestock, or pets.

Co-op is among the most popular and respected businesses in towns and cities of all sizes — from Moscow (population 384) to Clarksville (75,494) to Nashville (487,969). Regardless of the size of the town in which it operates, Co-op is seen as a cornerstone of the community, owned and operated by the people who do business with it.

It is the responsibility of Tennessee Farmers Cooperative (TFC), headquartered at LaVergne near Nashville, to manufacture, procure, and distribute top-quality products for the Co-ops to sell to their customers. TFC has 71 member Co-ops that operate nearly 150 retail outlets in 85 of Tennessee's 95 counties.

Chartered on September 27, 1945, TFC has manufacturing, distribution, and research facilities to serve member Co-ops and their customers across the state. At the LaVergne complex are the corporate offices, two feed mills, fertilizer plant, distribution center, testing laboratory, tire shop, material handling facility, and metal fabrication plant.

Co-ops in West Tennessee are served from a Jackson complex that's made up of a feed mill, distribution center, and fertilizer plant. TFC also operates a seed plant at Halls in West Tennessee, and one of FFR Cooperative's soybean research facilities is at Jackson.

TFC's Tenco complex — with two feed mills, fertilizer plant, and distribution center — near Maryville serves Co-ops in East Tennessee.

Co-op is proud of the record of service it has established during its 50-year history. The spirit of cooperation that breathed life into the Co-op system has nurtured it through the years and will help it grow and prosper in the future.

Member Co-ops

Anderson Farmers Cooperative — *Clinton*

Bedford Farmers Cooperative —
Shelbyville – Lynchburg

Benton Farmers Cooperative — *Camden*

Bledsoe Farmers Cooperative —
Pikeville – Dayton

Blount Greenback Farmers Cooperative —
Maryville – Greenback

Bradley Farmers Cooperative — *Cleveland*

Carroll Farmers Cooperative —
Huntingdon – Trezevant

Claiborne Farmers Cooperative —
New Tazewell – LaFollette – Speedwell

Cocke Farmers Cooperative — *Newport*

Coffee Farmers Cooperative — *Manchester*

Crockett Farmers Cooperative — *Alamo*

Cumberland Farmers Cooperative — *Crossville*

Davidson Farmers Cooperative — *Nashville*

Decatur Farmers Cooperative — *Decaturville*

DeKalb Farmers Cooperative — *Smithville*

Dickson Farmers Cooperative — *Dickson*

Dyer-Lauderdale Farmers, Inc. —
Dyersburg – Newbern – Ripley – Halls

Fentress Farmers Cooperative — *Jamestown*

Franklin Farmers Cooperative —
Decherd – Huntland

Gibson Farmers Cooperative —
Trenton – Dyer – Humboldt

Giles Farmers Cooperative —
Pulaski – Lynnville

Grainger Farmers Cooperative — *Rutledge*

Greene Farmers Cooperative — *Greeneville*

Grundy Farmers Cooperative —
Pelham – Coalmont

Hamblen Farmers Cooperative — *Morristown*

Hancock Farmers Cooperative — *Sneedville*

Hardeman Fayette Farmers Cooperative —
*Bolivar – Grand Junction – Moscow
– Somerville*

Hardin Farmers Cooperative — *Savannah*

Hawkins Farmers Cooperative — *Rogersville*

Haywood Farmers Cooperative — *Brownsville*

Henderson Chester Farmers Cooperative —
Lexington – Henderson

Henry Farmers Cooperative —
Paris – Cottage Grove – Henry

Hickman Farmers Cooperative — *Centerville*

Houston Farmers Cooperative — *Erin*

Humphreys Farmers Cooperative — *Waverly*

Jefferson Farmers Cooperative —
Dandridge – Jefferson City

Knox Farmers Cooperative — *Knoxville*

Member Co-ops

Lawrence Farmers Cooperative —
Lawrenceburg – St. Joseph

Lewis Farmers Cooperative — Hohenwald

Lincoln Farmers Cooperative —
Fayetteville – Petersburg

Macon Trousdale Farmers Cooperative —
Lafayette – Hartsville

Madison Farmers Cooperative —
Jackson – Mercer

Marion Farmers Cooperative — Jasper

Marshall Farmers Cooperative —
Lewisburg – Chapel Hill

Maury Farmers Cooperative —
Columbia – Mt. Pleasant – Spring Hill

McMinn Loudon Farmers Cooperative —
Athens – Decatur – Loudon

McNairy Farmers Cooperative — Selmer

Monroe Farmers Cooperative —
Madisonville – Sweetwater – Tellico Plains

Montgomery Farmers Cooperative — Clarksville

Morgan Farmers Corporation — Wartburg

Obion Farmers Cooperative —
Union City – Kenton – Obion

Overton Farmers Cooperative —
Livingston – Bydstown

Perry Farmers Cooperative — Linden

Putnam Farmers Cooperative — Cookeville

Roane Farmers Cooperative — Harriman

Robertson Chatham Farmers Cooperative —
Springfield – Ashland City – Adams

Rutherford Farmers Cooperative —
Murfreesboro – Eagleville – Woodbury

Scott Farmers Cooperative — Oneida

Sequatchie Farmers Cooperative — Dunlap

Sevier Farmers Cooperative — Sevierville

Smith Farmers Cooperative — Carthage

Sumner Farmers Cooperative — Gallatin

Tipton Farmers Cooperative — Covington

Tri-State Growers — Mountain City

Union Farmers Cooperative — Maynardville

Warren Farmers Cooperative — McMinnville

Washington Farmers Cooperative —
Jonesborough – Erwin

Wayne Farmers Cooperative — Waynesboro

Weakley Farmers Cooperative —
Martin – Gleason – Greenfield

White County Farmers Cooperative — Sparta

Williamson Farmers Cooperative — Franklin

Wilson Farmers Cooperative — Lebanon

Nutritional Profile Guidelines

The editors have attempted to present family recipes in a form that allows approximate nutritional values to be computed. Persons with dietary or health problems or whose diets require close monitoring should not rely solely on the nutritional information provided. They should consult their physicians or a registered dietitian for specific information.

Abbreviations for Nutritional Profile

Cal — Calories	Fiber — Dietary Fiber	Sod — Sodium
Prot — Protein	T Fat — Total Fat	g — gram
Carbo — Carbohydrates	Chol — Cholesterol	mg — milligrams

Nutritional information for these recipes is computed from information derived from many sources, including materials supplied by the United States Department of Agriculture, computer databanks and journals in which the information is assumed to be in the public domain. However, many specialty items, new products and processed foods may not be available from these sources or may vary from the average values used in these profiles. More information on new and/or specific products may be obtained by reading the nutrient labels. Unless otherwise specified, the nutritional profile of these recipes is based on all measurements being level.

- **Artificial sweeteners** vary in use and strength so should be used "to taste," using the recipe ingredients as a guideline. Sweeteners using aspartame (Nutra-Sweet and Equal) should not be used as a sweetener in recipes involving prolonged heating which reduces the sweet taste. For further information, refer to package information.
- **Alcoholic ingredients** have been analyzed for the basic ingredients, although cooking causes the evaporation of alcohol thus decreasing caloric content.
- **Buttermilk, sour cream** and **yogurt** are the types available commercially.
- **Cake mixes** which are prepared using package directions include 3 eggs and 1/2 cup oil.
- **Chicken**, cooked for boning and chopping, has been roasted; this method yields the lowest caloric values.
- **Cottage cheese** is cream-style with 4.2% creaming mixture. Dry curd cottage cheese has no creaming mixture.
- **Eggs** are all large. To avoid raw eggs that may carry salmonella as in eggnog or 6-week muffin batter, use an equivalent amount of commercial egg substitute.
- **Flour** is unsifted all-purpose flour.
- **Garnishes**, serving suggestions and other optional additions and variations are not included in the profile.
- **Margarine** and **butter** are regular, not whipped or presoftened.
- **Milk** is whole milk, 3.5% butterfat. Lowfat milk is 1% butterfat. Evaporated milk is whole milk with 60% of the water removed.
- **Oil** is any type of vegetable cooking oil. Shortening is hydrogenated vegetable shortening.
- **Salt** and other ingredients to taste as noted in the ingredients have not been included in the nutritional profile.
- If a choice of ingredients has been given, the nutritional profile information reflects the first option. If a choice of amounts has been given, the nutritional profile reflects the greater amount.

CHAPTER 1

Appetizers, Snacks, & Beverages

Cat Nap

Shielding themselves from the
biting cold of winter, these
feline friends huddle together
for warmth and a little cat nap.

Alice Morrow's Cheese Ball

Mickey Clark, Hermitage

8 ounces Cheddar cheese, grated
1 tablespoon finely chopped pimento
1 tablespoon finely chopped greem
   bell pepper
1 tablespoon finely chopped onion
1/4 teaspoon salt
1 teaspoon Worcestershire sauce
1 cup chopped pecans
16 ounces cream cheese, softened

Combine Cheddar cheese, pimento, green pepper, onion, salt, Worcestershire sauce and 1/2 cup pecans in large bowl. Add cream cheese; mix well. Shape mixture into ball or log. Roll in remaining pecans. Yield: 48 servings.

Approx Per Serving: Cal 69; Prot 2 g; Carbo <1 g; Fiber <1 g; T Fat 7 g; 84% Calories from Fat; Chol 15 mg; Sod 70 mg.

Wafered Beef Cheese Ball

Jenny L. Harrell, Tullahoma

16 ounces cream cheese, softened
5 ounces wafered beef, finely chopped
2 green onions, finely chopped
2 teaspoons MSG
1 teaspoon Worcestershire sauce

Place cream cheese in large bowl; whip well by hand. Add half the beef and remaining ingredients; mix well. Chill, covered, for 2 hours or until firm. Shape into ball. Roll in remaining beef, coating completely. Cover with plastic wrap; chill until serving time. Serve with assorted crackers. May substitute wafered ham for wafered beef if desired. Yield: 32 servings.

Approx Per Serving: Cal 57; Prot 2 g; Carbo <1 g; Fiber <1 g; T Fat 5 g; 80% Calories from Fat; Chol 18 mg; Sod 465 mg.

Bacon Poles

Ernestine Jones, Gallatin

10 thin slices bacon
20 long thin garlic bread sticks

Cut bacon slices in half lengthwise, making 2 long thin strips from each slice. Wrap bacon strip in spiral "barber pole" fashion around each bread stick. Place 2 paper towels in bottom of 3-quart oblong glass baking dish. Arrange bread sticks, not touching, on towels. Cover with paper towel. Microwave at High for 8 to 10 minutes or until bacon is cooked, rotating dish 1/2 turn after 4 minutes. Remove poles as they are cooked. Arrange poles in circle spoke-fashioned on serving plate. May serve small squares Cheddar cheese in center if desired.
Yield: 20 servings.

Approx Per Serving: Cal 138; Prot 5 g; Carbo 23 g; Fiber 0 g; T Fat 3 g; 17% Calories from Fat; Chol 7 mg; Sod 301 mg.

Chicken Log

Joan Overton, Tazewell

1½ cups chopped cooked chicken
1 tablespoon Heinz 57 sauce
½ teaspoon curry powder
2 tablespoons dried parsley flakes
8 ounces cream cheese, softened
⅓ cup finely chopped celery
½ cup finely chopped pecans

Combine chicken, sauce, curry powder, parsley, cream cheese and celery in medium bowl; mix well. Shape into log. Roll in pecans. Chill, covered, for 2 hours. May serve with assorted crackers if desired. Yield: 32 servings.

Approx Per Serving: Cal 50; Prot 3 g; Carbo <1 g; Fiber <1 g; T Fat 4 g; 74% Calories from Fat; Chol 14 mg; Sod 36 mg.

Party Wieners

Mrs. Charlie Guy, Troy

2 cups barbecue sauce
½ cup catsup
3 tablespoons Worcestershire sauce
1 tablespoon dark brown sugar
½ cup grape jelly
½ cup water
3 pounds wieners, cut into small pieces

Combine barbecue sauce, catsup, Worcestershire sauce, brown sugar, grape jelly and water in Crock●Pot. Heat on Low. Add wieners. Simmer for 1 to 2 hours. Remove wieners from sauce; serve warm. Serve sauce as dip for wieners. Yield: 60 servings.

Approx Per Serving: Cal 88; Prot 3 g; Carbo 4 g; Fiber <1 g; T Fat 7 g; 69% Calories from Fat; Chol 11 mg; Sod 355 mg.

Easy Sausage Balls

Billie Ries, Smyrna

1½ pounds bulk hot pork sausage
10 ounces sharp Cheddar cheese, grated
3 cups baking mix

Preheat oven to 350 degrees. Crumble sausage in large bowl. Add cheese; mix well. Let stand at room temperature for 1 hour. Add baking mix, 1 cup at a time, mixing well after each addition. Shape into 1-inch balls. Place on ungreased cookie sheet. Bake for 13 to 15 minutes or until lightly browned. Serve warm.
Yield: 42 (2 balls) servings.

Approx Per Serving: Cal 85; Prot 4 g; Carbo 4 g; Fiber <1 g; T Fat 6 g; 63% Calories from Fat; Chol 14 mg; Sod 226 mg.

Sausage Balls

Mrs. Malcom Price, Sparta

2 pounds bulk sausage
12 ounces Cheddar cheese, shredded
5 cups baking mix

Preheat oven to 350 degrees. Combine sausage and cheese in large bowl. Let stand at room temperature for 1 hour. Add baking mix, 1 cup at a time, mixing well after each addition. Shape into 1-inch balls. Place on ungreased cookie sheet. Bake for 12 to 15 minutes or until lightly browned. Yield: 60 servings.

Approx Per Serving: Cal 89; Prot 4 g; Carbo 6 g; Fiber <1 g; T Fat 6 g; 56% Calories from Fat; Chol 12 mg; Sod 248 mg.

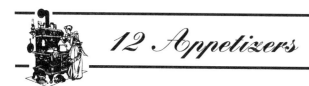

Tuna Roll

Annice Jones, Westmoreland

1 (6-ounce) can tuna, drained
8 ounces cream cheese, softened
1/8 teaspoon onion salt
1/4 cup chopped nuts
1/2 teaspoon lemon-pepper
1/2 teaspoon paprika
3 tablespoons parsley flakes

Combine tuna, cream cheese, onion salt and nuts in medium bowl; mix well. Place on waxed paper; shape into log. Sprinkle with lemon-pepper and paprika. Coat with parsley flakes. Yield: 32 servings.

Approx Per Serving: Cal 37; Prot 2 g; Carbo <1 g; Fiber <1 g; T Fat 3 g; 75% Calories from Fat; Chol 9 mg; Sod 58 mg.

Cheese Drops

Charlotte Shackelford, Strawberry Plains

1 cup butter
2 cups grated sharp Cheddar cheese
2 1/2 cups sifted flour
1/2 teaspoon cayenne pepper
2 cups Rice Krispies

Preheat oven to 350 degrees. Cream butter and cheese in large mixer bowl. Combine flour and cayenne pepper in medium bowl. Add to creamed mixture; blend well. Stir in Rice Krispies. Drop by teapoonfuls onto greased baking sheet. Bake for 15 to 20 minutes or until lightly browned. Yield: 48 servings.

Approx Per Serving: Cal 79; Prot 2 g; Carbo 6 g; Fiber <1 g; T Fat 5 g; 62% Calories from Fat; Chol 15 mg; Sod 82 mg.

Ham 'n' Fruit Sandwiches

Mauline Singleton, Adamsville

1 pound boiled ham slices
1 large red Delicious apple, finely chopped
1/3 cup raisins
1/4 cup mayonnaise
1 tablespoon apple juice
1/8 teaspoon ground allspice
4 lettuce leaves
4 French rolls, cut into halves

Place ham slices in stack; cut into 1/4-inch squares. Combine ham, apple, raisins, mayonnaise, apple juice and allspice in medium bowl; mix well. Cover; chill thoroughly. Spoon filling onto lettuce-lined rolls. May substitute pita bread for French rolls if desired. Yield: 4 servings.

Approx Per Serving: Cal 480; Prot 31 g; Carbo 45 g; Fiber 2 g; T Fat 20 g; 37% Calories from Fat; Chol 67 mg; Sod 2104 mg.

Bacon Roll-Ups

Cheryl Hinson, Linden

1 (12-ounce) package wieners
1 (12-ounce) package Sizzelean bacon
1 1/2 cups packed dark brown sugar

Cut wieners and bacon slices into halves. Wrap each bacon half around each wiener half; secure with toothpicks. Place in Crock•Pot. Add brown sugar. Cook on Low for 3 hours. Yield: 8 (2 roll-ups) servings.

Approx Per Serving: Cal 303; Prot 6 g; Carbo 35 g; Fiber <1 g; T Fat 16 g; 47% Calories from Fat; Chol 21 mg; Sod 676 mg.

Pigs-in-a-Biscuit

Mrs. Wiley Bowlin, Whitesburg

1 (8-count) can refrigerator biscuits
1 (5-ounce) can Vienna sausage

Preheat oven to 300 degrees. Roll out biscuits. Place 1 sausage on each biscuit. Roll up dough to enclose sausage; seal. Place in lightly greased baking pan. Bake for 10 minutes or until lightly browned. Yield: 8 servings.

Approx Per Serving: Cal 119; Prot 4 g; Carbo 11 g; Fiber 0 g; T Fat 8 g; 55% Calories from Fat; Chol 9 mg; Sod 431 mg.

Hot Mexican Dip

Mrs. Clyde Holloway, Crossville

1 pound ground beef
1/4 cup chopped onion
1/3 cup taco sauce
1 (16-ounce) can refried beans
1 1/2 cups shredded Monterey Jack cheese

Brown ground beef with onion in 10-inch skillet, stirring until crumbly; drain off fat. Stir in taco sauce, beans and 1 cup cheese. Heat, stirring, until cheese is melted. Pour into serving dish. Sprinkle remaining cheese on top. May serve with Bugles or corn chips if desired.
Yield: 46 (1 tablespoon) servings.

Approx Per Serving: Cal 47; Prot 4 g; Carbo 2 g; Fiber <1 g; T Fat 3 g; 50% Calories from Fat; Chol 11 mg; Sod 74 mg.

Meat and Cheese Dip

Ella Mae Guffey, Athens

1 pound bulk sausage
2 pounds Velveeta cheese, grated
1 (8-ounce) jar jalapeño relish

Cook sausage in skillet, stirring until crumbly; drain off fat. Add cheese and relish to skillet. Simmer on medium heat until cheese is melted, stirring constantly. Serve hot with corn chips. Yield: 48 (1 tablespoon) servings.

Approx per Serving: Cal 89; Prot 5 g; Carbo <1 g; Fiber <1 g; T Fat 7 g; 74% Calories from fat; Chol 22 mg; Sod 350 mg.

Honey-Baked Bananas

Mrs. Bobby Huff, Chestnut Mound

4 firm ripe bananas
2 teaspoons melted butter
1/4 cup honey
1 tablespoon orange juice
1/4 cup chopped pecans

Preheat oven to 375 degrees. Cut bananas in half crosswise. Brush with butter. Arrange in shallow baking dish. Combine honey and orange juice in small bowl; mix well. Pour over bananas. Sprinkle with pecans. Bake for 15 minutes. Yield: 8 servings.

Approx Per Serving: Cal 118; Prot <1 g; Carbo 23 g; Fiber 1 g; T Fat 4 g; 26% Calories from Fat; Chol 3 mg; Sod 11 mg.

Crunchy Banana Bits

Rena Bell, Cleveland

1/4 cup milk
1/4 cup honey
1/4 cup granola
3 bananas, cut into bite-sized pieces

Mix milk and honey in small bowl. Place granola in plastic bag. Dip each banana piece in milk mixture. Drop into granola; shake until well coated. Serve with toothpicks. Yield: 6 servings.

Approx Per Serving: Cal 122; Prot 1 g; Carbo 29 g; Fiber 2 g; T Fat 1 g; 10% Calories from Fat; Chol 1 mg; Sod 16 mg.

Candied Fruit Peel

Billie C. Dodson, Gallatin

"Rinds ordinarily thrown away can be made into a delicious treat to serve at parties, use for desserts or for any 'yummy snacks,'" says Billie C. Dodson of Gallatin.

Rinds of 4 grapefruit
3/4 cup water
2 cups sugar
1 (3-ounce) package favorite gelatin

Remove dividing membranes and all edible fruit from rinds, leaving white lining around inside of rinds. Accumulate rinds in plastic bag; store in refrigerator. Cut rinds with scissors to make strips 1/2 to 3/4 inches wide and 1 to 3 inches long. Place rinds in small saucepan. Cover with water; boil for 20 minutes. Pour off water. Repeat procedure twice more; drain rinds. Combine 3/4 cup water and 1 1/2 cups sugar in medium saucepan; bring to a boil. Add gelatin; bring to a boil. Add rinds; bring to a boil. Boil for 20 minutes or until rinds are tender and liquid is absorbed. Flatten rinds individually on cake rack; let dry overnight. Roll dried rinds in remaining sugar. Store in fairly tight metal container with waxed paper between layers. Rinds of oranges and lemons may be substituted for grapefruit or used in any combination. Yield: 8 servings.

Approx Per Serving: Cal 238; Prot 1 g; Carbo 61 g; Fiber <1 g; T Fat <1 g; <1% Calories from Fat; Chol 0 mg; Sod 28 mg.

Roasted Pumpkin Seeds

Mrs. Thelma Robinson, Lafayette

Seeds of 1 pumpkin
Butter to taste
Salt to taste

Preheat oven to 375 degrees. Remove seeds from pumpkin; wash well. Spread seeds on cookie sheet. Roast for 20 to 30 minutes or until dried. Dot with butter. Increase oven temperature to 400 degrees. Bake for 5 to 10 minutes or until browned, stirring often. Sprinkle with salt.

Nutritional information for this recipe is not available.

Boiled Chestnuts

Sam Spencer, Burns

Chestnuts
Water

Wash chestnuts in clear water. Puncture each chestnut with ice pick to prevent explosion. Place in saucepan; cover with water. Boil for 5 minutes or longer if desired. Let cool; serve.

Roasted Chestnuts:

Chestnuts   **Water**

Preheat oven to 275 degrees. Wash chestnuts in clear water. Puncture each chestnut with ice pick to prevent explosion. Place in baking pan. Bake for 25 minutes. Peel; serve.

Chestnut Meal:

Chestnuts   **Water**

Wash chestnuts in clear cold water. Blanch in boiling water for 2 to 3 minutes up to 5 minutes. Let cool; remove outer hull. Do not remove inner covering if bulk is desired in diet. Grind chestnut with medium blades in food chopper. Add 1 1/2 cups chestnut meal to mixture of chicken or turkey dressing at the time celery and onions are added. Bake in usual way. Ground chestnut meal can be frozen.

Nutritional information for this recipe is not available.

Cracker Jacks

Mrs. Joe Deakins, Pikeville

8 quarts popped corn
1 (16-ounce) package light brown sugar
1/2 cup light corn syrup
1 cup butter
1 teaspoon baking soda
1 teaspoon salt

Preheat oven to 250 degrees. Place popped corn in large baking pan. Combine sugar, syrup and butter in large saucepan. Boil until thickened and to hard-ball stage. Remove from heat. Add baking soda and salt; beat well. Pour over popped corn; mix well. Bake for 1 hour, stirring 2 or 3 times to coat; let cool. Yield: 32 servings.

Approx Per Serving: Cal 149; Prot 1 g; Carbo 24 g; Fiber 1 g; T Fat 6 g; 35% Calories from Fat; Chol 16 mg; Sod 163 mg.

Cracker Jacks

Mrs. Mai Cornwell, Dixon Springs

8 quarts popped popcorn
2 cups packed light brown sugar
1/2 cup light corn syrup
1 cup butter
2 teaspoons salt
1/2 teaspoon baking soda
1 teaspoon vanilla extract

Preheat oven to 250 degrees. Place popcorn in large buttered baking pan. Mix brown sugar, syrup and butter in medium saucepan; bring to a boil. Cook over medium heat for 5 minutes, adding salt, baking soda and vanilla during cooking. Remove from heat; pour over popcorn. May add nuts if desired. Bake for 1 hour, stirring at 15-minute intervals. Yield: 32 servings.

Approx Per Serving: Cal 138; Prot 1 g; Carbo 21 g; Fiber 1 g; T Fat 6 g; 38% Calories from Fat; Chol 16 mg; Sod 216 mg.

Peanut Buttered Popcorn

Mary Lynn Butler, Decaturville

3 quarts popped corn
1 1/2 cups unblanched whole almonds
1 tablespoon butter
1 cup sugar
1/2 cup honey
1/2 cup light corn syrup
1 cup peanut butter
1 teaspoon vanilla extract

Preheat oven to 250 degrees. Combine popcorn and almonds in large baking pan. Place in oven to keep warm. Butter side of heavy 1 1/2-quart saucepan. Combine sugar, honey and corn syrup in saucepan; bring to a boil. Boil, stirring constantly, for 2 minutes. Remove from heat; stir in peanut butter and vanilla. Pour over popcorn mixture, stirring to coat well; let cool. Break into bite-sized pieces. May substitute dry roasted peanuts or mixed nuts for almonds if desired. Yield: 24 servings.

Approx Per Serving: Cal 207; Prot 5 g; Carbo 27 g; Fiber 2 g; T Fat 11 g; 43% Calories from Fat; Chol 1 mg; Sod 65 mg.

Sandwich Spread

Mrs. Jewell Ellis, Bethel Springs

1 medium green bell pepper, chopped
1 medium cucumber, chopped
1 carrot, grated
1 medium onion, chopped
3/4 cup chopped celery
Salt to taste
8 ounces cream cheese, softened
1/2 cup mayonnaise

Combine green pepper, cucumber, carrot, onion and celery in large bowl. Add salt, cream cheese and mayonnaise; mix well. Spread on bread for sandwich.
Yield: 12 servings.

Approx Per Serving: Cal 144; Prot 2 g; Carbo 4 g; Fiber <1 g; T Fat 14 g; 85% Calories from Fat; Chol 26 mg; Sod 118 mg.

Grape Juice

Mrs. Toy Junior Bonds, Iuka, Mississippi

2 cups grapes
1/2 cup sugar
Boiling water

Wash grapes; place in 1-quart jar. Add sugar. Pour boiling water over top of grapes to fill jar. Place in water bath canner. Cook for 5 to 10 minutes. Remove lid; stir grapes. Drain juice. Chill. Yield: 4 servings.

Approx Per Serving: Cal 153; Prot <1 g; Carbo 39 g; Fiber 1 g; T Fat <1 g; 3% Calories from Fat; Chol 0 mg; Sod 2 mg.

Fruit Punch

Mrs. C. Ed Simpson, New Market

2 cups boiling water
1 (3-ounce) package lime gelatin
3 cups sugar
1 (6-ounce) can concentrated orange juice
1 cup pure lemon juice
1 (46-ounce) can pineapple juice
1 gallon ice water

Pour boiling water over gelatin in large container; stir until dissolved. Add sugar; stir for 1 minute. Let cool thoroughly. Add orange, lemon and pineapple juices. Pour into tightly covered container; chill. Add ice water; mix well. Add ice cubes tinted with green food coloring just before serving. Serve in chilled punch cups.
Yield: 56 (1/2-cup) servings.

Approx Per Serving: Cal 58; Prot <1 g; Carbo 15 g; Fiber <1 g; T Fat <1 g; <1% Calories from Fat; Chol 0 mg; Sod 4 mg.

Punch-for-100

Mrs. Harold Wilmore, Pleasant Shade

This is a very tasty summer cooler.

3 (3-ounce) packages strawberry gelatin
2 envelopes strawberry powdered drink mix
4 cups sugar
1 quart boiling water
1 1/2 gallons cold water
2 (12-ounce) cans frozen orange juice
2 (12-ounce) cans frozen lemonade
2 (46-ounce) cans pineapple juice
4 quarts ginger ale, chilled

Dissolve gelatin, drink mix and sugar in boiling water in large container. Add cold water, orange juice, lemonade and pineapple juice; mix well. Chill until serving time. Pour into punch bowl. Add ginger ale. Yield: 100 servings.

Approx Per Serving: Cal 92; Prot <1 g; Carbo 23 g; Fiber <1 g; T Fat <1 g; <1% Calories from Fat; Chol 0 mg; Sod 12 mg.

Percolator Punch

Mrs. Loran Whaley, Dandridge

3 cups cranberry juice cocktail
3 cups unsweetened pineapple juice
1 1/2 cups cold water
1/3 cup light brown sugar
1/8 teaspoon salt
1 cinnamon stick
1 1/2 teaspoons whole cloves

Combine cranberry juice, pineapple juice, water, brown sugar and salt in 10-cup percolator. Break cinnamon stick into small pieces. Place cinnamon and cloves in basket. Perk; serve hot. Yield: 12 servings.

Approx Per Serving: Cal 86; Prot <1 g; Carbo 22 g; Fiber <1 g; T Fat <1 g; 1% Calories from Fat; Chol 0 mg; Sod 26 mg.

Wanda's Strawberry Punch

Wanda W. Richardson, Gadsden, Alabama

Strawberries are special to Wanda Richardson of Gadsden where the sweet, luscious berries are said to have been grown for the first time in West Tennessee. "We have an historical marker on Highway 79 recognizing this," says Mrs. Richardson.

2 envelopes unsweetened strawberry
    powdered drink mix
1/2 gallon vanilla ice milk, cut into 8 blocks
2 pints fresh strawberries, sliced
2 quarts ginger ale, chilled

Mix powdered drink mix according to package directions; chill. Mix ice milk and strawberries in large punch bowl. Pour chilled drink mixture over strawberry mixture. Add ginger ale. Yield: 48 servings.

Approx Per Serving: Cal 48; Prot <1 g; Carbo 9 g; Fiber <1 g; T Fat <1 g; 18% Calories from Fat; Chol 3 mg; Sod 25 mg.

Strawberry-Banana Shake

Patricia Lynn Hickman, Mt. Pleasant

2 cups fresh strawberries
2 cups nonfat buttermilk
1 small ripe banana, sliced
3 tablespoons honey

Wash and cap strawberries; drain well. Place strawberries in single layer in shallow pan; freeze. Combine frozen strawberries and remaining ingredients in blender container; process until smooth. Serve immediately. Yield: 9 (1/2 cup) servings.

Approx Per Serving: Cal 62; Prot 2 g; Carbo 13 g; Fiber 1 g; T Fat <1 g; 9% Calories from Fat; Chol 2 mg; Sod 58 mg.

Quick Hot Drink

Charlene Sawyer Reeves, Lebanon

3/4 cup apple juice
1/4 cup orange juice
1/4 teaspoon ground cloves
1/4 teaspoon ground cinnamon

Mix ingredients in microwave-safe cup. Microwave for 1 minute or to desired temperature. Yield: 1 serving.

Approx Per Serving: Cal 115; Prot <1 g; Carbo 28 g; Fiber <1 g; T Fat <1 g; 3% Calories from Fat; Chol 0 mg; Sod 6 mg.

Hot Spiced Tea Mix

Romanza O. Johnson, Bowling Green, Kentucky

1/2 cup instant tea
2 cups orange instant breakfast drink mix
1 envelope sweetened lemonade mix
1 teaspoon ground cloves
1/2 teaspoon cinnamon
2 cups sugar

Combine all ingredients in large bowl; mix well. Store in wide-mouth jar with lid. Add 2 teaspoons mix to 1 cup boiling water for 1 serving; 8 heaping teaspoons for 1 quart. Yield: 72 servings.

Approx Per Serving: Cal 50; Prot <1 g; Carbo 13 g; Fiber <1 g; T Fat <1 g; <1% Calories from Fat; Chol 0 mg; Sod 2 mg.

CHAPTER 2

SOUPS & SALADS

This Old House

Draped in snow, an old abandoned
farmhouse serves as a gentle
reminder of simpler times when
farming was a way of life for almost
everyone who lived in the country.

Multi-Bean Soup

Mary Lou Brown, Thorn Hill

1/2 cup dried northern beans
1/2 cup dried pinto beans
1/2 cup dried navy beans
1/2 cup dried white kidney beans
1/2 cup dried black-eyed peas
1/2 cup dried green split peas
8 cups water
2 tablespoons cornstarch
1 pound Polish sausage
1/4 cup parsley
1/4 teaspoon garlic powder
1/2 teaspoon sage
1/4 teaspoon thyme
1/4 teaspoon celery salt
Salt and pepper to taste
1/4 cup lemon juice
1 quart tomatoes
1 large onion, chopped
1 clove of garlic, minced

Combine beans in large bowl; cover with water. Soak overnight; drain. Place in large stockpot; add 8 cups fresh water. Simmer for 1 1/2 to 3 hours. Remove a small amount of broth; stir in cornstarch. Return to beans. Slice sausage lengthwise; cut into small pieces. Add sausage, parsley, garlic powder, sage, thyme, celery salt, salt and pepper, lemon juice, tomatoes, onion and garlic; mix well. Simmer for 30 minutes. Serve hot. Refrigerate leftover soup. May use any combination of the following dried beans and peas: northern, pinto, black-eyed, white, pearl barley, pink, cranberry, navy, green split pea, yellow split pea, large and small lima, white kidney, red kidney, lentils, black or any dried bean or field pea from your garden. Reserve extra beans in plastic bag for future use. May substitute 1 teaspoon poultry seasoning for sage, thyme and celery salt if desired. Yield: 16 servings.

Approx Per Serving: Cal 187; Prot 11 g; Carbo 27 g; Fiber 8 g; T Fat 4 g; 21% Calories from Fat; Chol 9 mg; Sod 243 mg.

Beefy Black-Eyed Soup

Mary Wilburn, Nashville

2 pounds ground beef
1/2 cup chopped green pepper
1/2 cup butter
1/2 cup flour
2 quarts water
1 (28-ounce) can whole tomatoes
1 (16-ounce) package frozen
　black-eyed peas
1 cup chopped onions
1 cup diced carrots
1 cup chopped celery
2 tablespoons beef instant bouillon
1 tablespoon pepper
1/2 teaspoon salt
1/8 teaspoon garlic powder
1/8 teaspoon onion powder

Cook beef and green pepper in skillet until beef is browned, stirring until crumbly; drain. Melt butter in Dutch oven; add flour, stirring until smooth. Cook, stirring constantly, for 1 minute. Add water gradually; cook, stirring constantly, until bubbly. Stir in beef mixture, tomatoes, peas, onions, carrots, celery, bouillon, pepper, salt, garlic powder and onion powder; bring to a boil. Simmer, covered, for 45 minutes to 1 hour. Yield: 18 servings.

Approx Per Serving: Cal 219; Prot 15 g; Carbo 12 g; Fiber 3 g; T Fat 13 g; 51% Calories from Fat; Chol 51 mg; Sod 507 mg.

Cream of Chicken Soup

Gail Walker, Sparta

This recipe won fifth place in the 1987 Tennessee Dairy Recipe Contest.

1 bunch celery stalks with tops,
  cut into halves
4 medium onions, quartered
4 large tomatoes, quartered
4 large carrots, cut into halves
2 tablespoons salt
5 large chicken breasts
1 gallon water
1 pound lightly salted butter
3 bunches small green onions
  without tops, thinly sliced
1 cup plus 2 tablespoons flour
2 cups whipping cream
1 cup half and half
2 teaspoons sugar
1 teaspoon pepper
3/4 teaspoon nutmeg
1/2 teaspoon salt

Place celery, onions, tomatoes and carrots in 3-gallon heavy kettle. Sprinkle with 2 tablespoons salt. Arrange chicken breasts over vegetables. Add water; bring to a boil. Reduce heat; cook for 1 1/2 hours or until chicken is tender. Do not stir. Remove chicken. Cover; refrigerate. Cook vegetables for 3 hours longer, adding water as liquid reduces to maintain 3/4 gallon of liquid. Pour liquid and cooked vegetables into colander. Let drain. Press vegetable pulp lightly; dispose of remaining vegetable pulp. Remove skin, fat and bone from chicken. Break into bite-sized pieces. Cover; refrigerate. Wash kettle. Melt butter in kettle over low heat. Add green onions. Sauté over low heat, stirring constantly, until butter is reduced and onions are golden. Do not let onions or butter brown. Add flour slowly, stirring constantly, until smooth. Add gradually drained vegetable liquid, whipping cream and half and half. Liquid amount should not exceed 1 gallon. Add sugar, pepper, nutmeg and 1/2 teaspoon salt. Bring to a boil, stirring constantly, until thickened. Reduce heat; cook slowly for 30 minutes. Add chicken; cook until chicken is heated through. Yield: 18 servings.

Approx Per Serving: Cal 403; Prot 12 g; Carbo 16 g; Fiber 2 g; T Fat 33 g; 73% Calories from Fat; Chol 121 mg; Sod 1045 mg.

Margo's Lamb Soup

Margo Raymond and Julie Sherman Raymond, New Market

1 lamb shank, cut or cracked
  with marrow showing
1 pound lamb flank
4 packets beef bouillon
3 stalks celery with tops, cut in
  1/4-inch slices
1 medium yellow onion, chopped
3 sweet carrots, cut into 1-inch pieces
Salt and pepper to taste
Worcestershire sauce to taste
1/2 cup minute rice
1/2 cup peas

Fill stockpot half full with water. Place over medium heat; add lamb shank, lamb flank and bouillon. Bring to a boil; reduce to simmer. Add celery, onion and carrots. Add water until pot is almost full. Cook for 1 hour. Add salt and pepper and Worcestershire sauce. Cook for 2 hours or until meat is tender. Remove meat. Add rice, peas and small amount of water. Simmer until rice is cooked. Ladle into bowls. Serve with sliced meat and potatoes. Yield: 12 servings.

Approx Per Serving: Cal 99; Prot 10 g; Carbo 8 g; Fiber 1 g; T Fat 3 g; 27% Calories from Fat; Chol 28 mg; Sod 379 mg.

Golden Creamy Soup

Mrs. Maude Campbell, Elizabethton

This recipe won third place in the 1987 Tennessee Dairy Recipe Contest.

2 cups boiling water
3 cups diced potatoes
1/2 cup chopped celery
1/4 cup chopped onion
1 teaspoon minced parsley
1/2 teaspoon salt
1/8 teaspoon white pepper
1 chicken bouillon cube
2 tablespoons flour
2 cups milk
2 tablespoons butter
1/2 pound Velveeta cheese, cubed

Combine water, potatoes, celery, onion, parsley, salt, white pepper and bouillon cube in kettle. Cook, uncovered, until vegetables are tender. Blend flour with a small amount of milk in small bowl; stir into vegetable mixture. Add remaining milk and butter; cook until thickened. Add cheese; stir until melted. Yield: 8 servings.

Approx Per Serving: Cal 224; Prot 10 g; Carbo 16 g; Fiber 1 g; T Fat 14 g; 55% Calories from Fat; Chol 43 mg; Sod 751 mg.

Hearty Potato Soup

Lynn McNeely, Columbia

6 peeled medium potatoes
2 carrots, diced
6 stalks celery, diced
2 quarts water
1 onion, chopped
6 tablespoons butter
6 tablespoons flour
1 teaspoon salt
1/2 teaspoon pepper
1 1/2 cups milk

Combine potatoes, carrots and celery in large kettle; add water. Cook for 20 minutes or until tender. Drain, reserving liquid; set vegetables aside. Sauté onion in butter in kettle until softened. Stir in flour, salt and pepper. Add milk gradually, stirring gently. Add cooked vegetables. Add 1 cup or enough reserved liquid to make of desired consistency. Yield: 8 servings.

Approx Per Serving: Cal 228; Prot 5 g; Carbo 30 g; Fiber 3 g; T Fat 10 g; 40% Calories from Fat; Chol 30 mg; Sod 414 mg.

Sour Cream-Potato Soup

Ethel Hagler, Erin

This recipe won second place in the 1987 Tennessee Dairy Recipe Contest.

3 cups diced Irish potatoes
1/2 cup finely chopped celery
1/2 cup finely chopped onion
3 cups water
2 cups scalded milk
2 chicken bouillon cubes
3 tablespoons butter
1 cup sour cream
1 tablespoon flour
Salt and pepper to taste

Place potatoes, celery, onion and water in medium-sized kettle. Cook, covered, until potatoes are tender. Add milk, bouillon cubes and butter. Combine sour cream and flour in small bowl; mix until smooth. Add to soup mixture. Cook, stirring constantly, until thickened and bouillon cubes are dissolved. Stir in salt and pepper. Yield: 6 servings.

Approx Per Serving: Cal 256; Prot 6 g; Carbo 22 g; Fiber 2 g; T Fat 17 g; 57% Calories from Fat; Chol 44 mg; Sod 516 mg.

Potato Stew

E. A. Wilburn, Beech Grove

1 (2¹/2-pound) broiler chicken
1 teaspoon salt
3 cups water
2 cups diced potatoes
1¹/2 cups frozen lima beans
1 (16-ounce) can tomatoes
¹/4 cup chopped onion
1³/4 cups frozen corn
1 small green pepper, chopped
1 small red pepper, chopped
¹/8 teaspoon pepper
¹/4 teaspoon poultry seasoning
¹/4 cup water
2 tablespoons flour

Place chicken, salt and water in large kettle; simmer until tender. Drain, reserving broth; chill broth. Separate meat from skin and bones; cut into bite-sized pieces. Skim fat from reserved broth. Return broth to kettle. Add potatoes; simmer for 5 minutes. Add lima beans, tomatoes and onion; simmer for 7 minutes. Add chicken, corn, green pepper, red pepper, pepper and poultry seasoning. Cook for 4 minutes. Mix ¹/4 cup water with flour in small bowl until smooth. Add to stew; heat, stirring constantly, until thickened. Serve with French bread. Yield: 6 servings.

Approx Per Serving: Cal 337; Prot 34 g; Carbo 35 g; Fiber 7 g; T Fat 8 g; 20% Calories from Fat; Chol 84 mg; Sod 578 mg.

Mushroom-Potato Soup

Lou Conner, Algood

2 tablespoons butter
1 small onion, chopped
1 stalk celery, chopped
¹/2 small green pepper, chopped
1 (8-ounce) package fresh mushrooms,
   sliced
2 cups diced peeled potatoes
2 cups chicken broth
¹/2 teaspoon dried thyme
¹/2 teaspoon salt
¹/2 teaspoon pepper
2 cups milk
3 tablespoons flour

Melt butter in large kettle. Add onion, celery, green pepper and mushrooms. Cook until tender. Stir in potatoes, chicken broth and thyme. Bring to a boil; reduce heat. Simmer, covered, until vegetables are tender. Stir in salt, pepper and 1¹/2 cups milk. Combine ¹/2 cup milk with flour in small bowl, stirring until smooth. Stir into soup. Simmer, uncovered, until slightly thickened.
Yield: 6 servings.

Approx Per Serving: Cal 167; Prot 7 g; Carbo 19 g; Fiber 2 g; T Fat 7 g; 39% Calories from Fat; Chol 21 mg; Sod 526 mg.

Yellow Squash Soup

Jane Beverly, Fayetteville

1 small onion, diced
1 stalk celery, chopped
1 carrot, chopped
1¹/3 cups butter
1¹/2 pounds yellow squash, sliced
1 peeled medium potato, sliced
1 quart chicken broth
1 teaspoon caraway seeds
³/4 cup heavy cream
Salt and pepper to taste

Sauté onion, celery and carrot in butter in heavy kettle until softened; do not brown. Add squash, potato, broth and caraway seeds. Cook until squash is very tender. Pour ¹/4 hot mixture into blender container at a time; blend until smooth. Return to kettle. Stir cream and seasonings into mixture. Reheat gently. Sprinkle a few caraway seeds on top of individual servings. Yield: 8 servings.

Approx Per Serving: Cal 407; Prot 5 g; Carbo 10 g; Fiber 2 g; T Fat 40 g; 86% Calories from Fat; Chol 113 mg; Sod 719 mg.

Mama's Tomato Soup

Claudine Vanderpool, Hendersonville

1 pound bulk sausage
1 peeled large potato, chopped
1 large onion, chopped
3 cups water
3 cups canned tomatoes
3 hard-cooked eggs, chopped
Salt and pepper to taste
1 cup milk

Brown sausage in 3-quart saucepan, stirring until crumbly. Remove from skillet, reserving 2 tablespoons drippings. Add potato, onion and water to drippings; cook until vegetables are tender. Add tomatoes, eggs, salt and pepper and sausage. Simmer until heated through. Add 2 tablespoons milk to each individual serving bowl. Yield: 8 servings.

Approx Per Serving: Cal 224; Prot 10 g; Carbo 12 g; Fiber 2 g; T Fat 15 g; 60% Calories from Fat; Chol 109 mg; Sod 550 mg.

Creamy Vegetable-Cheese Soup

Nannie Quails, Manchester

This recipe won fourth place in the 1987 Tennessee Dairy Recipe Contest.

1/4 cup plus 1 tablespoon butter
1 cup chopped onion
2 cups hot water
2 cups shredded cabbage
1 (10-ounce) package frozen baby
   lima beans
1 cup sliced carrots
1 cup cubed potatoes
1 tablespoon chicken instant bouillon
3 tablespoons flour
2 cups milk
1 cup half and half
1/4 teaspoon paprika
1/4 teaspoon pepper
1 1/2 cups shredded Cheddar cheese
4 tablespoons Parmesan cheese

Melt 2 tablespoons butter in large heavy skillet; add onion. Sauté for 5 minutes or until tender. Add hot water, vegetables and bouillon; bring to a boil. Reduce heat; simmer, covered, for 20 minutes or until vegetables are tender. Melt remaining butter in heavy kettle over low heat. Add flour, stirring until smooth. Cook for 1 minute, stirring constantly. Add milk and half and half gradually; cook over medium heat, stirring constantly, until thickened and bubbly. Stir in paprika, pepper and Cheddar cheese. Stir in vegetable mixture gradually; cook, stirring constantly, until heated through. Sprinkle with Parmesan cheese. Garnish with sprigs of parsley. Yield: 6 servings.

Approx Per Serving: Cal 429; Prot 18 g; Carbo 28 g; Fiber 5 g; T Fat 28 g; 58% Calories from Fat; Chol 85 mg; Sod 1007 mg.

Vegetable Chowder

Mrs. Bill Russell, Wartrace

1 (10-ounce) can cream of celery soup
1 (10-ounce) can cream of mushroom soup
2 (10-ounce) soup cans milk
1 small onion, chopped
1 cup shredded sharp Cheddar cheese
1 cup fresh broccoli flowerets

Combine soups and milk in large saucepan. Add onion, cheese and broccoli; mix well. Bring to a boil. May substitute 1 small can asparagus or 1 can English peas for broccoli if desired. Yield: 8 servings.

Approx Per Serving: Cal 169; Prot 7 g; Carbo 10 g; Fiber <1 g; T Fat 11 g; 59% Calories from Fat; Chol 29 mg; Sod 718 mg.

Southern Vegetable Soup

Mamie Carson, Jefferson City

1 pound white navy beans
1 ham bone with 1 cup meat on it
3 cups canned tomatoes
3 quarts water
3/4 cup chopped onion
1 cup chopped celery
Salt and pepper to taste
2 cups diced peeled potatoes
1/2 cup mashed cooked potatoes

Soak beans overnight in large bowl in cold water; drain. Place in deep stockpot. Add ham bone, tomatoes, water, onion, celery, salt and pepper. Simmer, covered, for 2 hours or until beans are tender. Remove ham bone. Remove meat from bone; cut into small pieces. Add meat to soup. Add diced potatoes. Cook until potatoes are tender. Stir small amount of hot soup into mashed potatoes; add to soup, mixing well. Yield: 10 servings.

Approx Per Serving: Cal 239; Prot 14 g; Carbo 40 g; Fiber 11 g; T Fat 3 g; 12% Calories from Fat; Chol 9 mg; Sod 333 mg.

Taco Soup

Hilda Brown, Moss

2 pounds ground beef
1 small onion, chopped
3 (14-ounce) cans stewed tomatoes
1 (16-ounce) can pinto beans
1 (15-ounce) can kidney beans
1 (15-ounce) can yellow hominy
1 (4-ounce) can chopped green chilies
   with liquid
1 1/2 cups water
1 (1 1/4-ounce) package taco seasoning
1 envelope ranch salad dressing mix
1/4 teaspoon salt
1/2 teaspoon pepper

Cook ground beef and onion in heavy kettle until meat is browned, stirring until crumbly; drain off fat. Add tomatoes, pinto beans, kidney beans, hominy, green chilies and water; mix well. Stir in taco seasoning, dressing mix, salt and pepper. Reduce heat; simmer, covered, for 1 hour, stirring occasionally. Yield: 12 servings.

Approx Per Serving: Cal 316; Prot 22 g; Carbo 32 g; Fiber 5 g; T Fat 11 g; 32% Calories from Fat; Chol 56 mg; Sod 1740 mg.

Thirty-Minute Beef and Black Bean Soup

Terryl Propper, Nashville

1 pound coarsely ground beef chuck
1 (10-ounce) can black bean soup
1 (15-ounce) can black beans, rinsed,
   drained
1 1/3 cups water
1 cup prepared medium or hot chunky
   salsa
1/4 cup thinly sliced green onions
1/4 cup lite sour cream
4 fresh cilantro sprigs

Brown beef in heavy kettle over medium heat for 8 to 10 minutes, breaking into 3/4-inch crumbles. Pour off drippings. Stir in black bean soup, black beans, water and salsa. Bring to a boil; reduce heat to low. Simmer, uncovered, for 15 minutes. Stir in green onions; remove from heat. Garnish with sour cream and cilantro. Serve with corn muffins. May substitute 19-ounce for 10-ounce can black bean soup if desired. Yield: 4 servings.

Approx Per Serving: Cal 459; Prot 37 g; Carbo 35 g; Fiber 8 g; T Fat 20 g; 39% Calories from Fat; Chol 90 mg; Sod 1468 mg.

Poor Man's Stew

Wilma McMillan, Parrottsville

12 ears corn with shucks
12 unpeeled potatoes, washed
12 unpeeled carrots, washed
12 onions, washed
1 large head cabbage, quartered
2 pounds smoked sausages, cut into
  2-inch pieces

Clean and wash corn, leaving inner shucks in place. Place ingredients in order listed in clean lard can with pencil-sized hole punched in lid. Pour 1 gallon water over vegetables and meat. Place can over fire. Begin timing when steam begins to come out of hole in lid; cook for 1 hour. Serve with salt, pepper and butter. Yield: 12 servings.

Approx Per Serving: Cal 451; Prot 17 g; Carbo 73 g; Fiber 12 g; T Fat 13 g; 25% Calories from Fat; Chol 24 mg; Sod 601 mg.

Burgoo

Sophia A. Hudson, Lebanon

2 (4-pound) stewing chickens
1 (4-pound) chuck roast
1 (5-pound) lamb shoulder
1 (3-pound) veal shoulder
1 ham bone with 2 cups meat on it
Salt and pepper to taste
1 bunch carrots, peeled, chopped
1 bunch celery, sliced
1 small head cabbage, shredded
2 green bell peppers, chopped
2 red bell peppers, chopped
2 (10-ounce) packages frozen green beans
2 (10-ounce) packages frozen lima beans
6 medium onions, chopped
4 potatoes, chopped
4 (10-ounce) packages frozen corn
4 (28-ounce) cans tomatoes
4 (10-ounce) packages frozen English peas
1 (14-ounce) bottle catsup
1/2 cup vinegar
1 (5-ounce) bottle Worcestershire sauce

Place chickens, roast, lamb, veal and ham bone in large stockpot. Cover with water. Season with salt and pepper. Cook until meat is tender. Remove meat from stockpot; let cool. Remove meat from bones; refrigerate. Remove grease from top of broth; return to heat. Add meat and remaining ingredients. Cook until all vegetables are tender. Serve in mugs with garlic bread or corn bread. Freezes well. Yield: 36 servings.

Approx Per Serving: Cal 448; Prot 48 g; Carbo 31 g; Fiber 7 g; T Fat 15 g; 30% Calories from Fat; Chol 143 mg; Sod 571 mg.

French Salad Dressing

Mrs. Jo Nell Taubert, Allardt

1 (10-ounce) can tomato soup
1 1/2 cups vegetable oil
1/2 cup sugar
1 teaspoon each salt, pepper
2/3 cup apple cider vinegar
1/2 teaspoon whole oregano
Dash of onion salt
Dash of garlic salt

Combine all ingredients in blender container. Cover; blend well. Yield: 16 (2-ounce) servings.

Approx Per Serving: Cal 219; Prot <1 g; Carbo 9 g; Fiber <1 g; T Fat 21 g; 83% Calories from Fat; Chol 0 mg; Sod 266 mg.

Apple-Carrot Salad

Mrs. Archie L. Sticklin, Savannah

1 apple, cored
2 teaspoons fresh lemon juice
1 cup grated carrot
2 ounces Swiss cheese, cubed
2 tablespoons dark raisins

Grate apple into medium bowl. Add lemon juice; toss together to coat. Stir in remaining ingredients; mix well. Chill. Yield: 2 servings.

Approx Per Serving: Cal 202; Prot 9 g; Carbo 26 g; Fiber 4 g; T Fat 8 g; 35% Calories from Fat; Chol 26 mg; Sod 94 mg.

Apricot Salad

Helen W. Shelton, Marshall, North Carolina

1 (6-ounce) package apricot gelatin
2 cups hot water
1 1/2 cups cold water
1 (8-ounce) can crushed pineapple
4 bananas, sliced
1 cup miniature marshmallows
1/2 cup sugar
2 teaspoons flour
1 egg
4 ounces cream cheese, softened
1 tablespoon butter
2 cups whipped topping
1 cup shredded coconut

Dissolve gelatin in hot water in large bowl; add cold water. Drain pineapple, reserving juice. Stir in pineapple and bananas. Pour into 9-inch square pan. Cover with marshmallows. Chill until firm. Combine sugar, flour, egg and 1/2 cup reserved pineapple juice in large saucepan. Cook until thickened; remove from heat. Add cream cheese and butter. Blend in whipped topping. Spread on congealed salad; top with coconut. Yield: 8 servings.

Approx Per Serving: Cal 413; Prot 5 g; Carbo 66 g; Fiber 3 g; T Fat 16 g; 34% Calories from Fat; Chol 46 mg; Sod 157 mg.

Frozen Banana Salad

Mrs. Mildred Rogers, Livingston

1 (6-ounce) jar maraschino cherries, drained
4 bananas, mashed
1 (8-ounce) can crushed pineapple
1 tablespoon lemon juice
1/2 cup chopped pecans
3/4 cup sugar
1 teaspoon salt
2 cups sour cream

Cut cherries into squares. Combine cherries, bananas, pineapple, lemon juice, pecans, sugar, salt and sour cream in large bowl; mix well. Pour into 9-inch square pan. Freeze until firm; cut into squares. Serve on lettuce leaves. Yield: 8 servings.

Approx Per Serving: Cal 305; Prot 3 g; Carbo 38 g; Fiber 1 g; T Fat 17 g; 49% Calories from Fat; Chol 26 mg; Sod 298 mg.

Blueberry Salad

Mrs. Harold Shipe, Blaine

2 (3-ounce) packages grape gelatin
1¹/₂ cups boiling water
1 (20-ounce) can crushed pineapple
1 (21-ounce) can blueberry pie filling
6 ounces cream cheese, softened
¹/₂ cup sugar
1 cup sour cream
1 teaspoon vanilla extract
1 cup chopped pecans

Dissolve gelatin in boiling water in large bowl. Stir in pineapple and pie filling. Pour into 10-inch square pan. Chill until firm. Combine cream cheese and sugar in medium bowl. Add sour cream; mix well. Add vanilla and pecans. Spread over congealed mixture. Yield: 12 servings.

Approx Per Serving: Cal 331; Prot 4 g; Carbo 47 g; Fiber 2 g; T Fat 16 g; 41% Calories from Fat; Chol 24 mg; Sod 102 mg.

Champagne Salad

Ann W. Brown, Scottsville, Kentucky

8 ounces cream cheese, softened
³/₄ cup sugar
1 (15-ounce) can pineapple tidbits, drained
1 (10-ounce) package frozen strawberries
   with juice
¹/₂ cup chopped walnuts
2 bananas, mashed
1 (16-ounce) carton frozen whipped topping
8 lettuce leaves

Combine cream cheese and sugar in large bowl. Combine pineapple, strawberries, walnuts, bananas and whipped topping in large bowl; mix well gently. Add fruit mixture to cream cheese mixture. Spoon into large loaf pan; freeze until solid. Slice; serve on individual lettuce leaves. Remove salad from freezer 15 minutes before serving time to make removal from pan and slicing easier. Yield: 8 servings.

Approx Per Serving: Cal 468; Prot 5 g; Carbo 51 g; Fiber 2 g; T Fat 29 g; 54% Calories from Fat; Chol 31 mg; Sod 102 mg.

Cherry Salad

Bessie L. White, Fairview

1 (21-ounce) can cherry pie filling
1 (20-ounce) can crushed pineapple,
   drained
1 (16-ounce) carton whipped topping
1 (14-ounce) can sweetened condensed
   milk

Combine pie filling and pineapple in large bowl. Add whipped topping and condensed milk; mix well. Chill thoroughly. Yield: 12 servings.

Approx Per Serving: Cal 310; Prot 4 g; Carbo 47 g; Fiber <1 g; T Fat 13 g; 36% Calories from Fat; Chol 11 mg; Sod 78 mg.

Cherry-Pineapple Salad

Pauline M. Morris, LaVergne

1 (12-ounce) carton whipped topping
1 (14-ounce) can sweetened condensed
   milk
1 (20-ounce) can crushed pineapple
1 (21-ounce) can cherry pie filling

Combine whipped topping and condensed milk in large bowl. Add pineapple and pie filling; mix well. Chill until firm. Yield: 16 servings.

Approx Per Serving: Cal 219; Prot 3 g; Carbo 36 g; Fiber <1 g; T Fat 8 g; 31% Calories from Fat; Chol 8 mg; Sod 57 mg.

Cool Summer Salad

Mrs. Oscar Bragg, Meigs County

8 ounces cream cheese, softened
2 (15-ounce) cans pineapple chunks,
   drained
1³/₄ cups grated Cheddar cheese
1 quart vanilla ice cream, softened
Orange Cream Dressing

Combine cream cheese and pineapple in large bowl; blend until smooth. Add 1 cup grated cheese and ice cream; mix well. Pour into 9-by-12-inch dish; freeze. Cut into 12 squares. Serve on spinach or grape leaves. Top each square with 3 tablespoons Orange Cream Dressing. Sprinkle with 1 tablespoon Cheddar cheese. Yield: 12 servings.

Orange Cream Dressing:
¹/₃ cup orange juice
1 tablespoon
   lemon juice
¹/₄ cup sugar

2 egg yolks
1 cup heavy cream,
   whipped

Combine orange juice, lemon juice and sugar in medium saucepan. Heat until mixture comes to a boil; let cool. Add egg yolks, 1 at a time, beating well after each addition. Cook over low heat, stirring constantly, until mixture is creamy. Chill. Fold in whipped cream just before serving. Yield: 12 (3 tablespoons) servings.

Approx Per Serving: Cal 453; Prot 8 g; Carbo 32 g; Fiber <1 g; T Fat 33 g; 66% Calories from Fat; Chol 183 mg; Sod 213 mg.

Easy Fruit Salad

Maxine Pruitt, Burns

1 (16-ounce) can peaches with juice
1 (8-ounce) jar maraschino cherries with
   juice
1 (16-ounce) can pears, drained
1 (46-ounce) can pineapple juice
1 (4-ounce) package lemon instant
   pudding mix

Combine peaches, cherries, pears and pineapple juice in large bowl. Pour dry pudding mix over fruit mixture; mix well. Chill overnight. Yield: 8 servings.

Approx Per Serving: Cal 252; Prot <1 g; Carbo 64 g; Fiber 2 g; T Fat <1 g; 1% Calories from Fat; Chol 0 mg; Sod 197 mg.

Fruit Salad and Dressing

Mrs. Scottie Harding, Paris

1 (20-ounce) can pineapple chunks
1 egg
1 heaping tablespoon flour
¹/₂ cup sugar
1 tablespoon butter
4 bananas, sliced
1 cup chopped nuts
2 cups miniature marshmallows
1 (8-ounce) carton whipped topping
6 maraschino cherries

Drain pineapple, reserving juice. Combine reserved juice, egg, flour and sugar in top of double boiler. Place over boiling water; boil until thickened. Remove from heat. Add butter; let cool. Add pineapple, bananas, nuts and marshmallows. Fold in whipped topping. Garnish with cherries. Yield: 6 servings.

Approx Per Serving: Cal 549; Prot 5 g; Carbo 81 g; Fiber 3 g; T Fat 26 g; 41% Calories from Fat; Chol 41 mg; Sod 49 mg.

Fruit Salad

Mrs. Bill Fuqua, Springfield

1 (15-ounce) can pineapple tidbits
2 cups miniature marshmallows
1/2 cup sugar
1 tablespoon flour
1 egg, beaten
6 bananas, sliced

Drain pineapple, reserving juice. Combine pineapple and marshmallows in large bowl. Combine 1 cup reserved pineapple juice, sugar, flour and egg in medium saucepan. Cook over medium heat, stirring constantly, until thickened. Pour over pineapple mixture. Add bananas just before serving. Yield: 8 servings.

Approx Per Serving: Cal 217; Prot 2 g; Carbo 53 g; Fiber 2 g; T Fat 1 g; 4% Calories from Fat; Chol 27 mg; Sod 15 mg.

Frosted Salad

Earline Moran, Charlotte

2 (3-ounce) packages lemon gelatin
2 cups boiling water
2 cups 7-Up
1 1/2 cups pineapple tidbits, drained
3 large bananas, chopped
2 cups miniature marshmallows
1 1/2 cups sugar
1 cup pineapple tidbits, drained
1 egg, well beaten
2 tablespoons butter
2 envelopes whipped topping mix

Dissolve gelatin in boiling water in large bowl; add 7-Up. Chill until partly congealed. Add 1 1/2 cups pineapple, bananas and marshmallows. Chill until firm. Combine sugar, 1 cup pineapple and egg in medium saucepan. Cook, stirring, until thickened. Remove from heat. Add butter; chill. Prepare topping mix using package directions. Add gently to chilled sauce. Spread over congealed gelatin mixture; chill. Yield: 8 servings.

Approx Per Serving: Cal 488; Prot 5 g; Carbo 102 g; Fiber 2 g; T Fat 9 g; 16% Calories from Fat; Chol 38 mg; Sod 126 mg.

Gelatin Salad

Mrs. Jimmie Huff Grisham, Chestnut Mound

1 (3-ounce) package lime gelatin
1 (16-ounce) can fruit cocktail
1 (8-ounce) can crushed pineapple
1 (16-ounce) package marshmallows
3 ounces cream cheese, softened
1 cup whipped topping
1 cup chopped pecans

Combine gelatin, fruit cocktail, pineapple and marshmallows in large heavy saucepan. Bring to a boil over high heat. Boil until marshmallows are melted. Remove from heat; let cool thoroughly. Add cream cheese and whipped topping. Fold in pecans; chill. Yield: 8 servings.

Approx Per Serving: Cal 450; Prot 4 g; Carbo 77 g; Fiber 2 g; T Fat 16 g; 31% Calories from Fat; Chol 12 mg; Sod 91 mg.

Low-Calorie Salad

Zona Hilbert, Jonesborough

This is a colorful salad.

10 ounces whipped topping
12 ounces low-fat cottage cheese
1 (3-ounce) package orange gelatin
1 (20-ounce) can crushed pineapple,
    drained
1 (11-ounce) can mandarin oranges,
    drained

Combine whipped topping and cottage cheese in large bowl. Sprinkle dry gelatin over top. Fold in pineapple and oranges. May use other fruit and different flavor gelatin if desired. Yield: 8 servings.

Approx Per Serving: Cal 251; Prot 8 g; Carbo 35 g; Fiber <1 g; T Fat 10 g; 35% Calories from Fat; Chol 4 mg; Sod 212 mg.

Lemon Congealed Salad

Norma Barham, Calhoun

2 (3-ounce) packages lemon gelatin
2 cups boiling water
1 (14-ounce) can sweetened condensed
    milk
1 cup mayonnaise
1 (20-ounce) can crushed pineapple,
    drained
1 cup chopped pecans
2 cups shredded Cheddar cheese

Dissolve gelatin in boiling water in large bowl; let cool slightly. Combine condensed milk and mayonnaise in medium bowl. Fold into gelatin. Add pineapple, pecans and cheese. Pour into dish or mold. Chill until firm. Yield: 8 servings.

Approx Per Serving: Cal 687; Prot 14 g; Carbo 60 g; Fiber 1 g; T Fat 46 g; 58% Calories from Fat; Chol 63 mg; Sod 450 mg.

Lime Mist

Rebecca M. Cortner, Wartrace

2 cups applesauce
1 (3-ounce) package lime gelatin
1 (3-ounce) package lemon gelatin
1 cup chopped celery
1/2 cup chopped nuts
1/4 cup chopped maraschino cherries,
    well drained
2 cups ginger ale
1 cup evaporated milk
2 tablespoons lemon juice

Combine applesauce and gelatins in large saucepan. Heat over low heat until gelatins are dissolved; let cool. Stir in celery, nuts, cherries and ginger ale. Chill until syrupy. Chill evaporated milk in refrigerator tray until soft ice crystals form around edges of tray. Whip with chilled beaters until stiff. Add lemon juice; whip until very stiff. Fold into gelatin mixture. May add a few drops green food coloring if desired. Spoon into 2-quart mold. Chill until firm. Yield: 8 servings.

Approx Per Serving: Cal 256; Prot 5 g; Carbo 45 g; Fiber 2 g; T Fat 8 g; 25% Calories from Fat; Chol 9 mg; Sod 107 mg.

Polynesian Orange Salad Bowl

Rubye Bailey, Knoxville

2 cups mandarin oranges
1 cup chunk pineapple, drained
1 cup chopped pecans
1/2 cup maraschino cherries, quartered
1 cup diced apples
4 cups chopped cooked chicken breasts
1 1/2 cups mayonnaise
2 tablespoons lemon juice
1/2 teaspoon curry powder
1/2 teaspoon salt
8 lettuce leaves

Combine oranges, pineapple, pecans, cherries, apples and chicken in large bowl. Add mayonnaise, lemon juice, curry powder and salt; mix gently. Serve on lettuce leaves. Yield: 8 servings.

Approx Per Serving: Cal 584; Prot 24 g; Carbo 23 g; Fiber 2 g; T Fat 46 g; 69% Calories from Fat; Chol 84 mg; Sod 426 mg.

Diabetic Orange Salad

Mrs. Glenn Smelcer, Greeneville

8 ounces low-fat cottage cheese
1/2 cup mayonnaise
1 (11-ounce) can mandarin oranges, drained
1 (3-ounce) package artificially sweetened orange gelatin

Combine cottage cheese and mayonnaise in medium bowl. Add oranges and gelatin; mix well. Chill until firm. Exchanges: 1 lean meat, 1 1/2 fruit and 3 fat. Yield: 6 servings.

Approx Per Serving: Cal 203; Prot 7 g; Carbo 11 g; Fiber 0 g; T Fat 15 g; 67% Calories from Fat; Chol 14 mg; Sod 298 mg.

Evelyn's Pineapple-Cheese Salad

Evelyn Nutt, Waynesboro

2 cups crushed pineapple, canned in unsweetened juice
1 (3-ounce) package lime sugar-free gelatin
1 (3-ounce) package lemon sugar-free gelatin
1 cup reduced-calorie mayonnaise
1 cup low-fat cottage cheese
1/2 cup sliced almonds
1/2 cup low-fat sour cream
1/2 cup reduced-calorie mayonnaise

Drain pineapple, reserving juice. Add enough water to reserved juice to make 2 1/2 cups. Bring to a boil in saucepan. Add gelatins, stirring until dissolved. Chill until consistency of unbeaten egg whites. Fold in pineapple, 1 cup mayonnaise, cottage cheese and almonds. Pour into 8-by-12-inch dish. Chill until firm. Cut into squares. Serve on lettuce. Combine sour cream and 1/2 cup mayonnaise in small bowl; mix well. Place small amount on each square. Yield: 15 servings.

Approx Per Serving: Cal 125; Prot 4 g; Carbo 11 g; Fiber <1 g; T Fat 8 g; 53% Calories from Fat; Chol 10 mg; Sod 218 mg.

Pineapple-Lemon Salad

Mrs. Una F. Ring, Columbia

1 (20-ounce) can unsweetened
  crushed pineapple
1 (3-ounce) package sugar-free lemon
  gelatin
1 tablespoon fresh lemon juice
1 cup plain nonfat yogurt
9 lettuce leaves

Drain pineapple, reserving juice. Add enough water to reserved juice to make 2 cups liquid. Bring 1 cup liquid to a boil in saucepan. Add gelatin, stirring until dissolved. Add remaining liquid and lemon juice. Add yogurt gradually, mixing well. Chill until thickened but not set. Add pineapple. Pour into 5-cup mold or 9-inch square dish. Chill until firm. Cut into squares. Serve on lettuce leaves. Yield: 9 servings.

Approx Per Serving: Cal 61; Prot 2 g; Carbo 12 g; Fiber <1 g; T Fat <1 g; 13% Calories from Fat; Chol 3 mg; Sod 39 mg.

Pineapple-Cheese Salad

Mrs. Bennie Oliver, Ashland City

1 (8-ounce) can pineapple tidbits
8 ounces American cheese, cubed
1 (10-ounce) package miniature
  marshmallows
1 tablespoon flour
1 tablespoon vinegar
1/3 cup sugar
3 eggs, well beaten
1/2 cup maraschino cherries
1/2 cup chopped nuts

Drain pineapple, reserving juice. Combine pineapple, cheese and marshmallows in large bowl. Pour into 8-inch square dish. Combine reserved juice, flour, vinegar, sugar and eggs in top of double boiler. Cook until thickened; pour over pineapple mixture. Sprinkle cherries and nuts over top. Chill until firm. Cut into squares. May store in refrigerator for several days. Yield: 6 servings.

Approx Per Serving: Cal 480; Prot 13 g; Carbo 65 g; Fiber <1 g; T Fat 21 g; 39% Calories from Fat; Chol 142 mg; Sod 594 mg.

Pink Cloud Pineapple Salad

Mrs. Brentz Moore, Kenton

1 (20-ounce) can crushed pineapple,
  drained
1 (3-ounce) package cherry gelatin
16 ounces cottage cheese
1 (10-ounce) carton whipped topping

Combine pineapple and gelatin in large bowl; mix well. Add cottage cheese; mix well. Fold in whipped topping with spoon. Pour into large serving bowl; chill. May store in refrigerator for 1 week. Yield: 8 servings.

Approx Per Serving: Cal 248; Prot 9 g; Carbo 29 g; Fiber <1 g; T Fat 12 g; 41% Calories from Fat; Chol 8 mg; Sod 266 mg.

34 Salads

Seven-Step Low-Fat Salad

Helen Harris, Santa Fe

1 1/2 cups crushed vanilla wafers
8 ounces reduced-calorie cream cheese, softened
1/4 cup sugar
2 tablespoons low-fat milk
8 ounces no-fat cottage cheese
1 (20-ounce) can crushed pineapple, drained
1/2 cup grated low-fat Colby cheese
1/2 cup grated low-fat Monterey Jack cheese
2 cups whipped topping
1/4 cup confectioners' sugar
1 cup grated fat-free Cheddar cheese
16 ounces reduced-calorie sour cream
12 maraschino cherries
1 cup walnut halves

Combine vanilla wafers, cream cheese, sugar and milk in medium bowl; mix well. Press into 8-by-13-inch pan. Combine cottage cheese and pineapple in large bowl; mix well. Spread over first layer. Combine Colby and Monterey Jack cheeses in small bowl; mix well. Spread over second layer. Combine 1 cup whipped topping and confectioners' sugar; mix well. Spread over third layer. Sprinkle Cheddar cheese over fourth layer. Combine 1 cup whipped topping and sour cream; mix well. Spread over fifth layer. Garnish with cherries and walnuts. Yield: 12 servings.

Approx Per Serving: Cal 350; Prot 13 g; Carbo 33 g; Fiber <1 g; T Fat 20 g; 49% Calories from Fat; Chol 39 mg; Sod 287 mg.

Strawberry Salad

Mary J. Griffith, Palmersville

4 cups fresh strawberries
1 (6-ounce) package strawberry gelatin
1 cup boiling water
1 cup mashed bananas
1 (15-ounce) can crushed pineapple
1/2 cup chopped pecans
2 cups sour cream

Wash and hull strawberries; mash. Combine gelatin and boiling water in large bowl; stir until dissolved. Stir in strawberries, bananas, pineapple and pecans. Pour half of mixture into 9-by-13-inch dish. Chill for 1 hour or until set. Let remaining mixture stand at room temperature. Spread sour cream over congealed mixture. Spoon remaining gelatin mixture over sour cream layer. Cover; chill overnight. Cut into squares. Yield: 12 servings.

Approx Per Serving: Cal 228; Prot 3 g; Carbo 30 g; Fiber 2 g; T Fat 12 g; 44% Calories from Fat; Chol 17 mg; Sod 57 mg.

Strawberry Diabetic Salad

Rosanne Beasley, Covington

1 (3-ounce) package sugar-free strawberry gelatin
3/4 cup chopped fresh strawberries
1 cup plain low-fat yogurt
1 teaspoon vanilla extract
Sugar substitute to equal 2 teaspoons sugar
4 lettuce leaves

Prepare gelatin using package directions in large bowl; chill until slightly thickened. Crush strawberries in small bowl; add to gelatin mixture. Add yogurt, vanilla and sugar substitute; stir until well blended. Pour into 4 individual molds; chill until set. Remove from molds. Serve on lettuce leaves. Exchange for 1 fruit. Yield: 4 (1/2 cup) servings.

Approx Per Serving: Cal 60; Prot 5 g; Carbo 8 g; Fiber <1 g; T Fat 1 g; 16% Calories from Fat; Chol 4 mg; Sod 100 mg.

Strawberry Gelatin Salad

Melissa Meyer, Afton

1 (11-ounce) can mandarin oranges
1/2 cup sugar
1 envelope plain gelatin
1/2 cup orange juice
1/4 cup lemon juice
2 eggs, well beaten
1 cup sour cream
1 (3-ounce) package cream cheese, softened
1 banana, sliced
1 cup strawberries, sliced
1/3 cup chopped walnuts

Drain oranges, reserving syrup. Add enough water to syrup to make 3/4 cup liquid. Combine sugar and gelatin in large saucepan; add syrup, orange juice and lemon juice. Heat over medium heat until gelatin is dissolved. Remove from heat. Stir half of mixture gradually into eggs. Stir egg mixture back into hot mixture. Return to stove; cook, stirring constantly, for 2 minutes or until thickened. Remove from heat; add sour cream and cream cheese. Beat until smooth. Chill until partially set. Fold in oranges, banana, strawberries and walnuts. Pour into 8-inch square dish. Chill until firm. Yield: 8 servings.

Approx Per Serving: Cal 242; Prot 5 g; Carbo 26 g; Fiber 1 g; T Fat 14 g; 51% Calories from Fat; Chol 77 mg; Sod 67 mg.

Strawberry-Cream Congealed Salad

Mae Guffey, Athens

2 (3-ounce) packages strawberry gelatin
1 cup boiling water
2 (10-ounce) packages frozen strawberries
1 (8-ounce) can crushed pineapple
2 medium bananas, mashed
1 cup chopped nuts
2 cups sour cream

Dissolve gelatin in boiling water in large bowl. Add strawberries; stir until strawberries are thawed. Add pineapple, bananas and nuts. Pour half of mixture into gelatin mold. Chill for 1 1/2 hours or until set. Let remaining gelatin stand at room temperature. Spread sour cream over congealed gelatin mixture. Pour remaining gelatin over sour cream layer. Chill until set. Yield: 12 servings.

Approx Per Serving: Cal 251; Prot 4 g; Carbo 29 g; Fiber 2 g; T Fat 15 g; 51% Calories from Fat; Chol 17 mg; Sod 58 mg.

Congealed Strawberry-Buttermilk Salad

Mrs. J. B. Wisecarver, Bybee

1 (6-ounce) package strawberry gelatin
1 (20-ounce) can crushed pineapple
2 cups buttermilk
1 cup chopped pecans
1 (9-ounce) container whipped topping

Combine gelatin and pineapple in large saucepan; mix well. Heat until gelatin is dissolved; do not boil. Remove from heat; let cool. Add buttermilk, pecans and whipped topping. Mix well; do not beat. Pour into serving dish. Chill until firm. Yield: 12 servings.

Approx Per Serving: Cal 235; Prot 4 g; Carbo 31 g; Fiber <1 g; T Fat 12 g; 44% Calories from Fat; Chol 1 mg; Sod 85 mg.

Strawberry-Pretzel Salad

Janice Stafford, Dyersburg

2 cups coarsely crushed pretzels
3/4 cup melted butter
3 tablespoons sugar
1 (6-ounce) package strawberry gelatin
2 cups boiling water
1 cup sliced strawberries, drained
1 cup chopped pecans
8 ounces cream cheese, softened
1 cup sugar
1 (8-ounce) container whipped topping

Preheat oven to 400 degrees. Combine pretzels, butter and 3 tablespoons sugar in medium bowl; mix well. Press into 9-by-13-inch baking pan. Bake for 8 minutes. Let cool. Dissolve gelatin in boiling water in large bowl. Chill until partially set; stir in strawberries and pecans. Combine cream cheese and 1 cup sugar in saucepan; heat, stirring, until smooth. Remove from heat; stir in whipped topping. Spread carefully over crust. Spoon gelatin mixture over cream cheese mixture. Chill until firm. May substitute 1 cup chopped apple for strawberries if desired. Salad will keep longer with apples. Yield: 12 servings.

Approx Per Serving: Cal 483; Prot 5 g; Carbo 51 g; Fiber 1 g; T Fat 30 g; 55% Calories from Fat; Chol 52 mg; Sod 457 mg.

Delicious Pretzel Salad

Mrs. George Sargent, LaVergne

2 cups crushed pretzels
3/4 cup melted margarine
3 tablespoons sugar
8 ounces cream cheese, softened
1 cup sugar
1 (16-ounce) container whipped topping
1 (6-ounce) package strawberry gelatin
2 cups boiling water
2 (10-ounce) packages frozen strawberries

Preheat oven to 400 degrees. Combine pretzels, margarine and 3 tablespoons sugar in medium bowl; mix well. Press into 9-by-13-inch baking pan. Bake for 8 minutes. Do not overcook. Let cool thoroughly. Combine cream cheese and 1 cup sugar in large mixer bowl; beat until smooth. Fold in whipped topping. Spread over pretzel layer. Dissolve gelatin in boiling water in large bowl. Add strawberries. Chill until partially set. Pour over cream cheese layer. Chill until firm. Yield: 12 servings.

Approx Per Serving: Cal 489; Prot 5 g; Carbo 57 g; Fiber 1 g; T Fat 28 g; 50% Calories from Fat; Chol 21 mg; Sod 480 mg.

Luscious Pretzel Salad

Mrs. Alphus E. Keen, Westmoreland

2 cups crushed pretzels
3 tablespoons sugar
3/4 cup melted margarine
8 ounces cream cheese, softened
1 (8-ounce) container whipped topping
1 cup sugar
1 (6-ounce) package strawberry gelatin
2 cups hot water
1 (16-ounce) package frozen strawberries

Preheat oven to 350 degrees. Combine pretzels, 3 tablespoons sugar and margarine in large bowl; mix well. Press into 9-by-13-inch baking dish. Bake for 8 minutes. Let cool completely. Combine cream cheese, whipped topping and 1 cup sugar in large mixer bowl. Beat until sugar is dissolved. Spread over crust. Chill for 5 minutes. Dissolve gelatin in boiling water in large bowl; let cool. Add strawberries. Pour over cream cheese mixture. Chill for 4 hours or until firm. Yield: 12 servings.

Approx Per Serving: Cal 426; Prot 4 g; Carbo 52 g; Fiber 1 g; T Fat 23 g; 48% Calories from Fat; Chol 21 mg; Sod 475 mg.

Watergate Salad

Bertha E. Davis, Morrison

1 (3-ounce) package pistachio instant
   pudding mix
1 (20-ounce) can crushed pineapple
1/2 cup chopped nuts
2 cups miniature marshmallows
1 (9-ounce) container whipped topping

Combine pudding mix and pineapple in large bowl; mix well. Add nuts and marshmallows; mix well. Fold in whipped topping. Chill. Yield: 8 servings.

Approx Per Serving: Cal 281; Prot 1 g; Carbo 42 g; Fiber <1 g; T Fat 13 g; 41% Calories from Fat; Chol 0 mg; Sod 167 mg.

Creamy Waldorf Salad

Pat Dummett, Cumberland Gap

3 ounces cream cheese, softened
1 1/2 teaspoons sugar
1 1/2 teaspoons orange juice
3 large apples, cubed
1 (8-ounce) can pineapple tidbits, drained
2 tablespoons chopped celery
2 tablespoons chopped pecans
2 tablespoons raisins
8 lettuce leaves

Combine cream cheese, sugar and orange juice in small bowl; mix well. Combine apples, pineapple, celery, pecans and raisins in large bowl. Add cream cheese mixture; toss gently. Cover; chill. Toss again before serving. Serve on lettuce leaves. Yield: 8 servings.

Approx Per Serving: Cal 125; Prot 2 g; Carbo 20 g; Fiber 2 g; T Fat 5 g; 36% Calories from Fat; Chol 12 mg; Sod 35 mg.

Bean Salad

Mrs. A. W. Cavin, Martin

1 (16-ounce) can red kidney beans
1 (16-ounce) can French green beans,
   drained
1 (15-ounce) can yellow wax beans, drained
1 small onion, chopped
1 cup vinegar
1/2 cup vegetable oil
3/4 cup sugar
1/2 teaspoon salt

Wash kidney beans in cold water; drain. Combine beans and onion in large bowl. Mix vinegar, oil, sugar and salt in small saucepan. Bring to a rolling boil. Pour over vegetables; cover. Let stand for several hours or overnight in refrigerator. Salad will keep for several days.
Yield: 12 servings.

Approx Per Serving: Cal 180; Prot 3 g; Carbo 23 g; Fiber 4 g; T Fat 9 g; 44% Calories from Fat; Chol 0 mg; Sod 402 mg.

Three-Bean Salad

Mrs. John Walters, Springville

1 (16-ounce) can red kidney beans
1 (15-ounce) can slant-sliced wax beans,
   drained
1 (16-ounce) can green beans, drained
1 medium onion, chopped
1 celery stalk, sliced
3/4 cup sugar
Salt and pepper to taste
1/2 cup vegetable oil
2/3 cup white vinegar

Rinse kidney beans; drain. Combine beans in large bowl. Add onion and celery. Combine sugar, salt, pepper, oil and vinegar in small bowl. Pour over bean mixture; mix well. Chill, covered, for 24 hours. May store in refrigerator for several days. Yield: 12 servings.

Approx Per Serving: Cal 181; Prot 3 g; Carbo 23 g; Fiber 4 g; T Fat 9 g; 44% Calories from Fat; Chol 0 mg; Sod 493 mg.

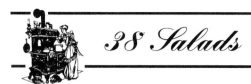

Crunchy Broccoli Salad

Betty Smith, Atwood

2 bunches fresh broccoli
1 cup mayonnaise
2 tablespoons vinegar
2 tablespoons sugar
1 cup sunflower seeds
1 cup crumbled crisp-fried bacon
1/2 cup raisins

Separate broccoli into bite-sized pieces. Peel and cut stems into bite-sized pieces. Place in large bowl. Combine mayonnaise, vinegar and sugar in small bowl; mix well. Pour over broccoli. Add sunflower seeds, bacon and raisins; mix well. Yield: 12 servings.

Approx Per Serving: Cal 253; Prot 6 g; Carbo 14 g; Fiber 3 g; T Fat 21 g; 71% Calories from Fat; Chol 13 mg; Sod 182 mg.

Broccoli Salad

Lou Anna Cumby, Cookeville

1 bunch broccoli
1 cup raisins
1/2 cup chopped green onions
1/2 cup mayonnaise-type salad dressing
2 tablespoons white vinegar
1/4 cup sugar
6 crisp-fried bacon slices, crumbled

Cut broccoli into bite-sized pieces. Peel stalk; cut into bite-sized pieces. Combine broccoli, raisins and onions in large bowl. Combine salad dressing, vinegar and sugar in small bowl; mix well. Pour over broccoli mixture; mix gently. Sprinkle bacon over top. Yield: 8 servings.

Approx Per Serving: Cal 209; Prot 4 g; Carbo 35 g; Fiber 2 g; T Fat 8 g; 30% Calories from Fat; Chol 8 mg; Sod 196 mg.

Broccoli Delight Salad

Vickie Ray, Bethel Springs

1 large bunch fresh broccoli
1 cup raisins
1 cup sunflower kernels
10 crisp-fried bacon slices, crumbled
1/4 cup diced red onion
1/2 cup mayonnaise-type salad dressing
3 tablespoons sugar
1 tablespoon white vinegar

Wash broccoli; drain. Cut into bite-sized pieces. Combine broccoli, raisins, sunflower kernels, bacon and onion in large bowl. Combine salad dressing, sugar and vinegar in small bowl; mix well. Pour over broccoli mixture; toss together gently. May store in refrigerator up to 2 days. Yield: 8 servings.

Approx Per Serving: Cal 302; Prot 9 g; Carbo 31 g; Fiber 4 g; T Fat 18 g; 50% Calories from Fat; Chol 11 mg; Sod 249 mg.

Broccoli-Cauliflower Salad

Nadine Turner, Fountain Run, Kentucky

1 bunch broccoli
1 head cauliflower
1 cup grated carrots
1 medium red onion, finely chopped
1 envelope ranch salad dressing mix
1 cup milk
1 cup mayonnaise

Wash broccoli and cauliflower; break into bite-sized pieces. Combine broccoli, cauliflower, carrots and onion in large serving bowl. Place dressing mix, milk and mayonnaise in blender container; blend until smooth. Pour over vegetables; mix gently. Yield: 10 servings.

Approx Per Serving: Cal 208; Prot 3 g; Carbo 9 g; Fiber 2 g; T Fat 19 g; 77% Calories from Fat; Chol 16 mg; Sod 357 mg.

Cabbage Salad

Mrs. Thurman Hurst, Bethel Springs

1 large head cabbage, chopped
2 medium onions, thinly sliced
1 small green bell pepper, thinly sliced
1 (2-ounce) jar pimentos, drained
1 cup vegetable oil
1 cup sugar
3/4 cup white vinegar
1 1/2 teaspoons salt
1 teaspoon celery seed

Layer cabbage, onions, green pepper and pimentos in large glass bowl; do not stir. Combine remaining ingredients in medium saucepan; mix well. Bring to a boil; boil for 2 minutes. Pour over vegetables; cover tightly. Refrigerate for 4 hours. May store up to 2 weeks in refrigerator. Yield: 8 servings.

Approx Per Serving: Cal 391; Prot 3 g; Carbo 37 g; Fiber 3 g; T Fat 28 g; 61% Calories from Fat; Chol 0 mg; Sod 428 mg.

Garden Cabbage Salad

Mrs. Henry G. Frazier, Dickson

1 small cabbage, finely shredded
1 bunch green onions, chopped
1 carrot, shredded
1/2 green bell pepper, finely chopped
6 radishes, thinly sliced
1 cucumber, finely chopped
3/4 cup mayonnaise-type salad dressing
1/4 cup vinegar
1/4 cup sugar
1 teaspoon celery seed
1/4 teaspoon salt
1/4 teaspoon pepper

Combine cabbage, green onions, carrot, green pepper, radishes and cucumber in large bowl; chill. Combine remaining ingredients in small bowl; blend well. Pour over salad just before serving; toss to coat.
Yield: 10 servings.

Approx Per Serving: Cal 118; Prot 2 g; Carbo 16 g; Fiber 2 g; T Fat 6 g; 44% Calories from Fat; Chol 5 mg; Sod 197 mg.

Bavarian Coleslaw

Mrs. Carrie E. Wilson, Crossville

This slaw will keep in refrigerator for up to 6 weeks and is so handy to have made before guests arrive.

1 medium head cabbage, finely chopped
1 tablespoon non-iodized salt
1 cup white vinegar
1 1/2 cups sugar
2 cups finely chopped celery
2 cups finely chopped green bell pepper
2 cups finely chopped carrots

Place cabbage in large bowl. Add salt; mix well. Chill for 1 hour. Mix vinegar and sugar in saucepan. Heat, stirring, until sugar is dissolved; let cool. Add celery, green pepper and carrots to cabbage; mix well. Pack in bowl with tight-fitting lid. Pour vinegar mixture over cabbage mixture. Cover tightly; refrigerate. Yield: 12 servings.

Approx Per Serving: Cal 131; Prot 2 g; Carbo 33 g; Fiber 2 g; T Fat <1 g; 2% Calories from Fat; Chol 0 mg; Sod 569 mg.

Freezer Coleslaw

Catherine Tate, Joelton

5 cups shredded cabbage
1 teaspoon salt
2 cups sugar
1 cup vinegar
1/2 cup water
1 teaspoon celery seed
2 cups chopped celery
1/2 cup chopped green bell pepper
1/2 cup thinly sliced carrot
1/4 cup chopped onion

Mix cabbage and salt in large bowl; let stand for 1 hour. Combine sugar, vinegar, water and celery seed in 1-quart saucepan. Bring to a boil; boil, stirring, for 1 minute. Let cool to lukewarm. Drain cabbage; add celery, green pepper, carrot and onion. Stir vinegar mixture into cabbage mixture. Spoon into three 1-pint freezer containers. Cover and label; freeze for up to 1 month. Thaw in refrigerator for 8 hours before serving; drain well. Garnish with sliced pimento-stuffed olives. Yield: 12 (1/2 cup) servings.

Approx Per Serving: Cal 147; Prot <1 g; Carbo 38 g; Fiber 1 g; T Fat <1 g; 1% Calories from Fat; Chol 0 mg; Sod 202 mg.

Freezer Slaw

Ida Robertson, Martin

1 medium head cabbage, grated
1 teaspoon pickling salt
1 medium carrot, grated
1 green bell pepper, chopped
1 cup white vinegar
1/4 cup water
1 teaspoon celery seed
1 teaspoon white mustard seed
2 cups sugar

Place cabbage in large bowl. Sprinkle pickling salt over cabbage; mix well. Let set for 1 hour. Drain; squeeze out liquid. Add carrot and green pepper; mix well. Combine remaining ingredients in mixer bowl; beat for 1 minute. Chill mixture. Pour over cabbage mixture; mix well. Pack in pint freezer containers; freeze. Yield: 8 servings.

Approx Per Serving: Cal 236; Prot 2 g; Carbo 60 g; Fiber 2 g; T Fat <1 g; 2% Calories from Fat; Chol 0 mg; Sod 291 mg.

Nine-Day Slaw

Mildred Barker, Dunlap

1 medium cabbage, shredded
2 stalks celery, finely chopped
2 medium onions, finely chopped
1 green bell pepper, finely chopped
2 cups sugar
1 cup vegetable oil
1 cup vinegar
2 tablespoons sugar
2 tablespoons salt

Combine cabbage, celery, onions and green pepper in large bowl. Add 2 cups sugar; mix well. Mix oil, vinegar, 2 tablespoons sugar and salt in medium saucepan. Bring to a boil, stirring constantly. Pour over cabbage mixture; chill. May be stored in refrigerator for up to 9 days. Yield: 8 servings.

Approx Per Serving: Cal 494; Prot 2 g; Carbo 64 g; Fiber 3 g; T Fat 28 g; 48% Calories from Fat; Chol 0 mg; Sod 1629 mg.

Wanda's Kraut Salad

Mrs. Wanda Cochran, Dickson

1 (16-ounce) can kraut, drained
2 cups shredded celery
1 large green pepper, chopped
1 large purple onion, chopped
1 large carrot, shredded
1/2 cup vinegar
1/2 cup vegetable oil
1 cup sugar

Combine kraut, celery, green pepper, onion and carrot in large bowl. Mix vinegar, oil and sugar in small saucepan. Bring to a boil; simmer for 10 minutes. Remove from heat; let cool. Pour over kraut mixture; mix well. Chill for 2 hours or overnight. Yield: 8 servings.

Approx Per Serving: Cal 249; Prot 1 g; Carbo 32 g; Fiber 3 g; T Fat 14 g; 48% Calories from Fat; Chol 0 mg; Sod 406 mg.

Blanche's Kraut Salad

Mrs. Blanche Lee, Ooltewah

1 (32-ounce) can kraut, drained
1 onion, chopped
1 cup chopped celery
1 cup chopped green bell pepper
1 (2-ounce) jar pimentos, drained
1 1/2 cups sugar
1 cup vinegar

Combine kraut, onion, celery, green pepper and pimentos in large bowl. Mix sugar and vinegar in medium bowl. Pour over kraut mixture; mix well. Chill. Yield: 8 servings.

Approx Per Serving: Cal 183; Prot 1 g; Carbo 47 g; Fiber 4 g; T Fat <1 g; 1% Calories from Fat; Chol 0 mg; Sod 764 mg.

Pool Room Slaw

Elaine Latham, Huntland

This slaw goes great on hamburgers.

1 gallon chopped cabbage
3 large onions, chopped
2 green bell peppers, chopped
1 cup vinegar
1 tablespoon salt
3 cups sugar
1 teaspoon pepper
1 quart prepared mustard

Combine cabbage, onions and green peppers in large bowl. Combine vinegar, salt, sugar and pepper in small saucepan. Bring to a boil; let cool. Stir into cabbage mixture. Add mustard; mix well. Store in containers in refrigerator. Yield: 24 servings.

Approx Per Serving: Cal 150; Prot 3 g; Carbo 33 g; Fiber 2 g; T Fat 2 g; 12% Calories from Fat; Chol 0 mg; Sod 798 mg.

Carrot Salad

Mrs. B. T. Atkisson, Jr., Columbia

1 (3-ounce) package orange gelatin
1 1/2 cups boiling water
1 (8-ounce) can crushed pineapple
2 cups grated carrots
1/2 cup flaked coconut
1/4 cup chopped pecans

Dissolve gelatin in boiling water in large bowl. Drain pineapple; add juice to gelatin mixture. Chill until gelatin is consistency of unbeaten egg white. Stir in pineapple, carrots, coconut and pecans. Pour into lightly greased 1-quart mold; chill. Yield: 8 servings.

Approx Per Serving: Cal 120; Prot 2 g; Carbo 21 g; Fiber 2 g; T Fat 4 g; 29% Calories from Fat; Chol 0 mg; Sod 38 mg.

Cauliflower Salad

Dailia Adams, Petersburg

1 head cauliflower, chopped
1 bunch green onions, chopped
1 bunch radishes, chopped
1 (10-ounce) package frozen green peas
1 cup mayonnaise
Salt and pepper to taste

Combine cauliflower, green onions and radishes in large bowl. Add frozen peas. Add mayonnaise, salt and pepper; toss together gently. May be stored in refrigerator overnight. Yield: 8 servings.

Approx Per Serving: Cal 242; Prot 3 g; Carbo 9 g; Fiber 3 g; T Fat 22 g; 80% Calories from Fat; Chol 16 mg; Sod 215 mg.

Shoe Peg Corn Salad

Sandra Lyons, Ethridge

1 cup chopped onions
1 cup chopped green bell pepper
1 cup chopped celery
1 (11-ounce) can white shoe peg corn, drained
1 (15-ounce) can green English peas, drained
1 (15-ounce) can French-cut green beans, drained
1 (4-ounce) jar chopped pimentos, drained
1 cup sugar
3/4 cup vinegar
1/2 cup vegetable oil
1 teaspoon each salt, pepper

Combine onions, green pepper, celery, corn, peas, green beans and pimentos in large bowl. Mix sugar, vinegar, oil, salt and pepper in small bowl. Pour over vegetables; mix well. Refrigerate until chilled or until serving time. Yield: 12 servings.

Approx Per Serving: Cal 211; Prot 3 g; Carbo 31 g; Fiber 3 g; T Fat 10 g; 39% Calories from Fat; Chol 0 mg; Sod 439 mg.

Chick-Pea Fantasy Salad

Lora Robbins, Henry County

1/3 cup vegetable oil
1/4 teaspoon salt
2 tablespoons lemon juice
4 cups cooked chick-peas
1/2 cup crumbled feta cheese
1/2 cup cubed Monterey Jack cheese
1/2 cup cubed sharp Cheddar cheese
3 medium tomatoes, chopped
2 green onions, chopped
1/4 cup finely minced fresh parsley
1/2 cup finely chopped celery
8 ounces plain yogurt
2 tablespoons mayonnaise
2 tablespoons buttermilk
6 radishes, thinly sliced
6 black olives, sliced
1/2 cup alfalfa sprouts

Combine oil, salt and lemon juice in large mixer bowl; beat well. Add chick-peas, cheeses, tomatoes, green onions, parsley and celery; mix gently until well coated. Chill for a few hours or overnight. Combine yogurt, mayonnaise and buttermilk in small bowl; mix gently. Add half of mixture to salad mixture just before serving; toss gently. Serve on bed of lettuce. Garnish with radishes and olives. Sprinkle alfalfa sprouts over top. Serve remaining dressing with individual servings. Yield: 8 servings.

Approx Per Serving: Cal 380; Prot 15 g; Carbo 28 g; Fiber 6 g; T Fat 24 g; 55% Calories from Fat; Chol 36 mg; Sod 410 mg.

Crunchy Pea Salad

Lucille Bivens, Lynnville

1 (10-ounce) package frozen English peas, thawed
1 cup cauliflowerets
1 cup finely chopped celery
1/4 cup sliced green onions
1/2 cup sour cream
1/2 cup mayonnaise
1 cup coarsely chopped pecans
3 crisp-fried bacon slices, crumbled

Combine peas, cauliflower, celery and green onions in large bowl. Combine sour cream and mayonnaise in small bowl; mix well. Pour over vegetable mixture; toss to coat. Stir in pecans; sprinkle with bacon. Chill.
Yield: 10 servings.

Approx Per Serving: Cal 221; Prot 4 g; Carbo 8 g; Fiber 3 g; T Fat 20 g; 80% Calories from Fat; Chol 13 mg; Sod 145 mg.

Green Pea Salad

Bonnye Catron, Shelbyville

2 (15-ounce) cans green peas, drained
3/4 cup chopped salad olives with pimentos
3 hard-cooked eggs, chopped
1 tablespoon dehydrated onion
1/4 teaspoon pepper
1/4 teaspoon onion powder
1/2 cup mayonnaise
3/4 cup grated cheese

Combine peas, olives, eggs, onion, pepper and onion powder in large serving bowl. Add mayonnaise; mix well. Sprinkle cheese over top. Chill for 3 hours or overnight.
Yield: 8 servings.

Approx Per Serving: Cal 262; Prot 10 g; Carbo 15 g; Fiber 4 g; T Fat 19 g; 63% Calories from Fat; Chol 99 mg; Sod 730 mg.

English Pea Salad

Mrs. Edd Quinn, Parsons

1 (20-ounce) can English peas, drained
4 ounces Velvetta cheese, cubed
3 medium pickles, chopped
2 hard-cooked eggs, chopped
1/2 medium onion, chopped
1/4 cup vinegar
1/2 teaspoon dry mustard
1/2 cup water
1 egg, beaten
1/4 cup sugar
1/2 teaspoon flour

Combine peas, cheese, pickles, hard-cooked eggs and onion in salad bowl. Mix vinegar, mustard, water, beaten egg, sugar and flour in small saucepan. Bring to a boil; let cool. Pour over salad; mix gently. Yield: 6 servings.

Approx Per Serving: Cal 219; Prot 12 g; Carbo 24 g; Fiber 4 g; T Fat 9 g; 36% Calories from Fat; Chol 124 mg; Sod 925 mg.

Pea Salad

Pat Hinton, Knoxville

1 cup sugar
$^1/_2$ cup vinegar
$^1/_2$ cup canola oil
$^1/_2$ teaspoon salt
$^1/_4$ teaspoon pepper
1 (15-ounce) can green peas
1 (15-ounce) can French-style green beans
1 (4-ounce) jar chopped pimentos
4 stalks celery, cut into bite-sized pieces
1 green bell pepper, chopped
1 cup chopped onion

Combine sugar, vinegar, oil, salt and pepper in saucepan; bring to a boil, stirring, until sugar is melted. Remove from heat; let cool. Place peas, green beans and pimentos in colander in sink; drain thoroughly. Combine drained vegetables, celery, green pepper and onion in large bowl. Pour vinegar mixture over vegetables; chill. Serve with cottage cheese or baked ham. Yield: 12 servings.

Approx Per Serving: Cal 180; Prot 2 g; Carbo 24 g; Fiber 2 g; T Fat 9 g; 45% Calories from Fat; Chol 0 mg; Sod 330 mg.

Country Potato Salad

Helen McCarley, Nashville

4 cups cubed cooked potatoes
$^1/_4$ cup creamy French dressing
1 cup chopped celery
3 hard-cooked eggs, chopped
2 tablespoons grated onion
1 cup sour cream
2 tablespoons chopped parsley
2 tablespoons chopped dill pickle
2 tablespoons chopped pimento
1 tablespoon prepared mustard
1 teaspoon salt
$^1/_8$ teaspoon pepper

Combine potatoes and dressing in large bowl; mix lightly. Chill for 1 hour. Add celery and eggs. Mix onion, sour cream, parsley, pickle, pimento, mustard, salt and pepper in small bowl. Pour over potato mixture; mix lightly. Chill. Yield: 8 servings.

Approx Per Serving: Cal 199; Prot 5 g; Carbo 20 g; Fiber 2 g; T Fat 11 g; 50% Calories from Fat; Chol 92 mg; Sod 476 mg.

Danish Potato Salad

Mrs. George Wheat, Savannah

$^1/_4$ cup vinegar
$^1/_4$ cup water
$^1/_4$ cup sugar
$^1/_4$ teaspoon salt
$^1/_4$ teaspoon pepper
1 teaspoon prepared mustard
2 eggs, well beaten
1 cup mayonnaise-type salad dressing
4 cups cubed cooked potatoes
2 hard-cooked eggs, chopped
$^1/_2$ cup chopped pickles
1 tablespoon minced onion
1 tablespoon chopped sweet pepper

Combine vinegar, water, sugar, salt, pepper and mustard in medium saucepan; bring to a boil. Reduce heat gradually. Stir small amount of hot mixture into beaten eggs; return to mixture. Cook, stirring constantly, for 5 minutes or until slightly thickened. Beat in salad dressing. Place potatoes in large bowl. Add hard-cooked eggs, pickles, onion and sweet pepper. Add dressing; toss gently. Yield: 6 servings.

Approx Per Serving: Cal 330; Prot 6 g; Carbo 40 g; Fiber 2 g; T Fat 17 g; 45% Calories from Fat; Chol 152 mg; Sod 630 mg.

Great American Potato Salad

Juanita Beaty, Albany, Kentucky

1 cup mayonnaise-type salad dressing
1 teaspoon prepared mustard
1/2 teaspoon celery seed
1/2 teaspoon salt
1/8 teaspoon pepper
4 cups cubed cooked potatoes
2 hard-cooked eggs, chopped
1/2 cup chopped onion
1/2 cup sliced celery
1/2 cup chopped sweet pickles

Combine salad dressing, mustard, celery seed, salt and pepper in large bowl; mix well. Add potatoes, eggs, onion, celery and pickles; mix lightly. Chill.
Yield: 6 servings.

Approx Per Serving: Cal 294; Prot 5 g; Carbo 37 g; Fiber 2 g; T Fat 15 g; 45% Calories from Fat; Chol 81 mg; Sod 652 mg.

Quick New Potato Salad

Shawn Lee and Shannon Dee Bolden, Lynnville

5 cups 1/4-inch thick sliced new potatoes
1/3 cup cold water
1 cup mayonnaise
1/2 cup chopped onion
1/2 cup sliced celery
1/2 cup chopped sweet pickles
1 tablespoon prepared mustard
1/2 teaspoon each celery seed, salt

Combine potatoes and water in 2-quart glass casserole; cover. Microwave on High for 10 to 12 minutes or until tender, stirring after 6 minutes; drain. Combine mayonnaise, onion, celery, pickles, mustard, celery seed and salt in large bowl. Add potatoes; mix lightly. Chill.
Yield: 6 servings.

Approx Per Serving: Cal 385; Prot 3 g; Carbo 30 g; Fiber 2 g; T Fat 30 g; 67% Calories from Fat; Chol 22 mg; Sod 583 mg.

Stuffed Tomato Salad

Gerry Hickman, Mt. Pleasant

4 well-shaped medium tomatoes
1/2 teaspoon salt
2 cups chicken salad
1 hard-cooked egg, chopped
Parsley sprigs

Scald tomatoes in boiling water for 1 minute. Remove skins; scoop out part of centers. Sprinkle with salt. Turn upside down in shallow dish; chill. Fill centers with chicken salad. Garnish with egg and parsley sprigs. May fill with mixture of cottage cheese, grated American cheese and stuffed olives if desired. Yield: 4 servings.

Approx Per Serving: Cal 313; Prot 13 g; Carbo 7 g; Fiber 2 g; T Fat 26 g; 74% Calories from Fat; Chol 101 mg; Sod 494 mg.

Spinach Salad

Tena Carmack, Ripley

8 cups bite-sized pieces spinach
1 cucumber, sliced
1 bunch green onions with tops, chopped
1 (16-ounce) can sliced beets, drained
1 pound fresh mushrooms, sliced
1/2 cup vinegar
1/2 cup vegetable oil

Combine spinach, cucumber, green onions, beets and mushrooms in large bowl. Combine vinegar and vegetable oil in small bowl. Pour over salad just before serving. Toss to coat. Yield: 8 servings.

Approx Per Serving: Cal 176; Prot 4 g; Carbo 12 g; Fiber 4 g; T Fat 14 g; 68% Calories from Fat; Chol 0 mg; Sod 204 mg.

Crisp Vegetable Salad

Irene Cameron, Rutledge

1 cauliflower
1 bunch broccoli, cut into bite-sized pieces
2 cups diced celery
1 medium onion, chopped
1 green pepper, chopped
1 cucumber, chopped
1 (16-ounce) can kidney beans, drained
1/3 cup vinegar
1/3 cup vegetable oil
1/4 cup sugar
1/2 cup mayonnaise
Salt and pepper to taste
1 cup shredded cheese
3/4 cup bacon bits

Separate cauliflower into small flowerets. Cut broccoli into bite-sized pieces; peel and dice stem. Combine cauliflower, broccoli, celery, onion, green pepper, cucumber and kidney beans in large bowl; toss together to mix. Combine vinegar, oil, sugar, mayonnaise, salt and pepper in mixer bowl; beat until creamy. Drizzle over vegetables; toss together lightly. Store, covered, in refrigerator overnight. Layer cheese and bacon bits over top just before serving. Yield: 12 servings.

Approx Per Serving: Cal 240; Prot 7 g; Carbo 17 g; Fiber 5 g; T Fat 17 g; 62% Calories from Fat; Chol 17 mg; Sod 321 mg.

Out-of-This-World Salad

Mrs. S. E. Shipe, Knoxville

1 (6-ounce) package lemon gelatin
1 (3-ounce) package lime gelatin
1 1/2 cups boiling water
2 cucumbers, finely chopped
1 medium onion, finely chopped
1 cup mayonnaise
2 1/2 teaspoons vinegar
3/4 teaspoon salt
1 (24-ounce) carton cottage cheese
1 cup chopped pecans

Dissolve gelatins in boiling water in large bowl; let cool. Stir in cucumbers, onion, mayonnaise, vinegar, salt, cottage cheese and pecans. Chill for 4 to 6 hours or until firm. Yield: 10 servings.

Approx Per Serving: Cal 417; Prot 12 g; Carbo 30 g; Fiber 1 g; T Fat 29 g; 60% Calories from Fat; Chol 23 mg; Sod 628 mg.

Veggies Salad

Geraldine Hickman, Mt. Pleasant

1 (8-count) can crescent dinner rolls
6 ounces cream cheese, softened
3/4 cup mayonnaise
1 cup chopped carrots
1 cup chopped celery
1 cup chopped radishes
1 cup chopped green and red bell peppers
1 cup broccoli flowerets
1 cup cauliflower flowerets
1 cup chopped onion
1/2 cup chopped cucumber

Preheat oven to 425 degrees. Unroll rolls; press into bottom of greased 9-by-13-inch baking pan, sealing perforations. Bake for 10 minutes or until golden brown; let cool. Combine cream cheese and mayonnaise in small bowl; mix well. Spread on crust. Layer vegetables over top. Chill; cut into squares. Yield: 12 servings.

Approx Per Serving: Cal 223; Prot 3 g; Carbo 13 g; Fiber 1 g; T Fat 18 g; 71% Calories from Fat; Chol 25 mg; Sod 305 mg.

Seven-Layer Salad

Marilyn Garner, Greenfield

1 medium red onion, thinly sliced
1 head lettuce, torn into bite-sized pieces
1 (10-ounce) package frozen green peas, uncooked
4 hard-cooked eggs, sliced
1 pound crisp-fried bacon, crumbled
2 tablespoons sugar
3/4 cup mayonnaise
1 cup shredded Cheddar cheese

Separate onion into rings. Layer lettuce, peas, onion rings, egg slices and 12 ounces bacon in 9-by-13-inch dish. Sprinkle with sugar. Cover with mayonnaise. Top with cheese. Garnish with remaining bacon. Chill, covered, for 2 hours or overnight. Yield: 12 servings.

Approx Per Serving: Cal 263; Prot 10 g; Carbo 8 g; Fiber 2 g; T Fat 22 g; 74% Calories from Fat; Chol 98 mg; Sod 369 mg.

Chicken-Fruit Salad

Mrs. James S. O'Neal, Oneida

3 cups chopped cooked chicken
3/4 cup chopped celery
3/4 cup seedless red grapes, cut into halves
1 (20-ounce) can pineapple chunks, drained
1 (11-ounce) can mandarin oranges, drained
1/4 cup chopped pecans
1/4 cup mayonnaise-type salad dressing
1/8 teaspoon salt
6 lettuce leaves

Combine chicken, celery, grapes, pineapple, oranges and 3 tablespoons pecans in large bowl; toss together gently. Add salad dressing and salt; mix well. Chill. Serve on lettuce leaves. Garnish with remaining pecans. Yield: 6 servings.

Approx Per Serving: Cal 304; Prot 22 g; Carbo 29 g; Fiber 2 g; T Fat 12 g; 35% Calories from Fat; Chol 65 mg; Sod 194 mg.

Crunchy Fruited Chicken Salad

Mrs. Chris Stallings, Cleveland

4 cups chopped cooked chicken
1 (20-ounce) can pineapple chunks, drained
1 (11-ounce) can mandarin oranges, drained
1/2 cup seedless white or purple grapes, cut into halves
1 cup chopped celery
1/2 cup sliced ripe olives
1/2 cup chopped green pepper
2 tablespoons grated onion
1 cup mayonnaise
1 tablespoon prepared mustard
1/4 teaspoon salt
1 (3-ounce) can chow mein noodles

Combine chicken, pineapple, oranges, grapes, celery, olives, green pepper and onion in large bowl; mix gently. Combine mayonnaise, mustard and salt in small bowl; mix well. Add to chicken mixture; toss together gently. Cover; chill thoroughly. Stir in chow mein noodles just before serving. Yield: 12 servings.

Approx Per Serving: Cal 315; Prot 15 g; Carbo 18 g; Fiber 1 g; T Fat 21 g; 60% Calories from Fat; Chol 52 mg; Sod 293 mg.

Chinese Chicken Salad

Mrs. Edward Felknor, Dandridge

This recipe may be combined the day before serving and mayonnaise added at serving time.

1 (8-ounce) can bamboo shoots, drained
1 (8-ounce) can water chestnuts, drained
2 tablespoons minced onion
1 cup slivered almonds
2 (11-ounce) cans mandarin oranges, drained
4 cups cubed cooked chicken breasts
2 cups mayonnaise
1 (5-ounce) can Chinese noodles

Chop bamboo shoots and water chestnuts into large bowl. Add onion, almonds, oranges and chicken. Add mayonnaise; mix gently. Chill for several hours. Serve on nest of Chinese noodles. Yield: 12 servings.

Approx Per Serving: Cal 514; Prot 19 g; Carbo 22 g; Fiber 2 g; T Fat 41 g; 72% Calories from Fat; Chol 61 mg; Sod 303 mg.

Turkey Salad

Ruth B. Hardin, Lexington

2 1/2 cups cubed cold cooked turkey
2 tablespoons vinegar
2 teaspoons water
1/2 teaspoon salt
1/4 teaspoon sugar
1/2 cup coarsely chopped celery, chilled
1/2 cup Toray seeded grape halves, chilled
1/2 cup mayonnaise, chilled
2 cups crisp salad greens
8 stuffed olives, sliced
2 hard-cooked eggs, sliced

Place turkey in large bowl. Combine vinegar, water, salt and sugar in small bowl; mix well. Drizzle over turkey; toss lightly. Chill, covered, for 2 to 3 hours. Add celery, grapes and mayonnaise; toss lightly with fork. Arrange on salad greens. Garnish with olives and eggs. Serve immediately. Yield: 4 servings.

Approx Per Serving: Cal 430; Prot 30 g; Carbo 10 g; Fiber 1 g; T Fat 30 g; 63% Calories from Fat; Chol 189 mg; Sod 697 mg.

Dairyman's Salad Supreme

Mrs. Carl Steadman, Whitesburg

4 cups salad greens, broken into bite-sized
    pieces
1/2 cup crumbled blue cheese
1 cup chopped ham
1 (8-ounce) can water chestnuts, sliced
1 cup cherry tomatoes
1 cup grated Cheddar cheese
1 cup grated Mozzarella cheese
2 (10-ounce) packages frozen peas
1 cup sour cream
1/2 cup buttermilk
1/2 cup parsley sprigs
2 hard-cooked eggs, sliced
1/2 cup grated Parmesan cheese

Layer salad greens, blue cheese, ham, water chestnuts, 3/4 cup tomatoes, Cheddar cheese, Mozzarella cheese and frozen peas in 3-quart glass bowl. Mix sour cream and buttermilk in small bowl; blend well. Spread over layered mixture. Garnish with remaining tomatoes, parsley, egg slices and Parmesan cheese. Chill. Yield: 12 servings.

Approx Per Serving: Cal 230; Prot 15 g; Carbo 12 g; Fiber 3 g; T Fat 14 g; 54% Calories from Fat; Chol 75 mg; Sod 493 mg.

Imperial Salad

Lillian M. White, Knoxville

1 (8-ounce) jar pimentos
6 pounds shredded cabbage
1 medium onion, chopped
3 large cucumbers, chopped
3 green bell peppers, chopped
2 red bell peppers, chopped
2 pounds boiled ham, chopped
4 ounces mixed sweet pickles, chopped
Salt and pepper to taste
2 cups mayonnaise

Mash pimentos with fork to fine consistency in large bowl. Add cabbage, onion, cucumbers, green peppers, red peppers, ham and pickles; toss together gently. Add salt, pepper and mayonnaise; mix well. Yield: 16 servings.

Approx Per Serving: Cal 359; Prot 18 g; Carbo 17 g; Fiber 5 g; T Fat 26 g; 62% Calories from Fat; Chol 48 mg; Sod 1010 mg.

Chinese Pork Salad

Tonya Jackson, West Point

1 pound pork strips
1/2 cup oriental stir-fry sauce
3 green onions, sliced
1/2 red bell pepper, diced
2 (10-ounce) packages frozen pea pods,
    thawed, drained
1 (8-ounce) can mandarin oranges, drained
1 (3-ounce) can chow mein noodles

Marinate pork strips in stir-fry sauce for 30 minutes; drain. Stir-fry pork in large nonstick skillet over medium-high heat for 4 to 5 minutes. Remove from skillet to large bowl. Add green onions, red pepper, pea pods, oranges and noodles. Toss together gently. Serve with hot French bread. Yield: 4 servings.

Approx Per Serving: Cal 423; Prot 29 g; Carbo 41 g; Fiber 5 g; T Fat 16 g; 35% Calories from Fat; Chol 69 mg; Sod 1299 mg.

Taco Salad

Mrs. Patsy Cox, Mosheim

1 small onion, thinly sliced
1 pound ground beef
1/4 cup dry onion soup mix
3/4 cup water
1 medium head lettuce, torn into
    bite-sized pieces
1 large tomato, cut into wedges
1/4 cup chopped green pepper
1/2 cup sliced green olives
1 cup shredded sharp natural Cheddar
    cheese
1 (6-ounce) package corn chips

Separate onion slices into rings. Brown beef in medium skillet, stirring until crumbly; drain off excess fat. Sprinkle soup mix over beef. Stir in water. Simmer, uncovered, for 10 minutes. Combine onion rings, lettuce, tomato, green pepper, olives and cheese in salad bowl; toss together. Place lettuce mixture on individual salad plates. Spoon meat mixture on lettuce. Top with corn chips.
Yield: 6 servings.

Approx Per Serving: Cal 453; Prot 26 g; Carbo 25 g; Fiber 3 g; T Fat 29 g; 56% Calories from Fat; Chol 76 mg; Sod 1285 mg.

Dale Hollow Bass Salad

Mrs. Dewey Wells, Celina

1 fresh bass
1 green bell pepper, chopped
1 red bell pepper, chopped
1 small onion, chopped
1 medium cucumber, chopped
2 hard-cooked eggs, chopped
1/4 cup chopped olives
1/4 cup mayonnaise
Salt and pepper to taste

Boil fish in saucepan until tender; let cool. Remove all bones. Chop into bite-sized pieces. Combine fish, green pepper, red pepper, onion, cucumber, eggs and olives in large bowl. Add mayonnaise, salt and pepper. Toss lightly until well mixed. Yield: 6 servings.

Approx Per Serving: Cal 159; Prot 10 g; Carbo 5 g; Fiber 1 g; T Fat 11 g; 63% Calories from Fat; Chol 101 mg; Sod 146 mg.

Shrimp Salad

Jenny B. Milam, Decaturville

1 (5-ounce) can small shrimp, drained
2 cups cooked macaroni
2 hard-cooked eggs, chopped
1 cup chopped celery
1 tablespoon chopped pimento
1/4 cup French dressing
1/2 cup mayonnaise

Combine shrimp, macaroni, eggs, celery, pimento and French dressing in large bowl. Add mayonnaise; mix gently. Chill thoroughly. Yield: 6 servings.

Approx Per Serving: Cal 300; Prot 10 g; Carbo 17 g; Fiber 1 g; T Fat 22 g; 64% Calories from Fat; Chol 128 mg; Sod 326 mg.

Low-Cal Pasta Salad

Mrs. William Booker, Dickson

1 cup cooked shell macaroni, drained
1 cup cherry tomato halves
1 cup cooked green beans, drained
1/4 cup cucumber slices
1/4 cup radish slices
1/2 cup Italian reduced-calorie dressing
4 slices cheese, chopped
4 lettuce leaves

Combine macaroni, tomatoes, green beans, cucumber and radishes in large bowl. Pour dressing over mixture. Marinate, covered, in refrigerator overnight. Add cheese; toss lightly. Serve on lettuce leaves.
Yield: 4 servings.

Approx Per Serving: Cal 178; Prot 7 g; Carbo 19 g; Fiber 3 g; T Fat 9 g; 43% Calories from Fat; Chol 13 mg; Sod 496 mg.

Vegetable-Macaroni Salad

Carolyn Aaron, Lexington

1 (16-ounce) package medium macaroni
1 large green pepper, chopped
4 carrots, shredded
1 onion, chopped
1 (14-ounce) can sweetened condensed milk
1 cup white vinegar
1 cup sugar
1 teaspoon salt
1/4 teaspoon pepper
1 cup mayonnaise
1 (16-ounce) can English peas, drained

Cook macaroni according to package directions; drain and let cool. Combine macaroni, green pepper, carrots and onion in large bowl. Combine condensed milk, vinegar, sugar, salt, pepper, mayonnaise and peas in large bowl. Add to macaroni mixture; mix gently. Cover; chill thoroughly. May store in refrigerator for 3 to 4 days.
Yield: 12 servings.

Approx Per Serving: Cal 487; Prot 10 g; Carbo 73 g; Fiber 3 g; T Fat 18 g; 33% Calories from Fat; Chol 22 mg; Sod 419 mg.

Spaghetti Salad

Bertie Watkins, Maryville

1 (12-ounce) package thin spaghetti
1 (16-ounce) bottle Italian dressing
1 (2-ounce) bottle salad supreme
5 green onions, chopped
1/2 green pepper, chopped
1 cup chopped broccoli
4 tomatoes, chopped
1 cup chopped cauliflower
3 stalks celery, chopped
1 carrot, chopped

Cook spaghetti according to package directions for 9 minutes; rinse and drain. Combine spaghetti, Italian dressing and salad supreme in large bowl. Marinate, covered, in refrigerator overnight. Add remaining ingredients; mix gently. May be stored in refrigerator for several days. Yield: 8 servings.

Approx Per Serving: Cal 467; Prot 10 g; Carbo 45 g; Fiber 3 g; T Fat 29 g; 54% Calories from Fat; Chol 0 mg; Sod 802 mg.

Ri-Salad

Jean Baird, Pine Knot, Kentucky

1 cup minute rice
2 cups mayonnaise
2 cups sliced celery
1 medium onion, finely chopped
4 teaspoons prepared mustard
1/2 teaspoon salt
4 hard-cooked eggs, chopped
8 radishes, sliced
1 cucumber, chopped

Cook rice according to package directions; chill. Combine rice, mayonnaise, celery, onion, mustard and salt in large bowl; mix well. Chill thoroughly. Stir in eggs, radishes and cucumber just before serving. Yield: 8 servings.

Approx Per Serving: Cal 497; Prot 5 g; Carbo 15 g; Fiber 1 g; T Fat 47 g; 84% Calories from Fat; Chol 139 mg; Sod 539 mg.

Rice Salad

Mrs. Molly Morgan, Soddy-Daisy

3 cups cooked cold rice
1 cup sweet pickle relish
4 hard-cooked eggs, chopped
1/2 cup finely chopped onion
2 tablespoons chopped pimento
1 1/2 cups mayonnaise
2 hard-cooked eggs, sliced

Combine rice, relish, chopped eggs, onion, pimento and mayonnaise in large bowl; toss together lightly. Chill thoroughly. Garnish with egg slices before serving. Yield: 8 servings.

Approx Per Serving: Cal 502; Prot 8 g; Carbo 35 g; Fiber 1 g; T Fat 37 g; 67% Calories from Fat; Chol 185 mg; Sod 501 mg.

Corn Bread Salad

Shirley Joiner, Lexington, Alabama

4 tomatoes, finely chopped
1 small green bell pepper, finely chopped
1 tablespoon sugar
1/2 pound crisp-fried bacon, crumbled
1 small onion, finely chopped
1/2 cup sweet pickles
1/4 cup pickle juice
6 cups crumbled corn bread
1 cup mayonnaise

Combine tomatoes, green pepper, sugar, bacon, onion, pickles and pickle juice in large bowl. Add corn bread. Stir in mayonnaise; mix well. Yield: 12 servings.

Approx Per Serving: Cal 334; Prot 6 g; Carbo 27 g; Fiber 2 g; T Fat 24 g; 63% Calories from Fat; Chol 36 mg; Sod 537 mg.

Saltine Salad

Mrs. H. G. Bryant, Cleveland

8 ounces saltine crackers, finely crushed
1/4 cup sweet pickle relish with juice
1/4 cup dill pickle relish with juice
5 hard-cooked eggs, chopped
1/2 green bell pepper, chopped
1 (4-ounce) jar chopped pimentos with juice
3/4 cup mayonnaise

Combine crackers, relishes, eggs, green pepper, pimentos and mayonnaise in large bowl; mix well. Serve on lettuce leaves. Yield: 8 servings.

Approx Per Serving: Cal 347; Prot 7 g; Carbo 28 g; Fiber 2 g; T Fat 23 g; 61% Calories from Fat; Chol 145 mg; Sod 637 mg.

Meat Dishes

Blacksmith

Ensuring that the craft of making
horseshoes doesn't become a lost art,
David Gibson of Lexington, Ky. teaches
a shoeing clinic for blacksmiths and
farriers at Bloomington Springs.

Corned Beef and Cabbage Casserole

Mrs. Betty Walls, Rockwood

5 medium potatoes, thinly sliced
1 small onion, chopped
4 cups chopped cabbage
1 teaspoon salt
1/2 teaspoon pepper
1 (12-ounce) can corned beef
1 (10-ounce) can cream of celery soup
1 1/4 cups milk

Preheat oven to 350 degrees. Layer potatoes, onion and cabbage in large casserole. Sprinkle with salt and pepper. Crumble corned beef over layers. Combine soup and milk in large bowl; pour over top. Bake, covered, for 1 hour. Yield: 8 servings.

Approx Per Serving: Cal 239; Prot 15 g; Carbo 24 g; Fiber 2 g; T Fat 10 g; 35% Calories from Fat; Chol 46 mg; Sod 1011 mg.

Barbecued Beef

Mrs. Pat Lipscomb, Springfield

1 (4-pound) cooked boneless beef roast
1 cup catsup
1/3 cup red wine vinegar
1/4 cup vegetable oil
1 tablespoon dark brown sugar
1 tablespoon Worcestershire sauce
1 tablespoon whole mustard seed
2 teaspoons paprika
1 teaspoon dried oregano
1 teaspoon chili powder
1/2 teaspoon salt
1/4 teaspoon ground cloves
1 bay leaf
1/8 teaspoon garlic salt

Preheat oven to 300 degrees. Slice roast into serving pieces. Place in large baking pan. Combine 1/2 cup water and remaining ingredients in large saucepan; mix well. Bring to a rolling boil; remove from heat. Pour sauce over roast. Bake for 45 minutes. This barbecue sauce is good on beef, pork or chicken. Yield: 16 servings.

Approx Per Serving: Cal 228; Prot 21 g; Carbo 5 g; Fiber <1 g; T Fat 13 g; 53% Calories from Fat; Chol 71 mg; Sod 322 mg.

Mexican Pot Roast with Black Bean Salsa

Elaine Fronczek, Knoxville

1 (3-pound) boneless chuck roast
1 teaspoon salt
2 tablespoons olive oil
1 large dried ancho chili
1/4 cup tomato paste
1 teaspoon cinnamon
2 tablespoons chili powder
1 teaspoon cocoa powder
1 teaspoon oregano
1/2 cup red wine
3 cloves of garlic, crushed
1 cup beef broth
1 (12-ounce) jar salsa

Preheat oven to 425 degrees. Sprinkle roast with salt. Add oil to bottom of Dutch oven. Place roast in pan; roast for 15 minutes, turning once. Split ancho chili; remove seed. Soak in water in small bowl for 5 minutes; mince. Combine with tomato paste and spices in medium bowl; blend well. Add to wine in large bowl; whisk. Add garlic and beef broth. Pour mixture over roast; cover. Reduce oven temperature to 350 degrees. Roast for 2 to 2 1/2 hours or until tender. Remove to cutting board; let stand for 5 minutes. Carve into 1/4-inch thick slices. Arrange slices in center of serving platter. Pour sauce into small bowl; skim off excess fat. Spoon sauce over roast. Arrange salsa on either side of roast. Garnish with parsley or cilantro. Yield: 8 servings.

Approx Per Serving: Cal 326; Prot 33 g; Carbo 7 g; Fiber 1 g; T Fat 18 g; 49% Calories from Fat; Chol 106 mg; Sod 687 mg.

Beef Steak-Potato Scallop

Mrs. Charley Henley, Limestone

1 (1-pound) 1-inch thick beef round steak
1/2 cup flour
3 tablespoons vegetable shortening
3 small onions, thinly sliced
3 tablespoons flour
1 1/2 teaspoons salt
1/4 teaspoon pepper
1/4 teaspoon thyme
1/4 teaspoon garlic salt
2 cups water
3 peeled medium potatoes, thinly sliced
Salt to taste
Paprika to taste

Preheat oven to 350 degrees. Cut steak into 1-inch cubes; coat with 1/2 cup flour. Melt shortening in skillet. Add meat; cook, stirring, until browned. Add onions; cook, stirring, until onions are tender. Pour into ungreased 2-quart casserole; sprinkle with 3 tablespoons flour, 1 1/2 teaspoons salt, pepper, thyme and garlic salt. Pour water over mixture. Bake, covered, for 45 minutes to 1 hour or until meat is tender. Increase oven temperature to 450 degrees. Arrange potatoes over meat; sprinkle with salt to taste and paprika. Bake, uncovered, for 30 minutes or until potatoes are tender. Yield: 4 servings.

Approx Per Serving: Cal 389; Prot 26 g; Carbo 41 g; Fiber 3 g; T Fat 13 g; 31% Calories from Fat; Chol 56 mg; Sod 975 mg.

Hot Beef and Hazelnut Salad

Joan Benton, Education Coordinator, Tennessee Beef Industry Council, Franklin

1/4 cup chopped green onions
2 cloves of garlic, minced
2 tablespoons Japanese light soy sauce
1 tablespoon safflower oil
1 tablespoon sherry
1 tablespoon water
1 pound beef sirloin steak, cut crossgrain into 1/8-inch strips
2 tablespoons cider vinegar
2 tablespoons wine vinegar
2 tablespoons Japanese light soy sauce
1 clove of garlic, minced
1 teaspoon sugar
1/4 teaspoon curry
1/4 teaspoon cayenne pepper
1/4 teaspoon ginger
6 cups mixed salad greens
1 red bell pepper
1 (8-ounce) can sliced water chestnuts, drained
1 tablespoon safflower oil

Combine green onions, 2 cloves of garlic, 2 tablespoons soy sauce, 1 tablespoon safflower oil, 1 tablespoon sherry and 1 tablespoon water in large bowl; mix well. Add beef strips. Let marinate at room temperature for 20 to 30 minutes. Combine vinegars, 2 tablespoons soy sauce, 1 clove of garlic, sugar, curry, cayenne pepper and ginger in small skillet; mix well. Let stand at room temperature for 30 minutes. Tear salad greens into bite-sized pieces. Cut half of red pepper into rings; cut remaining half into slivers. Combine salad greens, red pepper slivers and water chestnuts in large bowl. Heat 1 tablespoon safflower oil in large skillet. Brown steak quickly, half at a time. Add steak to salad mixture. Heat dressing in skillet; pour over salad. Toss together to mix well. Arrange reserved red pepper rings over salad. Garnish with lettuce leaves, chopped toasted hazelnuts or almonds. Yield: 4 servings.

Approx Per Serving: Cal 269; Prot 24 g; Carbo 16 g; Fiber 4 g; T Fat 13 g; 41% Calories from Fat; Chol 60 mg; Sod 139 mg.

Chinese Pepper Steak

Mrs. Grace Smith, Spring City

1 (1 1/2-pound) 1-inch thick sirloin or
   round steak
1/4 cup vegetable oil
1 clove of garlic, crushed
1 teaspoon salt
1 teaspoon ground ginger
1/2 teaspoon ground pepper
2 1/2 cups sliced green peppers
2 cups thinly sliced onions
1 tablespoon cornstarch
1/4 cup cold water
1/4 cup soy sauce
1/2 teaspoon sugar
1/2 cup beef bouillon
1 (6-ounce) can water chestnuts, sliced
4 green onions, cut into 1-inch pieces

Freeze steak for 1 hour. Cut into 1/8-inch slices. Heat oil in heavy skillet or wok. Add garlic, salt, ginger and pepper. Sauté until garlic is golden. Add steak; stir-fry for 2 minutes or until lightly browned. Remove beef from skillet. Add green peppers and onions. Cook, stirring constantly, for 3 minutes. Dissolve cornstarch in cold water in small bowl. Return beef to skillet; add soy sauce, sugar, bouillon, water chestnuts and cornstarch mixture. Add green onions. Simmer for 2 minutes or until sauce is thickened. Serve over hot rice. Yield: 8 servings.

Approx Per Serving: Cal 202; Prot 17 g; Carbo 9 g; Fiber 1 g; T Fat 11 g; 49% Calories from Fat; Chol 45 mg; Sod 866 mg.

Lynchburg-Laced Sirloin Strip Steaks

Del Tinsley, Nashville

2 tablespoons sour mash whiskey
2 tablespoons low-sodium soy sauce
2 tablespoons honey
1 tablespoon vegetable oil
1/4 teaspoon five-spice powder
1/4 teaspoon freshly ground pepper
4 (4-ounce) boneless New York sirloin strip
   steaks, trimmed
1 kiwifruit
1/4 cup small fresh mushrooms

Combine whiskey, soy sauce, honey, oil, five-spice powder and pepper in small bowl. Place steaks in plastic food bag. Add marinade; shake to coat evenly. Marinate for 2 to 4 hours, turning occasionally. Remove steaks from bag; reserve marinade. Place steaks on broiler pan; grill in oven 3 inches from broiler unit for 5 minutes on each side. Reserve several slices kiwifruit; chop remaining kiwifruit. Reserve several whole mushrooms; slice remaining mushrooms into thin slices. Add chopped kiwifruit and sliced mushrooms to marinade in plastic bag; shake to coat. Spoon over steaks. Grill for 1 to 2 minutes. Place steaks on serving platter. Arrange kiwifruit slices and whole mushrooms on steaks. Garnish with cherry tomatoes and cilantro. Pour pan juices into small bowl; serve separately. Yield: 4 servings.

Approx Per Serving: Cal 231; Prot 21 g; Carbo 13 g; Fiber <1 g; T Fat 9 g; 35% Calories from Fat; Chol 60 mg; Sod 71 mg.

Herb-Stuffed Flank Steak with Sauce

Barbara Jones, Memphis

This recipe won third place in the 1988 Tennessee Beef Cook-Off.

1 (1½-pound) flank steak
¼ cup butter
1 small onion, chopped
1 teaspoon chervil
1 teaspoon sage
1 teaspoon tarragon
1 teaspoon basil
1 teaspoon cilantro
1 teaspoon pepper
2 cups soft bread crumbs
1 (15-ounce) can herb tomato sauce
½ cup bourbon

Butterfly steak by slicing along grain, cutting carefully so steak will lay flat. Melt butter in small skillet. Add onion; sauté for 3 to 4 minutes. Combine onion, chervil, sage, tarragon, basil, cilantro, pepper and bread crumbs in medium bowl. Spread mixture over steak to within 1 inch of sides. Roll up, jelly-roll fashion. Tie with string; place in shallow dish. Mix tomato sauce and bourbon in medium bowl. Pour over steak; refrigerate for several hours or overnight. Preheat oven to 325 degrees. Transfer steak to baking dish. Bake for 1½ to 2 hours. Remove to serving platter. Let cool for 20 minutes. Slice across grain, making 8 equal slices. Serve sauce in separate dish.
Yield: 4 servings.

Approx Per Serving: Cal 472; Prot 31 g; Carbo 21 g; Fiber 3 g; T Fat 23 g; 43% Calories from Fat; Chol 99 mg; Sod 958 mg.

Southwestern Chuck-Eye Steaks with Sauce

Stanley Fronczek, Knoxville

1 teaspoon salt
¼ teaspoon cayenne pepper
½ teaspoon cumin
2 teaspoons minced fresh cilantro
1 large clove of garlic, crushed
1 tablespoon lime juice
2 tablespoons vegetable oil
4 (6-ounce) 1-inch thick chuck-eye steaks, well trimmed
2 medium red bell peppers
2 tablespoons minced fresh cilantro
1 tablespoon lime juice
½ teaspoon salt
½ teaspoon freshly ground pepper
¾ cup lite sour cream

Combine 1 teaspoon salt, cayenne pepper, cumin, 2 teaspoons cilantro, garlic, 1 tablespoon lime juice and 1 tablespoon oil in small bowl. Brush on steaks. Let stand for 30 minutes. Heat large skillet over high heat for 2 to 3 minutes. Add remaining oil to skillet. Add steaks; cook for 6 to 8 minutes or until steaks are cooked to medium degree of doneness, turning once. Split red peppers into quarters; remove seeds. Place skin side up on broiler pan 3 to 4 inches from heat. Broil until skin blisters and begins to blacken. Remove from pan; place pepper sections in brown bag for 5 minutes. Remove from bag; peel off skin. Cut into 1-inch pieces. Purée peppers, 2 tablespoons cilantro, 1 tablespoon lime juice, ½ teaspoon salt and pepper in blender. Fold pepper mixture into sour cream. Arrange steaks on serving platter. Spoon 1 to 2 tablespoons sauce on each steak. Garnish with cilantro, lime slices and cherry tomatoes. Serve remaining sauce on side.
Yield: 4 servings.

Approx Per Serving: Cal 361; Prot 30 g; Carbo 5 g; Fiber <1 g; T Fat 24 g; 61% Calories from Fat; Chol 98 mg; Sod 888 mg.

Saucy Pepper Steak

Besse Lovvorn Gentry, Christiana

1 cup flour
1/2 teaspoon salt
1/2 teaspoon paprika
1/4 teaspoon pepper
1/2 teaspoon chili powder
1/2 teaspoon celery seed
1 1/2 pounds round steak
1 cup vegetable oil
1/2 cup chopped green onions
1/4 cup Worcestershire sauce
1/3 cup tomato sauce
1/2 cup chopped red bell pepper
2 cups hot water

Combine flour, salt, paprika, pepper, chili powder and celery seed in shallow bowl; mix well. Cut steak into 1-inch serving pieces; dredge with flour mixture. Heat oil in 10-inch heavy skillet. Add steak; brown slowly on both sides, turning often. Add onions during last few minutes of browning. Pour off oil. Add Worcestershire sauce, tomato sauce, red pepper and water. Cover skillet tightly; cook on low heat for 1 1/2 hours or until tender. May add 1 can baked or barbecued beans to turn dish into meal-in-one favorite if desired. Yield: 6 servings.

Approx Per Serving: Cal 530; Prot 22 g; Carbo 20 g; Fiber 1 g; T Fat 40 g; 68% Calories from Fat; Chol 46 mg; Sod 414 mg.

Stuffed Steak

Shirley Stubblefield, Christiana

1 (3-pound) 1/4-inch thick sirloin steak
2 tablespoons butter
2 green onions, chopped
1 (8-ounce) can mushrooms, drained
1 tablespoon flour
1 tablespoon lemon juice
1 tablespoon Worcestershire sauce
2 tablespoons snipped parsley
Salt and pepper to taste

Cut pocket in steak with sharp knife. Pocket should be length of steak and almost all the way from side to side. Melt butter in heavy skillet. Add onions and mushrooms; sauté until onions are soft. Stir in flour. Add lemon juice and Worcestershire sauce, stirring until thickened. Add parsley, salt and pepper. Fill pocket in steak with stuffing. Place 4 toothpicks along edge to keep pocket closed. Broil for 10 to 12 minutes on each side or until desired doneness. May also be cooked on grill. Yield: 8 servings.

Approx Per Serving: Cal 241; Prot 31 g; Carbo 3 g; Fiber <1 g; T Fat 11 g; 42% Calories from Fat; Chol 97 mg; Sod 238 mg.

Tournedos ''Scarborough Fair''

Joel Stephens, Nashville

This recipe won second place in the 1988 Tennessee Beef Cook-Off.

1/4 cup chopped parsley
1/2 teaspoon dry ground sage
1/2 teaspoon dry crushed rosemary
1/2 teaspoon dry ground thyme
1/2 cup dry white wine
1/4 cup butter
1 pound beef tenderloin, cut into 1-inch thick slices
Garlic salt to taste
Freshly ground pepper to taste
1/3 cup sour cream

Combine parsley, sage, rosemary, thyme and wine in small bowl. Let stand for 15 minutes. Melt butter in large skillet on high heat. Sprinkle meat with garlic salt and pepper. Cook meat in butter for 1 minute. Turn; cook for 1 minute longer. Remove meat to warm platter. Add herb and wine mixture to skillet. Reduce heat to medium; cook for 1 minute, scraping up any bits that cling to pan. Add sour cream; cook for 1 minute longer. Spoon sauce over meat. Garnish with herbs if desired. Yield: 4 servings.

Approx Per Serving: Cal 305; Prot 20 g; Carbo 1 g; Fiber <1 g; T Fat 22 g; 66% Calories from Fat; Chol 96 mg; Sod 173 mg.

Louisiana Bake with Yam Dumplings

Mrs. J. W. Yarbro, Camden

2 cups chopped cooked chicken
2 cups chopped cooked ham
1/4 cup butter
1/4 cup flour
1 (3-ounce) can sliced mushrooms, drained
1 cup chicken broth
1 cup lite cream
1/4 cup finely chopped onion
Dash of cayenne pepper
1 cup mashed cooked yams
1/3 cup melted butter
1 egg, beaten
1 cup flour
2 teaspoons baking powder
1/2 teaspoon salt
1/2 teaspoon cinnamon

Preheat oven to 350 degrees. Arrange chicken and ham in lightly greased 2-quart casserole. Melt 1/4 cup butter in medium saucepan; blend in 1/4 cup flour. Add mushrooms, broth, cream, onion and cayenne pepper; cook, stirring, until thickened. Pour over ham and chicken. Bake for 20 minutes. Blend yams, 1/3 cup melted butter and egg in large bowl. Sift 1 cup flour, baking powder, salt and cinnamon together in medium bowl; add to yam mixture, mixing well. Drop by tablespoonfuls onto hot casserole. Bake for 25 to 30 minutes longer or until dumplings are lightly browned. Yield: 8 servings

Approx Per Serving: Cal 444; Prot 24 g; Carbo 23 g; Fiber 2 g; T Fat 28 g; 57% Calories from Fat; Chol 146 mg; Sod 1010 mg.

Crock•Pot Chili

Mrs. Diane Kaylor, Cleveland

1 1/2 pounds ground beef
1 medium onion, finely chopped
2 (15-ounce) cans pinto beans
1 envelope chili seasoning mix
1 (15-ounce) can tomato sauce with garlic, herbs and spices
1 (8-ounce) can tomato sauce
1 (15-ounce) can light red kidney beans
1/2 green bell pepper, finely chopped
2 teaspoons chili powder
1 teaspoon pepper

Brown ground beef in large skillet, stirring until crumbly. Add onion; pour off fat. Remove fat meat from pinto beans. Combine ground beef mixture, pinto beans and remaining ingredients in Crock•Pot. Cook on Low for 10 to 12 hours. Yield: 8 servings.

Approx Per Serving: Cal 349; Prot 28 g; Carbo 32 g; Fiber 6 g; T Fat 12 g; 32% Calories from Fat; Chol 63 mg; Sod 1182 mg.

Larry's Crock•Pot Chili

Larry R. Whitford, Brentwood

4 pounds ground beef
2 large onions, chopped
2 (6-ounce) cans chopped green chilies
1 (32-ounce) jar spaghetti sauce
1 (28-ounce) can tomatoes
2 packages chili mix
2 (16-ounce) cans chili beans
Chili powder to taste

Brown ground beef in large skillet, stirring until crumbly; drain. Combine ground beef and remaining ingredients in large Crock•Pot. Cook on Low for 6 to 8 hours. May remove lid near end of cooking to thicken. Serve with grated Cheddar cheese. May substitute chopped green peppers for chopped green chilies if desired. Yield: 12 servings.

Approx Per Serving: Cal 533; Prot 40 g; Carbo 29 g; Fiber 5 g; T Fat 29 g; 48% Calories from Fat; Chol 125 mg; Sod 1318 mg.

Mama's Chili

Tonia Wallace, Parsons

2 pounds ground beef
1/2 cup chopped onion
1 clove of garlic, minced
1 tablespoon salt
1 (6-ounce) can tomato paste
2 cups Dr. Pepper
1 cup water
2 tablespoons chili powder
2 cups hot chili beans
1/8 teaspoon oregano
1 teaspoon pepper
1 tablespoon paprika

Brown ground beef, onion and garlic in large skillet, stirring until crumbly; drain off fat. Add salt, tomato paste, Dr. Pepper and water; let simmer for 30 minutes. Add remaining ingredients. Simmer for 20 minutes.
Yield: 8 servings.

Approx Per Serving: Cal 375; Prot 30 g; Carbo 21 g; Fiber 4 g; T Fat 20 g; 47% Calories from Fat; Chol 95 mg; Sod 1386 mg.

Mexican Chili with Beans

Mrs. H. L. Liles, Bruceton

3 tablespoons vegetable oil
1 pound ground beef
1 large onion, chopped
2 cups canned tomatoes
1 (29-ounce) can kidney beans
1/2 teaspoon salt
1/2 teaspoon paprika
1 clove of garlic, crushed
Chili powder to taste

Heat oil in large heavy skillet. Add ground beef and onion. Brown, stirring until crumbly; drain off fat. Stir in remaining ingredients. Simmer for 2 hours. May add more tomatoes if more liquid is needed. Serve hot with corn chips or corn bread. Yield: 8 servings.

Approx Per Serving: Cal 276; Prot 19 g; Carbo 20 g; Fiber 7 g; T Fat 14 g; 44% Calories from Fat; Chol 42 mg; Sod 612 mg.

Special Chili

Mrs. Gwen V. Bailey, Burnsville, North Carolina

1 onion, finely chopped
1 green pepper, finely chopped
2 tablespoons vegetable oil
1 pound ground beef
3 1/2 cups tomatoes
1 1/2 teaspoons salt
1 bay leaf
1/4 teaspoon paprika
1/8 teaspoon cayenne pepper
2 whole cloves
1 tablespoon chili powder
1 teaspoon cumin

Brown onion and green pepper in oil in large heavy skillet. Add ground beef. Cook, stirring, until browned and crumbly. Add tomatoes, salt, bay leaf, paprika, cayenne pepper, cloves, chili powder and cumin; mix well. Cook over low heat for 3 to 4 hours. Yield: 4 servings.

Approx Per Serving: Cal 363; Prot 27 g; Carbo 12 g; Fiber 3 g; T Fat 23 g; 57% Calories from Fat; Chol 84 mg; Sod 894 mg.

Crafty Crescent Lasagna

Mrs. Ann Baumgartner, Shelby County

This recipe won first place and a microwave oven in the Tennessee Dairy Recipe Contest.

1/2 pound bulk sausage
1/2 pound ground beef
3/4 cup chopped onion
1/2 clove of garlic, minced
1 tablespoon minced parsley
1/2 teaspoon basil leaves
1/2 teaspoon oregano leaves
1/2 teaspoon salt
1/4 teaspoon pepper
1 (6-ounce) can tomato paste
1/4 cup grated Parmesan cheese
1 cup creamed cottage cheese
1 egg
2 (8-ounce) cans crescent dinner rolls
2 (4-by-7-inch) slices mozzarella cheese
1 tablespoon milk
2 tablespoons melted butter
1 tablespoon sesame seed

Preheat oven to 350 degrees. Brown sausage and ground beef in large skillet; drain off fat. Add onion, garlic, parsley, basil, oregano, salt, pepper and tomato paste; mix well. Simmer, uncovered, for 5 minutes. Combine Parmesan cheese, cottage cheese and egg in small bowl; mix well. Unroll crescent dough; separate into 8 rectangles. Place rectangles on ungreased cookie sheet, overlapping edges to form 13-by-15-inch rectangle. Press edges and perforations to seal. Spread half of meat mixture lengthwise down center third of dough to within 1 inch of each 13-inch end. Top meat mixture with cheese mixture; spoon remaining meat mixture over top, forming 3 layers. Place mozzarella cheese slices over meat mixture. Fold 13-inch ends of dough over filling 1 inch. Pull long sides of dough over filling, being careful to overlap edges only 1/4 inch. Pinch edges to seal. Brush with milk and butter; sprinkle with sesame seed. Bake for 20 to 25 minutes or until deep golden brown. Meat mixture may be made ahead and refrigerated. Yield: 6 servings.

Approx Per Serving: Cal 546; Prot 27 g; Carbo 44 g; Fiber 2 g; T Fat 30 g; 49% Calories from Fat; Chol 112 mg; Sod 1627 mg.

Lasagna

Jane Barham, Maryville

This recipe is even better the next day. It will keep in refrigerator for several days and freezes beautifully.

1 pound ground beef
1 large onion, chopped
3 tablespoons unsalted butter
1 tablespoon parsley flakes
1/2 teaspoon salt
2 cups chopped canned tomatoes
1 (12-ounce) can tomato paste
1 cup water
8 lasagna noodles
1 (24-ounce) carton cottage cheese
2 eggs, beaten
1 1/2 teaspoons salt
1/2 teaspoon pepper
2 tablespoons parsley flakes
1/2 cup Parmesan cheese
8 ounces shredded mild Cheddar cheese
8 ounces shredded mozzarella cheese

Preheat oven to 350 degrees. Brown ground beef in large heavy skillet, stirring until crumbly; drain off fat. Sauté onion in butter in small saucepan until lightly browned. Add to ground beef. Add 1 tablespoon parsley flakes, 1/2 teaspoon salt, tomatoes, tomato paste and water; mix well. Simmer for 45 minutes. Prepare lasagna noodles according to package directions. Combine cottage cheese, eggs, 1 1/2 teaspoons salt, pepper, 2 tablespoons parsley flakes, Parmesan cheese and Cheddar cheese in large bowl; mix well. Arrange 4 noodles in lightly greased 9-by-13-inch baking dish. Spread half cheese mixture over noodles. Top with half mozzarella cheese. Spread half meat mixture over mozzarella cheese. Repeat layers. Bake for 30 minutes. Let stand for 15 minutes before serving. Yield: 8 servings.

Approx Per Serving: Cal 623; Prot 45 g; Carbo 32 g; Fiber 4 g; T Fat 36 g; 51% Calories from Fat; Chol 176 mg; Sod 1756 mg.

Mexican Lasagna

Faye Burchett, Cookeville

1 1/2 pounds ground beef
1 1/2 teaspoons ground cumin
1 tablespoon chili powder
1/4 teaspoon red pepper
Salt to taste
1/4 teaspoon pepper
1 (16-ounce) can tomatoes, chopped
12 corn tortillas
2 cups small curd cottage cheese, drained
1 cup grated Monterey Jack cheese
1 egg
1/2 cup shredded Cheddar cheese
2 cups shredded lettuce
1/2 cup chopped tomatoes
3 green onions, chopped
1/4 cup sliced black olives

Preheat oven to 350 degrees. Brown ground beef in large skillet, stirring until crumbly; drain off fat. Add cumin, chili powder, red pepper, salt, pepper and tomatoes; heat thoroughly. Arrange enough tortillas in 9-by-13-inch baking dish to cover bottom and sides. Spread meat mixture over tortillas. Layer remaining tortillas over meat mixture. Combine cottage cheese, Monterey Jack cheese and egg in medium bowl; pour over tortillas. Bake for 30 minutes. Sprinkle rows of Cheddar cheese, lettuce, tomatoes, green onions and olives diagonally across center of casserole. Yield: 8 servings.

Approx Per Serving: Cal 457; Prot 35 g; Carbo 27 g; Fiber 4 g; T Fat 23 g; 46% Calories from Fat; Chol 118 mg; Sod 597 mg.

Spaghetti and Meatballs

Mrs. Willis Sugg, Newport

1 pound ground chuck
2 eggs
2 teaspoons minced garlic
1 1/2 teaspoons oregano
1 teaspoon salt
1/4 teaspoon pepper
2 tablespoons vegetable oil
3/4 cup chopped onion
1/2 teaspoon pepper
1 bay leaf
5 cups tomato sauce
1 (16-ounce) package spaghetti
1/2 cup Parmesan cheese

Combine meat, eggs, 1 teaspoon garlic, 1/2 teaspoon oregano, salt and 1/4 teaspoon pepper in large bowl; mix well. Form into 1-inch balls. Brown in oil in heavy skillet. Remove from skillet; drain. Cook onion and 1 teaspoon garlic in hot oil in skillet until tender; do not brown. Stir in 1/2 teaspoon pepper, 1 teaspoon oregano, bay leaf, tomato sauce and 1/4 cup water. Add meatballs; cook over medium heat for 30 minutes. Cook spaghetti according to package directions. Remove bay leaf from sauce. Serve over hot spaghetti. Sprinkle with Parmesan cheese. Yield: 6 servings.

Approx Per Serving: Cal 619; Prot 35 g; Carbo 74 g; Fiber 6 g; T Fat 21 g; 30% Calories from Fat; Chol 133 mg; Sod 1813 mg.

One-Dish Spaghetti

Frances Crossman, Cookeville

1 pound ground beef
3 1/2 cups cooked tomatoes
1/3 cup chopped onion
1/3 cup chopped green pepper
1/2 cup catsup
1 teaspoon salt
1 cup uncooked bite-sized spaghetti pieces

Brown beef lightly in large skillet over medium heat, stirring until crumbly; drain off fat. Add remaining ingredients; mix well. Cook, covered, over high heat for 5 minutes, stirring frequently. Reduce heat; simmer for 30 minutes or until spaghetti is tender, stirring occasionally. Serve hot. Yield: 6 servings.

Approx Per Serving: Cal 279; Prot 20 g; Carbo 25 g; Fiber 3 g; T Fat 11 g; 36% Calories from Fat; Chol 56 mg; Sod 654 mg.

Spaghetti Casserole

Mary Ann Crowell, Franklin

2 pounds ground beef
2 tablespoons butter
5 green onions, chopped
1 medium green pepper, chopped
1 teaspoon salt
1 teaspoon pepper
1 teaspoon garlic salt
1/2 teaspoon red pepper
1 (6-ounce) can tomato paste
1 (8-ounce) Italian-style spaghetti dinner
8 ounces cream cheese, softened
1 (16-ounce) container small curd
   cottage cheese
1 cup sour cream
8 ounces mozzarella cheese, grated

Preheat oven to 375 degrees. Brown beef in butter in large skillet, stirring until crumbly. Add green onions, green pepper, salt, pepper, garlic salt and red pepper. Add tomato paste and herb mix package from dinner box. Cook spaghetti according to package directions. Arrange in bottom of 9-by-13-inch casserole dish. Mix cream cheese, cottage cheese and sour cream in medium bowl; spread over spaghetti. Spoon meat sauce over cheese mixture. Sprinkle Parmesan cheese from dinner box and mozzarella cheese over top. Bake for 45 minutes.
Yield: 10 servings.

Approx Per Serving: Cal 581; Prot 38 g; Carbo 27 g; Fiber 2 g; T Fat 36 g; 56% Calories from Fat; Chol 137 mg; Sod 1256 mg.

Spaghetti Pizza Casserole

Lynne Pigue, Centerville

1/4 cup butter
1 cup grated Parmesan cheese
10 ounces spaghetti, cooked
24 ounces grated mozzarella cheese
1 (3-ounce) package sliced pepperoni
1 (32-ounce) jar spaghetti sauce

Preheat oven to 350 degrees. Melt butter in 9-by-13-inch baking pan. Sprinkle with Parmesan cheese. Add spaghetti; mix well. Arrange in layer. Sprinkle 12 ounces mozzarella cheese over spaghetti. Top with half pepperoni. Add spaghetti sauce. Sprinkle with remaining mozzarella cheese. Top with remaining pepperoni. Bake for 30 minutes or until all cheese is melted. Mixture also fits into two 8-inch square baking pans. Freezes well.
Yield: 12 servings.

Approx Per Serving: Cal 436; Prot 20 g; Carbo 31 g; Fiber 1 g; T Fat 26 g; 53% Calories from Fat; Chol 67 mg; Sod 925 mg.

Porcupine Balls

Mrs. Ina Bayless, Jefferson City

2 pounds ground beef
1 cup chopped onions
1 cup uncooked rice
1 tablespoon pepper
2 teaspoons salt
2 (10-ounce) cans tomato soup
2 (10-ounce) soup cans water

Preheat oven to 350 degrees. Combine beef, onions, rice, pepper and salt in large bowl; mix well. Shape into egg-sized balls. Combine soup and water in large baking dish; mix well. Drop meatballs into soup mixture. Bake, covered, for 1 1/2 hours. Yield: 8 servings.

Approx Per Serving: Cal 392; Prot 28 g; Carbo 30 g; Fiber <1 g; T Fat 17 g; 40% Calories from Fat; Chol 84 mg; Sod 1125 mg.

Meatballs

Mrs. Dudley Hesson, Lafayette

1 pound ground beef
1/3 cup uncooked rice
1/2 cup chopped onion
3/4 cup water
1 teaspoon salt
1/4 teaspoon pepper
1 (10-ounce) can condensed tomato soup
1/2 teaspoon chili powder

Combine beef, rice, onion, 1/4 cup water, salt and pepper in large bowl. Shape into 1-inch balls. Blend soup and chili powder in large saucepan. Stir in 1/2 cup water; bring to a boil. Add meatballs. Simmer, covered, for 1 hour, stirring occasionally. Yield: 4 servings.

Approx Per Serving: Cal 364; Prot 28 g; Carbo 24 g; Fiber <1 g; T Fat 17 g; 42% Calories from Fat; Chol 84 mg; Sod 1124 mg.

Meatballs in Mushroom Sauce

Mrs. J. D. Prince, Estill Springs

1 1/2 pounds ground beef
Salt and pepper to taste
1/4 cup minced onion
1 cup crushed cornflakes
1/2 (10-ounce) can golden mushroom soup
1/2 (10-ounce) can cream of mushroom soup
1/4 cup water

Preheat oven to 350 degrees. Combine beef, salt, pepper, onion and cornflakes in large bowl; mix well. Shape into 1-inch balls. Brown meatballs in skillet; drain. Place in 8-inch square baking dish. Combine soups and water in medium bowl; mix well. Pour over meatballs. Bake for 1 hour or until hot and bubbly. Yield: 6 servings.

Approx Per Serving: Cal 342; Prot 27 g; Carbo 15 g; Fiber <1 g; T Fat 18 g; 49% Calories from Fat; Chol 85 mg; Sod 584 mg.

Grandmother's Meat Loaf

Mrs. Marie Mayes, Nashville

1 pound ground beef
1 (10-ounce) can vegetable soup
2 eggs
1 cup cracker crumbs
1/2 teaspoon each salt, pepper
2 stalks celery, finely chopped
2 green bell peppers, finely chopped
1 cup milk

Preheat oven to 375 degrees. Combine beef, soup, eggs, cracker crumbs, salt, pepper, celery and green peppers in large bowl; mix well. Add milk; mix well. Press into loaf pan. Bake for 40 minutes. Yield: 4 servings.

Approx Per Serving: Cal 471; Prot 34 g; Carbo 29 g; Fiber 2 g; T Fat 24 g; 46% Calories from Fat; Chol 199 mg; Sod 1180 mg.

Mexican Meat Loaf

Margaret L. Davis, Decherd

1 1/2 pounds ground beef
1 (8-ounce) can tomato sauce
1 cup broken corn tortilla chips
1/2 cup chopped onion
1 (4-ounce) can diced green chilies
1 egg
1 tablespoon chili powder
1/2 teaspoon salt

Preheat oven to 375 degrees. Combine beef, 1/2 can tomato sauce, tortilla chips, onion, chilies, egg, chili powder and salt in large bowl; mix well. Shape into loaf. Place in shallow baking dish. Bake for 1 hour; drain. Pour remaining tomato sauce over meat loaf. Bake for 5 minutes longer. Let stand for 10 minutes before slicing. Yield: 6 servings.

Approx Per Serving: Cal 345; Prot 28 g; Carbo 13 g; Fiber 2 g; T Fat 20 g; 52% Calories from Fat; Chol 120 mg; Sod 774 mg.

Cattlemen's Meat Loaf

Kathryn Nowell, Maryville

3/4 cup milk
1 1/2 cups soft bread crumbs
2 pounds lean ground beef
2 teaspoons salt
1/8 teaspoon pepper
1 medium carrot, grated
1 small onion, chopped
2 eggs, beaten
1/4 cup catsup
3 tablespoons dark brown sugar
2 tablespoons prepared mustard

Preheat oven to 325 degrees. Pour milk over bread crumbs in large bowl. Add ground beef, salt, pepper, carrot, onion and eggs; mix well. Press into 5-by-9-inch loaf pan. Combine catsup, brown sugar and mustard in small bowl; spread over meat loaf. Bake for 1 1/2 hours. Let stand for 10 minutes before serving. Yield: 8 servings.

Approx Per Serving: Cal 335; Prot 29 g; Carbo 13 g; Fiber <1 g; T Fat 18 g; 50% Calories from Fat; Chol 141 mg; Sod 807 mg.

Depression Meat Loaf

Helen Anderson, Morristown

2 pounds ground beef
2 (10-ounce) cans tomato soup
1 cup crumbled corn bread
1/2 cup chopped onion
1/4 cup chopped green pepper
1 egg, slightly beaten
1 teaspoon salt
1/4 teaspoon pepper
1/4 cup meat loaf drippings

Preheat oven to 350 degrees. Combine beef, 1 can tomato soup, corn bread, onion, green pepper, egg, salt and pepper in large bowl; mix well. Shape firmly into loaf. Place in shallow baking pan. Bake for 1 hour and 45 minutes. Combine 1 can tomato soup and drippings in small saucepan; heat. Serve with meat loaf. Yield: 8 servings.

Approx Per Serving: Cal 408; Prot 28 g; Carbo 16 g; Fiber <1 g; T Fat 25 g; 56% Calories from Fat; Chol 123 mg; Sod 931 mg.

Delicious Microwave Meat Loaf

Kathy Keicher, Midway

1 egg, slightly beaten
16 squares saltine crackers, crushed
1/4 cup Worcestershire sauce
1 cup chopped canned tomatoes,
    drained
Seasoned salt to taste
1 medium onion, chopped
1 teaspoon garlic powder
2 pounds ground beef
1/2 cup catsup
1 large green pepper, cut into strips

Stir egg into crackers in large bowl. Add Worcestershire sauce, tomatoes, seasoned salt, onion and garlic powder; mix well. Add ground beef; mix well. Shape and flatten into ungreased 8-inch square microwave-safe baking dish. Spread catsup over top. Decorate with green pepper strips. Cover with glass lid or plastic wrap with a couple of slits cut into it. Microwave on High for 20 minutes, turning every 5 minutes. Test in 15 minutes or on third turn for doneness. Lift out with two spatulas; drain. Yield: 8 servings.

Approx Per Serving: Cal 320; Prot 27 g; Carbo 13 g; Fiber 1 g; T Fat 17 g; 49% Calories from Fat; Chol 111 mg; Sod 461 mg.

Pot Roast Meat Loaf

Joyce Hall, Clarkrange

1/2 cup catsup
1 pound ground chuck
2/3 cup evaporated milk
2/3 cup cracker crumbs
1 teaspoon salt
2 teaspoons Worcestershire sauce
1/4 teaspoon pepper
1/2 cup chopped onion
1/3 cup chopped green pepper
3 peeled potatoes, chopped
3 peeled carrots, chopped
2 onions, chopped
2 teaspoons parsley flakes
1/2 teaspoon salt
1/4 teaspoon pepper

Preheat oven to 375 degrees. Combine catsup, meat, milk, crumbs, 1 teaspoon salt, Worcestershire sauce, 1/4 teaspoon pepper, 1/2 cup onion and green pepper in large bowl; mix well. Shape into loaf. Place in large baking dish. Layer potatoes, carrots and 2 onions over loaf. Sprinkle with parsley flakes, 1/2 teaspoon salt and 1/4 teaspoon pepper. Bake, covered, for 1 hour. Remove lid; bake for 10 minutes longer. May substitute ground turkey for ground chuck if desired. Yield: 6 servings.

Approx Per Serving: Cal 359; Prot 22 g; Carbo 37 g; Fiber 4 g; T Fat 14 g; 35% Calories from Fat; Chol 64 mg; Sod 1002 mg.

Top-of-the-Stove Meat Loaves

Anne Henderson, Dandridge

1 pound ground beef
1 teaspoon salt
1/2 onion, chopped
1/2 cup uncooked oats
1/4 cup milk
1 egg, slightly beaten
2 cups tomatoes
2 tablespoons dark brown sugar
1 tablespoon vinegar

Combine beef, salt, onion, oats, milk and egg in large bowl; mix well. Shape into 6 small loaves. Brown on both sides in large skillet. Mix tomatoes, brown sugar and vinegar in medium bowl. Pour over meat loaves. Cook over medium heat for 30 minutes or until sauce is thickened. Yield: 6 servings.

Approx Per Serving: Cal 242; Prot 20 g; Carbo 13 g; Fiber 2 g; T Fat 12 g; 46% Calories from Fat; Chol 93 mg; Sod 420 mg.

Meat-Za-Pie

Mrs. Inita McPeake, Lexington

1 pound ground beef
1 teaspoon garlic salt
1/2 cup fine dry bread crumbs
2/3 cup evaporated milk
1/3 cup catsup
1 (2-ounce) can sliced mushrooms, drained
3 (4-by-7-inch) slices processed cheese, cut into strips
1/4 teaspoon oregano
2 tablespoons grated Parmesan cheese

Preheat oven to 400 degrees. Place beef, garlic salt and bread crumbs in 9-inch pie pan. Add evaporated milk; mix together with fork. Spread mixture evenly over bottom of pan with fork, raising rim 1/2 inch high around edge. Spread catsup over meat to rim. Arrange mushrooms over catsup. Place cheese strips in crisscross pattern over top. Sprinkle with oregano and Parmesan cheese. Bake for 20 minutes or until cheese is melted and lightly browned. Cut into wedges. May substitute 1/4 cup finely chopped green pepper for mushrooms if desired. Yield: 4 servings.

Approx Per Serving: Cal 473; Prot 36 g; Carbo 20 g; Fiber 1 g; T Fat 27 g; 52% Calories from Fat; Chol 119 mg; Sod 1389 mg.

Hamburger Pie

Sherrell Hickman, Mt. Pleasant

1 1/4 pounds ground beef
1 large onion, chopped
1 (11-ounce) can whole kernel corn,
  drained
1 (14-ounce) can Mexican-style stewed
  tomatoes
1 cup sour cream
1 tablespoon chili powder
1 teaspoon salt
1/4 teaspoon pepper
1/2 cup chopped green pepper
1 cup self-rising cornmeal
3 tablespoons flour
1 cup buttermilk
1 tablespoon vegetable oil
2 ounces shredded Cheddar cheese
1/4 teaspoon paprika

Preheat oven to 350 degrees. Brown ground beef and onion in large skillet; drain off fat. Add corn, tomatoes, sour cream, chili powder, salt, pepper and green pepper; mix well. Pour into 2-quart casserole. Combine cornmeal, flour, buttermilk and oil in large bowl; mix well. Pour over meat mixture. Bake for 30 to 40 minutes or until golden brown. Remove from oven; sprinkle with Cheddar cheese and paprika. Return to oven; bake for 2 minutes or until cheese is melted. Yield: 8 servings.

Approx Per Serving: Cal 401; Prot 23 g; Carbo 31 g; Fiber 3 g; T Fat 21 g; 47% Calories from Fat; Chol 74 mg; Sod 890 mg.

Spoon Bread Tamale Pie

Mrs. K. E. Givens, Fairview

1 1/2 pounds lean ground beef
1/4 cup vegetable oil
1 cup chopped onion
1/2 cup chopped green pepper
1 cup tomatoes
1 tablespoon salt
1 1/2 tablespoons chili powder
1/4 teaspoon pepper
1/2 cup white cornmeal
1 cup water
1 1/2 cups milk
1 teaspoon salt
2 tablespoons butter
1/2 cup cornmeal
1 cup grated Cheddar cheese
2 eggs

Preheat oven to 375 degrees. Brown beef in oil in large skillet, stirring until crumbly. Add onion and green pepper; cook until onion is golden. Stir in tomatoes, 1 tablespoon salt, chili powder and pepper. Simmer for 5 minutes. Mix 1/2 cup cornmeal and 1 cup water in small bowl. Stir into beef mixture. Simmer, covered, for 10 minutes. Pour into casserole. Combine milk, 1 teaspoon salt and butter in medium saucepan; place over medium heat. Stir 1/2 cup cornmeal slowly into mixture. Cook, stirring, until thickened. Remove from heat. Stir in cheese. Stir in eggs. Pour over meat mixture. Bake for 30 to 40 minutes or until golden brown. Yield: 6 servings.

Approx Per Serving: Cal 606; Prot 37 g; Carbo 26 g; Fiber 3 g; T Fat 40 g; 59% Calories from Fat; Chol 193 mg; Sod 1715 mg.

Upside Down Meat Pie

Patsy A. Crum, Greeneville

1 1/2 cups flour
1 tablespoon baking powder
1 teaspoon salt
1 teaspoon paprika
1 teaspoon celery salt
1/4 teaspoon pepper
5 tablespoons vegetable shortening
3/4 cup milk
1/4 cup sliced onion
1 (10-ounce) can tomato soup
1 pound ground beef

Preheat oven to 450 degrees. Sift together flour, baking powder, 1/2 teaspoon salt, paprika, celery salt and pepper into large bowl. Add 3 tablespoons shortening; mix in thoroughly with fork. Add milk; stir until blended. Melt remaining shortening in 9-inch pan. Add onion; cook until softened. Add tomato soup, 1/2 teaspoon salt and ground beef; bring to a boil. Spread flour mixture over meat mixture. Bake for 20 minutes or until tests done. Turn upside down on serving plate. Yield: 8 servings.

Approx Per Serving: Cal 323; Prot 16 g; Carbo 25 g; Fiber <1 g; T Fat 17 g; 49% Calories from Fat; Chol 45 mg; Sod 884 mg.

Blackened Cajun Steak

Marydee J. Richardson, Gallatin

This recipe won second place in the 1987 Tennessee Beef Cook-Off. The seasoning is wonderful on rib-eye, sirloin or T-bone steak as well as rump roast cooked on rotisserie. Rub roast with 2 or 3 cloves of crushed garlic before rubbing in seasoning mixture.

1 teaspoon garlic powder
1 tablespoon rosemary
2 teaspoons hot chilies
2 teaspoons black peppercorns
2 teaspoons white peppercorns
1 1/2 teaspoons coriander seed
1 teaspoon caraway seed
1 teaspoon cumin seed
1 teaspoon fennel seed
1 teaspoon dried thyme
1 1/2 teaspoons Hungarian sweet paprika
2 pounds ground round

Heat cast iron skillet over medium-high heat. Add first 10 ingredients, stirring for 2 to 3 minutes or just until spices begin to darken. Remove from heat; transfer to blender container. Grind until very fine texture. Remove from blender container; stir in paprika. Store in tightly covered jar. Shape meat into 1/2-inch thick patties. Sprinkle spice mixture generously on both sides of meat, rubbing into meat. Heat iron skillet until almost white. Spray with non-stick cooking spray. Add patties, leaving enough space to turn. Cook for 3 minutes or until darkened. Turn; cook other side. Meat will be medium. Yield: 6 servings.

Approx Per Serving: Cal 333; Prot 34 g; Carbo <1 g; Fiber <1 g; T Fat 21 g; 58% Calories from Fat; Chol 112 mg; Sod 81 mg.

Scrum-Delicious Burgers

Mychele Roberts, Allardt

1 1/2 pounds ground beef
3 tablespoons finely chopped onion
1/2 teaspoon each garlic salt, pepper
1 cup shredded Cheddar cheese
1/2 cup canned sliced mushrooms
6 crisp-fried bacon slices, crumbled
1/4 cup mayonnaise
6 hamburger buns, split
6 lettuce leaves
6 tomato slices

Combine beef, onion, garlic salt and pepper in medium bowl; mix well. Shape into six 3/4-inch-thick patties. Combine cheese, mushrooms, bacon and mayonnaise in small bowl; refrigerate. Grill patties over medium-hot coals for 10 to 12 minutes, turning once. Spoon 1/4 cup cheese mixture onto each burger during last 3 minutes of cooking. Serve on buns with lettuce and tomato slices. Yield: 6 servings.

Approx Per Serving: Cal 567; Prot 36 g; Carbo 26 g; Fiber 2 g; T Fat 35 g; 56% Calories from Fat; Chol 115 mg; Sod 812 mg.

Ground Beef Steaks

Castella Love, Five Points

1 pound ground beef
1/2 cup soft bread crumbs
1/2 teaspoon salt
1/4 teaspoon pepper
1 (8-ounce) can tomato sauce
2 tablespoons chopped green onions
2 tablespoons dark brown sugar
1 teaspoon Worcestershire sauce
1 teaspoon prepared mustard

Combine beef, crumbs, salt and pepper in large bowl; shape into 4 steaks. Brown in large skillet; pour off excess fat. Combine tomato sauce, green onions, brown sugar, Worcestershire sauce and mustard in medium bowl; mix well. Pour over steaks. Simmer for 10 minutes.
Yield: 4 servings.

Approx Per Serving: Cal 300; Prot 27 g; Carbo 12 g; Fiber 1 g; T Fat 16 g; 48% Calories from Fat; Chol 84 mg; Sod 731 mg.

Barbecue Cups

Ruby A. Watson, Madisonville

1 pound ground beef
1/2 cup barbecue sauce
1 tablespoon minced onion
1 1/2 tablespoons dark brown sugar
1 (8-ounce) can flaky refrigerator biscuits
3/4 cup shredded Cheddar cheese

Preheat oven to 400 degrees. Brown ground beef in heavy skillet, stirring until crumbly; drain off fat. Stir in barbecue sauce, onion and brown sugar. Press each biscuit into greased muffin cup. Spoon meat mixture into each cup. Sprinkle with cheese. Bake for 12 minutes.
Yield: 10 servings.

Approx Per Serving: Cal 239; Prot 15 g; Carbo 17 g; Fiber <1 g; T Fat 14 g; 50% Calories from Fat; Chol 43 mg; Sod 519 mg.

Frying Pan Supper

Leah Habegger, Monterey

1 pound ground beef
1 small onion, chopped
2 cups potato strips
2 cups shredded cabbage
2 cups chopped celery
1/2 teaspoon salt

Cook beef with onion in large skillet, stirring until crumbly; drain off fat. Add potatoes, cabbage and celery. Sprinkle with salt. Add 1/2 cup water. Simmer, covered, for 20 minutes or until vegetables are tender. Yield: 6 servings.

Approx Per Serving: Cal 220; Prot 18 g; Carbo 13 g; Fiber 2 g; T Fat 11 g; 44% Calories from Fat; Chol 56 mg; Sod 259 mg.

Beef 'n' Bean Barbecue Bake

Mrs. Roger Mazelin, Clarkrange

1 pound ground beef
1 (16-ounce) can pork and beans
1/2 cup barbecue sauce
1/2 cup chopped onion
1 teaspoon salt
1/4 pound Velveeta cheese cubes
1 (8-ounce) can refrigerator biscuits

Preheat oven to 375 degrees. Brown beef in large skillet, stirring until crumbly; drain off fat. Add pork and beans, barbecue sauce, onion and salt; simmer for 5 minutes. Stir in cheese. Pour into 7-by-11-inch baking dish. Cut biscuits into halves to form half circles. Place, cut side down, around edge of casserole. Bake for 20 minutes.
Yield: 6 servings.

Approx Per Serving: Cal 492; Prot 29 g; Carbo 43 g; Fiber 4 g; T Fat 25 g; 44% Calories from Fat; Chol 79 mg; Sod 1657 mg.

Slumgullia

Carolyn Franks, Savannah

1 pound ground beef
1 small onion, chopped
1 (6-ounce) can tomato paste
1 (10-ounce) can corn niblets
1 tablespoon margarine
1 (8-ounce) can green peas
6 slices American cheese

Preheat oven to 350 degrees. Cook beef in large skillet, stirring until crumbly; drain off fat. Add onion and tomato paste. Simmer, covered, until onion is transparent. Cook corn with 1/2 tablespoon margarine in small saucepan until tender; drain. Cook peas in small saucepan with 1/2 tablespoon margarine until tender; drain. Spread meat mixture in ungreased casserole. Layer corn over mixture. Layer peas over corn. Arrange cheese over top with edges just touching. Bake until cheese is melted. Serve warm with salad and rolls. Yield: 6 servings.

Approx Per Serving: Cal 327; Prot 24 g; Carbo 18 g; Fiber 3 g; T Fat 18 g; 49% Calories from Fat; Chol 70 mg; Sod 758 mg.

Calico Beans

Sheri Edmonds, Humboldt

1 1/2 pounds ground beef
1 medium onion, chopped
1 (15-ounce) can pork and beans
1 (15-ounce) can kidney beans, drained
1 (15-ounce) can small green lima beans, drained
1 (15-ounce) can speckled butter beans, drained
1/2 cup dark brown sugar
1 cup catsup
1 tablespoon dark corn syrup
2 tablespoons vinegar
1 tablespoon mustard
Salt and pepper to taste
1/2 pound crisp-fried bacon, crumbled

Brown ground beef and onion in large skillet, stirring until crumbly; drain. Place in Crock•Pot. Stir in pork and beans, kidney beans, lima beans, butter beans, brown sugar, catsup, corn syrup, vinegar, mustard, salt and pepper. Cook on Low for 4 to 6 hours. Stir in bacon just before serving. Yield: 12 servings.

Approx Per Serving: Cal 348; Prot 22 g; Carbo 40 g; Fiber 9 g; T Fat 12 g; 30% Calories from Fat; Chol 50 mg; Sod 791 mg.

Cowboy Beans

Timmy L. Buckingham, Gray

1 (15-ounce) can pinto beans
1 (16-ounce) can pork and beans
1 (16-ounce) can baby lima beans
1 (15-ounce) can great northern beans
1 (16-ounce) can kidney beans
1 small onion, chopped
1/3 cup chopped green pepper
1 (18-ounce) bottle barbecue sauce
2 1/2 pounds ground chuck

Combine beans, onion, green pepper and barbecue sauce in large Crock•Pot. Brown beef in large skillet, stirring until crumbly; drain well. Spoon over mixture in Crock•Pot; do not stir. Cover; cook on High for 4 hours. Yield: 12 servings.

Approx Per Serving: Cal 403; Prot 31 g; Carbo 36 g; Fiber 9 g; T Fat 15 g; 33% Calories from Fat; Chol 73 mg; Sod 1048 mg.

Meat and Black-Eyed Pea Casserole

Mrs. Robert Herndon, Troy

1 pound ground chuck
1 large onion, chopped
1 small green pepper, chopped
2 cups cooked black-eyed peas
1 cup canned tomatoes
1 teaspoon oregano
1 teaspoon parsley
Salt and pepper to taste

Preheat oven to 350 degrees. Brown beef with onion and green pepper in large skillet, stirring until crumbly; drain off fat. Add remaining ingredients; mix well. Pour into large casserole. Bake for 30 minutes. Yield: 6 servings.

Approx Per Serving: Cal 239; Prot 19 g; Carbo 16 g; Fiber 5 g; T Fat 11 g; 41% Calories from Fat; Chol 56 mg; Sod 109 mg.

Soybean-Hamburger Casserole

Mrs. D. L. McGee, Fayetteville

2¹/₂ cups dry soybeans
1 tablespoon vegetable oil
¹/₂ pound ground beef
¹/₂ cup chopped onion
1 cup chopped celery
¹/₄ cup chopped green bell pepper
1 beef bouillon cube
1 cup hot water
1 (10-ounce) can tomato soup
2 cups cooked rice
Salt and pepper to taste
1 cup shredded Cheddar cheese

Soak soybeans in water to cover in large saucepan overnight. Add oil; bring to a boil. Reduce heat; simmer for 3 hours or until tender. Preheat oven to 350 degrees. Sauté beef, onion, celery and green pepper in large skillet until beef loses its red color and vegetables are glossy; drain off fat. Dissolve bouillon cube in hot water in small bowl. Stir bouillon, soup, rice, salt and pepper into beef mixture. Add soybeans; mix gently. Pour into 2¹/₂-quart baking dish. Bake for 45 minutes. Top with cheese. Bake for 5 minutes longer. Cooked soybeans may be stored in refrigerator for 1 week or in freezer for 3 months. Yield: 10 servings.

Approx Per Serving: Cal 381; Prot 27 g; Carbo 31 g; Fiber 8 g; T Fat 18 g; 41% Calories from Fat; Chol 29 g; Sod 393 mg.

Beef and Cabbage Casserole

Mrs. Helen Stanley, Ripley

1 tablespoon vegetable oil
1 pound lean ground beef
1 onion, finely chopped
1 (10-ounce) can tomato soup
1 (10-ounce) soup can water
Salt and pepper to taste
¹/₄ cup uncooked rice
4 cups finely shredded cabbage

Preheat oven to 350 degrees. Heat oil in large skillet. Add beef and onion. Cook until beef is browned and onion is tender, stirring until crumbly; drain off fat. Add soup, water, salt, pepper and rice. Bring to a boil; reduce heat. Simmer for 3 minutes, stirring constantly. Place cabbage in 3-quart casserole. Spoon beef mixture over cabbage. Bake, covered, for 1 hour. Yield: 8 servings.

Approx Per Serving: Cal 200; Prot 14 g; Carbo 13 g; Fiber 1 g; T Fat 10 g; 46% Calories from Fat; Chol 42 mg; Sod 302 mg.

Beef-Potato Casserole

Mary Bingham, Bell Buckle

6 large potatoes, peeled
Salt and pepper to taste
2 pounds ground beef
2 (19-ounce) cans vegetable beef soup

Preheat oven to 400 degrees. Slice potatoes; place in 5-quart baking dish. Add salt and pepper. Crumble uncooked beef over potatoes. Sprinkle salt and pepper over beef. Pour soup over beef. Bake, covered, for 1 hour. Remove cover; bake for 30 minutes longer. Serve hot. Yield: 12 servings.

Approx Per Serving: Cal 308; Prot 23 g; Carbo 27 g; Fiber 2 g; T Fat 11 g; 32% Calories from Fat; Chol 58 mg; Sod 596 mg.

Hamburger Beef Casserole

Mrs. John Roy Williams, Monterey

1 pound ground beef
1 large onion, chopped
Salt and pepper to taste
Garlic salt to taste
6 beef bouillon cubes
2 cups boiling water
4 large potatoes, cubed

Preheat oven to 350 degrees. Brown beef with onion in large skillet, stirring until crumbly; drain off fat. Add salt, pepper and garlic salt. Dissolve bouillon cubes in boiling water in small bowl. Place potatoes in 2-quart casserole. Pour beef mixture over potatoes. Top with bouillon; mix gently, lifting lightly. Bake for 1 to 1 1/2 hours or until potatoes are done. Yield: 8 servings.

Approx Per Serving: Cal 221; Prot 15 g; Carbo 22 g; Fiber 2 g; T Fat 8 g; 33% Calories from Fat; Chol 42 mg; Sod 683 mg.

Stuffed Cabbage

Frances Milliken, Ashland City

12 large outer cabbage leaves
1 tablespoon salt
1 cup chopped onions
1 clove of garlic, crushed
1 pound lean ground beef
2 cups cooked rice
2 eggs, beaten
1/4 teaspoon pepper
1 (8-ounce) can tomato sauce
1 (16-ounce) can tomatoes, chopped
Juice of 1 lemon
1/4 teaspoon pepper
2 tablespoons dark brown sugar

Preheat oven to 375 degrees. Trim off thick part of each cabbage leaf. Add leaves and 1 teaspoon salt to boiling water in saucepan. Let stand for 5 minutes or until leaves become pliable; drain. Combine onions, garlic, ground beef, rice, eggs, pepper and 1 teaspoon salt in large bowl; mix well. Place 1/2 cup meat mixture in hollow of each leaf. Fold sides of leaf over mixture; roll up from thick end of leaf to make neat roll. Arrange cabbage rolls, seam sides down, in single layer in lightly buttered 3-quart shallow baking pan. Combine tomato sauce, tomatoes, lemon juice, 1 teaspoon salt and pepper in large saucepan; bring to a boil. Pour over cabbage rolls. Sprinkle with brown sugar. Bake, covered, for 50 minutes. Uncover; bake for 10 minutes longer. Remove to warm serving platter. Spoon sauce over rolls. Yield: 8 servings.

Approx Per Serving: Cal 257; Prot 17 g; Carbo 26 g; Fiber 3 g; T Fat 10 g; 33% Calories from Fat; Chol 95 mg; Sod 1118 mg.

Plain and Pleasing

Mrs. Charles Murrell, Newport

1 pound lean ground beef
2 envelopes brown gravy mix
1 small onion, thinly sliced
4 medium potatoes, thinly sliced
Salt and pepper to taste

Preheat oven to 400 degrees. Shape beef into 4 patties of equal size. Place in 9-by-13-inch baking pan. Broil for 10 minutes on each side. Mix gravy using package directions. Pour over patties. Place onion and potato slices over patties. Cover pan with cooking foil. Bake for 40 minutes. Yield: 4 servings.

Approx Per Serving: Cal 405; Prot 29 g; Carbo 34 g; Fiber 2 g; T Fat 17 g; 37% Calories from Fat; Chol 85 mg; Sod 603 mg.

Stuffed Pepper Cups

Mrs. Preston Pruett, Sardis

6 medium green peppers
Salt to taste
1 pound ground beef
1/2 cup chopped onion
1 tablespoon vegetable oil
2 cups stewed tomatoes
3/4 cup cooked rice
2 tablespoons Worcestershire sauce
1/4 teaspoon pepper
1 1/2 cups shredded sharp process
   American cheese

Cut off tops of green peppers; remove seeds and membranes. Preheat oven to 350 degrees. Cook green peppers in boiling salted water in large saucepan for 5 minutes; drain. Sprinkle insides with salt. Brown beef with onion in hot oil in large skillet. Add tomatoes, rice, Worcestershire sauce, salt and pepper. Simmer, covered, for 5 minutes. Add 1 cup cheese; stuff peppers. Stand stuffed peppers upright in baking dish or muffin cups. Bake, uncovered, for 25 minutes or until hot. Sprinkle with remaining cheese. Yield: 6 servings.

Approx Per Serving: Cal 376; Prot 25 g; Carbo 20 g; Fiber 3 g; T Fat 22 g; 52% Calories from fat; Chol 83 mg; Sod 719 mg.

Stuffed Green Peppers

Mrs. Margaret Smithson, Centerville

Mrs. Smithson's peppers can be frozen. "These can be removed from freezer and put immediately in oven with a little longer cooking," she advises.

8 green peppers
2 cups ground beef
1 1/2 teaspoons salt
1 cup white sauce
1 cup cooked corn
1/4 teaspoon dry mustard
1 cup water
1/2 cup bread crumbs
2 tablespoons butter

Preheat oven to 350 degrees. Cut tops off green peppers; remove membranes and seeds. Place peppers in salted water in large saucepan. Cover; boil for 5 minutes. Do not overboil; drain. Brown beef in skillet, stirring until crumbly; drain off fat. Add salt, sauce, corn, mustard and water; mix well. Stuff peppers. Sprinkle bread crumbs over tops. Dot with butter. Bake for 20 minutes. Yield: 8 servings.

Approx Per Serving: Cal 210; Prot 11 g; Carbo 17 g; Fiber 3 g; T Fat 12 g; 49% Calories from Fat; Chol 36 mg; Sod 552 mg.

German-Style Casserole

Mrs. J. Franklin Nix, Smyrna

2 eggs
8 ounces cream cheese, softened
12 ounces creamed cottage cheese
1 teaspoon salt
1/2 teaspoon pepper
1 teaspoon garlic salt
1 teaspoon dried parsley flakes
1 teaspoon dried sweet basil
1 (16-ounce) can whole tomatoes, drained
1 1/2 pounds lean ground beef
1 tablespoon vegetable oil
2 large potatoes, sliced
1 large onion, sliced
4 ribs celery, coarsely chopped
3 medium carrots, sliced
1 cup cola beverage
4 ounces bleu cheese, crumbled

Preheat oven to 350 degrees. Combine eggs, cream cheese and cottage cheese in large mixer bowl; beat until smooth. Mix salt, pepper, garlic salt, parsley flakes and basil in small bowl. Chop tomatoes. Cook beef in oil in large skillet until no longer pink, stirring until crumbly; drain. Layer meat, potatoes, onion, celery, carrots, tomatoes, seasoning mixture and cream cheese mixture 1/2 at a time in greased 3-quart casserole. Repeat layers. Pour cola beverage carefully around edges, opening space with knife. Top with bleu cheese. Bake on bottom shelf of oven for 1 1/4 hours. May be prepared ahead and refrigerated until baking time. Yield: 10 servings.

Approx Per Serving: Cal 401; Prot 26 g; Carbo 19 g; Fiber 2 g; T Fat 25 g; 55% Calories from Fat; Chol 132 mg; Sod 928 mg.

Mexican Casserole

Mrs. Fred Shrock, Monterey

2 pounds ground beef
1 teaspoon salt
1/2 teaspoon cayenne pepper
1 stalk celery, chopped
1/2 green pepper, chopped
1/3 cup chopped onion
1/2 teaspoon pepper
1 teaspoon chili powder
3 beef bouillon cubes
2 tablespoons taco seasoning
1 tablespoon catsup
1 (10-ounce) can cream of mushroom soup
1 cup water
2 tablespoons flour
3/4 cup sour cream
1 cup rice
3 cups grated cheese
2 cups chopped lettuce
1 cucumber, chopped
2 tablespoons chopped onion
1/2 cup chopped celery
2 tomatoes, chopped

Combine ground beef, salt, cayenne pepper, 1 stalk celery, green pepper, 1/3 cup onion, pepper and chili powder in large skillet. Cook until meat is browned, stirring until crumbly; drain off fat. Add bouillon cubes, taco seasoning, catsup, soup, water and flour; mix well. Bring to a boil; remove from heat. Add sour cream. Keep hot; do not allow to boil again. Cook rice according to package directions. Place cooked rice in bottom of greased 9-by-13-inch pan. Spread meat mixture over rice. Sprinkle cheese over meat mixture. Combine lettuce, cucumber, 2 tablespoons onion and 1/2 cup celery in medium bowl; sprinkle over cheese. Top with tomatoes. Serve immediately.
Yield: 8 servings.

Approx Per Serving: Cal 631; Prot 40 g; Carbo 32 g; Fiber 2 g; T Fat 38 g; 54% Calories from Fat; Chol 139 mg; Sod 1520 mg.

Chow Mein Casserole

Pat Hinson, Lobelville

1 pound ground beef
1 onion, chopped
1 1/2 cups chopped celery
1 (10-ounce) can cream of chicken soup
1 (10-ounce) can cream of mushroom soup
1 1/2 cups water
3 tablespoons soy sauce
1/2 cup uncooked minute rice
Salt and pepper to taste
1 (5-ounce) can chow mein noodles

Brown ground beef in large skillet, stirring until crumbly; drain off fat. Add onion and celery. Add soups, water, soy sauce, rice, salt and pepper; mix well. Pour into microwave-safe 3-quart casserole. Microwave, uncovered, on High for 15 minutes. Top with chow mein noodles. Microwave on High for 3 minutes longer.
Yield: 8 servings.

Approx Per Serving: Cal 327; Prot 17 g; Carbo 23 g; Fiber 2 g; T Fat 19 g; 51% Calories from Fat; Chol 46 mg; Sod 1122 mg.

Beef Casserole

Mrs. John Taylor, Benton

1 (8-ounce) package macaroni
1 pound ground beef
1 medium onion, minced
1 green pepper, chopped
2 cups canned tomatoes
1/4 cup catsup
1/2 teaspoon salt
1/8 teaspoon pepper
6 slices Cheddar cheese

Preheat oven to 350 degrees. Cook macaroni according to package directions; drain. Brown beef with onion and green pepper lightly in large skillet, stirring until crumbly; drain off fat. Add macaroni, tomatoes, catsup, salt and pepper; mix well. Pour into ungreased casserole. Arrange cheese slices over top. Bake, covered, for 30 minutes. Yield: 6 servings.

Approx Per Serving: Cal 456; Prot 30 g; Carbo 37 g; Fiber 3 g; T Fat 21 g; 41% Calories from Fat; Chol 86 mg; Sod 649 mg.

Company Beef Stew Casserole

Hayden Thornton, Brownsville

1 pound ground beef
2 tablespoons vegetable oil
1 medium onion, chopped
2 cups canned tomatoes
1 tablespoon catsup
1 tablespoon steak sauce
1/4 cup chopped green pepper
2 tablespoons chopped parsley
Salt and pepper to taste
5 ounces elbow macaroni
1 (10-ounce) can cream of mushroom soup
1 cup grated Cheddar cheese

Preheat oven to 350 degrees. Brown ground beef in oil in skillet until all red color disappears, stirring until crumbly; drain off fat. Add onion, tomatoes, catsup, steak sauce, green pepper, parsley, salt and pepper; mix well. Simmer for 30 minutes. Cook macaroni according to package directions. Combine macaroni and ground beef mixture in baking dish. Spoon soup gently into mixture, lifting from bottom. Sprinkle cheese over top. Bake for 30 minutes or until bubbly and cheese is melted. Yield: 8 servings.

Approx Per Serving: Cal 337; Prot 20 g; Carbo 21 g; Fiber 2 g; T Fat 19 g; 51% Calories from Fat; Chol 57 mg; Sod 578 mg.

Twisty Bake Beef Casserole

Carol Taylor, Madisonville

4 ounces corkscrew macaroni
1 pound ground beef
1 (10-ounce) can cream of mushroom soup
2/3 cup water
3/4 cup catsup
3/4 cup shredded Cheddar cheese
1/2 cup chopped green pepper
1/4 teaspoon salt
1 (6-ounce) can French fried onions

Preheat oven to 350 degrees. Cook macaroni according to package directions; drain. Brown ground beef in large skillet, stirring until crumbly; drain off fat. Add macaroni, soup, water, catsup, cheese, green pepper and salt; mix well. Pour into 2-quart casserole. Sprinkle onions over top. Bake for 35 minutes. Yield: 8 servings.

Approx Per Serving: Cal 415; Prot 20 g; Carbo 28 g; Fiber <1 g; T Fat 24 g; 53% Calories from Fat; Chol 54 mg; Sod 884 mg.

Hamburger-Noodle Casserole

Mary Gitchell, Ripley

1 (12-ounce) package noodles
1 1/2 pounds ground beef
1 small onion, chopped
1 (16-ounce) can tomatoes
1 (10-ounce) can cream of celery soup
1 (10-ounce) can Cheddar cheese soup

Preheat oven to 350 degrees. Cook noodles according to package directions; drain. Cook ground beef with onion in large skillet, stirring until crumbly; drain off fat. Add tomatoes and celery soup; mix well. Spread half the noodles in bottom of 3-quart lightly greased casserole. Spoon half the meat mixture over noodles. Repeat layers. Bake for 30 minutes. Spoon cheese soup over top. Bake for 10 minutes longer or until heated through.
Yield: 8 servings.

Approx Per Serving: Cal 277; Prot 28 g; Carbo 39 g; Fiber 1 g; T Fat 19 g; 39% Calories from Fat; Chol 151 mg; Sod 724 mg.

Ground Beef Casserole

Mrs. Edra White, Morris Chapel

1 (16-ounce) package elbow macaroni
1 1/2 pounds ground beef
1 medium onion, chopped
1 (10-ounce) can tomato soup
1 (10-ounce) can cream of mushroom soup
1 (16-ounce) can whole kernel corn, drained
Salt and pepper to taste
1 cup grated Cheddar cheese

Preheat oven to 325 degrees. Cook macaroni according to package directions; drain. Brown ground beef with onion in large skillet, stirring until crumbly; drain off fat. Add soups, corn, macaroni, salt and pepper; mix well. Pour into lightly greased 3-quart casserole. Sprinkle cheese over top. Bake for 15 to 20 minutes or until cheese is melted.
Yield: 12 servings.

Approx Per Serving: Cal 379; Prot 22 g; Carbo 41 g; Fiber 2 g; T Fat 14 g; 34% Calories from Fat; Chol 52 mg; Sod 596 mg.

Chuckwagon Dinner

Dersie Amonette, Byrdstown

1 pound ground beef
2 cups uncooked noodles
1 (16-ounce) can stewed tomatoes
1 small onion, chopped
1 cup chopped celery
1/2 cup water
1 teaspoon salt
2 slices cheese, cut into small pieces

Brown beef in large skillet, stirring until crumbly; drain off fat. Add noodles, tomatoes, onion, celery, water and salt; mix well. Simmer, covered, for 30 minutes. Remove from heat. Garnish with cheese. Yield: 8 servings.

Approx Per Serving: Cal 162; Prot 15 g; Carbo 10 g; Fiber 1 g; T Fat 10 g; 46% Calories from Fat; Chol 58 mg; Sod 517 mg.

Beef-Parmesan Casserole

Mrs. Bobby Vannatta, Bell Buckle

"This recipe freezes well and is a favorite at pot luck suppers," says Mrs. Vannatta.

1 1/2 pounds lean ground beef
1 large green pepper, chopped
2 onions, chopped
3 (8-ounce) cans tomato sauce
1 (6-ounce) can tomato paste
1 (4-ounce) can sliced mushrooms
1/2 teaspoon oregano
1 bay leaf
1/2 teaspoon sweet basil
1/2 teaspoon celery seed
1 teaspoon light brown sugar
1 teaspoon mustard
Salt and pepper to taste
1 (8-ounce) package egg noodles
4 ounces grated Cheddar cheese
1/2 cup grated Parmesan cheese

Brown beef with green pepper and onions in large skillet, stirring until crumbly; drain off fat. Add tomato sauce, tomato paste, mushrooms, oregano, bay leaf, basil, celery seed, brown sugar, mustard, salt and pepper; mix well. Bring to a boil; reduce heat. Simmer, covered, for 3 to 4 hours. Preheat oven to 350 degrees. Cook noodles according to package directions; drain. Place alternate layers of noodles, beef mixture and Cheddar cheese in lightly greased 3-quart casserole. Top with Parmesan cheese. Bake for 15 minutes. Yield: 6 servings.

Approx Per Serving: Cal 447; Prot 42 g; Carbo 46 g; Fiber 5 g; T Fat 27 g; 41% Calories from Fat; Chol 177 mg; Sod 1341 mg.

Dinner-in-a-Dish

Mrs. Lealand Noland, Bedford County

1 pound ground beef
1 onion, chopped
2 tablespoons vegetable oil
2 eggs
1 (16-ounce) can whole kernel corn
1 (16-ounce) can tomatoes
2 cups crushed soda crackers
2 tablespoons butter

Preheat oven to 350 degrees. Brown ground beef with onion in oil in large skillet, stirring until crumbly; drain off fat. Let cool for 5 minutes. Stir eggs into beef mixture. Layer beef mixture, corn, tomatoes and crackers 1/2 at a time in lightly greased 3-quart casserole. Dot with butter. Bake for 1 hour. Yield: 8 servings.

Approx Per Serving: Cal 341; Prot 18 g; Carbo 27 g; Fiber 2 g; T Fat 18 g; 48% Calories from Fat; Chol 103 mg; Sod 584 mg.

One-Dish Casserole

Mrs. Alvin Lackey, Mt. Juliet

1 pound ground beef
1 small onion, chopped
1 cup uncooked rice
1 (10-ounce) can tomato soup
1 (10-ounce) can cream of mushroom soup
1 (16-ounce) can English peas
1/2 cup Parmesan cheese

Preheat oven to 350 degrees. Brown ground beef in large skillet, stirring until crumbly; drain off fat. Add onion, rice, soups and peas; mix gently. Pour into lightly greased 3-quart casserole. Sprinkle Parmesan cheese over top. Bake for 40 minutes or until rice is tender.
Yield: 8 servings.

Approx Per Serving: Cal 333; Prot 20 g; Carbo 32 g; Fiber 2 g; T Fat 14 g; 37% Calories from Fat; Chol 47 mg; Sod 877 mg.

Hamburger Casserole

Mrs. Milton Cleek, Troy

1/2 pound ground beef
1/2 cup cornflakes
1 3/4 cups milk
3/4 teaspoon salt
1/4 teaspoon pepper
1/4 cup catsup
2 tablespoons vegetable shortening
3 tablespoons flour
1 tablespoon mustard
1/4 pound grated Cheddar cheese

Preheat oven to 300 degrees. Combine beef, cornflakes, 1/4 cup milk, 1/4 teaspoon salt, pepper and catsup in large bowl. Shape into 6 patties. Brown on both sides in 1 tablespoon shortening in large skillet. Melt remaining shortening in saucepan. Stir in flour and mustard. Add remaining milk and 1/2 teaspoon salt, stirring until smooth. Add cheese; cook until melted. Arrange patties in baking dish. Pour sauce over patties; bake for 20 minutes.
Yield: 6 servings.

Approx Per Serving: Cal 275; Prot 16 g; Carbo 11 g; Fiber <1 g; T Fat 18 g; 60% Calories from Fat; Chol 58 mg; Sod 613 mg.

Easy Beef Stew

Mrs. Remus Dunn, Greeneville

1 pound ground beef
2 cups chopped onions
2 cups chopped potatoes
2 cups chopped carrots
2 cups chopped celery
1 (6-ounce) can sliced mushrooms
1 tablespoon salt
1/2 teaspoon pepper
5 tablespoons quick-cooking tapioca
1 teaspoon sugar
3 cups V-8 juice

Preheat oven to 250 degrees. Layer ground beef, onions, potatoes, carrots, celery and mushrooms in 3-quart casserole. Combine salt, pepper, tapioca, sugar and juice in medium bowl; mix well. Pour over layered mixture. Bake, covered, for 5 hours. May cook in Crock•Pot or slow cooker on High for 3 hours. Yield: 8 servings.

Approx Per Serving: Cal 226; Prot 15 g; Carbo 24 g; Fiber 3 g; T Fat 8 g; 32% Calories from Fat; Chol 42 mg; Sod 1287 mg.

Ham Casserole

Mrs. Millard Harville, Savannah

2 cups chopped cooked ham
2 cups cooked rice
1/2 cup grated American cheese
1 (10-ounce) can cream of celery soup
3 tablespoons chopped onion
1/2 cup milk
3 tablespoons butter, softened
3/4 cup crushed cornflakes

Preheat oven to 350 degrees. Combine ham, rice, cheese, soup, onion, milk and butter in large bowl; mix well. Pour into lightly greased 3-quart casserole. Sprinkle cornflakes over top. Bake for 20 minutes or until mixture is hot and bubbly. Yield: 10 servings.

Approx Per Serving: Cal 201; Prot 11 g; Carbo 20 g; Fiber <1 g; T Fat 9 g; 39% Calories from Fat; Chol 35 mg; Sod 782 mg.

Ham and Asparagus Mornay

Mae Guffy, Athens

50 cooked asparagus spears
10 thin slices ham
4 tablespoons butter
3 tablespoons flour
2 cups milk
1/4 cup dry white wine
1/4 teaspoon salt
1/4 teaspoon white pepper
1/2 cup grated Parmesan cheese
2 cups cream, whipped
2 tablespoons grated Swiss cheese

Preheat oven to 350 degrees. Wrap 5 warm asparagus spears in each ham slice. Place in large shallow baking dish, seam side down. Melt butter in saucepan. Blend in flour. Add milk, stirring constantly, until smooth and starts to boil. Add wine, salt, pepper and Parmesan cheese. Remove from heat; let cool. Fold in whipped cream. Spread sauce over ham and asparagus rolls. Sprinkle Swiss cheese over rolls. Bake for 12 minutes. Broil for 1 minute. Yield: 5 servings.

Approx Per Serving: Cal 674; Prot 29 g; Carbo 18 g; Fiber 3 g; T Fat 55 g; 72% Calories from Fat; Chol 210 mg; Sod 1246 mg.

Fettucini with Peas and Ham

Dixie Jones, Gallatin

This recipe won third place in the 1988 Tennessee Dairy Recipe Contest.

1 (16-ounce) package fettucini
5 tablespoons unsalted butter
6 shallots, minced
8 ounces fresh mushrooms, sliced
1 1/4 cups cream, whipped
1 (10-ounce) package frozen tiny peas, thawed
4 ounces boiled ham, chopped
1 cup freshly grated Parmesan cheese
Salt to taste
Freshly ground pepper to taste

Cook fettucini according to package directions; drain. Heat butter in large heavy non-aluminum skillet. Add shallots; sauté until softened. Add mushrooms. Increase heat to high; cook until lightly browned. Add cream; let boil for 2 minutes. Stir in peas; cook for 30 seconds. Reduce heat to low; blend in ham, cheese and fettucini. Toss until heated, well combined and sauce clings to pasta. Season with salt and pepper. Serve on heated platter. Garnish with additional Parmesan cheese and parsley. Yield: 8 servings.

Approx Per Serving: Cal 558; Prot 21 g; Carbo 60 g; Fiber 4 g; T Fat 27 g; 43% Calories from Fat; Chol 88 mg; Sod 487 mg.

Southern Ham-Batter Pudding

Dorothy Peavyhouse, Jamestown

2 (10-ounce) packages frozen succotash
1/4 cup yellow cornmeal
1/4 cup flour
1/2 teaspoon salt
1 teaspoon baking powder
1 egg
1/2 cup milk
1 tablespoon melted butter
3 cups chopped cooked ham
1/2 cup sour cream
2 teaspoons prepared mustard
1/4 cup grated onion

Preheat oven to 375 degrees. Cook succotash according to package directions; drain. Sift together cornmeal, flour, salt and baking powder in medium bowl. Beat egg lightly in small bowl; mix in milk and butter. Add to dry ingredients, stirring only until moistened. Mix ham, succotash, sour cream, mustard and onion in greased 2-quart casserole. Spread cornmeal batter over mixture. Bake for 30 minutes or until top is set and golden in color.
Yield: 6 servings.

Approx Per Serving: Cal 324; Prot 25 g; Carbo 30 g; Fiber 6 g; T Fat 12 g; 34% Calories from Fat; Chol 90 mg; Sod 1275 mg.

Ham Casserole

Eydie Foster, Petersburg

1 (8-ounce) package wide egg noodles
1/2 cup chopped onion
4 tablespoons butter
3 cups chopped cooked ham
2 (10-ounce) cans creamy chicken mushroom soup
1 1/2 cups water
1 pound Velveeta cheese, cubed
1 (2-ounce) jar chopped pimentos
1 (8-ounce) can English peas

Preheat oven to 350 degrees. Cook noodles according to package directions, omitting salt. Sauté onion in butter in 10-inch skillet. Add ham, soup, water, cheese, pimentos and peas. Cook over low heat until cheese is melted. Layer noodles and sauce alternately in oblong casserole. Bake for 45 minutes. Yield: 12 servings.

Approx Per Serving: Cal 298; Prot 22 g; Carbo 20 g; Fiber <1 g; T Fat 22 g; 54% Calories from Fat; Chol 102 mg; Sod 1491 mg.

Pineapple-Glazed Ham

Patricia Matthews, Athens

1 (10-pound) smoked ham
1 cup packed dark brown sugar
1 tablespoon cornstarch
1/4 teaspoon salt
1 tablespoon mustard
1 (8-ounce) can crushed pineapple
1 (10-ounce) can sliced pineapple
1 (4-ounce) jar maraschino cherries

Preheat oven to 325 degrees. Bake ham in large baking pan for 3 hours or until tender. Mix sugar, cornstarch, salt, mustard and crushed pineapple in small saucepan. Cook over medium heat until mixture is thickened and has boiled for 1 minute. Slice ham; layer in 9-by-13-inch baking dish. Arrange sliced pineapple and cherries in center. Pour mixture over ham. Place in oven; broil until pineapple is lightly browned. Yield: 24 servings.

Approx Per Serving: Cal 346; Prot 48 g; Carbo 13 g; Fiber <1 g; T Fat 11 g; 28% Calories from Fat; Chol 104 mg; Sod 2539 mg.

Souse or Hog's Head Cheese

Louise Ervin, Winchester

The success of this recipe depends on preparation of the meat.

1 hog's head
2 pig's feet
2 tablespoons salt
2 teaspoons pepper
3 pods red pepper

Clean head and feet thoroughly. Remove eyeballs. Cut ears from head. Singe lining and hairs. Scrape meat; wash thoroughly. Split and scrape pig's snout. Remove hooves. Meat will have pink color when properly prepared. Place head and feet in deep pan. Cover with water; add salt. Simmer for 6 hours or until meat will slip easily from bone. Add water as needed. Remove from heat; let stand until cold. Skim will form. Remove meat from bone by hand, working up meat until fine. Add pepper. Return meat to deep pan; heat meat until boiling. Cook for 20 minutes. Break up pepper pods; add to boiling mixture. Pour into china glass molds. Let congeal in cold place. Must use within 2 weeks. To can, pack boiling mixture into quart jars; seal. Process in pressure canner for 40 minutes. To serve, unmold; cut into 1/2-inch slices. Yield: 36 servings.

Nutritional information for this recipe is not available.

Barbecue Ribs

Jan Wyatt, Camden

2 (2 1/4-pound) strips spareribs
1 cup catsup
4 tablespoons dark brown sugar
2 tablespoons soy sauce
1 clove of garlic, crushed
1 tablespoon mustard
1 tablespoon vinegar
1/4 cup water
Salt and pepper to taste

Cut sparerib strips in half; place in large stockpot. Cover with water; cook for 1 hour. Combine catsup, brown sugar, soy sauce, garlic, mustard, vinegar and water in small bowl; mix well. Remove ribs from stockpot; drain well. Sprinkle salt and pepper on both sides. Cook on grill over medium heat until fork-tender, turning often and basting with sauce. Yield: 8 servings.

Approx Per Serving: Cal 281; Prot 26 g; Carbo 14 g; Fiber <1 g; T Fat 13 g; 43% Calories from Fat; Chol 83 mg; Sod 707 mg.

Barbecued Pork Shoulder

Martha Jean Burris, Unionville

1 (4-pound) pork shoulder roast
1 teaspoon salt
1 cup catsup
1/2 cup packed dark brown sugar
1 teaspoon each salt, pepper
2 teaspoons chili powder
6 tablespoons vinegar
2 tablespoons lemon juice
1/4 cup Worcestershire sauce
2 teaspoons prepared mustard

Cover roast with water in large heavy kettle. Add 1 teaspoon salt. Cook for 2 to 2 1/2 hours or until tender. Drain; slice thinly. Place slices in shallow 2-quart baking dish. Combine remaining ingredients in medium bowl; mix well. Spoon mixture over sliced roast, turning slices to coat. Yield: 12 servings.

Approx Per Serving: Cal 288; Prot 31 g; Carbo 15 g; Fiber <1 g; T Fat 12 g; 37% Calories from Fat; Chol 107 mg; Sod 762 mg.

Roast Pork

Retta H. Iddins, Loudon

1 (4-pound) boneless pork roast, trimmed
2 cups sugar
1 cup vinegar
1 cup water
2 tablespoons chopped green pepper
1/2 teaspoon salt
4 teaspoons cornstarch
2 tablespoons water
2 teaspoons paprika
2 teaspoons finely chopped parsley

Preheat oven to 450 degrees. Place roast in roasting pan; roast for 30 minutes or until browned. Reduce oven temperature to 300 degrees. Combine sugar, vinegar, 1 cup water, green pepper and salt in saucepan; mix well. Simmer for 5 minutes. Mix cornstarch and 2 tablespoons water in small bowl to make smooth paste. Add paste to sauce mixture; cook over low heat, stirring constantly, until thickened. Stir in paprika and parsley. Transfer roast into deep baking dish; pour sauce over roast. Cover; bake, basting occasionally, for 2 1/2 hours or until tender. Serve roast on warm platter. Pour sauce over roast or serve in gravy boat. Yield: 12 servings.

Approx Per Serving: Cal 342; Prot 27 g; Carbo 35 g; Fiber <1 g; T Fat 10 g; 27% Calories from Fat; Chol 90 mg; Sod 151 mg.

Honey-Gingered Pork Tenderloin

Katy Pat Bellar, Springfield

2 (12-ounce) pork tenderloins
1/4 cup honey
1/4 cup soy sauce
1/4 cup oyster sauce
2 tablespoons dark brown sugar
4 teaspoons minced fresh gingerroot
1 tablespoon minced garlic
1 tablespoon catsup
1/4 teaspoon ground red pepper
1/4 teaspoon ground cinnamon

Place tenderloins in 7-by-11-inch baking dish. Combine honey and remaining ingredients in small bowl; mix well. Pour over tenderloins. Marinate, covered, in refrigerator for 8 hours, turning occasionally. Remove tenderloins from marinade, reserving marinade. Grill tenderloins over medium hot coals for 25 to 35 minutes or until meat thermometer inserted into thickest portion of tenderloin registers 160 degrees. Turn often, basting with reserved marinade. Slice tenderloins thinly. Arrange on serving platter. Garnish with fresh parsley sprigs. Yield: 6 servings.

Approx Per Serving: Cal 196; Prot 21 g; Carbo 18 g; Fiber <1 g; T Fat 4 g; 20% Calories from Fat; Chol 59 mg; Sod 783 mg.

Pork Chop Skillet Dinner

Rosalene Melhorn, Harriman

6 lean pork chops
2 tablespoons vegetable shortening
Salt and pepper to taste
1/4 teaspoon savory
1 cup tomato juice
3 medium onions, sliced
6 carrots, sliced
3 medium potatoes, sliced
6 cabbage wedges
Paprika to taste

Brown chops lightly in shortening in large skillet. Sprinkle with salt, pepper and savory. Add tomato juice. Simmer, covered tightly, for 45 minutes. Add vegetables. Sprinkle with paprika and additional salt. Cook for 30 minutes or until vegetables are tender and small amount of liquid remains in pan. Yield: 6 servings.

Approx Per Serving: Cal 401; Prot 36 g; Carbo 31 g; Fiber 6 g; T Fat 15 g; 34% Calories from Fat; Chol 97 mg; Sod 268 mg.

Pork Chop Bake

Lenora Durrett, Cottontown

6 lean ½-inch thick lean pork chops
½ teaspoon salt
2 tablespoons water
3 cups herb-seasoned stuffing mix
1 cup water
⅓ cup butter
1 (1-ounce) package brown gravy mix
¼ cup dry red wine

Preheat oven to 350 degrees. Trim fat from pork chops. Sprinkle salt on 1 side of each chop. Place chops, salted sides down, in ungreased 9-by-13-inch baking dish; add 2 tablespoons water. Prepare stuffing mix according to package directions, using 1 cup water and ⅓ cup butter with 3 cups mix. Spoon stuffing onto pork chops. Bake, covered, for 45 minutes. Uncover; bake for 15 minutes. Prepare gravy according to package directions, substituting ¼ cup dry red wine for ¼ cup water. Yield: 6 servings.

Approx Per Serving: Cal 469; Prot 36 g; Carbo 29 g; Fiber <1 g; T Fat 22 g; 43% Calories from Fat; Chol 126 mg; Sod 1095 mg.

Benefield's Creole Pork

Mrs. Jack N. Benefield, Summertown

¾ pound lean pork
1 medium onion, chopped
½ medium green bell pepper, chopped
1 stalk celery, chopped
½ cup water
1 clove of garlic, crushed
Salt and pepper to taste
2 cups tomato juice
3 tablespoons cornstarch

Chill meat; slice into very thin slices, then into strips. Place onion, green pepper and celery in nonstick pan sprayed with nonstick cooking spray. Add water. Cook over medium heat until water is absorbed and vegetables are tender. Increase heat; add meat. Cook, stirring, until meat is white. Add garlic, salt, pepper and tomato juice. Simmer, covered, for 20 minutes. Add cornstarch; simmer until thickened. Serve on bed of rice. Yield: 4 servings.

Approx Per Serving: Cal 181; Prot 18 g; Carbo 14 g; Fiber 2 g; T Fat 6 g; 28% Calories from Fat; Chol 52 mg; Sod 492 mg.

Pork Stir-Fry

Mrs. Fredrick J. Schrock, Monterey

3 tablespoons vegetable oil
3 tablespoons soy sauce
5½ tablespoons cornstarch
½ teaspoon garlic powder
¼ teaspoon pepper
1½ pounds boneless pork loin chops, cut into thin strips
1 green bell pepper, cut into 1-inch pieces
4 carrots, thinly sliced
8 green onions, cut into ½-inch slices
2 cups water
1¾ teaspoons chicken-flavored bouillon
⅛ teaspoon ground ginger

Combine 1 tablespoon oil, 1 tablespoon soy sauce, 1½ teaspoons cornstarch, garlic powder and pepper in shallow dish; mix well. Add pork; stir. Let stand for 20 minutes. Pour remaining oil around top of preheated wok or skillet, coating sides. Heat at medium high or to 325 degrees for 2 minutes. Add green pepper and carrots; stir-fry for 4 minutes. Add onions; stir-fry for 2 minutes. Remove vegetables. Combine remaining soy sauce, remaining cornstarch, water, bouillon and ginger in medium bowl. Add pork to wok; stir-fry for 4 minutes. Return vegetables to wok. Add bouillon mixture. Stir-fry for 3 minutes or until thickened. Serve over hot rice. Yield: 6 servings.

Approx Per Serving: Cal 287; Prot 24 g; Carbo 15 g; Fiber 2 g; T Fat 14 g; 46% Calories from Fat; Chol 69 mg; Sod 925 mg.

Crunchy Sausage Casserole

John W. Gentry, Jr., Christiana

2 (6-ounce) packages long grain and wild
  rice mix
1 pound bulk pork sausage
1/2 pound ground beef
1 (8-ounce) can sliced water chestnuts,
  drained
1 large onion, chopped
1 (8-ounce) can sliced mushrooms, drained
4 stalks celery, chopped
3/4 cup red and green bell peppers,
  chopped
3 tablespoons light soy sauce
1 (2-ounce) package sliced almonds

Preheat oven to 325 degrees. Cook rice according to package directions. Brown sausage and ground beef in large skillet, stirring until crumbly; drain off fat. Add rice to meat mixture. Add chestnuts, onion, mushrooms, celery, red and green peppers and soy sauce; mix well. Spoon into ungreased 3-quart casserole; sprinkle with almonds. Bake for 50 minutes. Yield: 8 servings.

Approx Per Serving: Cal 352; Prot 17 g; Carbo 29 g; Fiber 3 g; T Fat 19 g; 48% Calories from Fat; Chol 43 mg; Sod 948 mg.

Corn Bread Casserole

Evelyn Cable, Greenback

2 1/2 cups cornmeal
1/2 cup flour
3 tablespoons vegetable oil
1 teaspoon baking soda
1 teaspoon salt
1 tablespoon baking powder
2 eggs, slightly beaten
1 cup buttermilk
1 pound link sausage
1 cup chopped green onions
1 cup chopped cucumbers
1 cup chopped green peppers
1 cup chopped tomatoes
Salt and pepper to taste
1 3/4 cups ranch-style dressing
1 teaspoon paprika

Preheat oven to 450 degrees. Combine cornmeal, flour, oil, baking soda, salt, baking powder, eggs and buttermilk in large bowl. Pour into greased iron skillet. Bake for 30 minutes or until browned. Let cool; crumble into baking pan. Bake until golden brown. Cook sausage in large skillet; drain. Cut sausage into bite-sized pieces. Combine corn bread, sausage, vegetables, salt and pepper in large bowl. Place in casserole. Pour dressing over mixture to moisten. Sprinkle paprika over top. Serve hot or cold. Yield: 8 servings.

Approx Per Serving: Cal 569; Prot 15 g; Carbo 48 g; Fiber 3 g; T Fat 36 g; 56% Calories from Fat; Chol 97 mg; Sod 1119 mg.

Sausage Casserole

Mrs. Tom Bullifin, Brownsville

1 (8-ounce) package elbow macaroni
2 pounds hot or mild sausage
1 large onion, chopped
1 (10-ounce) can cream of mushroom soup
1 (10-ounce) can Cheddar cheese soup
1 (12-ounce) can evaporated milk

Preheat oven to 350 degrees. Cook macaroni according to package directions; drain. Brown sausage with onion in large skillet, stirring until crumbly; do not drain. Add macaroni, soups and milk; mix well. Pour into 3-quart casserole. Bake for 30 minutes or until hot and bubbly. Serve hot. Yield: 12 servings.

Approx Per Serving: Cal 302; Prot 13 g; Carbo 22 g; Fiber <1 g; T Fat 18 g; 53% Calories from Fat; Chol 44 mg; Sod 891 mg.

Sausage Casserole

Nettie Ellis, Westport

1 pound mild bulk sausage
1 small onion, finely chopped
1 cup uncooked rice
1 cup shredded Cheddar cheese
1 (10-ounce) can cream of chicken soup
1 (10-ounce) can cream of mushroom soup
1/2 cup water

Preheat oven to 350 degrees. Cook sausage with onion in skillet, stirring until crumbly; drain. Combine sausage mixture and remaining ingredients in bowl; mix well. Pour into 2 1/2-quart casserole. Bake for 45 minutes. Yield: 8 servings.

Approx Per Serving: Cal 317; Prot 12 g; Carbo 25 g; Fiber <1 g; T Fat 18 g; 52% Calories from Fat; Chol 40 mg; Sod 1042 mg.

Crunchy Sausage Casserole

Jean Holland, Mosheim

1 pound bulk pork sausage
1 medium onion, chopped
2 green bell peppers, chopped
2 (10-ounce) cans cream of mushroom soup
1 1/2 cups milk
1 (2-ounce) jar chopped pimento
1 (4-ounce) can sliced mushrooms, drained
1 (8-ounce) can sliced water chestnuts, drained
2/3 cup uncooked long grain rice

Preheat oven to 350 degrees. Cook sausage in large skillet, stirring until crumbly. Add onion; cook until transparent. Drain off fat. Add remaining ingredients; mix well. Pour into 9-by-13-inch baking dish sprayed with nonstick cooking spray. Cover; bake for 30 minutes. Uncover; stir. Bake for 30 minutes longer. Let stand for 10 minutes. Garnish with pepper strips and mushrooms. Yield: 12 servings.

Approx Per Serving: Cal 194; Prot 7 g; Carbo 18 g; Fiber 1 g; T Fat 11 g; 49% Calories from Fat; Chol 19 mg; Sod 699 mg.

Sausage Breakfast Casserole

Geneva Brotherton, Bulls Gap

2 pounds bulk sausage
8 slices white bread, crust removed
1/4 cup butter, softened
2 cups shredded sharp cheese
5 eggs
1 cup cream
1 cup milk
1 1/2 teaspoons each salt, dry mustard

Cook sausage in large skillet, stirring until crumbly; drain. Spread bread with butter; cut into cubes. Place in 9-by-13-inch baking dish. Sprinkle with sausage; top with cheese. Combine remaining ingredients in bowl; beat well. Pour over mixture. Cover with foil. Chill overnight. Preheat oven to 350 degrees. Bake for 1 hour. Yield: 12 servings.

Approx Per Serving: Cal 389; Prot 17 g; Carbo 9 g; Fiber <1 g; T Fat 32 g; 74% Calories from Fat; Chol 178 mg; Sod 993 mg.

Squash-Sausage Casserole

Dona F. Bender, Columbia

1 pound bulk sausage
1 medium onion, chopped
2 pounds yellow squash, sliced
1 carrot, grated
1 cup sour cream
4 ounces seasoned bread crumbs
1/2 cup butter, melted
1 (10-ounce) can cream of chicken soup

Preheat oven to 375 degrees. Cook sausage with onion in skillet, stirring until crumbly. Cook squash in small amount of water until tender; drain. Stir squash and remaining ingredients into sausage mixture; mix well. Pour into baking dish. Bake for 30 minutes. Yield: 6 servings.

Approx Per Serving: Cal 508; Prot 15 g; Carbo 28 g; Fiber 3 g; T Fat 38 g; 67% Calories from Fat; Chol 92 mg; Sod 1544 mg.

Sausage-Squash Special

Joyce Brookshire, Wing, Alabama

1 pound bulk pork sausage
1 clove of garlic, crushed
4 cups sliced summer squash
1/2 cup dry bread crumbs
1/2 cup grated Parmesan cheese
1/2 cup milk
1 tablespoon snipped parsley
1/2 teaspoon salt
1/2 teaspoon crushed dried oregano
2 eggs, beaten

Preheat oven to 325 degrees. Brown sausage with garlic in large skillet, stirring until crumbly; drain off excess fat. Cook squash in small amount of water in covered saucepan until tender; drain. Stir squash, bread crumbs, Parmesan cheese, milk, parsley, salt and oregano into sausage mixture; fold in eggs. Pour into 6-by-10-inch baking dish. Bake for 25 to 30 minutes or until bubbly. Yield: 6 servings.

Approx Per Serving: Cal 257; Prot 15 g; Carbo 12 g; Fiber 1 g; T Fat 17 g; 58% Calories from Fat; Chol 109 mg; Sod 897 mg.

Quiche

Pam Huddleston, Lebanon

3/4 pound bulk sausage
1/2 cup chopped onion
1/3 cup chopped green pepper
1 1/2 cups sharp shredded cheese
1 tablespoon flour
1 (9-inch) deep pie shell
2 eggs, beaten
1 cup evaporated milk
1 tablespoon parsley flakes
3/4 teaspoon seasoned salt
1/4 teaspoon garlic salt
1/4 teaspoon pepper

Brown sausage with onion and green pepper in large skillet, stirring until crumbly; drain. Combine cheese and flour in large bowl. Stir in sausage mixture; pour into pie shell. Mix eggs, milk, parsley flakes, seasoned salt, garlic salt and pepper in medium bowl. Pour over sausage mixture. Place on cookie sheet. Bake for 30 to 40 minutes or until bubbly. Yield: 6 servings.

Approx Per Serving: Cal 470; Prot 20 g; Carbo 22 g; Fiber 1 g; T Fat 34 g; 64% Calories from Fat; Chol 135 mg; Sod 1036 mg.

Southwestern Chowder

Krista Doxey, Greenfield

1 pound mild bulk sausage
2 (16-ounce) cans kidney beans
2 (14-ounce) cans tomatoes
2 cups tomato juice
1 cup whole kernel corn
1 stalk celery, chopped
1 large onion, finely chopped
1 green pepper, chopped
1 bay leaf
1 1/2 teaspoons seasoned salt
1/2 teaspoon garlic salt
1 teaspoon chili powder
1/2 teaspoon thyme
1/4 teaspoon pepper

Brown sausage in large skillet, stirring until crumbly; drain. Combine sausage, beans, tomatoes, tomato juice, corn, celery, onion and green pepper in large kettle. Add remaining ingredients; mix well. Simmer, covered, for 1 hour. Remove bay leaf. Serve hot with corn bread. Yield: 12 servings.

Approx Per Serving: Cal 168; Prot 9 g; Carbo 21 g; Fiber 6 g; T Fat 6 g; 32% Calories from Fat; Chol 15 mg; Sod 995 mg.

Sausage Spaghetti Delight

Loraine Yarbro, Camden

1 pound bulk pork sausage
1/2 cup chopped onion
1/2 cup chopped green pepper
2 cups chopped tomatoes
1 cup buttermilk
1 teaspoon sugar
1 tablespoon chili powder
1 teaspoon salt
4 ounces uncooked spaghetti, broken
    into 4-inch pieces

Brown sausage with onion and green pepper in large skillet over medium heat, stirring until crumbly; drain well. Add remaining ingredients. Cook, covered, over low heat for 25 to 30 minutes or until spaghetti is done, stirring occasionally. Yield: 4 servings.

Approx Per Serving: Cal 366; Prot 18 g; Carbo 33 g; Fiber 3 g; T Fat 18 g; 45% Calories from Fat; Chol 46 mg; Sod 1316 mg.

Stir-Fry Vegetables and Sausage

Arlene Rasnake, Madisonville

4 slices bacon
4 potatoes, sliced
3 carrots, sliced
1 onion, sliced
1 green pepper, thinly sliced
1/4 bunch broccoli, chopped
1/2 small head cabbage, cut up
1 pound smoked sausage, sliced

Fry bacon in large skillet until crisp. Remove bacon from skillet; drain and crumble. Add potatoes, carrots, onion, green pepper, broccoli and cabbage to drippings in skillet. Cook for 20 minutes, stirring occasionally. Arrange sausage over vegetables. Cook, covered, for 10 minutes longer. Transfer to serving dish; top with bacon. Yield: 10 servings.

Approx Per Serving: Cal 169; Prot 8 g; Carbo 17 g; Fiber 3 g; T Fat 8 g; 43% Calories from Fat; Chol 17 mg; Sod 379 mg.

Individual Lamb Roasts

Linda Welch, Decatur

4 (16-ounce) lamb shanks, well trimmed
1 clove of garlic, cut into quarters
1/4 cup flour
2 teaspoons salt
1 teaspoon paprika
2 tablespoons vegetable oil
1/2 cup lemon juice
2 tablespoons grated lemon rind
2 bay leaves
4 whole black peppers
4 medium sweet potatoes, pared
1 (9-ounce) package frozen cut green
    beans, partially thawed

Preheat oven to 350 degrees. Make slit in each lamb shank; insert piece of garlic in each slit. Combine flour, salt and paprika in shallow bowl. Coat shanks with mixture. Brown shanks well on all sides in hot oil in skillet for 15 to 20 minutes. Place in 3-quart casserole. Add lemon juice to skillet, stirring to loosen brown bits; pour over shanks. Add lemon rind, bay leaves and peppers. Bake, covered, for 1 hour. Cut potatoes into halves. Add potatoes and beans. Bake, covered, for 45 minutes to 1 hour or until fork-tender. Yield: 4 servings.

Approx Per Serving: Cal 722; Prot 81 g; Carbo 41 g; Fiber 6 g; T Fat 25 g; 32% Calories from Fat; Chol 237 mg; Sod 1266 mg.

Roast Leg of Lamb

Alice Brehm Williamson, Knoxville

1 clove of garlic, minced
1 teaspoon salt
1/2 teaspoon pepper
1 bay leaf, crushed
1/2 teaspoon each ginger, thyme
1/2 teaspoon each sage, marjoram
1 (5-pound) leg of lamb
1/4 cup vegetable oil

Preheat oven to 500 degrees. Combine first 8 ingredients in small bowl; mix well. Cut irregular slits in leg of lamb. Rub spice mixture into slits. Rub leg with vegetable oil. Roast in oven for 5 minutes. Reduce heat to 325 degrees. Bake for 2 1/2 hours. Yield: 12 servings.

Approx Per Serving: Cal 257; Prot 32 g; Carbo <1 g; Fiber <1 g; T Fat 13 g; 48% Calories from Fat; Chol 101 mg; Sod 255 mg.

Creole Lamb

Mrs. Leon Thomas, Hillsboro

4 lamb chops
3 tablespoons vegetable shortening
2 medium potatoes, peeled
3 tablespoons chopped green pepper
3 tablespoons chopped onion
Salt and pepper to taste
2 (8-ounce) cans tomato sauce

Brown chops in shortening in large skillet; drain. Cut potatoes in half lengthwise. Place 1 potato half on each chop. Add remaining ingredients. Simmer, covered, for 1 hour, basting occasionally. Yield: 4 servings.

Approx Per Serving: Cal 321; Prot 24 g; Carbo 19 g; Fiber 3 g; T Fat 17 g; 47% Calories from Fat; Chol 67 mg; Sod 514 mg.

Curried Lamb with Rice

Juanita Swaggerty, Kodak

2 pounds lean lamb shoulder, cubed
2 tablespoons vegetable shortening
Salt and pepper to taste
1 bay leaf
6 whole black peppers
2 small onions, sliced
1 teaspoon chopped parsley
1/4 cup flour
1 teaspoon curry powder

Brown meat in hot shortening in skillet. Cover with boiling water. Add next 6 ingredients; cover. Cook slowly for 2 hours. Pour 2 cups strained stock into saucepan. Mix flour and curry powder. Add 2 tablespoons cold water; blend well. Stir into stock; cook, stirring, until thickened. Add meat mixture. Serve with fluffy rice. Yield: 6 servings.

Approx Per Serving: Cal 250; Prot 23 g; Carbo 6 g; Fiber <1 g; T Fat 14 g; 52% Calories from Fat; Chol 79 mg; Sod 63 mg.

Modern Cottage Pie

Harriet Rothfeldt, Lynchburg

2 1/2 cups cubed cooked lamb
1/3 cup chopped onion
1/8 teaspoon crushed rosemary
2 tablespoons margarine
1 (10-ounce) can cream of mushroom soup
1/3 cup milk
1 tablespoon chopped parsley
1/4 teaspoon each salt, pepper
1 cup frozen peas
4 servings mashed potatoes

Preheat oven to 400 degrees. Cook lamb and onion with rosemary in margarine in skillet until lamb is browned and onion is tender. Add soup, milk, parsley, salt, pepper and peas; mix well. Pour into 1 1/2-quart casserole. Spoon potatoes around edge. Bake for 25 minutes or until hot. May substitute garlic salt for salt to add different flavor. Yield: 4 servings.

Approx Per Serving: Cal 390; Prot 20 g; Carbo 28 g; Fiber 3 g; T Fat 22 g; 51% Calories from Fat; Chol 63 mg; Sod 1178 mg.

Lamb Chop-Apple Sauté

Elizabeth Wilburn, Manchester

4 large shoulder lamb chops
3 tablespoons vegetable oil
6 green onions, thinly sliced
2 apples, cored
1/4 cup vegetable stock
Salt and pepper to taste
1 tablespoon cornstarch

Preheat oven to 300 degrees. Trim excess fat from lamb chops. Brown chops in oil in large skillet. Remove to large heavy saucepan. Sauté green onions in skillet until golden; sprinkle over chops. Slice apples into 1/4-inch thick slices. Sauté apple slices in skillet until brown on both sides, adding more oil if necessary. Arrange apple slices over chops. Pour stock over chops. Season with salt and pepper. Cook, covered, over low heat for 45 minutes. Remove chops to platter. Blend cornstarch with 2 tablespoons pan drippings. Add back to pan drippings, stirring constantly, until thickened. Pour sauce over chops. Yield: 4 servings.

Approx Per Serving: Cal 333; Prot 27 g; Carbo 13 g; Fiber 2 g; T Fat 19 g; 52% Calories from Fat; Chol 84 mg; Sod 141 mg.

Ragout of Lamb

Carman Alexander, Rockvale

2 pounds lamb shoulder, cut into cubes
3 tablespoons vegetable oil
1/2 teaspoon salt
1 bay leaf, crushed
1/2 teaspoon basil
1/4 teaspoon thyme
2 small onions, sliced
8 ounces small fresh mushrooms, sliced
2 tablespoons margarine
1 1/2 tablespoons whole wheat flour
2 cups beef stock
2 egg yolks
1 cup yogurt

Brown lamb in oil in large skillet. Transfer to Crock•Pot. Add salt, bay leaf, basil and thyme. Sauté onions in skillet; add to Crock•Pot. Sauté mushrooms in skillet; add to Crock•Pot. Melt margarine in skillet; add flour, blending thoroughly. Add beef stock, stirring until sauce is smooth. Add sauce to lamb mixture; mix gently. Cook, covered, on Low for 6 to 7 hours. Remove lamb to serving platter; keep warm. Pour liquid from Crock•Pot into saucepan. Mix egg yolks with yogurt in small bowl. Stir into hot liquid until smooth; pour over lamb. Garnish with chopped parsley. Serve immediately. Yield: 8 servings.

Approx Per Serving: Cal 265; Prot 20 g; Carbo 5 g; Fiber <1 g; T Fat 18 g; 61% Calories from Fat; Chol 116 mg; Sod 426 mg.

Lamb Stew

Marla Gordon, Shelbyville

1/3 cup flour
1 1/2 teaspoons salt
1/8 teaspoon pepper
1 1/2 pounds boneless stew lamb, cut into
    1-inch cubes
2 tablespoons vegetable oil
3 medium onions, sliced
4 medium potatoes, cut into 1-inch cubes
5 medium carrots, quartered
1 1/2 cups frozen peas

Combine flour, salt and pepper in shallow dish. Coat lamb with flour mixture. Brown lamb in moderately hot oil in large deep pot. Sprinkle remaining seasoned flour over browned lamb; stir. Add 3 1/4 cups water; cover tightly. Simmer for 1 1/2 to 2 hours or until lamb is tender. Add onions, potatoes and carrots. Simmer, covered, for 15 minutes. Add peas. Simmer, covered, until vegetables are tender, stirring occasionally. Yield: 8 servings.

Approx Per Serving: Cal 275; Prot 21 g; Carbo 29 g; Fiber 5 g; T Fat 8 g; 27% Calories from Fat; Chol 55 mg; Sod 486 mg.

Kate's Skillet Dinner

Mossie Kate Campbell, Sneedville

1 pound ground venison
2 tablespoons vegetable oil
1 cup chopped potatoes
1 cup canned tomatoes
1 large onion, chopped
1/2 cup chopped celery
1 tablespoon vinegar
1 teaspoon salt

Brown venison in oil in large skillet. Add potatoes, tomatoes, onion, celery, vinegar and salt; mix well. Cover; cook slowly for 45 minutes or until vegetables are tender. Yield: 6 servings.

Approx Per Serving: Cal 169; Prot 18 g; Carbo 9 g; Fiber 1 g; T Fat 7 g; 35% Calories from Fat; Chol 64 mg; Sod 462 mg.

David's Venison Supreme

David Nutt, Waynesboro

1 cup flour
Salt and pepper to taste
Garlic salt to taste
2 pounds lean venison, cut into
    2-by-4-inch pieces
1 cup bacon drippings
2 large carrots, cut into julienne strips
1 (8-ounce) package fresh mushrooms,
    cut into halves
4 green onions, cut into spears
3 stalks celery, cut into 2-inch spears
1 (30-ounce) can whole tomatoes
1 (10-ounce) can whole Ro-Tel tomatoes
3/4 cup grated Parmesan cheese
1 tablespoon Worcestershire sauce
1 (6-ounce) package mozzarella cheese
    slices

Preheat oven to 300 degrees. Combine flour, salt, pepper and garlic salt in shallow dish; mix well. Dredge venison in flour mixture. Brown in bacon drippings in large skillet. Transfer meat and drippings to Dutch oven. Layer carrots, mushrooms, green onions and celery over venison. Pour tomatoes over vegetables. Cover with Parmesan cheese. Sprinkle with Worcestershire sauce; cover tightly. Bake for 3 to 3 1/2 hours or until venison and vegetables are tender. Add mozzarella slices 30 minutes before serving. Serve over rice or egg noodles. Yield: 8 servings.

Approx Per Serving: Cal 566; Prot 32 g; Carbo 24 g; Fiber 4 g; T Fat 38 g; 61% Calories from Fat; Chol 128 mg; Sod 801 mg.

Barbecued Venison

Mrs. Mary Lynn Butler, Decaturville

1/2 cup catsup
1/4 cup red wine vinegar
2 tablespoons dark brown sugar
2 tablespoons Worcestershire sauce
1 clove of garlic, minced
1/2 cup water
1 teaspoon salt
1/8 teaspoon pepper
1 pound boneless venison, cut into
    1-inch cubes
1/2 cup chopped onion
2 crisp-fried slices bacon, crumbled

Combine catsup, vinegar, brown sugar, Worcestershire sauce, garlic, water, salt and pepper in large saucepan; mix well. Stir in venison, onion and bacon. Cover; cook for 45 to 55 minutes or until meat is tender. Yield: 4 servings.

Approx Per Serving: Cal 189; Prot 22 g; Carbo 17 g; Fiber <1 g; T Fat 4 g; 18% Calories from Fat; Chol 78 mg; Sod 1068 mg.

Marinated Venison Roast

Catherine Lankford, Dickson

2 cloves of garlic, minced
2 tablespoons vegetable oil
1 cup Dr. Pepper
1/4 teaspoon dry mustard
2 tablespoons catsup
1 1/4 teaspoons salt
1/4 teaspoon pepper
1 tablespoon vinegar
2 tablespoons soy sauce
1 (4-pound) venison roast

Sauté garlic in oil in large skillet. Add Dr. Pepper, mustard, catsup, salt, pepper, vinegar and soy sauce; mix well. Pour over roast in shallow baking dish. Refrigerate for 6 to 24 hours, turning several times. Preheat oven to 325 degrees. Place meat on large piece cooking foil in roasting pan. Bring foil up around roast, leaving top open. Pour marinade over meat. Bake for 2 1/2 hours or until tender, gently turning several times during cooking.
Yield: 12 servings.

Approx Per Serving: Cal 175; Prot 27 g; Carbo 3 g; Fiber <1 g; T Fat 5 g; 28% Calories from Fat; Chol 100 mg; Sod 474 mg.

Venison Parmesan

Mrs. Edna Barnes, Crossville

1 pound 1/4-inch thick venison steak
Salt and pepper to taste
1 egg
2 teaspoons water
1/3 cup grated Parmesan cheese
1/3 cup fine dried bread crumbs
1/4 cup olive oil
1 onion, finely chopped
2 tablespoons butter
1 (6-ounce) can tomato paste
2 cups hot water
1 teaspoon salt
1/2 teaspoon marjoram
1/2 pound mozzarella cheese, thinly sliced

Preheat oven to 350 degrees. Cut steak into 8 pieces. Sprinkle with salt and pepper. Beat egg with 2 teaspoons water in shallow bowl. Dip steaks in egg; roll in mixture of Parmesan cheese and bread crumbs. Heat oil in large skillet. Fry steaks until golden brown on each side. Place in wide shallow baking dish. Sauté onion in butter in same skillet until softened. Add tomato paste mixed with hot water, salt and marjoram. Boil for a few minutes, scraping brown bits from bottom. Pour most of sauce over steaks. Top with cheese; cover with remaining sauce. Bake for 30 minutes. Yield: 4 servings.

Approx Per Serving: Cal 571; Prot 39 g; Carbo 18 g; Fiber 3 g; T Fat 38 g; 60% Calories from Fat; Chol 195 mg; Sod 1416 mg.

Venison Pepper Steak

Mrs. Clifford Leonard, Dandridge

2 pounds stew venison
3 tablespoons vegetable shortening
2 1/2 cups water
2 beef bouillon cubes
2 red bell peppers, cut into eighths
2 green bell peppers, cut into eighths
3 tablespoons cornstarch
2 tablespoons soy sauce

Cut venison into thin 1-by-2-inch strips. Brown in shortening in large skillet. Add 2 cups water and bouillon cubes; bring to a boil. Cover; simmer for 1 hour or until venison is tender. Add red and green peppers; simmer for 5 minutes longer. Blend cornstarch, soy sauce and 1/2 cup water in small bowl. Add to meat mixture. Cook until thickened, stirring slowly. Serve with rice and additional soy sauce. Yield: 6 servings.

Approx Per Serving: Cal 231; Prot 28 g; Carbo 8 g; Fiber <1 g; T Fat 9 g; 37% Calories from Fat; Chol 100 mg; Sod 680 mg.

Venison Stew

Cindy Smith, Friendship

Salt and pepper to taste
1 (3-pound) venison roast
1 pound carrots, sliced
6 medium potatoes, cubed
1 cup lima beans
1 cup corn
1 large onion, chopped

Salt and pepper roast in large Dutch oven. Cover with water. Cook for 2 to 3 hours or until tender. Remove roast from broth; let cool. Reserve broth in Dutch oven. Tear roast into small pieces. Place roast, carrots, potatoes, beans, corn, onion, salt and pepper in broth. Simmer for 1 hour or until vegetables are tender. Serve with hot corn bread. Yield: 8 servings.

Approx Per Serving: Cal 313; Prot 35 g; Carbo 35 g; Fiber 4 g; T Fat 4 g; 11% Calories from Fat; Chol 112 mg; Sod 84 mg.

Texas-Fried Venison

Jane Cowan, Chestnut Mound

2 pounds venison
Salt to taste
3 tablespoons vinegar
1/2 cup bacon fat
1/2 cup flour
1 teaspoon pepper
1/4 cup sliced celery
1 large onion, sliced
1/2 cup chopped green pepper
2 tablespoons Worcestershire sauce
2 tablespoons steak sauce
2 tablespoons soy sauce
2 cups canned tomatoes

Soak venison in salt water with vinegar in large bowl overnight. Cut venison into serving-sized pieces. Heat bacon fat in large skillet. Mix flour and pepper in shallow dish. Coat venison with flour mixture. Brown on both sides. Add celery, onion, green pepper, Worcestershire sauce, steak sauce, soy sauce and tomatoes. Cover; cook slowly for 1 or 2 hours or until meat is done. May substitute tomato juice for tomatoes. Yield: 8 servings.

Approx Per Serving: Cal 290; Prot 22 g; Carbo 13 g; Fiber 2 g; T Fat 16 g; 51% Calories from Fat; Chol 89 mg; Sod 569 mg.

Aunt Earlene's Deer Summer Sausage

Pamela Taylor, Saulsbury

5 pounds ground venison
1 pound ground pork
3 tablespoons quick-tender salt
1 teaspoon liquid smoke
1/2 teaspoon crushed red pepper
2 1/2 teaspoons garlic salt
2 1/2 teaspoons mustard seed
2 teaspoons pepper

Combine all ingredients in large bowl; mix well. Refrigerate for 24 hours. Mix again; refrigerate for 24 hours longer. Preheat oven to 150 degrees. Shape into rolls 2 inches thick and 6 inches long. Place on oven rack over cookie sheet so logs can drain well. Bake for 8 hours. Turn each roll after first 4 hours. Sausage will keep in refrigerator for 2 to 3 weeks. Place in freezer to keep longer. Yield: 24 servings.

Approx Per Serving: Cal 145; Prot 26 g; Carbo <1 g; Fiber 0 g; T Fat 4 g; 24% Calories from Fat; Chol 93 mg; Sod 1062 mg.

Poultry, Seafood, Egg and Cheese Dishes

Horsin' Around

Expressing their delight for life, these two foals devote almost every moment to fun and frolic. As they mature, they'll receive the guidance they need to channel their energies into training.

Braised Doves

Mrs. Howard Hudson, Humboldt

6 doves
1/4 cup flour
1/2 teaspoon salt
1/8 teaspoon pepper
3 tablespoons vegetable oil
1 (10-ounce) can cream of mushroom soup
1 (10-ounce) soup can water

Clean and dress doves. Combine flour, salt and pepper in shallow dish. Roll doves in flour mixture. Brown doves in oil in skillet. Add soup and water. Simmer over low heat for 1 hour or until done. Yield: 4 servings.

Approx Per Serving: Cal 449; Prot 58 g; Carbo 12 g; Fiber <1 g; T Fat 19 g; 38% Calories from Fat; Chol 164 mg; Sod 884 mg.

Barbecued Chicken

Michael DeGeorge, Pegram

2 cups vinegar
1/2 cup plus 2 tablespoons vegetable shortening
1/2 cup butter
3 tablespoons pepper
2 tablespoons red pepper
1 1/2 tablespoons salt
8 chicken breast halves

Soak hickory chips in water for 1 to 12 hours. Combine vinegar, shortening, butter, pepper, red pepper and salt in saucepan; bring to a boil. Cook until shortening and butter are melted. Remove from heat. Prepare charcoal fire in grill; let burn for 15 to 20 minutes. Cover coals with soaked hickory chips. Coat chicken breasts with sauce. Grill chicken over medium coals for 45 to 55 minutes or until test done, turning and basting every 10 minutes. Refrigerate any leftover sauce to use with other meats. Yield: 8 servings.

Approx Per Serving: Cal 401; Prot 27 g; Carbo 6 g; Fiber 1 g; T Fat 31 g; 68% Calories from Fat; Chol 103 mg; Sod 1381 mg.

Easy and Delicious Chicken Casserole

Ola Tompkins, Allardt

4 chicken breasts
1 cup sour cream
1 (10-ounce) can cream of chicken soup
1 stack buttery crackers, crumbled
1/2 cup margarine, melted

Preheat oven to 400 degrees. Boil chicken in small amount of water in saucepan until tender. Remove from bone in small chunks. Place in 8-inch square glass dish. Mix sour cream and soup together in medium bowl; spoon over chicken. Mix cracker crumbs and margarine in small bowl; sprinkle over chicken. Bake, uncovered, for 20 minutes. Yield: 4 servings.

Approx Per Serving: Cal 658; Prot 32 g; Carbo 23 g; Fiber <1 g; T Fat 49 g; 66% Calories from Fat; Chol 104 mg; Sod 1164 mg.

Parmesan Chicken Bake

Mrs. Claude Hart, Cedar Hill

1/4 cup Parmesan cheese
1 tablespoon parsley flakes
1/4 teaspoon garlic salt
1/8 teaspoon pepper
3 skinless chicken breasts, split
1/4 cup margarine, melted
12 buttery crackers, crushed
Paprika to taste

Combine Parmesan cheese, parsley flakes, garlic salt and pepper in shallow bowl. Dip breasts in margarine. Roll in cracker crumbs and spice mixture. Arrange in circle in microwave-safe dish, overlapping thinnest parts. Sprinkle with paprika. Cover with waxed paper. Microwave on Medium-High for 13 to 15 minutes or until test done. Microwave boneless breasts on Medium-High for 10 to 12 minutes. Let stand uncovered for 5 minutes.
Yield: 6 servings.

Approx Per Serving: Cal 187; Prot 16 g; Carbo 4 g; Fiber <1 g; T Fat 12 g; 58% Calories from Fat; Chol 39 mg; Sod 335 mg.

Party Chicken

Mrs. A. J. Stafford, Limestone

This recipe can be made ahead and refrigerated until baking time.

8 boneless chicken breasts
8 slices bacon
4 ounces chipped beef
1 (10-ounce) can cream of
   mushroom soup
1 cup sour cream

Preheat oven to 275 degrees. Wrap each chicken breast with slice of bacon. Sprinkle chipped beef in bottom of 8-by-12-inch casserole. Arrange chicken over beef. Mix soup and sour cream in medium bowl; pour over chicken. Bake, uncovered, for 3 hours. Serve over rice.
Yield: 8 servings.

Approx Per Serving: Cal 390; Prot 34 g; Carbo 4 g; Fiber <1 g; T Fat 26 g; 60% Calories from Fat; Chol 107 mg; Sod 1034 mg.

Pineapple Chicken

Marlene Knox, Graysville

1 1/2 whole chicken breasts
1/2 cup cornstarch
1/2 cup flour
1 egg
1/2 cup water
Salt to taste
Oil for deep frying
1 1/2 tablespoons cornstarch
1/2 cup water
1/2 cup dark brown sugar
1/4 cup cider vinegar
1 cup pineapple chunks with juice
1/4 cup red maraschino cherries

Slice chicken breasts into 1-by-2-by-1/4-inch pieces; dredge in 1/2 cup cornstarch. Combine flour, egg, 1/2 cup water and salt in small bowl. Heat oil in skillet. Dip chicken pieces into batter. Fry in oil for 3 minutes on each side; drain. Dissolve 1 1/2 tablespoons cornstarch in 1/2 cup water in small bowl. Combine brown sugar and vinegar in separate skillet. Heat until sugar is dissolved. Add pineapple with juice. Stir in cornstarch mixture. Cook for 5 minutes. Add cherries. Pour over chicken pieces.
Yield: 2 servings.

Nutritional information does not include oil for deep frying.
Approx Per Serving: Cal 766; Prot 47 g; Carbo 127 g; Fiber 2 g; T Fat 8 g; 9% Calories from Fat; Chol 214 mg; Sod 146 mg.

Chicken Mazzetti Casserole

Mrs. R. T. DeMarcus, Knoxville

1 pound onions, chopped
1 1/2 cups chopped green peppers
1 1/2 cups chopped celery
1 clove of garlic, minced
2 (6-ounce) cans tomato paste
3 (8-ounce) cans tomato sauce
1 (10-ounce) can tomato soup
5 pounds chicken breasts and thighs
1 teaspoon salt
1 tablespoon Accent
2 (5-ounce) packages wide egg noodles
1 (4-ounce) can grated Parmesan cheese
1 1/2 pounds grated sharp Cheddar cheese
1 (8-ounce) can mushroom stems and
   pieces
1 (12-ounce) bottle stuffed salad olives
   and juice
1 (3-ounce) can sliced ripe olives
16 ounces natural mozzarella cheese,
   cubed
Paprika to taste

Preheat oven to 300 degrees. Combine onions, green peppers, celery, garlic, tomato paste, tomato sauce and tomato soup in large saucepan. Simmer until vegetables are tender. Cook chicken in water to cover with salt and Accent for 25 minutes or until test done. Remove chicken; let cool. Add noodles to chicken broth; cook for 7 minutes. Remove from heat; do not drain. Debone chicken; cut into 1/2-inch cubes. Add to tomato sauce mixture. Add Parmesan cheese and 1 1/4 pounds Cheddar cheese. Add mushrooms and olives. Alternate layers of drained noodles and chicken-tomato mixture in wide deep casserole. Top with remaining Cheddar cheese. Sprinkle with mozzarella cheese. Decorate with paprika. Bake for 1 hour.
Yield: 12 servings.

Approx Per Serving: Cal 677; Prot 60 g; Carbo 38 g; Fiber 4 g; T Fat 43 g; 57% Calories from Fat; Chol 222 mg; Sod 3472 mg.

Mexican Pinto Beans

Mrs. Sophia Hudson, Lebanon

1 pound dried pinto beans
2 medium onions, chopped
2 tablespoons olive oil
4 cups hot water
2 cloves of garlic, minced
2 teaspoons salt
1 tablespoon chili powder
1 (4-ounce) can diced green chilies
1 sweet red pepper, sliced into 1-inch
   strips
3 whole skinless boneless chicken breasts,
   cut into 1-inch strips
4 ounces grated Monterey Jack cheese

Wash beans. Soak beans in water to cover in large bowl overnight; drain. Sauté onions in olive oil in large kettle until golden. Add hot water, beans, garlic, salt and chili powder. Simmer for 1 hour or until done. Add chilies, red pepper and chicken; simmer for 30 minutes longer. Stir in cheese. Remove from heat. Serve in deep 2-quart casserole. Yield: 8 servings.

Approx Per Serving: Cal 399; Prot 37 g; Carbo 39 g; Fiber 14 g; T Fat 11 g; 24% Calories from Fat; Chol 67 mg; Sod 839 mg.

Chicken with Rice

Mrs. Dan (Vondie) Smith, Lebanon

Mrs. Smith enjoys preparing and serving this quick-but-tasty chicken with rice combination that has proven to be a hit with those lucky enough to sample it.

1 1/3 cups minute rice
1 (10-ounce) can celery soup
1 (10-ounce) can cream of mushroom soup
1 (5-ounce) can evaporated milk
1/2 cup water
1/2 envelope dried onion soup mix
4 skinless chicken breast halves

Preheat oven to 325 degrees. Sprinkle rice over bottom of buttered 9-by-13-inch baking dish. Combine soups, milk and water in large bowl; mix well. Pour over rice. Arrange chicken over mixture. Sprinkle onion soup mix over chicken. Seal with cooking foil. Bake for 2 hours and 15 minutes. Do not uncover during baking time. Yield: 4 servings.

Approx Per Serving: Cal 443; Prot 34 g; Carbo 42 g; Fiber 1 g; T Fat 15 g; 31% Calories from Fat; Chol 92 mg; Sod 1376 mg.

Countryside Chicken Bake

Maxine Beckwith, Lebanon

3 cups cooked rice
1 cup chopped celery
1/3 cup chopped onion
2 tablespoons margarine, melted
2 teaspoons parsley flakes
1/4 teaspoon salt
3 chicken breasts, split
1 (10-ounce) can cream of mushroom soup
2/3 cup mayonnaise-type salad dressing
1/4 cup milk
1 (16-ounce) can small whole carrots, drained
Paprika to taste

Preheat oven to 350 degrees. Combine rice, celery, onion, margarine, parsley flakes and salt in large bowl; mix lightly. Spoon into greased 3-quart baking dish; top with chicken breasts. Combine soup, salad dressing and milk in medium bowl; blend well. Pour over chicken. Bake for 45 minutes. Arrange carrots over top. Bake for 15 minutes longer or until chicken is tender. Sprinkle with paprika. Yield: 6 servings.

Approx Per Serving: Cal 421; Prot 18 g; Carbo 45 g; Fiber 2 g; T Fat 19 g; 40% Calories from Fat; Chol 45 mg; Sod 967 mg.

Clinch Mountain-Style Chicken

Blonde Mynatt, Luttrell

1 (3-pound) fryer chicken, cut up
1 teaspoon salt
1/4 teaspoon pepper
1/2 teaspoon minced onion
1/4 cup corn oil
1 clove of garlic, minced
1 cup tomato paste
2 cups chicken broth
1 cup uncooked long-grain rice
1 cup drained canned peas
1 (2-ounce) jar pimentos, chopped

Season chicken with salt, pepper and minced onion. Brown in hot oil in large skillet. Add garlic, tomato paste and 1/2 cup chicken broth. Reduce heat. Simmer, covered, for 20 minutes. Add rice and remaining broth, stirring until broth covers rice. Simmer, covered, for 20 minutes. Add peas and pimentos. Simmer for 5 minutes longer. Yield: 4 servings.

Approx Per Serving: Cal 721; Prot 60 g; Carbo 56 g; Fiber 5 g; T Fat 28 g; 35% Calories from Fat; Chol 151 mg; Sod 1681 mg.

Chicken Creole

Mary Getchell, Ripley

1 (3-pound) fryer chicken
1/4 cup margarine
3/4 cup chopped celery
3/4 cup chopped green bell pepper
3/4 cup chopped onion
3 cloves of garlic, chopped
3 tablespoons chili powder
1 teaspoon salt
1 (16-ounce) can tomatoes, mashed
1/2 (8-ounce) can tomato sauce
1/2 cup chicken broth

Cook chicken in water to cover in large saucepan for 1 hour or until tender; let cool. Debone; cut into bite-sized pieces. Melt margarine in skillet. Add celery, green pepper, onion and garlic. Sauté over medium heat until tender; do not boil. Add chili powder, salt, tomatoes, tomato sauce and broth. Cook for 3 minutes. Add chicken pieces. Simmer until chicken is heated; do not boil. Let stand for several hours to blend flavor. Spoon over cooked rice. Yield: 8 servings.

Approx Per Serving: Cal 251; Prot 27 g; Carbo 8 g; Fiber 3 g; T Fat 13 g; 46% Calories from Fat; Chol 75 mg; Sod 672 mg.

Chicken Potpie

Maggie S. Smith, Morrison

1 (3-pound) fryer chicken
2 (10-ounce) cans cream of chicken soup
1 (10-ounce) can cream of mushroom soup
1 (10-ounce) can cream of celery soup
2 (16-ounce) cans mixed vegetables with liquid
1 (8-ounce) can sweet peas, drained
1 1/2 cups chicken broth
1 cup self-rising flour
2 teaspoons baking powder
1/2 cup butter, melted

Preheat oven to 350 degrees. Boil chicken in large saucepan for 1 hour or until tender; let cool. Remove chicken from bones; cut into bite-sized pieces. Arrange chicken in bottom of 9-by-13-inch baking dish. Combine soups, mixed vegetables, peas and broth in large bowl; pour over chicken. Combine flour, baking powder and butter in medium bowl. Pour over casserole. Bake for 1 hour. Yield: 12 servings.

Approx Per Serving: Cal 350; Prot 22 g; Carbo 23 g; Fiber 1 g; T Fat 19 g; 48% Calories from Fat; Chol 78 mg; Sod 1419 mg.

Chicken Pie

Lila Walker, Petersburg

3/4 cup vegetable shortening
2 cups self-rising flour
5 tablespoons water
1 cup cubed cooked chicken
2/3 cup chopped celery
1/3 cup chopped onion
1/3 cup mayonnaise-type salad dressing
3 tablespoons sour cream
1 tablespoon prepared mustard
5 teaspoons butter

Preheat oven to 425 degrees. Cut shortening into flour in medium bowl. Add water; combine. Divide into 2 balls; roll each ball into crust. Place 1 crust in deep 9-inch pie plate. Combine chicken, celery, onion, salad dressing, sour cream and mustard in large bowl; mix well. Pour into pie crust. Dot with butter. Top with remaining crust; seal edges. Cut slits in crust so steam can escape. Bake for 1 hour or until golden brown. Yield: 6 servings.

Approx Per Serving: Cal 520; Prot 12 g; Carbo 36 g; Fiber 2 g; T Fat 37 g; 64% Calories from Fat; Chol 36 mg; Sod 722 mg.

Microwave Chicken and Rice

Barbara Lester, Lascassas

3¹/₂ pounds cut-up chicken
¹/₄ cup mayonnaise
¹/₂ cup Russian dressing
1 cup apricot preserves
1 envelope dry onion soup mix
6 cups cooked rice

Arrange chicken in microwave-safe baking dish with thickest parts to outside. Combine mayonnaise, dressing, preserves and soup mix in medium bowl; mix well. Coat chicken with mixture. Microwave on High for 18 to 22 minutes or until test done. Let stand for 5 minutes. Serve with rice. Yield: 8 servings.

Approx Per Serving: Cal 613; Prot 34 g; Carbo 71 g; Fiber 1 g; T Fat 21 g; 31% Calories from Fat; Chol 95 mg; Sod 354 mg.

Randell's Baked Chicken

Randell Cottrell, Crossville

3 cups Rice Krispies, finely crushed
1 teaspoon paprika
¹/₂ teaspoon salt
¹/₄ teaspoon pepper
3 pounds chicken pieces
¹/₂ cup mayonnaise

Preheat oven to 425 degrees. Mix Rice Krispies, paprika, salt and pepper in shaker bag. Brush chicken with mayonnaise. Coat with Rice Krispies mixture. Bake for 40 to 45 minutes or until test done. Yield: 8 servings.

Approx Per Serving: Cal 302; Prot 26 g; Carbo 10 g; Fiber <1 g; T Fat 17 g; 53% Calories from Fat; Chol 84 mg; Sod 411 mg.

Chicken Casserole Deluxe

Mrs. Ernest Taylor Logan, Murfreesboro

2 cups chopped cooked chicken
2 tablespoons grated onion
1 tablespoon lemon juice
¹/₂ cup mayonnaise
1 teaspoon salt
¹/₂ teaspoon pepper
¹/₂ cup cracker crumbs
3 hard-cooked eggs, chopped
¹/₂ cup chopped almonds
1 cup chopped celery
1 cup grated mild Cheddar cheese
1 (10-ounce) can cream of chicken soup
¹/₂ cup water
1 cup crushed potato chips

Preheat oven to 350 degrees. Combine chicken, onion, lemon juice, mayonnaise, salt, pepper, crumbs, eggs, almonds, celery, Cheddar cheese and soup in large bowl. Rinse soup can with water; add to mixture, mixing well. Pour into greased baking dish. Top with potato chips. Bake for 25 minutes. Yield: 6 servings.

Approx Per Serving: Cal 532; Prot 27 g; Carbo 18 g; Fiber 2 g; T Fat 40 g; 67% Calories from Fat; Chol 182 mg; Sod 1213 mg.

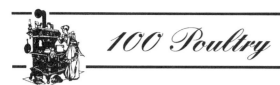

Chicken Casserole

Mrs. Allen Fine, Lenoir City

3 cups large boneless cooked chicken
   pieces
2 (10-ounce) cans cream of chicken soup
1 cup mayonnaise
2 cups chopped celery
1 cup chopped onions
8 saltine crackers, crumbled
6 hard-cooked eggs, chopped
Salt and pepper to taste
1 (5-ounce) can chow mein noodles

Preheat oven to 350 degrees. Combine chicken, soup, mayonnaise, celery, onions, crackers, eggs, salt and pepper in large baking dish; mix gently. Top with noodles. Bake for 25 minutes or until hot and bubbly.
Yield: 6 servings.

Approx Per Serving: Cal 727; Prot 33 g; Carbo 29 g; Fiber 2 g; T Fat 54 g; 66% Calories from Fat; Chol 304 mg; Sod 1321 mg.

Dorris' Chicken Casserole

Mrs. Dorris Harris, Clarksville

1 cup cooked chicken
1 cup chopped cooked celery
1 cup cooked rice
1 (10-ounce) can cream of chicken soup
1/3 cup evaporated milk
3/4 cup mayonnaise
1 tablespoon chopped onion
1/2 cup slivered almonds
1 cup crushed cornflakes
2 tablespoons melted butter

Preheat oven to 350 degrees. Combine chicken, celery, rice, soup, milk, mayonnaise, onion and almonds in large bowl; mix well. Pour into casserole. Mix cornflakes and butter in small bowl. Sprinkle over top. Bake for 40 minutes. Yield: 6 servings.

Approx Per Serving: Cal 505; Prot 14 g; Carbo 30 g; Fiber 2 g; T Fat 38 g; 66% Calories from Fat; Chol 56 mg; Sod 777 mg.

Hot Chicken Salad Casserole

Mrs. Elmer Arnold, Obion

2 cups chopped cooked chicken breasts
2 cups thinly sliced celery
1 (10-ounce) can cream of chicken soup
1 teaspoon salt
2 tablespoons minced onion
1/2 cup chopped almonds
1/4 teaspoon pepper
2 tablespoons lemon juice
3/4 cup mayonnaise
6 hard-cooked eggs, chopped
2 tablespoons chopped pimento
2 cups Chinese noodles

Preheat oven to 350 degrees. Combine chicken, celery, soup, salt, onion, almonds, pepper, lemon juice, mayonnaise, eggs and pimento in large bowl; mix well. Arrange half the noodles in bottom of well-greased casserole. Pour chicken mixture over noodles. Top with remaining noodles. Bake for 15 to 25 minutes or until bubbly.
Yield: 6 servings.

Approx Per Serving: Cal 552; Prot 26 g; Carbo 18 g; Fiber 3 g; T Fat 42 g; 68% Calories from Fat; Chol 272 mg; Sod 1110 mg.

Country Gentleman

Mrs. Troy Edwards, Cumberland Gap

1 (4-pound) hen
1 teaspoon salt
1 large onion, chopped
4 potatoes, sliced
1 cup chopped celery
1 (20-ounce) can tomatoes
1 (20-ounce) can green peas
1 cup uncooked rice
2 (10-ounce) cans cream of chicken soup

Preheat oven to 300 degrees. Sprinkle hen with salt. Boil in large saucepan for 1 1/2 hours or until tender. Remove chicken; let cool. Reserve broth. Remove meat from bones. Layer chicken, onion, potatoes, celery, tomatoes, peas and rice in alternating layers in large roaster. Mix soup with enough reserved broth to make 1 quart liquid. Pour over layered mixture. Bake, covered, for 1 hour. Mixture should be moist. Add more broth if needed; cook for a few minutes longer. Yield: 8 servings.

Approx Per Serving: Cal 486; Prot 41 g; Carbo 49 g; Fiber 4 g; T Fat 14 g; 25% Calories from Fat; Chol 107 mg; Sod 1290 mg.

Garden Chicken Casserole

Margaret Gallimore, Puryear

2 cups chicken broth
1 (4.8-ounce) package long grain
 wild rice mix
1 small onion, chopped
1 small carrot, grated
1 small green pepper, chopped
2 tablespoons butter
1 1/2 cups chopped cooked chicken
1 (4-ounce) can mushrooms
1 (3-ounce) package lite cream cheese
1 cup shredded American cheese
1 (10-ounce) can cream of chicken soup
1/2 cup evaporated skim milk
1/4 cup Parmesan cheese
1/4 cup sliced almonds

Preheat oven to 350 degrees. Bring broth to a boil in medium saucepan. Add contents of rice package. Simmer, covered, over low heat for 25 to 30 minutes or until liquid is absorbed. Sauté onion, carrot and green pepper in butter in Dutch oven for 5 minutes or until softened. Add rice, chicken and mushrooms; mix well. Combine cream cheese, American cheese, soup and milk in saucepan. Cook over medium heat, stirring until smooth; add to Dutch oven. Pour into buttered casserole. Top with Parmesan cheese and almonds. Cover; bake for 35 minutes. Uncover; bake for 15 minutes longer or until bubbly. Garnish with carrots and green onions. Casserole may be refrigerated overnight before baking. Increase baking time to 45 minutes covered and 15 minutes uncovered. Yield: 6 servings.

Approx Per Serving: Cal 416; Prot 26 g; Carbo 30 g; Fiber 2 g; T Fat 22 g; 47% Calories from Fat; Chol 75 mg; Sod 1602 mg.

Old-Fashioned Chicken and Dressing

Mrs. H. D. Rochelle, Bon Aqua

1 (3-pound) hen
1/2 cup chopped onion
1 cup chopped celery
2 tablespoons margarine
4 cups corn bread crumbs
4 cups bread crumbs
1 tablespoon mustard seed
4 hard-cooked eggs, chopped

Boil hen in large saucepan for 1 1/2 hours or until tender. Preheat oven to 425 degrees. Cook onion and celery in margarine in Dutch oven until tender but not brown; remove from heat. Add bread crumbs, mustard seed and eggs. Add enough broth from boiled chicken to make of desired consistency; mix well. Pour into baking pan. Bake for 30 minutes or until lightly browned. Yield: 8 servings.

Approx Per Serving: Cal 580; Prot 38 g; Carbo 58 g; Fiber 4 g; T Fat 21 g; 33% Calories from Fat; Chol 202 mg; Sod 845 mg.

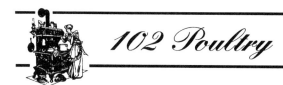

Chicken-Rice Casserole

Marie Gilliam, Lexington

1 (6-ounce) box long-grain and wild rice
1/2 cup low-calorie cholesterol-free
    mayonnaise
3 tablespoons white wine
Dash of nutmeg
2 cups chopped boneless cooked chicken
1 (8-ounce) can pineapple in unsweetened
    juice
1/2 cup slivered almonds

Preheat oven to 350 degrees. Prepare rice according to package directions. Combine rice, mayonnaise, wine, nutmeg, chicken and pineapple with juice in large bowl; mix well. Pour into 8-inch square baking dish sprayed with nonstick cooking spray. Sprinkle almonds over top. Bake for 20 to 30 minutes or until casserole is hot throughout. Cover with tent of cooking foil during last minutes of cooking if necessary to prevent overbrowning.
Yield: 6 servings.

Approx Per Serving: Cal 393; Prot 20 g; Carbo 35 g; Fiber 2 g; T Fat 19 g; 43% Calories from Fat; Chol 41 mg; Sod 745 mg.

Turkey Stroganoff

Cindy Patterson, Murfreesboro

1 1/2 pounds ground turkey
1/2 teaspoon garlic powder
1 small onion, finely chopped
Salt and pepper to taste
2 (10-ounce) cans cream of mushroom soup
16 ounces non-fat plain yogurt
1 (6-ounce) can mushroom pieces

Brown turkey in large skillet, adding garlic powder, onion, salt and pepper during cooking, stirring until crumbly. Add soup, yogurt and mushrooms; mix gently. Cook until heated through. Serve over rice or noodles.
Yield: 8 servings.

Approx Per Serving: Cal 269; Prot 23 g; Carbo 12 g; Fiber <1 g; T Fat 14 g; 49% Calories from Fat; Chol 67 mg; Sod 820 mg.

Turkey-Vegetable Bake

Mrs. Roger Helmuth, Whiteville

1 cup chopped carrots
1 cup sliced celery
1/2 cup chopped celery
1/2 cup chopped onion
1/2 cup chopped green pepper
1 1/2 cups chopped cooked turkey
1 (4-ounce) can sliced mushrooms, drained
1/2 teaspoon dried marjoram, crushed
1/4 teaspoon ground sage
1/4 teaspoon salt
1/4 teaspoon pepper
2 eggs, beaten
1/2 cup skim milk
1/4 cup shredded Cheddar cheese

Preheat oven to 325 degrees. Cook carrots, celery, onion and green pepper in small amount of boiling water in covered saucepan for 10 minutes or until tender; drain. Combine vegetable mixture, turkey, mushrooms, marjoram, sage, salt and pepper in 8-inch square baking dish. Combine eggs and milk in small bowl. Pour over turkey mixture. Sprinkle cheese over top. Bake for 30 to 35 minutes or until set. Let stand for 5 minutes. Cut into 6 squares. Yield: 6 servings.

Approx Per Serving: Cal 132; Prot 15 g; Carbo 6 g; Fiber 2 g; T Fat 5 g; 35% Calories from Fat; Chol 102 mg; Sod 285 mg.

Baked Fish and Rice

Mrs. James Blazier, Knoxville

1 1/2 cups chicken broth
1/2 cup uncooked rice
1/4 teaspoon garlic salt
1 (10-ounce) package frozen broccoli
1/2 (3-ounce) can French-fried onions
1 tablespoon grated Parmesan cheese
1 pound fish filets, thawed
Paprika to taste
1/2 cup shredded Cheddar cheese

Preheat oven to 375 degrees. Heat chicken broth in 8-by-12-inch baking dish. Stir in rice and garlic salt. Cover; bake for 10 minutes. Top with broccoli, half the onions and Parmesan cheese. Arrange fish over top. Sprinkle with paprika. Bake, uncovered, for 25 minutes or until fish flakes. Cover with remaining onions and Cheddar cheese. Bake for 3 minutes. Yield: 4 servings.

Approx Per Serving: Cal 335; Prot 30 g; Carbo 23 g; Fiber <1 g; T Fat 12 g; 34% Calories from Fat; Chol 78 mg; Sod 702 mg.

Crumb-Topped Baked Fish Filets

Hazel Luther, Telford

1/4 cup milk
2 teaspoons salt
1/2 cup packaged bread crumbs
1/2 teaspoon paprika
1/2 cup grated Parmesan cheese
2 pounds thawed quick-frozen or fresh fish filets
1/4 cup melted butter

Preheat oven to 375 degrees. Combine milk and salt in small shallow bowl. Combine crumbs, paprika and cheese in shallow bowl. Dip each filet in milk mixture, then in crumb mixture. Arrange filets side by side in buttered 8-by-12-inch baking dish. Drizzle with melted butter. Bake for 25 to 30 minutes or until easily flaked. Yield: 4 servings.

Approx Per Serving: Cal 430; Prot 51 g; Carbo 10 g; Fiber <1 g; T Fat 19 g; 41% Calories from Fat; Chol 166 mg; Sod 1721 mg.

Impossible Salmon Pie

Edna Barnes, Crossville

1 (15-ounce) can salmon, drained
1 small onion, chopped
1 small green bell pepper, chopped
4 ounces Swiss cheese, grated
3/4 cup baking mix
3 eggs
1 1/4 cups milk

Preheat oven to 350 degrees. Layer salmon, onion, green pepper and cheese in 8-by-10-inch casserole. Combine baking mix, eggs and milk in medium bowl; mix well. Pour over layered mixture. Bake, uncovered, for 30 to 35 minutes or until hot and bubbly. Yield: 6 servings.

Approx Per Serving: Cal 315; Prot 26 g; Carbo 14 g; Fiber <1 g; T Fat 17 g; 49% Calories from Fat; Chol 161 mg; Sod 668 mg.

Salmon Loaf

Gladys P. Easley, Springville

1 (15-ounce) can pink salmon
1 tablespoon lemon juice
1/4 teaspoon salt
8 ounces cream cheese
2 teaspoons grated onion
1/2 teaspoon liquid smoke
3/4 cup finely chopped nuts
3 tablespoons chopped parsley

Skin and bone salmon. Combine salmon, lemon juice, salt, cream cheese, onion and liquid smoke in large bowl; mix well. Refrigerate overnight. Shape mixture into 2 small loaves. Roll in nuts and parsley. Roll in plastic wrap. Chill until ready to serve. Serve with crackers. Yield: 24 servings.

Approx Per Serving: Cal 85; Prot 5 g; Carbo 1 g; Fiber <1 g; T Fat 7 g; 74% Calories from Fat; Chol 18 mg; Sod 146 mg.

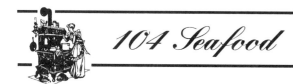

Salmon Spaghetti

Ann Watson, Brownsville

1 (8-ounce) package spaghetti
1/2 teaspoon salt
1 green bell pepper, chopped
2 large stalks celery, chopped
1 large onion, chopped
1 (16-ounce) can pink salmon
1 (4-ounce) can mushrooms
1 (10-ounce) can Ro-Tel tomatoes
8 ounces sharp Cheddar cheese, grated

Preheat oven to 350 degrees. Cook spaghetti with salt according to package directions. Sauté green pepper, celery and onion in microwave-safe dish in microwave until onion is transparent and soft. Drain salmon; crumble in large bowl. Add sautéed vegetables, mushrooms, tomatoes and cheese. Add spaghetti; mix well. Pour into casserole. Bake for 30 minutes or until hot and bubbly. Yield: 8 servings.

Approx Per Serving: Cal 325; Prot 23 g; Carbo 26 g; Fiber 2 g; T Fat 14 g; 39% Calories from Fat; Chol 55 mg; Sod 828 mg.

Tuna Patties

Mrs. Dwain Hollowell, Trezevant

1 (6-ounce) can tuna
1 egg, slightly beaten
3 tablespoons cornmeal
3 tablespoons vegetable oil

Combine tuna and egg in small bowl. Add cornmeal. Shape into 4 equal-sized patties. Fry in hot oil in skillet until golden brown. Yield: 4 servings.

Approx Per Serving: Cal 182; Prot 13 g; Carbo 5 g; Fiber <1 g; T Fat 12 g; 60% Calories from Fat; Chol 66 mg; Sod 160 mg.

Cheesy Crab and Pasta Surprise

Sue Cox, Cumberland County

This recipe won fifth place in the 1988 Tennessee Dairy Recipe Contest.

8 ounces frozen Alaskan king crab meat
7 ounces small pasta shells
2/3 cup chopped celery
1/3 cup chopped green onions
1/3 cup chopped red sweet pepper
1 clove of garlic, minced
1/4 cup butter
1 1/2 cups sour cream
1 1/2 cups small curd cottage cheese
1 1/2 cups grated sharp Cheddar cheese
3/4 teaspoon Mrs. Dash seasonings
1/4 cup fine dry bread crumbs
1 tablespoon grated Parmesan cheese

Preheat oven to 350 degrees. Thaw crab meat; drain and flake. Cook pasta according to package directions; drain well. Sauté celery, green onions, red pepper and garlic in 2 tablespoons butter for 3 minutes. Combine sour cream, cottage cheese, Cheddar cheese and seasonings in 4-quart saucepan. Heat over medium heat until Cheddar cheese starts to melt; remove from heat. Add pasta shells, crab meat and sautéed vegetables; mix gently. Spoon mixture into buttered 8-inch square baking dish. Melt remaining butter. Combine butter, bread crumbs and Parmesan cheese in small bowl. Sprinkle over pasta mixture. Bake for 30 to 35 minutes or until thoroughly heated. Garnish with red pepper and green onions. Yield: 6 servings.

Approx Per Serving: Cal 546; Prot 29 g; Carbo 33 g; Fiber 1 g; T Fat 33 g; 55% Calories from Fat; Chol 122 mg; Sod 672 mg.

Egg and Seafood Bake

Teresa Buck, Jackson

This recipe won third place in the Junior-Senior Category at the 1987 Tennessee Egg Cooking Contest.

1 cup crab meat, drained
1 cup soft bread crumbs
1 cup mayonnaise
3/4 cup milk
6 hard-cooked eggs, finely chopped
1/3 cup chopped green onions
1/4 cup chopped stuffed green olives
3/4 teaspoon salt
1/4 teaspoon pepper
1/2 cup buttered soft bread crumbs

Preheat oven to 350 degrees. Break crab meat into chunks. Combine crab meat, bread crumbs, mayonnaise, milk, eggs, green onions, olives, salt and pepper in large bowl. Pour into 1-quart casserole. Top with buttered bread crumbs. Bake for 25 minutes. Garnish with olive slices. Yield: 6 servings.

Approx Per Serving: Cal 428; Prot 13 g; Carbo 9 g; Fiber <1 g; T Fat 38 g; 80% Calories from Fat; Chol 260 mg; Sod 821 mg.

Seafood Fettucini

Dorothea Laycock, Athens

This recipe won second place in the 1988 Tennessee Dairy Recipe Contest.

12 ounces fettucini
1 envelope creamy herb soup mix
2 1/2 cups milk
1 cup half and half
1 cup shredded Monterey Jack cheese
8 ounces frozen shrimp, partially thawed
8 ounces snow crab, partially thawed
1 cup frozen peas, partially thawed
1/4 cup chopped pimento
1/3 cup grated Parmesan cheese

Cook fettucini according to package directions; drain. Blend soup mix with milk and half and half with fork or wire whip in 2-quart saucepan. Bring just to a boil. Add Monterey Jack cheese. Cook over low heat, stirring, until cheese is melted. Add shrimp, snow crab, peas and pimento. Simmer for 3 to 4 minutes or until shrimp and crab are tender. Toss sauce with hot fettucini and Parmesan cheese. Yield: 6 servings.

Approx Per Serving: Cal 527; Prot 35 g; Carbo 57 g; Fiber 3 g; T Fat 18 g; 30% Calories from Fat; Chol 147 mg; Sod 765 mg.

Music City's Sea 'n' Egg Supper

Mrs. F. A. Tinsley, Nashville

This recipe won second place in the 1988 Tennessee Egg Cooking Contest.

2 tablespoons margarine
1/3 cup sour cream
1 tablespoon dark mustard
1 teaspoon chopped garlic
8 eggs, beaten
1 pound fresh crab meat, cut into 1/2-inch
   pieces
8 ounces cream cheese, cut into small
   pieces
4 croissants, split

Melt margarine in small saucepan. Add sour cream, mustard and garlic, stirring until combined; set aside. Place eggs in skillet; warm slightly on very low heat until eggs take on soft-scrambled appearance. Add crab meat and cream cheese pieces. Stir until cream cheese is just about, but not quite, melted. Spoon evenly onto 4 croissant bottoms. Top with other halves of croissants; spoon sauce over croissants. Garnish with sliced tomatoes or fresh fruit. Yield: 4 servings.

Approx Per Serving: Cal 788; Prot 45 g; Carbo 30 g; Fiber 2 g; T Fat 54 g; 62% Calories from Fat; Chol 651 mg; Sod 1160 mg.

Scalloped Oysters

Mrs. Lewis Stinson, Lafayette

1 pint oysters
1 cup cream
2 cups cracker crumbs
1/2 cup melted butter
1 tablespoon Worcestershire sauce
1/2 teaspoon salt
1/4 teaspoon pepper

Preheat oven to 350 degrees. Place oysters with liquid in casserole. Combine cream, crumbs, butter, Worcestershire sauce, salt and pepper in large bowl. Add to oysters; mix well. Bake for 40 minutes or until firm.
Yield: 4 servings.

Approx Per Serving: Cal 731; Prot 20 g; Carbo 40 g; Fiber 1 g; T Fat 55 g; 67% Calories from Fat; Chol 249 mg; Sod 1534 mg.

Eggs Artichoke Delight

Reaba LaVelle, Burlison

1 (12-ounce) can artichokes, drained
1 large onion, chopped
2 tablespoons flour
5 eggs, slightly beaten
1 ounce grated Parmesan cheese
6 ounces grated Cheddar cheese

Preheat oven to 350 degrees. Combine artichokes, onion and flour in large bowl. Add eggs; mix well. Pour into buttered casserole. Sprinkle with cheeses. Bake for 25 minutes. Yield: 4 servings.

Approx Per Serving: Cal 347; Prot 24 g; Carbo 12 g; Fiber <1 g; T Fat 23 g; 59% Calories from Fat; Chol 315 mg; Sod 753 mg.

Egg Baskets

Kathleen F. Cole, Rockwood

This recipe won second place in the Adult Category in the 1987 Tennessee Egg Cooking Contest.

3 medium tomatoes
6 hard-cooked eggs
1/4 cup lite mayonnaise
3/4 teaspoon dry mustard
1 tablespoon Dijon mustard
1/4 teaspoon paprika
Salt to taste
2 tablespoons butter
2 tablespoons flour
1 cup milk
1/2 cup shredded processed Swiss cheese
1 tablespoon chopped pimento

Preheat oven to 350 degrees. Cut tomatoes into halves. Hollow out centers of tomato halves; reserve tomato pulp for another use. Cut eggs in half lengthwise. Remove and mash yolks in medium bowl. Stir in mayonnaise, dry and Dijon mustards, paprika and salt. Stuff whites with yolk mixture. Place 2 halves together to form egg. Place each egg in tomato basket. Arrange baskets in 8-inch square baking dish. Melt butter in saucepan; stir in flour. Add milk all at once. Cook, stirring, over medium heat until thickened and bubbly. Stir in cheese and pimento until cheese is melted. Pour sauce around stuffed baskets in baking dish. Bake, uncovered, for 10 to 15 minutes or until heated through. To serve, spoon some sauce onto each serving plate; place 1 basket on top of sauce. Spoon remaining sauce in an attractive stripe to crisscross eggs in each basket. Add 1/4 cup milk for thinner consistency if sauce is too thick. Yield: 6 servings.

Approx Per Serving: Cal 219; Prot 11 g; Carbo 10 g; Fiber <1 g; T Fat 15 g; 63% Calories from Fat; Chol 238 mg; Sod 368 mg.

Chili Pepper Eggs in Pita Pockets

Nancy Wortham, Indian Mound

4 eggs
6 egg whites
1/2 teaspoon salt
1/4 teaspoon chili powder
1/8 teaspoon pepper
1 (4-ounce) can chopped green chili
    peppers, drained
1/2 cup chopped roasted red peppers
1 tablespoon olive oil
4 (6-inch) pita breads

Beat together eggs, egg whites, salt, chili powder and pepper in large mixer bowl. Stir in chili peppers and red peppers. Heat olive oil in large skillet over moderate low heat. Pour in egg mixture; cook, stirring occasionally, for 8 to 10 minutes or until soft-set. Split open top third of pita. Fill each pita with 1/4 egg mixture. Serve immediately. Yield: 4 servings.

Approx Per Serving: Cal 305; Prot 17 g; Carbo 37 g; Fiber 2 g; T Fat 9 g; 27% Calories from Fat; Chol 212 mg; Sod 1066 mg.

Egg and Cheese Casserole

Marty Schuele, Maryville

1/4 cup margarine, melted
1/4 cup flour
1/4 teaspoon salt
4 eggs, beaten
1 cup small-curd cottage cheese
1 (4-ounce) can chopped green chilies
2 cups shredded Colby and Monterey Jack
    cheeses
4 cooked slices bacon, crumbled
2 tablespoons finely chopped green pepper

Preheat oven to 375 degrees. Combine margarine, flour and salt in large bowl. Add eggs, cottage cheese, green chilies, cheeses and bacon; mix well. Pour into greased baking dish. Sprinkle green pepper over top. Bake, uncovered, for 30 to 45 minutes or until set. To make a version lower in cholesterol and fat, use 2 whole eggs and 4 egg whites, non-fat or low-fat cottage cheese and light cheese. Real bacon bits may be used. Yield: 6 servings.

Approx Per Serving: Cal 346; Prot 20 g; Carbo 7 g; Fiber <1 g; T Fat 26 g; 69% Calories from Fat; Chol 185 mg; Sod 865 mg.

Eggs Deluxe

Joyce Swann, Pulaski

3 medium potatoes
Oil for deep frying
1/2 medium onion, chopped
1/2 green pepper, chopped
4 eggs, slightly beaten
Salt and pepper to taste

Peel potatoes; cut into 1/2-inch cubes. Add enough oil in skillet to fry potatoes. Fry potatoes until half done; add onion and green pepper. Cook vegetables together until done and potatoes are browned as desired. Add eggs; cook to desired consistency. Serve as main dish with toast or hot biscuits. For a one-dish meal, add chopped ham before eggs, allowing ham to heat thoroughly before adding eggs. Yield: 4 servings.

Nutritional analysis does not include oil for deep frying.
Approx Per Serving: Cal 167; Prot 8 g; Carbo 22 g; Fiber 2 g; T Fat 5 g; 28% Calories from Fat; Chol 212 mg; Sod 68 mg.

Herb and Vegetable Frittata

Margaret S. McClure, Maryville

This recipe won third place in the 1988 Tennessee Egg Cooking Contest.

8 ounces cream cheese
1/2 cup coarsely grated carrot
1/2 cup chopped green onions
1/2 cup chopped green pepper
1/2 cup sliced mushrooms
2 tablespoons olive oil
8 eggs
3/4 cup milk
1/2 cup grated Cheddar cheese
1 teaspoon oregano
1 teaspoon basil
1 teaspoon thyme
Garlic salt to taste
Pepper to taste
1 firm red tomato, coarsely chopped

Preheat oven to 350 degrees. Cut cream cheese into bits the size of large peas; keep chilled. Sauté carrot, green onions, green pepper and mushrooms in olive oil in large skillet. Whisk together eggs, milk, Cheddar cheese, oregano, basil, thyme, garlic salt and pepper in large bowl. Add tomato to vegetables in skillet. Fold vegetables into egg mixture. Add cream cheese. Pour into generously greased 9-by-13-inch glass baking dish. Bake for 25 to 30 minutes or until eggs are set and top is lightly browned. Yield: 6 servings.

Approx Per Serving: Cal 342; Prot 15 g; Carbo 7 g; Fiber <1 g; T Fat 29 g; 75% Calories from Fat; Chol 338 mg; Sod 276 mg.

Macaroni and Cheese Casserole

Mrs. C. B. Martin, Alexandria

1 1/4 cups milk
1/4 cup butter, melted
1/4 cup chopped pimento
1 cup cooked macaroni
1 1/2 cups grated Cheddar cheese
1 tablespoon chopped onion
1 (10-ounce) can cream of mushroom soup
Salt and pepper to taste

Preheat oven to 350 degrees. Combine milk, butter, pimento, macaroni, cheese and onion in large bowl. Add soup, salt and pepper; mix well. Pour into casserole. Bake for 1 hour. Yield: 4 servings.

Approx Per Serving: Cal 450; Prot 16 g; Carbo 21 g; Fiber 1 g; T Fat 34 g; 68% Calories from Fat; Chol 87 mg; Sod 1037 mg.

Cheese Omelet

Vera Stewart, Lawrenceburg

2 eggs
1 tablespoon water
Salt and pepper to taste
1/2 teaspoon butter
1/4 cup grated Cheddar cheese

Beat eggs with fork in medium bowl until frothy. Add water, salt and pepper; beat again. Melt butter in 10-inch skillet until sizzling hot. Reduce heat; add eggs. Eggs will immediately start to set. Scrape set edges of eggs toward center using fork, tilting pan at same time, so liquid egg seeps underneath cooked eggs. Add cheese when bottom is cooked and top is still runny. Fold over 1/3 of omelet toward center. Rest edge of pan on plate. Turn pan quickly upside down so omelet slides out on plate, folded in thirds. Yield: 1 serving.

Approx Per Serving: Cal 279; Prot 20 g; Carbo 2 g; Fiber 0 g; T Fat 21 g; 69% Calories from Fat; Chol 459 mg; Sod 321 mg.

CHAPTER 5

Vegetables & Side Dishes

Helping Hands

While Holly Jones of Washington County busies herself shelling corn in the barn, her cat watches with curiosity. Like so many other children who are raised on the farm, Holly learns valuable lessons of responsibility early in life.

Asparagus Casserole

Connie Haun, Russellville

1 (20-ounce) can asparagus with juice
1 (10-ounce) can cream of mushroom soup
1 (10-ounce) box Cheese Its crackers, crushed
2 or 3 hard-cooked eggs, sliced

Preheat oven to 350 degrees. Combine asparagus, juice and soup in saucepan; heat. Place enough crushed crackers in buttered 9-by-13-inch baking dish to cover bottom. Spread soup mixture over crackers. Layer eggs over mixture. Top with remaining crackers. Bake for 30 minutes. Yield: 4 servings.

Approx Per Serving: Cal 513; Prot 16 g; Carbo 51 g; Fiber 2 g; T Fat 28 g; 49% Calories from Fat; Chol 169 mg; Sod 1863 mg.

Asparagus and Egg Casserole

Magdalene Allen, Smithville

1 (20-ounce) can asparagus spears, drained
6 hard-cooked eggs, peeled and sliced
1/2 cup grated mild Cheddar cheese
1 (10-ounce) can cream of asparagus soup
1/2 cup buttered bread crumbs

Preheat oven to 350 degrees. Layer half the asparagus in 2-quart casserole. Layer half the egg slices over asparagus. Sprinkle with cheese. Spoon half the soup over top. Repeat layers. Sprinkle crumbs over top. Bake for 30 minutes. Yield: 6 servings.

Approx Per Serving: Cal 210; Prot 13 g; Carbo 13 g; Fiber 2 g; T Fat 12 g; 51% Calories from Fat; Chol 227 mg; Sod 968 mg.

Green Bean Casserole

Mrs. Richard D. Bonner, Pelham

1 (16-ounce) can French-style green beans
1 (12-ounce) can shoe peg corn
8 ounces sour cream
1 (10-ounce) can cream of celery soup
1 medium onion, finely chopped
1 cup grated Cheddar cheese
1 cup Ritz cracker crumbs
1/2 cup butter

Preheat oven to 350 degrees. Combine beans and corn in bowl. Place in greased casserole. Combine sour cream, soup, onion and cheese in bowl; mix well. Pour over beans and corn. Spread cracker crumbs over top. Dot with butter. Bake for 30 minutes. Yield: 8 servings.

Approx Per Serving: Cal 331; Prot 7 g; Carbo 19 g; Fiber 2 g; T Fat 26 g; 69% Calories from Fat; Chol 63 mg; Sod 901 mg.

Old-Fashioned Baked Beans

Claryce Faulkner, Ethridge

1 medium onion, chopped
1 1/2 teaspoons vegetable oil
2 cups cooked great northern beans
1/4 cup each molasses, catsup
1 tablespoon mustard
4 slices bacon, partially cooked

Preheat oven to 350 to 400 degrees. Sauté onion in oil in skillet. Add beans, molasses, catsup and mustard; mix well. Pour into casserole. Top with cooked bacon. Bake for 20 to 30 minutes. Yield: 6 servings.

Approx Per Serving: Cal 160 ; Prot 7 g; Carbo 26 g; Fiber 4 g; T Fat 4 g; 20% Calories from Fat; Chol 4 mg; Sod 228 mg.

Barbecued Beans

Mrs. Bruce Morelock, Chuckey

1 pound ground beef
1/2 cup chopped onion
1/2 teaspoon salt
1/4 teaspoon pepper
1 (28-ounce) can pork and beans
1/2 cup catsup
1 tablespoon Worcestershire sauce
2 tablespoons vinegar
1/4 teaspoon Tabasco sauce

Preheat oven to 350 degrees. Brown ground beef and onion in skillet; drain. Add remaining ingredients; mix well. Pour into 1 1/2-quart casserole. Bake for 30 minutes. Yield: 6 servings.

Approx Per Serving: Cal 341; Prot 24 g; Carbo 35 g; Fiber 8 g; T Fat 13 g; 32% Calories from Fat; Chol 65 mg; Sod 934 mg.

Harvard Beets

Louise Scruggs, Humboldt

1 (16-ounce) can beets
1/4 cup sugar
2 tablespoons cornstarch
1/2 cup vinegar
1 teaspoon salt
2 tablespoons butter

Drain beets, reserving 1/4 cup liquid. Combine sugar and cornstarch in saucepan; blend in reserved beet liquid, vinegar and salt. Bring to a boil, stirring constantly. Reduce heat; simmer for 2 minutes. Add beets; simmer for 15 minutes longer. Stir in butter just before serving. Yield: 4 servings.

Approx Per Serving: Cal 154; Prot 1 g; Carbo 26 g; Fiber 2 g; T Fat 6 g; 33% Calories from Fat; Chol 16 mg; Sod 902 mg.

Broccoli Casserole

Mrs. Paul D. Bryan, Hillsboro

1 (8-ounce) package Uncle Ben's Wild Rice
   with seasonings
1 bunch broccoli
1 (10-ounce) can cream of mushroom soup
1 (4-ounce) jar Cheez Whiz

Preheat oven to 350 degrees. Cook rice according to package directions. Cook broccoli in salted water in saucepan until tender; drain. Combine soup and Cheez Whiz in bowl. Place rice in bottom of greased casserole. Add broccoli. Pour soup mixture over top. Bake for 10 minutes. Yield: 8 servings.

Approx Per Serving: Cal 205; Prot 7 g; Carbo 25 g; Fiber 1 g; T Fat 9 g; 39% Calories from Fat; Chol 8 mg; Sod 938 mg.

Broccoli Corn Bread

Reba Harris, Union City

1/2 cup butter
2 (6-ounce) packages corn muffin mix
1 cup cottage cheese
4 eggs
1 medium onion, chopped
1 (10-ounce) package frozen chopped
   broccoli, thawed

Preheat oven to 375 degrees. Melt butter in 9-by-13-inch baking pan. Combine remaining ingredients in bowl; mix well. Pour over butter. Bake for 30 minutes or until browned. Yield: 8 servings.

Approx Per Serving: Cal 339 ; Prot 10 g; Carbo 35 g; Fiber 1 g; T Fat 18 g; 48% Calories from Fat; Chol 141 mg; Sod 541 mg.

Broccoli-Rice Casserole

Mrs. Dennis Taylor, Fall Branch

1 cup water
1 cup minute rice, uncooked
1/2 cup chopped onion
3/8 cup chopped celery
1 (10-ounce) package frozen chopped
  broccoli, thawed
1/2 cup butter, melted
1 (10-ounce) can cream of mushroom soup
1 (4-ounce) jar Cheez Whiz

Preheat oven to 350 degrees. Layer ingredients in order listed in casserole. Bake for 45 minutes to 1 hour. Yield: 8 servings.

Approx Per Serving: Cal 242; Prot 5 g; Carbo 17 g; Fiber 2 g; T Fat 18 g; 64% Calories from Fat; Chol 39 mg; Sod 631 mg.

Broccoli-Mushroom Casserole

Helen Shepherd, Clarksville

2 (10-ounce) packages frozen chopped
  broccoli
1 cup mayonnaise
2 eggs, beaten
1 medium onion, finely chopped
1 (10-ounce) can cream of mushroom soup
1 cup grated Cheddar cheese

Preheat oven to 350 degrees. Cook broccoli according to package directions; drain. Add remaining ingredients; mix well. Pour into greased casserole. Bake for 30 minutes. Yield: 8 servings.

Approx Per Serving: Cal 337; Prot 8 g; Carbo 9; Fiber 2 g; T Fat 31 g; 80% Calories from Fat; Chol 85 mg; Sod 586 mg.

Broccoli-Cheese Casserole

Mrs. Larry Davis, Hollow Rock

1 (10-ounce) package frozen chopped
  broccoli
1 (10-ounce) can cream of mushroom soup
1/2 cup shredded sharp cheese
1/4 cup milk
1/4 cup mayonnaise
1 egg, beaten
1/4 cup cornflake crumbs
1 tablespoon margarine, melted

Preheat oven to 350 degrees. Cook broccoli according to package directions. Place in 9-by-13-inch casserole. Combine soup and cheese in bowl. Add milk, mayonnaise and egg, stirring until well blended. Pour over broccoli. Combine crumbs and melted butter. Sprinkle evenly over soup mixture. Bake for 45 minutes. Yield: 6 servings.

Approx Per Serving: Cal 217; Prot 6 g; Carbo 10 g; Fiber 2 g; T Fat 17 g; 71% Calories from Fat; Chol 53 mg; Sod 603 mg.

Fried Cabbage

Helen Stanley, Ripley

1 head cabbage, shredded
1 green pepper, chopped
1 onion, chopped
1 tomato, chopped
1 teaspoon salt
2 teaspoons sugar
1/2 teaspoon pepper
1/4 cup vegetable oil

Combine cabbage, green pepper, onion and tomato in large bowl. Sprinkle with salt, sugar and pepper; mix well. Refrigerate for 1 hour. Heat oil in heavy skillet. Add vegetables and 1/2 cup hot water; mix well. Cover. Cook for 20 to 30 minutes. Yield: 6 servings.

Approx Per Serving: Cal 138; Prot 3 g; Carbo 13 g; Fiber 3 g; T Fat 10 g; 58% Calories from Fat; Chol 0 mg; Sod 385 mg.

Cabbage Casserole

Mrs. Clyde Mullican, Sparta

2 medium onions, chopped
1 medium green pepper, chopped
1 clove of garlic, minced
1/4 cup butter, melted
2 medium cabbage heads, chopped,
    cooked and drained
2 1/2 cups shredded Cheddar cheese
1 cup bread crumbs
Salt and pepper to taste
1 cup half and half

Preheat oven to 350 degrees. Sauté onions, green pepper and garlic in butter in small skillet. Combine cabbage with 2 cups cheese, bread crumbs, salt and pepper in large mixing bowl. Pour into 3-quart casserole. Sprinkle with remaining cheese. Pour half and half over top. Bake for 30 to 40 minutes. Yield: 12 servings.

Approx Per Serving: Cal 234; Prot 10 g; Carbo 18 g; Fiber 3 g; T Fat 15 g; 55% Calories from Fat; Chol 43 mg; Sod 293 mg.

Scalloped Cabbage with Cheese

Imogene Smith, Clinton

1 small head cabbage
3 tablespoons butter
3 tablespoons flour
1 cup milk
2 cups grated cheese
1/2 to 3/4 cup buttered bread crumbs

Preheat oven to 350 degrees. Steam cabbage in small amount of boiling salted water until tender-crisp; drain. Melt butter in saucepan; stir in flour. Remove from heat. Blend in milk gradually. Layer half the cabbage, white sauce and cheese in baking dish. Repeat layers. Top with buttered crumbs. Bake for 20 minutes or until browned. Yield: 6 servings.

Approx Per Serving: Cal 331; Prot 14 g; Carbo 21 g; Fiber 3 g; T Fat 22 g; 59% Calories from Fat; Chol 65 mg; Sod 455 mg.

Wonderful Cauliflower Casserole

Carole Moss, Putnam County

3 cups cauliflower
1 (2-ounce) jar pimento
2 tablespoons green pepper, chopped
1 (8-ounce) can water chestnuts, sliced
2 hard-cooked eggs, chopped
1 small onion, chopped
1 cup grated Cheddar cheese
2 tablespoons flour
1/2 teaspoon salt
1/4 teaspoon pepper
4 tablespoons melted butter
2 cups half and half
1 cup cubed processed cheese
2 cups cheese crackers, crushed
3 tablespoons grated Parmesan cheese

Preheat oven to 350 degrees. Layer first 7 ingredients in order listed in 2-quart casserole. Blend flour, salt and pepper into butter in saucepan. Cook for 1 minute, stirring constantly. Add half and half with processed cheese, stirring until smooth. Pour over vegetables. Bake for 30 minutes. Top with cracker crumbs and Parmesan cheese. Bake for 3 minutes longer. Yield: 12 servings.

Approx Per Serving: Cal 284; Prot 10 g; Carbo 17 g; Fiber 1 g; T Fat 20 g; 63% Calories from Fat; Chol 83 mg; Sod 546 mg.

Extra Good Corn for the Freezer

Mrs. Pete Killebrew, Dresden

12 cups corn
2 cups milk
8 tablespoons butter
1/2 cup sugar

Combine all ingredients in saucepan. Simmer for 10 minutes. Let cool. Place in plastic freezer containers. Freeze. Yield: 24 servings.

Approx Per Serving: Cal 129; Prot 3 g; Carbo 20 g; Fiber 2 g; T Fat 5 g; 35% Calories from Fat; Chol 13 mg; Sod 61 mg.

Corn Casserole

Alice Childress, Franklin

2 (10-ounce) packages frozen white
   shoe peg corn
2 ((16-ounce)) cans French-style green
   beans, drained
2 cups grated mild Cheddar cheese
3/4 cup chopped onion
1/2 cup chopped celery
1 (10-ounce) can cream of celery soup
1/2 cup slivered almonds
1 cup Ritz crackers, crushed
1/2 cup butter, melted

Preheat oven to 350 degrees. Cook corn according to package directions. Combine with remaining ingredients except Ritz crackers and butter; mix well. Place in casserole. Combine cracker crumbs and butter. Place on top of casserole. Bake for 30 to 45 minutes or until bubbly. Yield: 12 servings.

Approx Per Serving: Cal 268; Prot 9 g; Carbo 19 g; Fiber 4 g; T Fat 19 g; 60% Calories from Fat; Chol 43 mg; Sod 610 mg.

Corn Fritters

Mary A. Crowder, Cottage Grove

1 cup flour, sifted
1 tablespoon sugar
1 teaspoon baking powder
1/2 teaspoon salt
1 egg, beaten
1/2 cup milk
1 tablespoon vegetable oil
1 1/2 cups cooked whole kernel corn
Vegetable oil for frying

Combine first 8 ingredients in bowl; mix well. Drop from tablespoon into hot oil. Cook until brown. Yield: 8 servings.

Nutritional information does not include oil for frying.
Approx Per Serving: Cal 130; Prot 4 g; Carbo 22 g; Fiber 2 g; T Fat 3 g; 23% Calories from Fat; Chol 29 mg; Sod 195 mg.

Okra and Cheese Casserole

Mrs. Marcelle Mash, Williamsport

1/2 pound sliced okra
4 medium tomatoes, peeled and sliced
1/2 cup chopped onion
1 pound Cheddar cheese, cubed
Salt and pepper to taste

Preheat oven to 325 degrees. Layer okra in 1-quart casserole. Add layer of tomatoes, onion and cheese cubes. Add salt and pepper; repeat layers, ending with cheese. Cover casserole. Bake for 40 minutes. Yield: 8 servings.

Approx Per Serving: Cal 253; Prot 15 g; Carbo 6 g; Fiber 2 g; T Fat 19 g; 66% Calories from Fat; Chol 60 mg; Sod 359 mg.

Stuffed Mushrooms

Louise Patterson, Gallatin

12 large fresh mushrooms
3 tablespoons butter
Salt and pepper to taste
1/4 cup butter
1/3 cup finely chopped onion
1 tablespoon flour
1/2 cup heavy cream
1/4 cup chopped parsley
1/4 cup grated Swiss cheese

Wipe mushrooms with damp cloth. Remove stems; set aside. Microwave 3 tablespoons butter in microwave-safe dish for 30 seconds. Brush mushroom caps with melted butter. Place, hollow-side up, in shallow microwave-safe baking dish. Sprinkle with salt and pepper. Chop reserved stems. Microwave 1/4 cup butter in microwave-safe bowl for 30 seconds. Add onion and stems; stir to combine. Microwave, uncovered, for 3 minutes. Blend in flour until smooth. Stir in heavy cream gradually until smooth. Microwave, uncovered, for 2 1/2 minutes. Stir in parsley. Fill each cap with mixture. Sprinkle with cheese. Place in microwave-safe pie pan. Microwave, uncovered, for 3 minutes. Yield: 6 servings.

Approx Per Serving: Cal 224; Prot 3 g; Carbo 5 g; Fiber <1 g; T Fat 22 g; 86% Calories from Fat; Chol 68 mg; Sod 159 mg.

Onion Pie

Margaret C. Lampkins, Paris

1 cup fine soda cracker crumbs
1/4 cup melted butter
2 cups finely chopped onions
2 tablespoons margarine
2 eggs, slightly beaten
3/4 cup milk
1/2 teaspoon salt
1/8 teaspoon pepper
1/2 cup grated sharp Cheddar cheese
Paprika

Preheat oven to 350 degrees. Combine cracker crumbs and 1/4 cup butter. Press in bottom and side of 8-inch pie pan. Sauté onions in 2 tablespoons margarine until tender, stirring constantly. Place onions in crumb shell. Combine eggs, milk, salt and pepper. Pour over onions. Spread cheese over top. Sprinkle with paprika. Bake for 30 minutes. Let set for 10 to 15 minutes. Serve warm. Yield: 4 servings.

Approx Per Serving: Cal 396; Prot 11 g; Carbo 25 g; Fiber 2 g; T Fat 29 g; 64% Calories from Fat; Chol 158 mg; Sod 868 mg.

Southern-Style Black-Eyed Peas

Velma Henry, Manchester

1 (1-pound) package dried black-eyed peas
2 teaspoons salt
1/4 teaspoon pepper
1 large onion, chopped
1 stalk celery, chopped
1/2 pound salt pork, sliced

Cover peas with water in bowl; soak overnight. Drain. Place in Crock•Pot. Add 4 cups water and remaining ingredients; cover. Cook on High for 1 to 2 hours. Turn to Low. Cook for 8 to 9 hours longer. Serve over fluffy rice. Yield: 8 servings.

Nutritional information does not include salt pork.
Approx Per Serving: Cal 198; Prot 14 g; Carbo 36 g; Fiber 16 g; T Fat <1 g; 3% Calories from Fat; Chol 0 mg; Sod 547 mg.

Pea Casserole

Glenda Stratton, Rutledge

2 (16-ounce) cans green peas
1 (10-ounce) can cream of mushroom soup
2 tablespoons butter
Salt and pepper to taste
1/3 cup shredded American cheese
2 slices toast
1 medium onion, chopped
1 (2-ounce) can pimento, chopped

Preheat oven to 350 degrees. Drain peas, reserving liquid. Combine peas, soup, butter, salt, pepper and cheese in saucepan. Cook over medium heat for 5 minutes. Place toast in baking dish. Pour pea mixture over toast. Add reserved pea liquid as needed. Top with onion and pimento. Bake for 10 minutes. Yield: 8 servings.

Approx Per Serving: Cal 164; Prot 6 g; Carbo 18 g; Fiber 3 g; T Fat 8 g; 42% Calories from Fat; Chol 13 mg; Sod 752 mg.

Deluxe Green Pea Casserole

Carol Ainsworth, Murfreesboro

2 (10-ounce) packages frozen green peas
1/4 cup chopped onion
1 clove of garlic, minced
3/4 cup chopped mushrooms
6 tablespoons butter
1 (10-ounce) can cream of mushroom soup
3 ounces cream cheese, softened
1 1/2 cups shredded sharp Cheddar cheese
1/4 cup chopped pimento
2 tablespoons butter
1/2 cup fine bread crumbs

Preheat oven to 350 degrees. Cook peas according to package directions; drain. Sauté onion, garlic and mushrooms in 6 tablespoons butter. Add soup; heat. Add cream cheese and Cheddar cheese; stir well. Add peas and pimento; mix well. Pour into buttered shallow 2-quart casserole. Combine 2 tablespoons butter with bread crumbs. Sprinkle over top of casserole. Bake for 30 to 40 minutes or until bubbly. Let cool for 15 minutes before serving. Yield: 16 servings.

Approx Per Serving: Cal 174; Prot 6 g; Carbo 9 g; Fiber 2 g; T Fat 13 g; 66% Calories from Fat; Chol 33 mg; Sod 362 mg.

Marinated Peas

Mrs. J. W. Yarbro, Camden

1 (10-ounce) package frozen peas
1/2 cup tarragon vinegar
1/4 cup water
3 tablespoons sugar
1/2 teaspoon dillweed
1/2 teaspoon caraway seed
1 1/4 teaspoons salt
1/4 teaspoon celery salt
3 small onions, sliced into thin rings

Cook peas according to package directions; drain. Combine vinegar, water, sugar, dillweed, caraway seed, salt and celery salt in saucepan. Heat until sugar dissolves; cool. Combine peas and onion rings in bowl. Add vinegar mixture. Chill for 2 to 3 hours. Drain. Yield: 4 servings.

Approx Per Serving: Cal 115; Prot 4 g; Carbo 25 g; Fiber 4 g; T Fat <1 g; 3% Calories from Fat; Chol 0 mg; Sod 841 mg.

Potato-Onion Casserole

Gayle L. Deaton, Jackson

1/2 cup melted butter
2 cups cornflakes, crushed
1 (32-ounce) package frozen hashed brown
    potatoes, thawed
1 teaspoon each salt, pepper
1/2 cup chopped onion
1 (10-ounce) can cream of chicken soup
1 (8-ounce) carton French onion dip
1 (4-ounce) jar Cheese Whiz

Preheat oven to 350 degrees. Combine 1/4 cup butter with crushed cornflakes in bowl; set aside. Combine remaining ingredients in bowl; mix well. Pour into 9-by-13-inch baking dish. Top with buttered cornflakes. Bake for 45 minutes. Yield: 6 servings.

Approx Per Serving: Cal 475; Prot 10 g; Carbo 43 g; Fiber 1 g; T Fat 30 g; 56% Calories from Fat; Chol 75 mg; Sod 1415 mg.

Frances' Potato Casserole

Mrs. Frances Holt, Fayetteville

1 (2-pound) package frozen hashed brown
    potatoes
1 (10-ounce) can cream of chicken soup
8 ounces cheese, grated
1/4 teaspoon each salt, pepper
1 cup sour cream
1 cup butter, melted
2 cups cornflakes, crushed

Preheat oven to 350 degrees. Combine first 6 ingredients with 1/2 cup melted butter in bowl; mix well. Pour into 3-quart baking dish. Combine cornflake crumbs with 1/2 cup melted butter in bowl. Sprinkle over top of casserole. Bake for 45 minutes. Yield: 8 servings.

Approx Per Serving: Cal 531; Prot 12 g; Carbo 30 g; Fiber <1 g; T Fat 41 g; 69% Calories from Fat; Chol 108 mg; Sod 881 mg.

Potato Casserole

Mrs. Ralph (Mary) Carter, Mosheim

1 (32-ounce) package frozen hashed brown
    potatoes, thawed
3 cups sour cream
1/2 cup chopped onions
1 (10-ounce) can cream of chicken soup
Salt and pepper to taste
2 cups shredded sharp Cheddar cheese
1/2 cup butter, melted
2 cups cornflakes, crushed

Preheat oven to 350 degrees. Combine first 6 ingredients in bowl; mix well. Place in casserole. Bake for 45 minutes. Combine butter and crushed cornflakes in bowl. Sprinkle over casserole. Bake for 15 minutes longer or until brown. Yield: 8 servings.

Approx Per Serving: Cal 553; Prot 14 g; Carbo 33 g; Fiber <1 g; T Fat 42 g; 67% Calories from Fat; Chol 102 mg; Sod 726 mg.

Supreme Potato Casserole

Mrs. Johnnie Rust, Kingston Springs

6 medium potatoes, cooked
2 cups cottage cheese
1 cup sour cream
2 tablespoons chopped green onions
1 teaspoon salt
2 teaspoons sugar
1/8 teaspoon garlic powder
1 cup grated Cheddar cheese

Preheat oven to 350 degrees. Peel and dice potatoes in bowl. Add next 6 ingredients; mix well. Pour into lightly greased 1 1/2-quart casserole. Top with cheese. Bake for 45 minutes. Yield: 10 servings.

Approx Per Serving: Cal 209; Prot 10 g; Carbo 19 g; Fiber 1 g; T Fat 11 g; 45% Calories from Fat; Chol 28 mg; Sod 470 mg.

Potatoes Anna

Sharon Dills, Dyersburg

2 pounds Russet potatoes, peeled
   and sliced
1/2 cup melted butter
Salt and pepper to taste

Preheat oven to 425 degrees. Layer potatoes, overlapping slices, in well buttered, 10-inch casserole. Brush each layer with butter. Sprinkle with salt and pepper. Bake, covered, for 40 minutes. Uncover; bake for 10 to 15 minutes longer or until potatoes are golden brown. Invert onto warm platter; serve. Yield: 6 servings.

Approx Per Serving: Cal 276; Prot 3 g; Carbo 33 g; Fiber 2 g; T Fat 16 g; 49% Calories from Fat; Chol 41 mg; Sod 164 mg.

Cheese Potatoes

Mrs. Steve Turner, Morris Chapel

6 medium potatoes, cooked
2 cups sour cream
1 (4-ounce) jar Cheez Whiz
1 teaspoon salt
1 teaspoon minced onion

Preheat oven to 350 degrees. Cube potatoes in bowl. Add remaining ingredients; mix well. Pour into greased casserole. Bake for 45 minutes. Yield: 6 servings.

Approx Per Serving: Cal 332; Prot 8 g; Carbo 31 g; Fiber 2 g; T Fat 20 g; 54% Calories from Fat; Chol 45 mg; Sod 655 mg.

Hot Cheese Potato Salad

Mrs. Kyle Kenyon, Sevierville

8 potatoes, cooked
1/2 pound sharp Cheddar cheese, grated
1 cup mayonnaise
1/3 cup chopped green onion
1 teaspoon celery seed
Salt and pepper to taste
1/2 cup chopped pecans
1/2 pound bacon, fried

Preheat oven to 325 degrees. Cube potatoes in bowl. Add next 5 ingredients; mix well. Pour into greased casserole. Top with pecans and chopped bacon. Bake for 30 minutes. Yield: 8 servings.

Approx Per Serving: Cal 525; Prot 13 g; Carbo 29 g; Fiber 2 g; T Fat 41 g; 69% Calories from Fat; Chol 53 mg; Sod 476 mg.

Creamed New Potatoes

Joan Rutherford, Luttrell

12 small new potatoes
1 (10-ounce) can cream of chicken soup
1 cup green peas, cooked
1/4 cup milk

Cook potatoes until tender in saucepan; drain. Combine remaining ingredients in saucepan; heat. Pour over potatoes. Serve hot. Yield: 6 servings.

Approx Per Serving: Cal 148; Prot 5 g; Carbo 25 g; Fiber 3 g; T Fat 4 g; 21% Calories from Fat; Chol 5 mg; Sod 410 mg.

Mashed Potatoes Supreme

John M. Clark, Newport

12 medium potatoes
8 ounces cream cheese, softened
1 cup sour cream
2 teaspoons salt
1/8 teaspoon pepper
1/8 teaspoon garlic salt
1/4 cup chopped chives
1 tablespoon butter
1/2 teaspoon paprika

Preheat oven to 350 degrees. Cook potatoes; mash. Combine with next 6 ingredients; mix well. Pour into greased 8-by-12-inch casserole. Dot with butter and paprika. Bake for 35 minutes. Yield: 12 servings.

Approx Per Serving: Cal 229; Prot 4 g; Carbo 28 g; Fiber 2 g; T Fat 12 g; 45% Calories from Fat; Chol 32 mg; Sod 458 mg.

Pimento-Cheese Potatoes

Mary Ferrell, Brentwood

5 medium potatoes, diced
1 medium onion, diced
1 (4-ounce) can pimentos, diced
3 tablespoons low-fat margarine
3 tablespoons flour
1 teaspoon salt
1 teaspoon pepper
2 cups skim milk
1/2 pound Cheddar cheese, grated

Preheat oven to 350 degrees. Combine potatoes, onion and pimentos. Pour into greased casserole. Melt margarine in saucepan. Blend in flour and seasonings. Add milk, stirring constantly, until thickened. Remove from heat. Add cheese; mix well. Pour over potato mixture in casserole. Bake, uncovered, for 1 hour. Yield: 6 servings.

Approx Per Serving: Cal 332; Prot 15 g; Carbo 32 g; Fiber 2 g; T Fat 17 g; 44% Calories from Fat; Chol 41 mg; Sod 675 mg.

Savory Scalloped Potatoes

Madlyn Bolen, Wildersville

4 cups sliced cooked potatoes
1/2 cup diced onion
1/4 cup celery leaves
2 sprigs parsley
3 tablespoons flour
1/4 cup butter
1/2 teaspoon salt
1/4 teaspoon pepper
1 clove of garlic, crushed
1 cup milk
1/4 cup grated American cheese
Paprika

Preheat oven to 350 degrees. Place potatoes in greased 1-quart casserole. Place next 8 ingredients in food processor. Add milk gradually until well blended. Pour over potatoes. Top with grated cheese and paprika. Bake for 45 minutes. Yield: 8 servings.

Approx Per Serving: Cal 154; Prot 3 g; Carbo 18 g; Fiber 1 g; T Fat 8 g; 46% Calories from Fat; Chol 23 mg; Sod 261 mg.

Sour Cream Potatoes

Mrs. Willis Tompkins, Allardt

4 medium Irish potatoes
1 cup sour cream
3/4 cup shredded Cheddar cheese
1 teaspoon salt
1/8 teaspoon pepper
3/4 cup shredded Cheddar or American
  cheese
Paprika

Preheat oven to 350 degrees. Cook potatoes in jackets until tender. Peel and shred. Combine potatoes with sour cream and 3/4 cup shredded cheese. Add salt and pepper. Turn mixture into greased 1 1/2-quart baking dish. Top with remaining shredded cheese and paprika. Bake for 30 to 40 minutes. Yield: 6 servings.

Approx Per Serving: Cal 252; Prot 9 g; Carbo 19 g; Fiber 1 g; T Fat 16 g; 56% Calories from Fat; Chol 42 mg; Sod 526 mg.

Potato Wedges

Marie Cox, Maynardville

4 medium Idaho potatoes
3 tablespoons olive oil
1/2 teaspoon dried oregano leaves
1/2 teaspoon onion powder
Salt and pepper to taste
1/4 cup grated Parmesan cheese

Preheat oven to 425 degrees. Cut each potato into 8 wedges. Combine next 4 ingredients in large bowl; mix well. Add potatoes; toss to coat. Place potatoes on ungreased jelly roll pan. Sprinkle wedges with cheese, turning to coat all sides. Bake for 40 minutes or until golden brown and tender, turning occasionally.
Yield: 4 servings.

Approx Per Serving: Cal 231; Prot 5 g; Carbo 26 g; Fiber 2 g; T Fat 12 g; 46% Calories from Fat; Chol 5 mg; Sod 122 mg.

Layered Cheese and Spinach Tart

Cheryl Luneack, Coffee County

1 (10-ounce) package frozen chopped
  spinach
1/2 cup plus 1 tablespoon fine bread
  crumbs
1/3 cup grated Parmesan cheese
2 tablespoons butter, melted
1 pound Ricotta or cottage cheese
1 cup sour cream
2 tablespoons flour
2 eggs
1/4 teaspoon salt
1/4 pound cooked ham, diced
1/4 teaspoon seasoned pepper

Preheat oven to 350 degrees. Cook spinach according to package directions; drain. Combine 1/2 cup bread crumbs with 2 tablespoons Parmesan cheese in bowl. Add melted butter. Press crumb mixture into bottom and side of 9-inch pie plate. Place Ricotta cheese, remaining Parmesan cheese, 2 tablespoons sour cream, flour and eggs in large mixer bowl. Beat at high speed until mixture is smooth. Add salt. Combine half the cheese mixture with spinach. Spread evenly in prepared pie shell. Add ham to remaining cheese mixture. Spread over spinach-cheese layer. Sprinkle seasoned pepper and remaining 1 tablespoon crumbs on top. Bake for 40 minutes. Serve immediately with remaining sour cream as a sauce.
Yield: 6 servings.

Approx Per Serving: Cal 385; Prot 22 g; Carbo 15 g; Fiber 1 g; T Fat 27 g; 62% Calories from Fat; Chol 151 mg; Sod 702 mg.

Summer Squash Casserole

Mrs. Ruby Rollins, Greeneville

1 (6-ounce) package Pepperidge Farm
   Stuffing Mix
2 tablespoons melted butter
4 cups cut-up summer squash
1 teaspoon salt
1 cup sour cream
1 (10-ounce) can cream of chicken soup

Preheat oven to 350 degrees. Combine stuffing mix with butter in bowl. Cook squash in boiling salted water in saucepan until tender; drain. Add sour cream and soup; mix well. Alternate layers of squash mixture and stuffing mixture in greased casserole. Bake for 30 minutes. Yield: 6 servings.

Approx Per Serving: Cal 290; Prot 7 g; Carbo 31 g; Fiber 1 g; T Fat 16 g; 49% Calories from Fat; Chol 32 mg; Sod 1267 mg.

Squash Casserole

Mrs. Aaron Miller, Ripley

1 onion, chopped
1 bell pepper, chopped
1/2 cup margarine
2 cups cooked squash, drained
1 cup milk
2 eggs, beaten
Salt and pepper to taste
1 cup cracker crumbs

Preheat oven to 350 degrees. Sauté onion and bell pepper in margarine. Combine with remaining ingredients; mix well. Pour into greased 1 1/2-quart baking dish. Bake for 1 hour. Yield: 6 servings.

Approx Per Serving: Cal 269; Prot 6 g; Carbo 17 g; Fiber 2 g; T Fat 20 g; 66% Calories from Fat; Chol 76 mg; Sod 403 mg.

Banana Squash Bake

Amos Cherry, Red Boiling Springs

1 (3- to 7-pound) banana squash
1/2 cup margarine
1 cup sugar
1 cup crushed potato chips

Preheat oven to 400 degrees. Peel squash lengthwise; split into halves lengthwise. Remove seeds. Melt 5 tablespoons margarine in 10-by-14-inch baking pan. Place squash in pan. Spread remaining margarine over squash halves. Sprinkle sugar over margarine. Top with crushed potato chips. Bake for 45 minutes or until brown. Let cool for 4 to 5 minutes. Cut each half lengthwise. Cut into 2-inch squares. Yield: 8 servings.

Approx Per Serving: Cal 343; Prot 3 g; Carbo 57 g; Fiber 8 g; T Fat 14 g; 35% Calories from Fat; Chol 0 mg; Sod 187 mg

Judy's Squash Casserole

Judy Henderson, Dandridge

2 cups yellow squash, cooked and drained
1 medium onion, diced
2 carrots, grated
1 cup sour cream
1 (10-ounce) can cream of chicken soup
1/2 cup butter, melted
1 (8-ounce) package corn bread stuffing
   mix

Preheat oven to 350 degrees. Combine first 5 ingredients in bowl; set aside. Add butter to stuffing mix; mix well. Place 1/4 stuffing mix in bottom of greased 9-by-13-inch casserole. Combine 1/4 stuffing mix with squash mixture. Pour squash mixture into casserole, spreading evenly. Sprinkle remaining stuffing mix over top. Bake for 20 to 30 minutes or until golden brown. Yield: 6 servings.

Approx Per Serving: Cal 438; Prot 8 g; Carbo 40 g; Fiber 2 g; T Fat 28 g; 57% Calories from Fat; Chol 63 mg; Sod 1071 mg.

Yellow Squash Casserole

Nancy Jo Hughes, Mt. Pleasant

2 pounds yellow squash, cubed
1 large onion, chopped
2 tablespoons butter, melted
1 (10-ounce) can cream of shrimp soup
1 (8-ounce) can water chestnuts, drained
3/4 teaspoon salt
1/4 teaspoon pepper
1 cup soft bread crumbs
2 tablespoons butter, melted

Preheat oven to 350 degrees. Sauté squash and onion in 2 tablespoons butter until tender. Stir in soup, water chestnuts, salt and pepper. Pour into lightly greased shallow 2-quart casserole. Combine bread crumbs and 2 tablespoons butter. Sprinkle over top of casserole. Bake for 30 minutes. Yield: 8 servings.

Approx Per Serving: Cal 137; Prot 3 g; Carbo 15 g; Fiber 2 g; T Fat 8 g; 49% Calories from Fat; Chol 21 mg; Sod 588 mg.

Yellow Squash Croquettes

Edna Solomon, Powell

2 pounds yellow squash, sliced
2 1/2 cups fine dry bread crumbs
1/2 cup minced green onions
2 eggs
2 tablespoons grated Parmesan cheese
1 teaspoon salt
1/2 teaspoon pepper
1 cup cornmeal
Vegetable oil for deep frying

Cook squash until tender; drain and mash. Add bread crumbs and next 5 ingredients. Shape mixture into 18 logs. Roll in cornmeal. Deep fry in hot oil until golden brown. Yield: 6 servings.

Nutritional information does not include oil for deep frying.
Approx Per Serving: Cal 316; Prot 12 g; Carbo 56 g; Fiber 5 g; T Fat 5 g; 15% Calories from Fat; Chol 72 mg; Sod 779 mg.

Garden-Stuffed Yellow Squash

Judy Harris, Ashland City

8 medium yellow squash
1/2 cup chopped green pepper
1 medium tomato, chopped
1 medium onion, chopped
1/2 teaspoon salt
2 slices crisp-fried bacon, crumbled
1/2 cup shredded Cheddar cheese
Pepper to taste
8 teaspoons butter

Preheat oven to 400 degrees. Simmer squash in water to cover for 8 minutes or until tender. Drain; cool slightly. Cut thin slice from top of each squash; remove seed. Place in baking dish. Combine next 7 ingredients; mix well. Spoon into squash shells. Dot each with pat of butter. Bake for 20 minutes. Yield: 8 servings.

Approx Per Serving: Cal 133; Prot 6 g; Carbo 14 g; Fiber 4 g; T Fat 8 g; 47% Calories from Fat; Chol 19 mg; Sod 248 mg.

Squash Medley

Betty Jo Rutledge, Church Hill

2 tablespoons bacon drippings
1 medium onion, thinly sliced
4 medium yellow squash, thinly sliced
1 large zucchini, thinly sliced
1 medium green pepper, cut into thin strips
3 medium tomatoes, peeled and quartered
1 teaspoon salt
Pepper to taste
6 slices bacon, fried
1 cup grated cheese

Heat bacon drippings in large skillet. Add onion. Stir-fry briefly. Stir in yellow squash, zucchini and green pepper. Cook for 2 to 3 minutes or until vegetables are tender-crisp. Add tomatoes, salt and pepper. Add crumbled bacon to mixture. Sprinkle cheese over mixture; toss gently until cheese melts. Yield: 6 servings.

Approx Per Serving: Cal 219; Prot 10 g; Carbo 15 g; Fiber 4 g; T Fat 15 g; 57% Calories from Fat; Chol 30 mg; Sod 610 mg.

Squash Patties

Mrs. Clyde Thompson, Columbia

1 cup flour
1 teaspoon sugar
1/2 teaspoon salt
3/4 cup milk
1 egg
1/4 cup vegetable oil
3 cups grated yellow squash
1 medium onion, chopped
1/4 to 1/2 teaspoon red pepper

Combine first 6 ingredients; mix until smooth. Add remaining ingredients; stir well. Drop mixture by tablespoonsful into hot greased skillet. Cook until golden brown, turning once. Drain on paper towels. Yield: 24 servings.

Approx Per Serving: Cal 56; Prot 1 g; Carbo 6 g; Fiber <1 g; T Fat 3 g; 45% Calories from Fat; Chol 10 mg; Sod 52 mg.

Summer Squash Casserole

Mrs. J. H. Runion, Cleveland

4 cups cooked squash
3 eggs, beaten
Salt and pepper to taste
1 medium onion, chopped
1/2 cup butter
2 1/2 cups cracker crumbs

Preheat oven to 375 to 400 degrees. Combine first 4 ingredients with 2 1/2 tablespoons butter and 1 cup cracker crumbs. Set aside. Melt remaining butter. Add remaining cracker crumbs; mix well. Place squash mixture in casserole. Top with cracker crumb mixture. Bake until firm and top is browned. Yield: 8 servings.

Approx Per Serving: Cal 262; Prot 6 g; Carbo 23 g; Fiber 2 g; T Fat 17 g; 57% Calories from Fat; Chol 111 mg; Sod 484 mg.

Coconutty Sweet Potato Casserole

Mrs. Bill Knowles, Knoxville

3 cups mashed cooked fresh sweet
   potatoes
1 teaspoon vanilla extract
1 cup sugar
2/3 cup cream
1/3 cup butter
1 cup coconut
1 cup pecans or black walnuts
1 cup packed light brown sugar
1/3 cup flour
1/3 cup butter

Preheat oven to 325 degrees. Combine first 4 ingredients with 1/3 cup butter. Pour into casserole. Combine remaining ingredients. Sprinkle as topping over casserole. Bake for 25 minutes or until brown on top. Yield: 6 servings.

Approx Per Serving: Cal 809; Prot 5 g; Carbo 102 g; Fiber 6 g; T Fat 46 g; 49% Calories from Fat; Chol 82 mg; Sod 241 mg.

Sweet Potato Bake

Mrs. Susie Tegethoff, McKenzie

3 cups mashed cooked sweet potatoes
1 cup sugar
2 eggs
1 tablespoon vanilla extract
1/3 cup milk
1/8 teaspoon black walnut flavoring
7 tablespoons butter
1/3 cup flour
1 cup chopped pecans
1 cup packed light brown sugar

Preheat oven to 350 degrees. Combine first 6 ingredients with 4 tablespoons butter. Beat until smooth. Spoon into greased shallow 2-quart casserole. Combine remaining ingredients. Blend well with fork. Spoon over sweet potato mixture. Bake, uncovered, for 30 minutes. Yield: 6 servings.

Approx Per Serving: Cal 662; Prot 7 g; Carbo 97 g; Fiber 4 g; T Fat 29 g; 39% Calories from Fat; Chol 109 mg; Sod 187 mg.

Crunchy Sweet Potato Casserole

Mary Sue Campbell, Milton

3 cups mashed cooked sweet potatoes
1 cup sugar
1/3 cup milk
1 teaspoon vanilla extract
1/3 cup butter, melted
1 cup packed light brown sugar
1/3 cup flour
1 cup pecans

Preheat oven to 350 degrees. Combine first 4 ingredients. Pour into casserole. Combine remaining ingredients in bowl. Pour mixture over sweet potato mixture. Bake for 30 minutes. Yield: 6 servings.

Approx Per Serving: Cal 868; Prot 7 g; Carbo 136 g; Fiber 7 g; T Fat 36 g; 36% Calories from Fat; Chol 44 mg; Sod 196 mg.

Dr. Pepper-Sweet Potato Casserole

Mrs. Bill Britton, Sr., Greeneville

4 medium sweet potatoes
1 cup Dr. Pepper
3/4 cup sugar
1/4 cup butter
1/4 teaspoon salt

Preheat oven to 300 degrees. Parboil sweet potatoes in skins for 10 minutes or until soft. Peel and slice crosswise. Place in 2-quart casserole. Combine remaining ingredients in saucepan. Bring to a slow boil. Cook for 10 minutes on medium heat. Pour syrup over sweet potatoes. Bake for 35 to 40 minutes, basting occasionally. Yield: 4 servings.

Approx Per Serving: Cal 389; Prot 2 g; Carbo 71 g; Fiber 3 g; T Fat 12 g; 26% Calories from Fat; Chol 31 mg; Sod 268 mg.

Grannie's Sweet Potato Casserole

Jenny B. Milam, Decaturville

3 large cooked sweet potatoes, mashed
1 cup sugar
1/2 cup butter
1/2 cup sweetened condensed milk
1/4 teaspoon salt
1/4 cup chopped pecans
1 cup small marshmallows
1/2 cup raisins
1/4 cup whiskey
24 large marshmallows

Preheat oven to 300 degrees. Blend sweet potatoes, sugar, butter, condensed milk and salt in bowl. Stir in pecans, small marshmallows, raisins and whiskey. Place mixture in large casserole. Top with large marshmallows. Bake for 15 minutes or until marshmallows are browned. Yield: 8 servings.

Approx Per Serving: Cal 472; Prot 4 g; Carbo 79 g; Fiber 2 g; T Fat 16 g; 29% Calories from Fat; Chol 38 mg; Sod 228 mg.

Candied Sweet Potatoes

Mrs. Jane Trull, McLemoresville

2 pounds small sweet potatoes
3 tablespoons butter, melted
1/3 cup firmly packed light brown sugar
3 tablespoons water
3 tablespoons frozen orange juice
  concentrate
1/2 teaspoon pumpkin pie spice
1/4 teaspoon salt
1/3 cup chopped dates
1/3 cup coarsely chopped pecans, toasted

Cube sweet potatoes. Sauté in butter in large skillet over medium heat for 15 minutes. Add next 5 ingredients; cover. Simmer for 15 minutes. Add dates; cover. Cook over medium heat for 5 minutes, stirring occasionally. Transfer to serving dish. Stir in pecans. Serve immediately. Yield: 8 servings.

Approx Per Serving: Cal 247; Prot 3 g; Carbo 44 g; Fiber 4 g; T Fat 8 g; 28% Calories from Fat; Chol 12 mg; Sod 125 mg.

Sweet Potato Delight

Juanita Beaty, Albany, Kentucky

8 pineapple rings
1/2 cup pineapple juice
1 (16-ounce) can sweet potatoes, mashed
2 tablespoons butter
1/4 cup packed light brown sugar
1 cup chopped pecans
Salt to taste
8 large marshmallows

Preheat oven to 450 degrees. Layer pineapple rings in bottom of casserole. Combine remaining ingredients, except marshmallows; mix well. Place large scoops sweet potato mixture on pineapple rings. Top each mound with marshmallow. Place on lower rack of oven. Bake until marshmallows are browned. Yield: 8 servings.

Approx Per Serving: Cal 276; Prot 3 g; Carbo 40 g; Fiber 3 g; T Fat 14 g; 42% Calories from Fat; Chol 8 mg; Sod 79 mg.

Hawaiian Sweet Potatoes

Christine Evans, Lebanon

6 medium sweet potatoes, mashed
2/3 cup crushed pineapple, drained
1/4 cup orange juice
1/3 cup half and half
1/4 cup packed light brown sugar
1/4 cup butter
1/4 teaspoon salt
1/2 teaspoon ground cinnamon
1/4 cup flaked coconut

Preheat oven to 400 degrees. Combine sweet potatoes, pineapple and orange juice in bowl; mix well. Combine half and half, brown sugar and butter in saucepan. Cook over low heat until butter is melted. Combine with sweet potato mixture; mix well. Add salt and cinnamon; mix well. Pour into lightly greased casserole. Top with coconut. Bake for 10 minutes or until coconut is toasted. Yield: 10 servings.

Approx Per Serving: Cal 158; Prot 2 g; Carbo 25 g; Fiber 2 g; T Fat 6 g; 34% Calories from Fat; Chol 15 mg; Sod 113 mg.

Orange-Glazed Sweet Potatoes

Mrs. Allen Wells, Philadelphia

8 medium sweet potatoes, peeled and
    halved
1 1/4 teaspoons salt
2 tablespoons butter
1 tablespoon grated orange peel
3/4 cup dark corn syrup
1 teaspoon cinnamon
1 teaspoon allspice

Preheat oven to 350 degrees. Boil sweet potatoes in water to cover for 30 to 40 minutes or until tender. Place in casserole. Combine remaining ingredients in saucepan. Bring to boil. Spoon over sweet potatoes. Bake for 30 minutes. Yield: 10 servings.

Approx Per Serving: Cal 184; Prot 2 g; Carbo 41 g; Fiber 3 g; T Fat 2 g; 11% Calories from Fat; Chol 6 mg; Sod 337 mg.

Sweet Potato Soufflé

Mrs. Leonard Stephens, Spring Hill

3 cups sweet potatoes, mashed
2 eggs
1/2 cup milk
1 1/2 cups sugar
1/4 cup butter
2 teaspoons vanilla extract
Salt to taste
1 cup packed light brown sugar
1/3 cup flour
1/2 cup butter
1/2 cup milk
1 cup pecans, chopped

Preheat oven to 350 degrees. Place sweet potatoes, eggs, 1/2 cup milk, sugar, 1/4 cup butter, vanilla and salt in mixer container. Process to mix well. Place in 3-quart casserole. Combine brown sugar, flour, 1/2 cup butter and 1/2 cup milk in saucepan. Bring to a boil, stirring constantly. Remove from heat; add pecans. Pour over top of potato mixture. Bake for 30 to 40 minutes. Yield: 8 servings.

Approx Per Serving: Cal 616; Prot 6 g; Carbo 86 g; Fiber 3 g; T Fat 30 g; 42% Calories from Fat; Chol 104 mg; Sod 223 mg.

Spiced Sweet Potatoes

Mrs. Roseanne Beasley, Covington

2 cups sliced sweet potatoes
Brown sugar substitute to equal 3
    tablespoons
1/4 teaspoon salt
1/4 teaspoon cinnamon
1/4 teaspoon nutmeg
3 tablespoons reduced-calorie margarine

Preheat oven to 350 degrees. Arrange sweet potatoes in non-stick casserole. Combine brown sugar substitute, salt and spices. Sprinkle over sweet potatoes. Bake for 10 to 15 minutes. Yield: 6 (1/4-cup) servings.

Approx Per Serving: Cal 72; Prot <1 g; Carbo 9 g; Fiber 1 g; T Fat 4 g; 45% Calories from Fat; Chol 0 mg; Sod 128 mg.

Easy Tomato Pudding

Mrs. Harley Moore, Chuckey

4 baked biscuits, cut up
1 (10-ounce) can tomatoes
1 cup packed light brown sugar
2 tablespoons butter
1 teaspoon spices

Preheat oven to 350 degrees. Place biscuits in baking dish. Place tomatoes, brown sugar, butter and spices over biscuits. Add enough water to cover bread. Bake until bread is jellied and browned. Yield: 4 servings.

Approx Per Serving: Cal 336; Prot 3 g; Carbo 60 g; Fiber 1 g; T Fat 11 g; 28% Calories from Fat; Chol 16 mg; Sod 357 mg.

Tasty Tomato Pudding

O. Garner, Maryville

1 (32-ounce) can tomatoes
6 leftover biscuits, crumbled
1 tablespoon minced onion
1/4 teaspoon ground allspice
1 cup sugar

Preheat oven to 325 degrees. Combine all ingredients; mix well. Pour into well buttered casserole. Bake for 20 to 30 minutes. Yield: 6 servings.

Approx Per Serving: Cal 261; Prot 3 g; Carbo 53 g; Fiber 2 g; T Fat 5 g; 17% Calories from Fat; Chol <1 mg; Sod 412 mg.

Green Tomato Pie

Lassie Riley, Tazewell

2 cups sliced peeled green tomatoes
2 cups sugar
1 1/2 tablespoons vinegar
3 tablespoons flour
1/2 teaspoon cinnamon
1/2 teaspoon salt
1 tablespoon water
4 tablespoons butter
1 (9-inch) unbaked pie shell
Top crust or lattice
1 teaspoon sugar

Preheat oven to 425 degrees. Combine first 8 ingredients; mix well. Pour mixture into unbaked pie shell. Add top crust. Sprinkle with 1 teaspoon sugar. Bake for 10 minutes. Reduce heat to 350 degrees. Bake for 30 minutes longer. Yield: 8 servings.

Approx Per Serving: Cal 479; Prot 3 g; Carbo 74 g; Fiber 1 g; T Fat 20 g; 36% Calories from Fat; Chol 16 mg; Sod 415 mg.

Tomato and Zucchini Casserole

Mrs. George Evans, Martin

1 medium onion, chopped
1/4 clove of garlic
2 tablespoons butter
1 medium zucchini, chopped
1 (10-ounce) can tomatoes, diced
1 teaspoon salt
1 teaspoon oregano
Pepper to taste
1 teaspoon wine vinegar
3 tablespoons sugar
1 (4-ounce) package mozzarella cheese, grated
1/2 cup grated Parmesan cheese

Preheat oven to 400 degrees. Sauté onion and garlic in butter in skillet. Add remaining ingredients, except cheeses. Heat to boiling. Simmer for 10 minutes. Pour mixture into greased casserole. Bake for 45 minutes. Stir in mozzarella cheese. Top with Parmesan cheese. Bake for 10 minutes longer. Yield: 6 servings.

Approx Per Serving: Cal 172; Prot 8 g; Carbo 12 g; Fiber 1 g; T Fat 11 g; 54% Calories from Fat; Chol 32 mg; Sod 698 mg.

Zucchini Crescent Pie

Dorothy Tubbs, Crockett County

4 cups sliced zucchini
1 cup chopped onions
1/2 cup butter
1/2 cup chopped parsley
1/2 teaspoon salt
1/4 teaspoon garlic powder
1/4 teaspoon oregano leaves
1/2 teaspoon pepper
1/4 teaspoon sweet basil leaves
2 eggs, beaten
2 cups shredded mozzarella cheese
1 (8-ounce) can crescent rolls
2 teaspoons Dijon mustard

Preheat oven to 375 degrees. Cook zucchini and onions in butter in 10-inch skillet until tender. Stir in parsley and seasonings. Blend eggs and cheese in large bowl. Stir in vegetable mixture. Separate rolls into 8-inch triangles. Press dough over bottom and up sides of 10-inch pie pan to form crust. Brush crust with mustard. Pour in vegetable mixture. Bake for 18 to 20 minutes or until a knife comes out clean. Cover with foil. Bake for 10 minutes longer. Let stand for 10 minutes. Cut into wedges. Serve hot. Yield: 8 servings.

Approx Per Serving: Cal 262; Prot 9 g; Carbo 11 g; Fiber 1 g; T Fat 21 g; 70% Calories from Fat; Chol 107 mg; Sod 533 mg.

Fried Zucchini Squash Blossoms

Margaret Nichols, Waverly

12 zucchini blossoms
2 eggs
1/2 teaspoon salt
1/4 teaspoon pepper
1 cup fine bread crumbs
Oil for frying

Place zucchini blossoms in large bowl. Wash gently and thoroughly in several changes of cool water. Make sure insides of blossoms are free of insects. Drain blossoms gently on paper towels. Combine eggs, salt and pepper in bowl. Whisk until frothy. Dip blossoms gently into eggs. Roll in bread crumbs. Fry a few at a time in 425-degree deep oil until golden brown; drain. Serve warm. Yield: 4 servings.

Nutritional information for this recipe is not available.

Italian Zucchini Crescent Pie

Mrs. Von M. Saylor, Knoxville

4 cups thinly sliced zucchini
1 cup coarsely chopped onions
1/2 cup margarine, melted
1 tablespoon parsley flakes
1/4 teaspoon garlic powder
1/4 teaspoon oregano leaves
1/4 teaspoon basil leaves
1/2 teaspoon each salt, pepper
2 eggs
2 cups shredded Muenster cheese
1 can refrigerated crescent rolls
2 teaspoons mustard

Preheat oven to 375 degrees. Cook zucchini, onions and margarine in large skillet for 10 minutes. Stir in spices. Blend eggs and cheese in large bowl. Pour into vegetable mixture. Press crescent rolls into 10-inch pie plate to form crust. Pour vegetable mixture evenly into crust. Bake for 18 to 20 minutes or until a knife comes out clean. Let cool for 10 minutes. Yield: 8 servings.

Approx Per Serving: Cal 327; Prot 11 g; Carbo 17 g; Fiber 1 g; T Fat 24 g; 66% Calories from Fat; Chol 83 mg; Sod 729 mg.

Grilled Vegetables

Annie Pearl Thurman, Lynnville

Asparagus spears
Small carrots
Eggplant
Sweet pepper
Leeks
New potatoes
Zucchini
Yellow squash

Wash and prepare vegetables. Precook for about 8 minutes. Eggplant, peppers and squash do not have to be precooked. Using skewers or wire mesh, grill vegetables to preferred doneness.

Nutritional information for this recipe is not available.

Creamy Vegetable Surprise

Marie Pepper, Montgomery County

3 (10-ounce) packages mixed vegetables
1/2 cup butter
8 slices crisp-fried bacon, crumbled
1/4 cup pimentos, chopped
1 cup water chestnuts, sliced
2 cup shredded Swiss cheese
2 cup shredded Cheddar cheese
1 (10-ounce) can cream of celery soup
1 (10-ounce) can cream of mushroom soup
3 cups half and half
1 teaspoon curry powder
Salt and pepper to taste
1/4 cup mayonnaise
1 1/2 cups water
1/2 teaspoon salt
2 (5-ounce) packages mashed potatoes
1 (6-ounce) can French fried onions

Preheat oven to 400 degrees. Cook mixed vegetables according to package directions; drain. Stir in 1/4 cup butter. Combine vegetables, bacon, pimentos, water chestnuts, Swiss and Cheddar cheeses in bowl; mix well. Pour into 9-by-13-inch casserole. Combine celery soup, mushroom soup, 1 cup half and half, curry powder, salt, pepper and mayonnaise in bowl; mix well. Pour over casserole; cover. Bake for 20 to 25 minutes or until bubbly. Heat water, remaining 2 cups half and half, remaining 1/4 cup butter and salt in saucepan. Slowly stir in potatoes; mix well. Pour over casserole. Spread potatoes to edges. Top with remaining Swiss and Cheddar cheeses. Sprinkle with fried onions. Bake, uncovered, for 10 to 15 minutes or until golden brown. Yield: 10 servings.

Approx Per Serving: Cal 737; Prot 23 g; Carbo 53 g; Fiber 6 g; T Fat 50 g; 60% Calories from Fat; Chol 106 mg; Sod 1178 mg.

Veg-All Casserole

Mrs. G. R. Baker, Michie

2 (16-ounce) cans Veg-All
1 (10-ounce) can water chestnuts
1 cup grated cheese
1 cup salad dressing
1/2 cup chopped celery
1/2 cup chopped onion
1 cup crushed Ritz crackers
1/4 cup butter

Preheat oven to 400 degrees. Combine first 6 ingredients. Place in casserole. Top with crackers. Dot with butter. Bake for 15 to 20 minutes. Yield: 6 servings.

Approx Per Serving: Cal 450; Prot 11 g; Carbo 31 g; Fiber 8 g; T Fat 32 g; 63% Calories from Fat; Chol 56 mg; Sod 707 mg.

Low-Fat Company Casserole

Mrs. Henry B. Harris, Santa Fe

1 (16-ounce) can yellow whole kernel corn, drained
1 1/2 cups cooked noodles, drained
8 ounces 98% fat-free ham, diced
1 1/2 cups green peas, drained
1 cup low-fat sour cream
1 cup grated low-fat sharp Cheddar cheese
1 (10-ounce) can cream of celery soup
2 tablespoons low-fat margarine
1/3 cup 1/2% butterfat milk
1/4 cup sliced almonds
1 cup canned French fried onions

Preheat oven to 350 degrees. Layer corn, noodles, ham and peas in 2-quart casserole. Combine next 6 ingredients in bowl. Pour over casserole. Bake for 30 minutes. Top with French fried onions. Bake for 5 minutes longer.
Yield: 8 servings.

Approx Per Serving: Cal 451; Prot 18 g; Carbo 39 g; Fiber 3 g; T Fat 25 g; 50% Calories from Fat; Chol 49 mg; Sod 1071 mg.

Cheese-Vegetable Casserole

Brenda Woodlee, McMinnville

2 cups diced potatoes
1/2 cup sliced carrots
1/4 cup chopped onion
1 cup green peas, drained
1/4 cup butter
3 tablespoons flour
1 teaspoon salt
1/4 teaspoon pepper
1 cup milk
1 cup grated Cheddar cheese
1 cup cottage cheese
2 tablespoons melted butter
1 cup bread crumbs
1/4 cup grated Cheddar cheese

Preheat oven to 350 degrees. Cook first 3 vegetables in small amount of water until tender. Add peas. Drain. Combine 1/4 cup butter, flour, salt and pepper in saucepan. Stir in milk. Cook over low heat until thick. Add 1 cup Cheddar cheese; stir until cheese melts. Add cottage cheese; mix well. Combine sauce and vegetables. Pour into greased 2-quart casserole. Combine 2 tablespoons butter, bread crumbs and 1/4 cup cheese in bowl; mix well. Arrange over top of casserole. Bake for 15 to 20 minutes.
Yield: 8 servings.

Approx Per Serving: Cal 301; Prot 13 g; Carbo 24 g; Fiber 2 g; T Fat 18 g; 52% Calories from Fat; Chol 50 mg; Sod 743 mg.

Mixed Vegetable Casserole

Mrs. Ralph H. Flynn, Sevierville

2 (10-ounce) packages frozen mixed vegetables
1 cup chopped onion
1 cup chopped celery
1 cup mayonnaise
1 cup shredded Cheddar cheese
2 cups crushed Ritz crackers
1/2 cup melted margarine

Preheat oven to 350 degrees. Cook mixed vegetables in small amount of water for 20 minutes; drain. Add onion, celery,, mayonnaise and 1/2 cup cheese; mix well. Place mixture in casserole. Combine crackers, margarine and remaining cheese in bowl; mix well. Sprinkle over casserole. Bake for 30 minutes. Yield: 8 servings.

Approx Per Serving: Cal 502; Prot 8 g; Carbo 24 g; Fiber <1 g; T Fat 43 g; 75% Calories from Fat; Chol 31 mg; Sod 578 mg.

Vegetable Squares

Joysan Collier, St. Joseph

1 (6-count) can crescent rolls
1/3 cup buttermilk salad dressing
8 ounces cream cheese, softened
1 teaspoon dillweed
Assorted vegetables, chopped
1 cup shredded Cheddar cheese

Spread crescent roll dough on small cookie sheet to form crust. Bake according to package directions. Let cool completely. Mix salad dressing, cream cheese and dillweed until smooth. Spread evenly over crust. Place assorted vegetables over cream cheese mixture. Top with Cheddar cheese. Press lightly into mixture. Chill. Cut into squares. Yield: 6 servings.

Approx Per Serving: Cal 341; Prot 9 g; Carbo 15 g; Fiber 0 g; T Fat 27 g; 72% Calories from Fat; Chol 69 mg; Sod 536 mg.

Vegetable Strata

Alma H. Whinery, Fall Branch

1/2 pound fresh asparagus, cut into 1-inch
  pieces
1 medium red bell pepper, chopped
1 tablespoon butter
1 small onion, chopped
6 cups 1/2-inch square French bread cubes
2 cups shredded Swiss cheese
2 cups milk
4 eggs, beaten
1/4 teaspoon paprika
1/4 teaspoon salt

Preheat oven to 350 degrees. Cook asparagus with red pepper in butter in saucepan over medium high heat for 2 minutes, stirring constantly. Add onion; continue cooking for 1 minute or until tender-crisp. Place half the asparagus mixture in greased casserole. Top with half the cheese. Repeat layers. Combine milk, eggs, paprika and salt in bowl. Pour over layers carefully. Push vegetable-cheese mixture into liquid with tablespoon. Bake, uncovered, for 50 to 55 minutes or until center is set.
Yield: 8 servings.

Approx Per Serving: Cal 262; Prot 16 g; Carbo 18 g; Fiber 1 g; T Fat 14 g; 48% Calories from Fat; Chol 143 mg; Sod 351 mg.

Wagon Wheel Pie

Grace Owens, Speedwell

1/2 cup chopped onions
2 tablespoons butter
1 (12-ounce) can Spam or other luncheon
  meat
1 1/2 (10-ounce) packages frozen mixed
  vegetables
1/2 cup grated Cheddar cheese
1 cup evaporated milk
2 eggs, beaten
2 tablespoons flour
1/2 teaspoon salt
1/4 teaspoon paprika
1 (10-inch) unbaked pastry shell

Preheat oven to 400 degrees. Steam onions in butter in covered saucepan over low heat for 10 minutes. Set aside. Cut Spam into strips. Reserve 5 strips. Cut remaining strips into bite-sized pieces. Cook frozen vegetables in small amount of water for 10 minutes; drain. Combine vegetables, cheese, evaporated milk, eggs, flour, salt and paprika in bowl; mix well. Pour into pastry shell. Cut remaining meat strips into bite-sized pieces. Arrange over filling. Bake for 30 minutes. Yield: 8 servings.

Approx Per Serving: Cal 421; Prot 15 g; Carbo 25 g; Fiber 3 g; T Fat 30 g; 62% Calories from Fat; Chol 78 mg; Sod 970 mg.

Vegetable Chili

Dorothy A. Cunningham, Morris Chapel

1 tablespoon olive oil
1 large onion, chopped
1 (28-ounce) can whole tomatoes
2/3 cup hot picante sauce
1 1/2 teaspoons chili powder
1 1/2 teaspoons cumin
3/4 teaspoon salt
1 (16-ounce) can pinto beans, drained
1 large zucchini, cubed
1 can whole kernel corn, drained

Heat oil in large saucepan over medium heat. Sauté onion for 2 to 3 minutes. Add tomatoes, picante sauce, chili powder, cumin and salt; cover. Simmer for 10 minutes. Add beans, zucchini and corn; cover. Simmer for 10 minutes longer. Serve with additional picante sauce, if desired. Yield: 8 servings.

Approx Per Serving: Cal 147; Prot 6 g; Carbo 28 g; Fiber 4 g; T Fat 3 g; 16% Calories from Fat; Chol <1 mg; Sod 888 mg.

Chili Casserole

Mrs. Clarence Bond, Mt. Juliet

1 chili stick
2 (16-ounce) cans Boone Co. beans
1 (12-ounce) package corn chips
1 onion, chopped
1/2 pound American cheese, grated

Preheat oven to 350 degrees. Melt chili stick in small amount of water in saucepan over medium heat. Add beans. Add more water if needed. Line casserole with corn chips and onion. Pour a layer of beans over corn chips. Add layer of cheese. Repeat layers. Bake for 30 to 40 minutes. Top with layer of cheese. Heat until cheese is melted. Yield: 8 servings.

Nutritional information for this recipe is not available.

Chilly Day Stew

Rebecca Beachy, Finger

1 large carrot, chopped
3 onions, chopped
1 quart potatoes, diced
2 tablespoons rice
2 tablespoons macaroni
1 teaspoon salt
2 cups cream

Bring 6 cups or more water to boil in large saucepan. Add chopped carrots to rapidly boiling water. Add onions and potatoes to mixture. Add rice, macaroni and salt. Cook slowly until tender, keeping vegetables covered with water. Add cream; mix well. Do not let mixture boil. Serve with crackers. Yield: 8 servings.

Approx Per Serving: Cal 299; Prot 3 g; Carbo 23 g; Fiber 2 g; T Fat 22 g; 65% Calories from Fat; Chol 82 mg; Sod 297 mg.

Grits Casserole

Charlotte H. White, Lenoir City

1¹/2 teaspoons salt
1¹/2 cups grits
³/4 cup margarine
1 pound Velveeta cheese
1 cup green chilies, chopped
   and seeded

Preheat oven to 350 degrees. Bring 6 cups water and salt to a boil. Add grits. Simmer for 10 minutes. Remove from heat. Add margarine, cheese and chilies. Stir over low heat until margarine and cheese are melted. Pour into 9-by-13-inch baking dish. Bake for 40 to 45 minutes.
Yield: 6 servings.

Approx Per Serving: Cal 636; Prot 21 g; Carbo 34 g; Fiber 5 g; T Fat 47 g; 66% Calories from Fat; Chol 71 mg; Sod 1882 mg.

Chili Spanish Rice

Mary Hayes, Maynardville

¹/2 cup chopped onions
¹/2 cup chopped green pepper
2 tablespoons butter
4 cups cooked rice
1 (15-ounce) can chili
¹/2 pound Mexican Velveeta cheese
   spread with jalapeños, cubed
1 cup chopped tomatoes

Sauté onions and green pepper in butter. Add rice, chili, cheese spread, and tomatoes; mix well. Heat until cheese spread is melted and mixture is hot, stirring occasionally. Yield: 6 servings.

Approx Per Serving: Cal 462; Prot 15 g; Carbo 49 g; Fiber 1 g; T Fat 23 g; 44% Calories from Fat; Chol 31 mg; Sod 1010 mg.

Rice Dish

Pam Hurt, Bruceton

¹/4 cup margarine
1 cup rice
1 (10-ounce) can onion soup
1 (10-ounce) can beef consommé
1 (3-ounce) can sliced mushrooms

Preheat oven to 350 degrees. Melt margarine in casserole. Mix remaining ingredients with margarine. Bake, uncovered, for 1 hour. Yield: 4 servings.

Approx Per Serving: Cal 328; Prot 9 g; Carbo 44 g; Fiber 1 g; T Fat 13 g; 35% Calories from Fat; Chol 0 mg; Sod 1254 mg.

Green Rice

Mary Anne Carlton, Brownsville

2 cups cooked rice
1 cup chopped parsley
1 medium onion, chopped
1 pound American cheese
2 eggs, beaten
2 cups milk
1 (4-ounce) jar pimentos
Salt and pepper to taste
1 clove of garlic

Preheat oven to 350 degrees. Combine all ingredients in bowl. Pour into baking dish. Bake for 1 hour. Stir before serving. This may be made in advance and frozen.
Yield: 8 servings.

Approx Per Serving: Cal 346; Prot 18 g; Carbo 21 g; Fiber 1 g; T Fat 21 g; 55% Calories from Fat; Chol 115 mg; Sod 863 mg.

Glorious Macaroni

Mrs. James V. Hatcher, Millington

1 (8-ounce) package baby sea shell
  macaroni
1 tablespoon butter
1/3 cup chopped onions
1 (2-ounce) jar pimento, drained
2 cups shredded Cheddar cheese
1 (10-ounce) can cream of mushroom soup
1/2 cup mayonnaise
1 (3-ounce) can sliced mushrooms, drained

Preheat oven to 350 degrees. Cook macaroni according to package instructions; drain. Combine all ingredients. Place in 2-quart casserole. Bake for 30 minutes. Yield: 8 servings

Approx Per Serving: Cal 376; Prot 12 g; Carbo 26 g; Fiber 1 g; T Fat 25 g; 60% Calories from Fat; Chol 42 mg; Sod 625 mg.

Make-Ahead Pasta-Rami

Charlene Sipes, Hardeman County

This recipe won fourth place in the 1988 Tennessee Dairy Recipe Contest

1 tablespoon salt
16 ounces rotini
1 cup plain yogurt
1 1/2 cups buttermilk
1/2 teaspoon dried oregano, crushed
1 (1-ounce) envelope reduced-calorie
  buttermilk salad dressing mix
2 cups chopped deli-style turkey pastrami
1 1/2 cups cucumber, thinly sliced lengthwise
1/2 cup medium pitted ripe olives
3/4 cup grated American cheese
3/4 cup grated medium Cheddar cheese
3 medium tomatoes, cut into small wedges
1 cup alfalfa sprouts
1/2 cup Italian-style croutons

Bring 4 quarts water to rapid boil in 8-quart stockpot. Add salt and rotini; return to boiling point. Reduce heat to medium high. Cook pasta, uncovered, stirring occasionally, for 6 to 9 minutes or until tender but slightly firm. Remove from heat. Drain immediately in colander. Rinse with cold water; drain well. Transfer to large bowl; set aside. Combine yogurt, buttermilk, oregano and salad dressing mix in 1-quart bowl. Blend well with wire whisk. Measure 1 cup prepared dressing; set remaining aside. Stir 1 cup dressing into drained pasta; blend well. Place mixture in bottom of clear 4-quart salad bowl. Layer pastrami, cucumbers, olives, cheeses and tomatoes on top. Pour reserved dressing over top. Top with sprouts. Cover tightly. Chill up to 24 hours. Sprinkle with croutons at serving time. Yield: 10 servings.

Approx Per Serving: Cal 322; Prot 16 g; Carbo 41 g; Fiber 2 g; T Fat 9 g; 27% Calories from Fat; Chol 32 mg; Sod 1493 mg.

Tennessee Caviar

Stella Thomas, Leoma

1 cup dried black-eyed peas
4 slices bacon
1/3 cup wine vinegar
1 cup vegetable oil
1 clove of garlic, crushed
1/2 teaspoon pepper
1/2 teaspoon pepper sauce
1 teaspoon savory salt

Soak peas overnight in water to cover. Add bacon. Simmer until peas are tender but not mushy; drain. Combine remaining ingredients. Marinate drained peas in vinegar mixture for 5 days. Drain thoroughly. Serve on thin slices of corn bread. Yield: 6 servings.

Approx Per Serving: Cal 442; Prot 8 g; Carbo 18 g; Fiber 8 g; T Fat 39 g; 77% Calories from Fat; Chol 4 mg; Sod 292 mg.

Hominy Casserole

Mrs. Robbie Stanfill, Henderson

2 (16-ounce) cans yellow hominy
1 small bell pepper, chopped
1 small onion, chopped
1 (6-ounce) can evaporated milk
2 tablespoons butter
2 tablespoons flour
Salt and pepper to taste
1 cup shredded Cheddar cheese
Paprika

Preheat oven to 325 degrees. Mix hominy, bell pepper and onion in 2-quart baking dish. Melt butter in small saucepan. Add flour, salt and pepper; mix well. Stir in evaporated milk; cook mixture until thickened. Add cheese; stir until melted. Pour cheese mixture over hominy. Sprinkle with paprika. Bake until bubbly. Yield: 8 servings.

Approx Per Serving: Cal 204; Prot 7 g; Carbo 21 g; Fiber 1 g; T Fat 10 g; 45% Calories from Fat; Chol 21 mg; Sod 382 mg.

Homemade Noodles

Dorothy C. Webb, Bells

2 cups sifted flour
3/4 teaspoon salt
2 egg yolks
4 tablespoons water

Sift together flour and salt in bowl. Combine egg yolks and water; stir into flour mixture. Add a small amount additional water if dough is too dry. Divide dough into 3 parts. Roll out each until paper thin. Wind dough jelly roll-fashion; slice into narrow strips, about 1/8 inch wide. Separate and straighten strips; let dry thoroughly. Cook as desired. Yield: 8 servings

Approx Per Serving: Cal 120; Prot 4 g; Carbo 22 g; Fiber <1 g; T Fat 2 g; 12% Calories from Fat; Chol 53 mg; Sod 202 mg.

Potato Dressing

Mrs. Judy Counts, Lynnville

4 cups hot mashed potatoes
1 1/2 cups dry bread crumbs
2/3 cup bacon fat
1/2 cup finely chopped onion
1/2 cup finely chopped celery
2 teaspoons salt
1/2 teaspoon pepper
1/2 teaspoon ground sage
1 egg, beaten

Preheat oven to 360 degrees. Beat potatoes until fluffy. Combine with remaining ingredients. Pour in 8-inch square baking pan. Bake for about 30 minutes or until brown. Yield: 8 servings.

Approx Per Serving: Cal 337; Prot 5 g; Carbo 33 g; Fiber 3 g; T Fat 21 g; 55% Calories from Fat; Chol 48 mg; Sod 1129 mg.

Tasty Squash Dressing

Lorine R. Woodfin, Harvest, Alabama

2 cups sliced yellow squash
1 medium onion, finely chopped
1 cup cold water
2 cups corn bread crumbs
1 (10-ounce) can cream of chicken soup
1/4 cup butter, melted
1/4 teaspoon pepper

Preheat oven to 350 degrees. Combine squash, onion and water in medium saucepan. Bring to a boil; cover. Reduce heat. Simmer for 10 minutes or until squash is tender. Drain well; mash. Combine squash mixture with remaining ingredients, stirring well. Spoon into greased, 1 1/2-quart casserole. Bake for 25 minutes or until browned. Yield: 8 servings.

Approx Per Serving: Cal 170; Prot 3 g; Carbo 15 g; Fiber 1 g; T Fat 11 g; 57% Calories from Fat; Chol 29 mg; Sod 491 mg.

Easy Squash Dressing

Louise Smith, Obion

2 cups cooked yellow squash, drained
2 cups corn bread crumbs
1 onion, chopped
1/2 cup butter
1 (10-ounce) can cream of mushroom soup
1 teaspoon sugar
1 teaspoon sage
1 egg, beaten

Preheat oven to 350 degrees. Combine first 7 ingredients in bowl; mix well. Add egg; mix thoroughly. Pour into baking dish. Bake for 30 minutes. Yield: 6 servings.

Approx Per Serving: Cal 315; Prot 5 g; Carbo 21 g; Fiber 2 g; T Fat 24 g; 67% Calories from Fat; Chol 91 mg; Sod 755 mg.

Turkey Dressing

Ann D. Keith, Springfield

1 pound mushrooms
2 cups chopped onions
1 cup butter
4 (8-ounce) packages herb seasoned
   stuffing mix
2 (10-ounce) packages frozen spinach,
   thawed and drained
1 (15-ounce) carton ricotta cheese
6 eggs, beaten
1 cup parsley
1/2 teaspoon salt
1/4 teaspoon pepper
1 cup chicken broth

Cook mushrooms and onions in butter in saucepan. Place stuffing mix in large mixing bowl. Pour mushrooms and onions over top. Mix to coat. Fold spinach into stuffing mixture. Combine cheese, eggs, parsley, salt and pepper in separate bowl. Add to stuffing mixture. Stuff turkey with dressing. Blend broth with remaining stuffing. Place stuffing mixture in casserole dish. Bake with turkey the last hour of baking time. Yield 12 servings.

Approx Per Serving: Cal 551; Prot 19 g; Carbo 65 g; Fiber 2 g; T Fat 26 g; 41% Calories from Fat; Chol 166 mg; Sod 1613 mg.

Squash Puppies

Mrs. Count Boyd III, Springfield

1 1/2 cups self-rising cornmeal
1/2 cup self-rising flour
1/2 teaspoon baking soda
1 cup cooked yellow squash, drained
1 egg, beaten
3 tablespoons chopped onion
1 cup buttermilk
Oil for frying

Mix dry ingredients. Mash squash. Mix with egg, onion and buttermilk. Add to dry ingredients. Drop from teaspoon into hot deep oil. Cook until float to top of oil. Remove from oil; drain on absorbent paper. Serve hot with fish. Yield: 10 servings.

Approx Per Serving: Cal 118; Prot 4 g; Carbo 22 g; Fiber 2 g; T Fat 1 g; 9% Calories from Fat; Chol 22 mg; Sod 431 mg.

Apple Rings

Mrs. Robert M. Renfro, Luttrell

1 cup sugar
1/2 cup packed light brown sugar
1/2 cup butter
2 cups water
4 cups finely diced apples
1 recipe pie pastry
Cinnamon to taste

Preheat oven to 400 degrees. Combine first 4 ingredients in baking dish. Bake until mixture is bubbly hot. Reduce oven to 350 degrees. Prepare pastry; roll as for jelly roll. Place diced apples on pastry. Roll up. Cut into 1 1/2-inch slices. Drop into hot syrup in baking dish. Sprinkle with cinnamon. Bake for 45 minutes. Yield: 8 servings.

Approx Per Serving: Cal 396; Prot 2 g; Carbo 56 g; Fiber 2 g; T Fat 20 g; 43% Calories from Fat; Chol 31 mg; Sod 244 mg.

Hot Baked Fruit

Margaret Brabston, Knoxville

1 (6-ounce) package pitted prunes
1 (6-ounce) package dried apricots
1 (20-ounce) can chunk pineapple, undrained
1 (20-ounce) can cherry pie filling
1 cup water
1/4 cup cooking sherry

Preheat oven to 350 degrees. Place prunes, apricots and pineapple in 9-by-13-inch casserole. Combine cherry pie filling, water and sherry. Pour over fruit; mix well. Bake for 1 1/2 hours. Yield: 12 servings.

Approx Per Serving: Cal 164; Prot 1 g; Carbo 41 g; Fiber 3 g; T Fat <1 g; 3% Calories from Fat; Chol 0 mg; Sod 27 mg.

Hot Fruit Casserole

Margaret Hix, Lafayette

1 (16-ounce) can pineapple slices
1 (16-ounce) can peach halves
1 (16-ounce) can apple rings
1 (16-ounce) can pear halves
1 (16-ounce) can apricot halves
1/2 cup margarine
1/2 cup packed light brown sugar
2 tablespoons flour
1 cup sherry

Drain all fruits. Place in 2-quart baking dish. Combine margarine, sugar, flour and sherry in saucepan. Cook over medium heat until slightly thick. Pour sauce over fruit. Refrigerate for at least 1 day. Preheat oven to 350 degrees. Bake for 25 minutes. Yield: 12 servings.

Approx Per Serving: Cal 225; Prot <1 g; Carbo 38 g; Fiber 3 g; T Fat 8 g; 30% Calories from Fat; Chol 0 mg; Sod 101 mg.

Pineapple Casserole

Nelle Pendergrass, Fayetteville

1 (8-ounce) can pineapple slices
1 (20-ounce) can pineapple chunks
3 tablespoons flour
3 tablespoons sugar
1 1/4 cups shredded Cheddar cheese
1 1/4 cups crushed Ritz crackers
3 tablespoons melted butter

Preheat oven to 350 degrees. Drain pineapple reserving 3 tablespoons liquid. Cut each pineapple ring in half. Arrange with pineapple chunks on bottom of greased 1 1/2-quart casserole. Combine flour and sugar; sprinkle over pineapple. Drizzle with reserved pineapple liquid. Top with Cheddar cheese. Combine crackers and melted butter; distribute over cheese. Bake, covered, for 15 minutes. Remove cover; bake for 10 minutes longer. Yield: 8 servings.

Approx Per Serving: Cal 271; Prot 6 g; Carbo 34 g; Fiber 1 g; T Fat 13 g; 43% Calories from Fat; Chol 30 mg; Sod 250 mg.

Delicious Processed Apples

Mrs. Dorothy C. Wolske, Manchester

6 quarts apples, peeled and sliced
3 cups sugar

Place apples in large container. Sprinkle with sugar; cover. Let set overnight. Drain apples, reserving juice. Pack apples in hot sterilized 1-quart jars, leaving 1/2-inch headspace. Seal. Process jars in pressure cooker at 10 pounds pressure for 3 minutes. Yield: 32 servings (4 quarts).

Approx Per Serving: Cal 127; Prot <1 g; Carbo 33 g; Fiber 2 g; T Fat <1 g; 2% Calories from Fat; Chol 0 mg; Sod <1 mg.

Apple Butter

Carolyn Brasfield, Stanton

4 pounds apples, cored and chopped
1/2 cup water
4 1/2 cups sugar
3/4 teaspoon allspice
3/4 teaspoon cinnamon
3/4 teaspoon clove

Place apples in 4-quart Crock•Pot. Add water. Cook on Low for 10 hours. Add sugar and spices; cover. Cook for 8 to 10 hours longer. Remove lid last hour of cooking time. Spoon into hot sterilized jars, leaving 1/2-inch headspace. Seal with 2-piece lids. Store in refrigerator. Yield: 160 (1 tablespoon) servings (5 pints).

Approx Per Serving: Cal 28; Prot <1 g; Carbo 7 g; Fiber <1 g; T Fat <1 g; 1% Calories from Fat; Chol 0 mg; Sod <1 mg.

Apple Relish

Mrs. J. R. Lawson, Maryville

14 large apples
6 large onions
3 pods hot pepper
6 pods sweet pepper
1 1/2 cups sugar
1 quart vinegar

Grind all ingredients in food processor or blender. Cook for 15 minutes in heavy saucepan. Pour into hot sterilized jars, leaving 1/2-inch headspace. Seal with 2-piece lids. Store in refrigerator. Yield: 40 (1/4-cup) servings (5 pints).

Approx Per Serving: Cal 77; Prot <1 g; Carbo 20 g; Fiber 2 g; T Fat <1 g; 3% Calories from Fat; Chol 0 mg; Sod 1 mg.

Old-Fashioned Blackberry Jelly

Mrs. James C. Haag, Talbott

Blackberries
7 cups sugar

Wash desired amount of blackberries; drain well. Mash berries. Cook a small portion of berries slowly over low heat. Add additional berries slowly until all are cooked. Remove from heat; cool. Strain. Add 7 cups sugar to 4 cups juice in saucepan. Heat just to dissolve sugar; do not boil. Pour into hot, sterilized jars, leaving 1/2-inch headspace. Seal.

Nutritional information for this recipe is not available.

Blackberry Shrub

Mrs. Charles F. Nixon, Crossville

4 quarts blackberries
1 quart cider vinegar
8 pounds (about) sugar

Wash 2 quarts blackberries; drain. Pour 1 quart cider vinegar over berries. Let stand overnight. Crush berries; strain. Pour strained liquid over 2 more quarts blackberries; let stand overnight. Crush; strain. Add 1 pound sugar to each pint of juice. Bring to a boil; cook for 5 minutes; skim. Pour into hot sterilized jars leaving 1/2-inch headspace. Seal. Yield: 48 (1/4-cup) servings (6 pints).

Approx Per Serving: Cal 320; Prot <1 g; Carbo 83 g; Fiber 2 g; T Fat <1 g; 1% Calories from Fat; Chol 0 mg; Sod <1 mg.

Fried Peach Pie Mix

Vonnie Walker, Walland

2 1/2 pounds sugar
1 cup vinegar
1 gallon ripe peaches with skins, finely
** chopped**

Bring sugar and vinegar to boil; boil until sugar is dissolved. Add peaches. Cook until mixture is of spreading consistency. Pour mixture into hot sterilized jars, leaving 1/2-inch headspace. Seal. Use as filling for fried pies. Yield: 20 (1/2-cup) servings (5 pints).

Approx Per Serving: Cal 562; Prot 2 g; Carbo 145 g; Fiber 4 g; T Fat <1 g; <1% Calories from Fat; Chol 0 mg; Sod 1 mg.

Strawberry Preserves

Mrs. Edison Cornwell, Dixon Springs

4 cups fresh strawberries
4 cups sugar

Cap and wash strawberries. Combine with 2 cups sugar in saucepan. Bring to a boil. Boil for 5 minutes. Remove from heat. Add 2 cups sugar. Bring to a boil. Boil for 10 minutes longer. Let cool; stir. Pour into sterilized jars. Seal. Yield: 64 (1 tablespoon) servings (2 pints).

Approx Per Serving: Cal 51; Prot <1 g; Carbo 32 g; Fiber <1 g; T Fat <1 g; <1% Calories from Fat; Chol 0 mg; Sod <1 mg.

Purple Pea Hull Jelly

Sophia Hester, Lobelville

"It is a shame that in the past we've been throwing away those valuable pea hulls, especially as jelly-making materials are scarce," says Sophia Hester of Lobelville. With that, she tells how to use those hulls.

Purple pea hulls, washed
4 cups juice
1 package Sure-Jell
7 cups sugar

Cover hulls with water in saucepan. Simmer for about 30 minutes. Strain; reserving juice. Bring juice to a boil in saucepan. Add Sure-Jell, stirring until dissolved. Add sugar. Boil for about 10 minutes longer. Remove from heat; skim. Pour into hot sterilized jars, leaving 1/2-inch headspace. Seal.

Nutritional information for this recipe is not available.

Zucchini Preserves

Mrs. Jack Jett, Cornersville

6 cups zucchini, peeled and grated
6 cups sugar
1/2 cup water
1 (20-ounce) can crushed pineapple
   with juice
2 (3-ounce) packages apricot gelatin

Combine zucchini, sugar and water. Bring to a boil. Boil for 6 minutes. Add pineapple and juice. Boil for 10 minutes, stirring often. Sprinkle gelatin over hot mixture; mix well. Place in hot sterilized jars, leaving 1/2-inch headspace; seal. Strawberry gelatin may be used if desired. Yield: 128 (1 tablespoon) servings (4 pints).

Approx Per Serving: Cal 45; Prot <1 g; Carbo 11 g; Fiber <1 g; T Fat <1 g; <1% Calories from Fat; Chol 0 mg; Sod 4 mg.

Tasty Zucchini Preserves

Mrs. Rachel Pack, Maryville

6 cups zucchini, cut into strips
5 cups sugar
1 (20-ounce) can crushed pineapple
1 (6-ounce) package apricot gelatin

Combine zucchini with small amount of water in saucepan. Cook over Low for 10 minutes. Drain. Add sugar and pineapple; mix well. Cook on High for 10 minutes longer. Remove from heat. Add gelatin, stirring well. Pour into hot sterilized jars, leaving 1/2-inch headspace. Seal. Yield: 128 (1 tablespoon) servings (4 pints).

Approx Per Serving: Cal 40; Prot <1 g; Carbo 10 g; Fiber <1 g; T Fat <1 g; <1% Calories from Fat; Chol 0 mg; Sod 4 mg.

Coleslaw Relish

Frances Hurst, Newport

1 small firm head of cabbage, chopped
1 small green pepper, chopped
2 tablespoons finely chopped onion
1/2 teaspoon celery seed
1/2 cup vinegar
1/3 cup sugar
1 teaspoon salt
1/4 teaspoon pepper
2 tablespoons sweet pickle relish

Combine cabbage, green pepper, onion and celery seed in bowl; chill. Combine vinegar, sugar, salt, pepper and relish in small saucepan. Cook until sugar is dissolved, stirring constantly. Chill. Blend vinegar mixture with cabbage mixture at serving time.
Yield: 64 (1 tablespoon) servings (4 cups).

Approx Per Serving: Cal 8; Prot <1 g; Carbo 2 g; Fiber <1 g; T Fat <1 g; 4% Calories from Fat; Chol 0 mg; Sod 39 mg.

Summer Corn Relish

Mrs. Turner Lowery, New Market

2 cups sugar
2 cups vinegar
1 1/2 teaspoons salt
1 1/2 teaspoons celery seed
1/2 teaspoon turmeric
2 cups chopped onion
2 cups chopped tomato
2 cups chopped cucumber
2 cups corn, cut from cob
2 cups chopped cabbage

Combine sugar, vinegar, salt, celery seed and turmeric in large Dutch oven. Bring to a boil. Add vegetables. Cook, uncovered, for 25 minutes, stirring occasionally. Pack in hot sterilized jars, leaving 1/2-inch headspace. Seal.
Yield: 12 (1/2-cup) servings (3 pints).

Approx Per Serving: Cal 179; Prot 2 g; Carbo 45 g; Fiber 2 g; T Fat <1 g; 3% Calories from Fat; Chol 0 mg; Sod 277 mg.

Cucumber Relish

Mrs. Lois Brooks, Middlesboro, Kentucky

"The Cucumber Relish has many uses — potato salad or macaroni salad, or it's just plain good with pinto beans and corn bread," says Mrs. Brooks.

4 quarts diced cucumbers
5 large onions, diced
1 red pepper, chopped
1 green pepper, chopped
1/2 cup salt
5 cups sugar
3 cups vinegar
1 1/2 teaspoons celery seed
1 1/2 teaspoons tumeric
2 tablespoons mustard seed

Combine first 5 ingredients in large bowl. Cover with ice. Let stand for 3 hours. Drain. Combine remaining ingredients in bowl. Combine with vegetable mixture in saucepan. Cook over low heat until just heated through; do not boil. Pour into hot, sterilized jars, leaving 1/2-inch headspace. Seal.
Yield: 96 (2 tablespoons) servings (6 pints).

Approx Per Serving: Cal 47; Prot <1 g; Carbo 12 g; Fiber <1 g; T Fat <1 g; 2% Calories from Fat; Chol 0 mg; Sod 533 mg.

Fresh Tomato Relish

Mrs. Thomas H. Brown, Columbia

2 tablespoons cider vinegar
1 teaspoon sugar
1/2 teaspoon salt
1/2 teaspoon celery seed
3 large ripe tomatoes, peeled and coarsely
    chopped
1 small onion, chopped
1 green bell pepper, chopped

Combine vinegar and seasonings. Pour over vegetables in bowl. Chill thoroughly. Drain before serving. This will keep several days in refrigerator. Yield: 8 servings (2 cups).

Approx Per Serving: Cal 23; Prot <1 g; Carbo 5 g; Fiber 1 g; T Fat <1 g; 10% Calories from Fat; Chol 0 mg; Sod 140 mg.

Uncooked Fresh Tomato Relish

Judy Jackson, LaFollette

3 cups diced fresh tomatoes
1/3 cup finely chopped onion
1 tablespoon fresh lemon juice
1 tablespoon vinegar
1 1/2 teaspoons salt
1/4 teaspoon pepper

Combine all ingredients in bowl. Chill for 2 to 3 hours. Serve as a relish with meats, fish, poultry, or pinto beans. Yield: 8 servings (2 cups).

Approx Per Serving: Cal 17; Prot <1 g; Carbo 4 g; Fiber 1 g; T Fat <1 g; 10% Calories from Fat; Chol 0 mg; Sod 406 mg.

Chopped Green Tomato Pickle

Mrs. Irvin Murff, Clarksville

10 pounds green tomatoes
1 cup salt
6 hot green peppers
5 sweet red peppers
6 medium onions
3 quarts vinegar
8 cups sugar
2 tablespoons celery seed
2 tablespoons mustard seed
1 tablespoon whole cloves

Place tomatoes through food chopper. Add salt to tomatoes. Place in colander. Let drain overnight. Place peppers and onions in food chopper. Combine tomatoes, peppers and onions with remaining ingredients in large saucepan; mix well. Cook for 20 minutes. Pour into hot sterilized jars, leaving 1/2-inch headspace. Seal.
Yield: 48 (1/4-cup) servings (3 quarts).

Approx Per Serving: Cal 173; Prot 2 g; Carbo 44 g; Fiber 2 g; T Fat <1 g; 2% Calories from Fat; Chol 0 mg; Sod 2146 mg.

Canned Green Tomatoes

Martha Bazzell, Adamsville

1 quart sliced green tomatoes
1/2 teaspoon salt
Boiling water

Pack tomatoes in 1-quart jar. Add 1/2 teaspoon salt. Pour boiling water over tomatoes, leaving 1/2-inch headspace. Seal. Preserves tomatoes until ready to fry.
Yield: 12 servings (1 quart).

Approx Per Serving: Cal 15; Prot <1 g; Carbo 3 g; Fiber <1 g; T Fat <1 g; 7% Calories from Fat; Chol 0 mg; Sod 97 mg.

Cucumber Pickles

Mrs. Harry Cumby, Cookeville

1 gallon whole cucumbers
2 tablespoons coarse salt
1 tablespoon alum
6 tablespoons pickling spice
1/2 gallon vinegar
4 cups sugar

Pack cucumbers in 1-gallon jar. Combine remaining ingredients except sugar. Pour over cucumbers, adding enough vinegar to cover cucumbers. Cover tightly. Let stand for 6 weeks. Drain. Slice cucumbers. Layer in gallon jar. Add sugar. Yield: 48 (1/4-cup) servings (6 pints).

Approx Per Serving: Cal 78; Prot <1 g; Carbo 21 g; Fiber <1 g; T Fat <1 g; <1% Calories from Fat; Chol 0 mg; Sod 269 mg.

Sweet Pickles

Mrs. G. W. Turnbow, Sr., Adamsville

10 pounds cucumbers
1 small box powdered alum
1/2 box whole allspice
1 gallon cider vinegar
10 pounds sugar

Soak cucumbers in brine for 14 days. Remove cucumbers. Slice and soak in alum water overnight. Soak in vinegar for 6 hours; drain. Place in container. Pour 10 pounds sugar over sliced cucumbers. Cover with lid until ready to use. No heating or sealing necessary.

Nutritional information for this recipe is not available.

Squash Pickles

Cleo Sensing, Cumberland Furnace

8 cups thinly sliced yellow squash
4 bell peppers, thinly sliced
3 large white onions, thinly sliced
1/4 cup coarse salt
3 cups sugar
2 cups white vinegar
2 tablespoons celery seed
2 teaspoons mustard seed
1 (3-ounce) jar pimentos

Combine squash, bell peppers and onions in container. Cover with ice for 4 hours. Rinse; drain. Combine remaining ingredients in saucepan. Bring to a boil. Pack squash mixture in hot sterilized jars. Add vinegar mixture, leaving 1/2-inch headspace. Seal.
Yield: 80 (1/4-cup) servings (10 pints).

Approx Per Serving: Cal 37; Prot <1 g; Carbo 9 g; Fiber <1 g; T Fat <1 g; 3% Calories from Fat; Chol 0 mg; Sod 321 mg.

Haden Salad

Mrs. Earlene Leath, Westmoreland

1 gallon ripe tomatoes
1 gallon cabbage
1 quart onions
1 cup hot peppers
1 quart vinegar
3 pints sugar
3 tablespoons salt
2 tablespoons each ginger, cinnamon
1 tablespoon cloves
4 tablespoons celery seed

Chop vegetables; drain if needed. Combine with remaining ingredients in saucepan. Cook over Low heat for 45 minutes or until mixture is thick. Pour into hot sterilized jars, leaving 1/2-inch headspace. Seal.
Yield: 60 (1/2-cup) servings (15 pints).

Approx Per Serving: Cal 112; Prot 2 g; Carbo 28 g; Fiber 2 g; T Fat <1 g; 4% Calories from Fat; Chol 0 mg; Sod 336 mg

Breads

Man About Town

Although he's quite a celebrity around Lynchburg, Herb Fanning, who appears in a number of advertisements for Jack Daniel products, enjoys the simple things in life – visiting with friends around town and a challenging day of fishing.

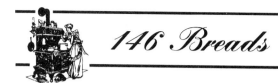

Biscuits with Less Fat

Mrs. Francis T. Davis, Old Fort

2 cups flour
3 teaspoons baking powder
1/4 teaspoon salt
1/4 teaspoon baking soda
1 cup buttermilk
4 tablespoons vegetable oil

Preheat oven to 425 degrees. Combine first 4 ingredients in bowl; mix well. Combine milk and oil in mixing bowl. Add enough flour mixture to make a soft dough. Roll out; cut with biscuit cutter. Place on baking pan. Bake for 8 to 10 minutes or until lightly browned. Yield: 10 servings.

Approx Per Serving: Cal 151; Prot 3 g; Carbo 21 g; Fiber 1 g; T Fat 6 g; 36% Calories from Fat; Chol 1 mg; Sod 199 mg.

Buttermilk Biscuits

Barbie Irvin, Dunlap

2 cups flour
1/2 teaspoon salt
1 teaspoon baking powder
1/2 teaspoon baking soda
3 tablespoons shortening
3/4 cup buttermilk

Preheat oven to 475 degrees. Combine flour, salt, baking powder and baking soda. Cut in shortening. Add buttermilk until blended. Roll 3/8 inch thick; cut into biscuits. Bake for 12 to 15 minutes. Yield: 10 servings.

Approx Per Serving: Cal 133; Prot 3 g; Carbo 20 g; Fiber g; T Fat 4 g; 29% Calories from Fat; Chol 1 mg; Sod 200 mg.

Banana-Honey-Nut Muffins

Thelma Robinson, Sparta

1 3/4 cups self-rising flour
1/2 cup pecans
1/3 cup sugar
3/4 cup mashed ripe banana
1/2 cup milk
1/3 cup vegetable oil
1 egg
1/4 cup honey
2 tablespoons butter, softened
1 cup pecans

Preheat oven to 400 degrees. Grease 12 muffin cups. Combine flour, 1/2 cup pecans and sugar in large mixing bowl. Mix bananas, milk, oil and egg in small bowl. Push flour mixture against sides of bowl to make well in center. Pour liquid mixture in all at once. Stir with fork until moistened. Do not over mix. Fill muffin cups 2/3 full. Bake for 15 minutes or until golden brown. Combine honey and butter; mix well. Dip tops of warm muffins into honey butter. Top with remaining pecans. Yield: 12 muffins.

Approx Per Serving: Cal 299; Prot 4 g; Carbo 31 g; Fiber 2 g; T Fat 19 g; 54% Calories from Fat; Chol 24 mg; Sod 262 mg.

Blackberry Muffins

Mrs. Ovid Essary, Enville

1 1/4 cups self-rising flour
3/4 cup sugar
1/4 teaspoon salt
1/4 teaspoon baking powder
1 egg
1/4 cup vegetable oil
1 1/4 cups milk
1 1/4 cups blackberries

Preheat oven to 400 degrees. Combine dry ingredients in bowl. Combine remaining ingredients. Add dry ingredients; mix with as little stirring as possible. Pour batter into well-greased muffin cups. Bake for 20 minutes. Yield: 12 servings.

Approx Per Serving: Cal 164; Prot 3 g; Carbo 25 g; Fiber 1 g; T Fat 6 g; 32% Calories from Fat; Chol 21 mg; Sod 234 mg.

Blueberry Streusel Muffins

Peggy Woodby, Mohawk

1/4 cup butter, softened
1/3 cup sugar
1 egg
2 1/3 cups flour
3 teaspoons baking powder
1/2 teaspoon salt
1 cup milk
1 teaspoon vanilla extract
1 1/2 cups blueberries
1/2 cup sugar
1/3 cup flour
1/2 teaspoon ground cinnamon
1/4 cup butter, softened

Preheat oven to 375 degrees. Cream 1/4 cup butter in mixer bowl; gradually add 1/3 cup sugar. Beat at medium speed until light and fluffy. Add egg, beating well. Combine 2 1/3 cups flour, baking powder and salt. Add to creamed mixture alternately with milk, stirring well after each addition. Stir in vanilla; fold in blueberries. Spoon batter into greased muffin cups, filling 2/3 full. Combine 1/2 cup sugar, 1/3 cup flour and cinnamon in bowl. Cut in 1/4 cup butter until mixture resembles crumbs. Sprinkle over muffin batter. Bake for 25 to 30 minutes or until golden brown. Yield: 18 servings.

Approx Per Serving: Cal 168; Prot 3 g; Carbo 26 g; Fiber 1 g; T Fat 6 g; 32% Calories from Fat; Chol 27 mg; Sod 177 mg.

Coffee Cake Muffins

Judy K. Grissom, McMinnville

1/2 cup packed light brown sugar
2 tablespoons flour
2 teaspoons cinnamon
2 tablespoons butter, softened
1/2 cup chopped pecans
1 1/2 cups flour
2 teaspoons baking powder
1/2 teaspoon salt
1/2 cup sugar
1/4 cup vegetable shortening
1 egg, beaten
1/2 cup milk

Preheat oven to 375 degrees. Combine brown sugar, 2 tablespoons flour and cinnamon. Cut butter into mixture until crumbly. Add pecans. Sift 1 1/2 cups flour, baking powder, salt and sugar in mixing bowl. Cut in shortening until crumbly. Combine egg and milk. Add to dry ingredients; stir quickly. Spoon layer of batter, then layer of pecan mixture into greased muffin cups. Repeat layers. Bake for 15 to 20 minutes. Yield: 12 servings.

Approx Per Serving: Cal 223; Prot 3 g; Carbo 30 g; Fiber 1 g; T Fat 11 g; 42% Calories from Fat; Chol 24 mg; Sod 177 mg.

Crullers

Mrs. Rachel B. Ferrell, Sevierville

Grated nutmeg to taste
2 teaspoons baking powder
1 3/4 cups flour
2 eggs
1 cup sugar
1 teaspoon butter
1/2 cup milk

Combine nutmeg and baking powder with 1 cup flour in bowl. Add remaining flour. Beat eggs in bowl, adding sugar gradually. Add butter. Add flour mixture alternately with milk beating well after each addition. Roll out on floured board to 1/3 inch thick. Cut with ring cutter. Fry in hot deep fat until brown. Drain. Yield: 16 servings.

Approx Per Serving: Cal 115; Prot 2 g; Carbo 24 g; Fiber <1 g; T Fat 1 g; 10% Calories from Fat; Chol 28 mg; Sod 56 mg.

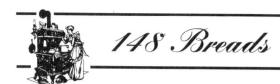

Angel Corn Sticks

Jo Whittaker, Portland

1 1/2 cups cornmeal
1 cup flour
1 tablespoon sugar
1 1/2 teaspoons baking powder
1 package dry yeast
1 teaspoon salt
1/2 teaspoon baking soda
2 eggs
2 cups buttermilk
1/2 cup vegetable oil

Preheat oven to 450 degrees. Combine dry ingredients in large bowl. Combine eggs, buttermilk and oil. Add to dry ingredients; stir well. Spoon into well-greased cast iron corn stick pans, filling one-half full. Bake for 12 to 15 minutes. Yield: 36 servings.

Approx Per Serving: Cal 73; Prot 2 g; Carbo 8 g; Fiber <1 g; T Fat 4 g; 45% Calories from Fat; Chol 12 mg; Sod 102 mg.

Cornmeal Muffins

Avo Anderson, Cookeville

1 1/4 cups self-rising cornmeal
2 tablespoons flour
1/8 teaspoon baking soda
1/8 teaspoon salt
1 egg white, unbeaten
1 cup low-fat buttermilk

Preheat oven to 450 degrees. Combine cornmeal, flour, baking soda and salt in bowl; mix well. Add unbeaten egg white and buttermilk; mix well. Fill greased muffin cups 2/3 full. Bake for 30 minutes or until brown. Yield: 6 servings.

Approx Per Serving: Cal 131; Prot 5 g; Carbo 26 g; Fiber 2 g; T Fat 1 g; 6% Calories from Fat; Chol 1 mg; Sod 501 mg.

Superb Spoonbread

Bettye T. Griffin, Centerville

1/2 cup cornmeal
2 cups hot milk
1/2 teaspoon salt
4 egg yolks, beaten
4 egg whites, stiffly beaten

Preheat oven to 350 degrees. Combine cornmeal, hot milk and salt in saucepan; mix well. Cook until thick. Cool slightly. Add egg yolks; mix well. Fold in egg whites. Pour into buttered 1 1/2-quart casserole. Bake for 45 minutes to 1 hour. Yield: 8 servings.

Approx Per serving: Cal 107; Prot 6 g; Carbo 10 g; Fiber <1 g; T Fat 5 g; 40% Calories from Fat; Chol 114 mg; Sod 194 mg.

Delicious Corn Bread

Mrs. B. Raymond Love, Savannah

1 cup butter, softened
1 cup sugar
2 cups cornmeal
1 cup flour
1/2 teaspoon salt
3 teaspoons baking powder
1 cup milk
2 eggs, beaten

Preheat oven to 350 degrees. Combine butter and sugar in bowl. Add cornmeal, flour, salt, baking powder and milk; mix well. Fold in eggs very slowly. Pour into 9-by-9-inch baking pan. Bake for 20 to 30 minutes. Yield: 8 servings.

Approx Per Serving: Cal 522; Prot 7 g; Carbo 66 g; Fiber 2 g; T Fat 26 g; 44% Calories from Fat; Chol 119 mg; Sod 523 mg.

Mexican Corn Bread

Mrs. Martin Young, Sr., Crossville

1/4 cup butter
1/4 cup sugar
2 eggs
1 (16-ounce) can cream-style corn
1/3 cup chopped mild Italian peppers
2 cups shredded Cheddar cheese
1 1/4 cups flour
4 teaspoons baking powder
1/4 teaspoon salt
1 cup cornmeal

Preheat oven to 325 degrees. Combine butter and sugar in large mixing bowl. Add eggs, one at a time; mix well. Add corn, peppers and cheese; mix well. Combine flour, baking powder, salt and cornmeal in small bowl. Add to cheese mixture; mix well. Pour into buttered 9-by-13-inch baking dish. Bake for 35 to 40 minutes. Remove to wire rack to cool. Yield: 8 servings.

Approx Per Serving: Cal 387; Prot 13 g; Carbo 47 g; Fiber 2 g; T Fat 17 g; 39% Calories from Fat; Chol 98 mg; Sod 644 mg.

Delicious Mexican Corn Bread

Mrs. Byron Cochran, Brownsville

1 1/2 cups self-rising cornmeal
1 cup grated Cheddar cheese
1 cup buttermilk
2/3 cup vegetable oil
3 eggs, beaten
1 onion, chopped
1 teaspoon salt
3 pods hot pepper, chopped
1 (8-ounce) can whole kernel corn

Preheat oven to 350 degrees. Combine all ingredients in bowl; mix lightly. Pour in 9-inch iron skillet. Bake for 45 minutes. Yield: 10 servings.

Approx Per Serving: Cal 303; Prot 8 g; Carbo 23 g; Fiber 2 g; T Fat 21 g; 60% Calories from Fat; Chol 76 mg; Sod 665 mg.

Soft Mexican Corn Muffins

Mrs. Harold Davison, Finley

1 cup cornmeal
3/4 teaspoon baking soda
1/2 teaspoon salt
1/4 cup vegetable oil
2 eggs
1 medium onion, chopped
1 cup buttermilk
1 (10-ounce) can cream-style corn
1/2 can chopped green chilies
1 cup grated sharp Cheddar cheese

Preheat oven to 425 degrees. Combine all ingredients in bowl; mix well. Pour into hot, greased muffin tins. Fill to 3/4 full. Bake for 25 to 30 minutes. Remove to wire rack to cool. Yield: 14 servings.

Approx Per Serving: Cal 139; Prot 5 g; Carbo 13 g; Fiber 1 g; T Fat 8 g; 49% Calories from Fat; Chol 39 mg; Sod 303 mg.

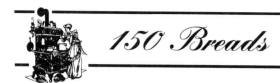

Three-Vegetable Corn Bread

Joyce Bell, Powell

2 cups self-rising cornmeal
2 eggs
1 medium onion, chopped
1 small green pepper, chopped
1 cup sour cream
1 (8-ounce) can cream-style corn
²/₃ cup vegetable oil

Preheat oven to 350 degrees. Combine all ingredients in bowl; mix well. Pour into well greased 9-inch pan. Bake for 45 to 50 minutes. Yield: 10 servings.

Approx Per Serving: Cal 312; Prot 5 g; Carbo 27 g; Fiber 2 g; T Fat 21 g; 60% Calories from Fat; Chol 53 mg; Sod 461 mg.

Diabetic Corn Bread

Mrs. Charles Smelcer, Parrottsville

1 cup cream of wheat
1 cup flour
¹/₃ cup vegetable oil
¹/₄ teaspoon salt
2 teaspoons baking powder
1 teaspoon baking soda
1 cup low-fat buttermilk

Preheat oven to 425 degrees. Combine all ingredients in bowl; mix well. Pour into greased skillet. Bake for 25 to 30 minutes. Yield: 8 servings.

Approx Per Serving: Cal 231; Prot 5 g; Carbo 31 g; Fiber 1 g; T Fat 10 g; 37% Calories from Fat; Chol 1 mg; Sod 348 mg.

Corn Light Bread

Sara S. Lowe, Rockvale

1³/₄ cups cornmeal
¹/₂ cup flour
¹/₂ teaspoon baking soda
¹/₄ cup sugar
1³/₄ cups buttermilk
1 egg, beaten
¹/₃ cup shortening

Preheat oven to 350 degrees. Combine all ingredients in order listed in bowl; mix well. Pour into greased loaf pan. Bake until slightly brown. Remove to wire rack to cool, covering with cloth. Yield: 8 servings.

Approx Per Serving: Cal 269; Prot 6 g; Carbo 38 g; Fiber 2 g; T Fat 10 g; 34% Calories from Fat; Chol 28 mg; Sod 117 mg.

4-H Corn Light Bread

Mrs. Ezra Sanders, Obion

1¹/₂ cups self-rising cornmeal
¹/₂ cup flour
¹/₂ cup corn oil
³/₄ cup sugar
1¹/₂ cups buttermilk
1 teaspoon dry yeast

Preheat oven to 350 degrees. Combine all ingredients in bowl; mix well. Pour into greased loaf pan. Bake for 1 hour. Remove to wire rack to cool. Yield: 8 servings.

Approx Per Serving: Cal 333; Prot 5 g; Carbo 46 g; Fiber 2 g; T Fat 15 g; 39% Calories from Fat; Chol 2 mg; Sod 397 mg.

Light Skillet Corn Bread

Helen Carpenter, Kingsport

¹/2 cup butter
2 tablespoons vegetable oil
1 cup self-rising cornmeal
2 cups self-rising flour
2 tablespoons sugar
1 cup milk

Preheat oven to 450 degrees. Melt butter in large skillet. Add oil; heat. Set aside. Combine dry ingredients. Add milk to make a medium thin batter. Reheat skillet. Pour in batter; do not overfill skillet. Shake skillet to allow oil to come to the top. Bake for 30 minutes or until brown. Yield: 10 servings.

Approx Per Serving: Cal 268; Prot 5 g; Carbo 32 g; Fiber 1 g; T Fat 13 g; 45% Calories from Fat; Chol 28 mg; Sod 609 mg.

Anadama Bread

John Wethington, Helenwood

¹/2 cup yellow cornmeal
3 tablespoons butter
¹/4 cup dark molasses
2 teaspoons salt
³/4 cup boiling water
1 package active dry yeast
¹/4 cup warm water
1 egg, slightly beaten
3 cups sifted flour

Preheat oven to 350 degrees. Combine cornmeal, butter, molasses, salt and boiling water in small bowl; mix well. Cool until lukewarm. Sprinkle yeast over warm water in large bowl. Set aside for 5 minutes. Add egg, cornmeal mixture and half the flour; mix well. Stir in remaining flour; mix well. Shape into ball. Turn in buttered bowl to coat entire surface; cover. Let rise until doubled in bulk; punch down. Turn into buttered 5-by-9-inch loaf pan; cover. Let rise until doubled in bulk. Sprinkle dough with cornmeal. Bake for 40 to 45 minutes. Remove to wire rack to cool. Yield: 8 servings.

Approx Per Serving: Cal 263; Prot 6 g; Carbo 46 g; Fiber 2 g; T Fat 6 g; 19% Calories from Fat; Chol 38 mg; Sod 592 mg.

Quick Banana Bread

Donna McGlothin, Seymour

¹/2 cup vegetable shortening
1 cup sugar
2 eggs, well beaten
3 bananas
1 teaspoon lemon juice
2 cups sifted flour
3 teaspoons baking powder
¹/2 teaspoon salt
1 cup chopped pecans

Preheat oven to 350 degrees. Blend shortening and sugar in bowl. Add eggs; mix well. Mash bananas until smooth. Add lemon juice. Add egg mixture; mix well. Combine flour, baking powder and salt in bowl. Add to banana mixture. Add pecans. Pour into greased loaf pan. Bake for 1 hour. Remove to wire rack to cool. Yield: 8 servings.

Approx Per Serving: Cal 474; Prot 6 g; Carbo 61 g; Fiber 3 g; T Fat 25 g; 46% Calories from Fat; Chol 53 mg; Sod 274 mg.

Banana-Nut Bread

Lib Beard, Franklin

1 cup sugar
²/₃ cup vegetable oil
2 eggs
¹/₃ cup buttermilk
2 cups flour
1 teaspoon baking soda
1 teaspoon baking powder
¹/₄ teaspoon salt
1 cup mashed bananas
1 teaspoon vanilla extract
1 cup chopped pecans

Preheat oven to 350 degrees. Combine sugar and oil in bowl. Add eggs; beat well. Add buttermilk and dry ingredients; mix well. Add bananas, vanilla and pecans. Pour mixture into large greased loaf pan. Bake for 50 to 55 minutes. Remove to wire rack to cool.
Yield: 8 servings.

Approx Per Serving: Cal 519; Prot 7 g; Carbo 59 g; Fiber 2 g; T Fat 30 g; 51% Calories from Fat; Chol 53 mg; Sod 238 mg.

Blueberry-Lemon Bread

Mrs. Vickie Whitworth, Camden

1¹/₂ cups flour
1 teaspoon baking powder
¹/₄ teaspoon salt
6 tablespoons butter
1 cup sugar
2 eggs
2 teaspoons grated lemon peel
¹/₂ cup milk
1¹/₂ cups blueberries
¹/₃ cup sugar
3 tablespoons fresh lemon juice

Preheat oven to 325 degrees. Butter 5-by-9-inch loaf pan. Combine flour, baking powder and salt in small bowl; set aside. Cream butter with 1 cup sugar in large mixer bowl. Mix until light and fluffy. Add eggs, one at a time, beating well after each addition. Add lemon peel. Add dry ingredients alternately with milk, beginning and ending with dry ingredients. Fold in blueberries. Spoon into loaf pan. Bake about 1 hour or until toothpick inserted in center comes out clean. Bring ¹/₃ cup sugar and lemon juice to boil in small saucepan, stirring until sugar dissolves. Pierce top of hot loaf with toothpick. Pour hot lemon mixture over loaf in pan. Cool for 30 minutes in pan. Remove to wire rack to cool completely. Yield: 8 servings.

Approx Per Serving: Cal 336; Prot 5 g; Carbo 57 g; Fiber 1 g; T Fat 11 g; 28% Calories from Fat; Chol 78 mg; Sod 221 mg.

Cherry-Pecan Bread

Geneva C. Hale, Lebanon

1 (4-ounce) jar maraschino cherries
1 egg, beaten
1 cup sugar
2 tablespoons melted butter
¹/₄ cup orange juice
¹/₄ cup water
2 cups sifted flour
3 teaspoons baking powder
¹/₄ teaspoon baking soda
³/₄ teaspoon salt
1 cup chopped pecans

Preheat oven to 350 degrees. Chop and drain cherries, reserving ¹/₄ cup juice. Combine egg and cherries in bowl. Add sugar and melted butter; mix well. Add cherry juice, orange juice and water; mix well. Combine flour, baking powder, baking soda and salt in small bowl. Add to cherry mixture; mix well. Add pecans. Pour into greased 5-by-9-inch loaf pan. Bake for 1 hour. Remove to wire rack to cool.
Yield: 8 servings.

Approx Per Serving: Cal 357; Prot 5 g; Carbo 55 g; Fiber 2 g; T Fat 14 g; 34% Calories from Fat; Chol 34 mg; Sod 387 mg.

Muscadine Bread

Mrs. John F. Morgan, Olive Hill

1/2 cup butter
1 cup sugar
2 eggs
2 cups flour
1 1/2 teaspoons baking powder
1/2 cup milk
1/2 cup muscadine sauce
1/2 cup chopped pecans

Preheat oven to 325 degrees. Cream butter and sugar in bowl until light and fluffy. Add eggs, one at a time, beating well after each addition. Combine flour and baking powder. Add alternately with milk and muscadine sauce, beating well after each addition. Stir in pecans. Pour into greased and floured loaf pan. Bake for 50 to 60 minutes, or until toothpick inserted in center comes out clean. Remove to wire rack to cool. Yield: 8 servings.

Nutritional information does not include muscadine sauce.
Approx Per Serving: Cal 391; Prot 6 g; Carbo 51 g; Fiber 1 g; T Fat 19 g; 42% Calories from Fat; Chol 86 mg; Sod 203 mg.

Pumpkin Bread

Mrs. John Guenther, Jr., Monterey

4 cups sugar
4 cups pumpkin
1 cup vegetable oil
5 cups flour
1 teaspoon cinnamon
1 1/2 teaspoons salt
1 teaspoon cloves
4 teaspoons baking soda
1 cup chopped pecans
1 egg
1 cup raisins

Preheat oven to 350 degrees. Combine first 3 ingredients in bowl; mix well. Sift flour, cinnamon, salt, cloves and baking soda in bowl. Add remaining ingredients; mix well. Combine with pumpkin mixture; mix well. Pour into 3 greased loaf pans. Bake for 1 hour. Remove to wire rack to cool. Yield: 24 servings.

Approx Per Serving: Cal 375; Prot 4 g; Carbo 63 g; Fiber 3 g; T Fat 13 g; 31% Calories from Fat; Chol 9 mg; Sod 276 mg.

Fall Pumpkin Bread

June Savage, Bedford County

3 1/2 cups flour
2 teaspoons baking soda
1 teaspoon salt
3 cups sugar
1 teaspoon cinnamon
1 teaspoon nutmeg
2 cups pumpkin
4 eggs
1 cup vegetable oil
2/3 cups water
1 teaspoon vanilla extract
1 cup pecans

Preheat oven to 350 degrees. Combine flour, baking soda, salt, sugar and spices in bowl; mix well. Make well in center of dry ingredients. Add pumpkin, eggs, oil, water and vanilla; mix until smooth. Add pecans. Pour into two 5-by-9-inch greased loaf pans. Bake for 1 hour. Remove to wire rack to cool. Yield: 16 servings.

Approx Per Serving: Cal 444; Prot 5 g; Carbo 62 g; Fiber 2 g; T Fat 20 g; 40% Calories from Fat; Chol 53 mg; Sod 254 mg.

Pumpkin-Nut Bread

Mrs. Jim Sullivan, Bells

2½ cups flour
1 tablespoon baking powder
1 teaspoon salt
1 teaspoon cloves
½ teaspoon mace
½ teaspoon baking soda
1 cup chopped pecans
½ cup vegetable oil
1 cup packed light brown sugar
2 eggs
1 cup buttermilk
¾ cup mashed pumpkin

Preheat oven to 350 degrees. Sift together first 6 ingredients in bowl. Make well in center. Add pecans, oil, brown sugar, eggs, buttermilk and pumpkin. Blend well. Pour into 2 greased loaf pans. Bake for 1 hour and 15 minutes. Remove to wire rack to cool.
Yield: 16 servings.

Approx Per Serving: Cal 242; Prot 4 g; Carbo 29 g; Fiber 1 g; T Fat 13 g; 47% Calories from Fat; Chol 27 mg; Sod 249 mg.

Zucchini Bread

Mrs. Wilson (Sue) Watts, Springfield

3 cups flour
¼ teaspoon salt
1½ teaspoons cinnamon
½ teaspoon nutmeg
2 teaspoons baking soda
¼ teaspoon baking powder
3 eggs
1 cup vegetable oil
2 cups sugar
2 cups grated raw zucchini
1 cup raisins
1 (4-ounce) can crushed pineapple
2 tablespoons vanilla extract
1 cup chopped pecans

Preheat oven to 350 degrees. Sift together first 6 ingredients in bowl. Beat eggs in bowl until frothy. Add oil and sugar; beat until thick. Add dry ingredients; mix well. Stir in zucchini, raisins, pineapple, vanilla and pecans; mix well. Pour into 2 greased loaf pans. Bake for 1 hour. Remove to wire rack to cool. Yield: 16 servings.

Approx Per Serving: Cal 413; Prot 5g; Carbo 55 g; Fiber 2 g; T Fat 20 g; 43% Calories from Fat; Chol 40 mg; Sod 156 mg.

Angel Biscuits

Annie Mae Reasons, Crockett County

1 package dry yeast
½ cup warm water
5 cups self-rising flour
½ teaspoon baking soda
2 tablespoons sugar
1 cup vegetable shortening
1½ cups buttermilk

Dissolve yeast in warm water. Combine dry ingredients in bowl. Add shortening; mix well. Add buttermilk and yeast; mix well. Add more buttermilk if dough seems to stiff. Place in large bowl; cover airtight. Refrigerate overnight. Preheat oven to 450 degrees. Pat dough out on floured surface. Do not knead. Cut with biscuit cutter. Place on baking sheet. Bake until golden brown. Yield: 24 servings.

Approx Per Serving: Cal 179; Prot 3 g; Carbo 21 g; Fiber 1 g; T Fat 9 g; 45% Calories from Fat; Chol 1 mg; Sod 364 mg.

Fluffy Angel Biscuits

Mrs. Edgar Bell, Jonesboro

2 packages dry yeast
4 tablespoons warm water
5 cups self-rising flour
4 tablespoons sugar
1 cup vegetable oil
2 cups buttermilk

Preheat oven to 400 degrees. Dissolve yeast in warm water. Combine flour, sugar, oil, buttermilk and yeast in large bowl; mix well. Roll out on floured surface; cut with biscuit cutter. Place on baking sheet. Bake until golden brown. Yield: 24 servings.

Approx Per Serving: Cal 191; Prot 4 g; Carbo 23 g; Fiber 1 g; T Fat 10 g; 45% Calories from Fat; Chol 1 mg; Sod 352 mg.

Old Farmhouse Biscuits

Kimberli Fisher, Murfreesboro

1 package dry yeast
1/4 cup warm water
5 cups self-rising flour
1/2 teaspoon baking soda
1 cup real lard
2 cups buttermilk

Dissolve yeast in warm water; set aside. Sift 4 cups flour and baking soda in large bowl. Cut in lard until mixture resembles coarse crumbs. Mix remaining 1 cup flour and buttermilk in bowl. Add yeast mixture. Add buttermilk and yeast mixture to flour mixture; mix well. Turn onto lightly floured surface and knead. Place in greased bowl; cover. Refrigerate until ready to bake. Preheat oven to 425 degrees. Roll out on floured surface. Cut with biscuit cutter. Place on baking sheet. Bake for about 15 minutes. Yield: 36 servings.

Approx Per Serving: Cal 119; Prot 2 g; Carbo 14 g; Fiber 1 g; T Fat 6 g; 46% Calories from Fat; Chol 6 mg; Sod 246 mg.

Working Girl Batter Rolls

Mrs. Kenneth Buchanan, Antioch

"This is a very simple roll recipe — one in which you don't have to let the batter rise before baking," says Mrs. Kenneth Buchanan of her Working Girl Batter Rolls.

1 package dry yeast
2 cups warm water
5 cups self-rising flour
1/4 cup sugar
3/4 cup vegetable shortening
1 egg
1 cup milk

Preheat oven to 450 degrees. Dissolve dry yeast in warm water. Combine flour, sugar, shortening and egg in bowl. Add milk and yeast slowly until mixture is sticky. Spoon batter into greased muffin tins. Bake for 20 minutes. Yield: 36 servings.

Approx Per Serving: Cal 111; Prot 2 g; Carbo 15 g; Fiber 1 g; T Fat 5 g; 39% Calories from Fat; Chol 7 mg; Sod 225 mg.

Idiot Sweet Rolls

Kittie L. Hankins, Greeneville

"Only an idiot would drop yeast batter into a pot of water," says Mrs. Kittie Hankins as she explains this unusual procedure.

1 teaspoon salt
1/2 cup butter
1 1/2 cups flour
1/2 cup milk
2 packages dry yeast
1 tablespoon sugar
3 eggs
1 teaspoon vanilla extract
1 1/2 cups flour
3/4 cup sugar
1 cup finely chopped pecans

Combine salt, butter and 1 1/2 cups flour in bowl; mix well. Heat milk in saucepan to lukewarm. Add yeast and 1 tablespoon sugar. Combine yeast mixture with first mixture; blend until smooth. Cover. Let stand for 20 minutes. Add eggs; beat well. Add vanilla and 1 1/2 cups flour; mix well. Loosely tie in square of cheesecloth. Drop into saucepan of lukewarm water; let stand for 1 hour. Preheat oven to 425 degrees. Dough will rise to top of water. Remove from water. Separate into 1 tablespoon-sized balls. Spread 3/4 cup sugar and pecans on board. Roll dough balls in sugar and pecans to make 6-inch logs. Twist into figure 8. Place on greased baking sheet. Let stand for 5 minutes. Bake for 13 minutes. Yield: 48 servings.

Approx Per Serving: Cal 82; Prot 2 g; Carbo 10 g; Fiber <1 g; T Fat 4 g; 44% Calories from Fat; Chol 19 mg; Sod 70 mg.

Classic Dinner Rolls

Liz Wilburn, Beech Grove

4 to 4 1/2 cups flour
1/4 cup sugar
2 packages dry yeast
1 1/2 teaspoons salt
3/4 cup warm milk
1/2 cup warm water
1/3 cup butter, softened
2 eggs

Combine 1 1/2 cups flour, sugar, undissolved yeast and salt in large mixer bowl. Gradually add milk, water and butter. Beat for 2 minutes, scraping bowl occasionally. Add eggs and 1/2 cup flour. Beat for 2 minutes, scraping bowl occasionally. Add additional flour to make soft dough. Grease top; cover tightly. Refrigerate for 2 to 24 hours. Divide dough into 18 equal pieces. Roll into balls. Place 9 balls each in 2 greased 8-inch round baking pans. Cover. Let rise until doubled in bulk. Bake in preheated 375-degree oven for 15 to 20 minutes. Yield: 18 servings.

Approx Per Serving: Cal 171; Prot 5 g; Carbo 28 g; Fiber 1 g; T Fat 5 g; 25% Calories from Fat; Chol 34 mg; Sod 225 mg.

Homemade Rolls

Mrs. Lynn Smith, Washburn

1 cup vegetable shortening
1 1/2 teaspoons salt
1 cup sugar
1 cup boiling water
2 packages dry yeast
1 cup lukewarm water
2 eggs, beaten
6 cups flour

Combine first 4 ingredients in bowl. Let cool. Dissolve yeast in lukewarm water. Pour into mixture. Add eggs. Add flour; mix well. Cover with wet paper towels. Chill. Roll out dough on floured surface. Cut into rolls. Place on greased baking sheet. Let rise for 1 to 2 hours. Bake in preheated 400-degree oven for 12 to 15 minutes. Yield: 48 servings.

Approx Per Serving: Cal 115; Prot 2 g; Carbo 16 g; Fiber 1 g; T Fat 5 g; 36% Calories from Fat; Chol 9 mg; Sod 70 mg.

Perfect Sunday Dinner Rolls

Mildred Sherrill, Hillsboro

1 package dry yeast
¹/₄ cup warm water
¹/₂ cup sugar
2 eggs
1 cup warm water
¹/₂ cup cooking oil
1 teaspoon salt
4 cups flour
¹/₄ melted butter

Dissolve yeast in ¹/₄ cup warm water. Add sugar. Beat eggs in 1 cup warm water; add oil and salt. Add to sugar and yeast mixture. Add flour gradually. Let stand overnight. Divide dough into 4 parts. Roll out each part; cut into pie-shaped wedges. Roll large end to small end; dip in melted butter. Place on lightly greased pans. Let rise for 1 hour. Bake in preheated 375-degree oven for 8 to 10 minutes. Yield: 18 servings.

Approx Per Serving: Cal 208; Prot 4 g; Carbo 27 g; Fiber 1 g; T Fat 10 g; 41% Calories from Fat; Chol 31 mg; Sod 152 mg.

Light Rolls

Sue Long, Whitesburg

1 cup buttermilk
1 yeast cake
3 tablespoons sugar
4 tablespoons shortening
2¹/₄ plain flour
¹/₂ teaspoon baking soda
¹/₂ teaspoon salt

Heat buttermilk to lukewarm in saucepan. Add yeast, sugar and shortening; mix well. Sift flour with baking soda and salt. Add dry ingredients to liquid mixture. Knead well. Let rise until doubled in bulk. Punch dough down. Shape into rolls. Place on baking sheet. Let rise again. Bake in preheated 375-degree oven for 15 to 20 minutes or until golden brown. Yield: 12 servings.

Approx Per Serving: Cal 145; Prot 3 g; Carbo 22 g; Fiber 1 g; T Fat 5 g; 29% Calories from Fat; Chol 1 mg; Sod 145 mg.

Party Refrigerator Rolls

Marie Swallows, Baxter

1 cup boiling water
1 cup vegetable shortening
1 cup sugar
1 teaspoon salt
2 packages yeast
1 cup warm water
4 eggs
7¹/₂ cups all-purpose flour

Pour water over shortening, sugar and salt. Let stand until lukewarm. Dissolve yeast in warm water for 5 minutes. Beat eggs in bowl. Add yeast mixture. Add sugar mixture. Stir in flour gradually; mixing well. Place in greased bowl; cover. Refrigerate for 12 hours or overnight. Remove 3 hours before baking. Knead; roll out onto floured surface. Cut into desired shape. Place on a lightly greased baking pan. Let rise in warm place. Bake in preheated 400-degree oven for about 15 minutes. Dough may be refrigerated for 1 week; bake as needed. Yield: 48 servings.

Approx Per Serving: Cal 132; Prot 3 g; Carbo 19 g; Fiber 1 g; T Fat 5 g; 33% Calories from Fat; Chol 18 mg; Sod 50 mg.

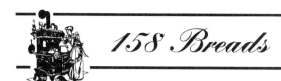

Refrigerator Rolls

Mary Louise Coleman, Charleston

1 package yeast
¹/₄ warm water
1 cup scalded milk
¹/₄ cup sugar
3¹/₂ cups sifted self-rising flour
¹/₄ cup vegetable shortening
1 egg

Dissolve yeast in warm water. Add milk. Combine sugar, flour, shortening and egg in greased bowl. Add yeast mixture; mix well. Cover; refrigerate. Remove from refrigerator 2 hours before baking. Shape into rolls. Place on baking sheet. Let rise for 1 hour. Bake in preheated 400-degree oven until brown. Yield: 24 servings.

Approx Per Serving: Cal 97; Prot 2 g; Carbo 15 g; Fiber 1 g; T Fat 3 g; 27% Calories from Fat; Chol 10 mg; Sod 221 mg.

Easy Spoon Rolls

Mrs. Esco Beaty, Jamestown

1 package yeast
2 cups warm water
4 cups self-rising flour
¹/₄ cup sugar
³/₄ cup vegetable oil
1 egg

Dissolve yeast in warm water in bowl. Combine with remaining ingredients in bowl; mix well. Spoon in greased muffin tins. Bake in preheated 425-degree oven for 20 minutes. Yield: 36 servings.

Approx Per Serving: Cal 97; Prot 2 g; Carbo 12 g; Fiber <1 g; T Fat 5 g; 45% Calories from Fat; Chol 6 mg; Sod 178 mg.

Spoon Rolls

Mrs. Jean Wood, Manchester

1 package dry yeast
2 cups warm water
¹/₄ cup sugar
³/₄ cup butter, softened
1 egg
4 cups self-rising flour

Preheat oven to 400 degrees. Dissolve yeast in 2 tablespoons warm water. Cream sugar and butter in bowl. Add egg, remaining water and yeast; mix well. Add flour, a little at a time; mix until blended. Drop batter into greased muffin tins. Bake for 20 minutes. Batter may be stored in an airtight container in the refrigerator for several days. Yield: 35 servings.

Approx Per Serving: Cal 94; Prot 2 g; Carbo 12 g; Fiber <1 g; T Fat 4 g; 41% Calories from Fat; Chol 17 mg; Sod 223 mg.

Tasty Spoon Rolls

Lettie Byrd, Counce

1 package dry yeast
2 cups warm water
¹/₄ cup sugar
1 egg, slightly beaten
¹/₄ cup vegetable oil
1 teaspoon salt
4 cups self-rising flour

Dissolve yeast in warm water. Add remaining ingredients; beat until well mixed. Place in airtight covered container. Refrigerate. Spoon into greased muffin tins. Bake in preheated 400-degree oven for 20 minutes. Dough may be refrigerated for 1 week. Bake as needed. Yield: 36 servings.

Approx Per Serving: Cal 71; Prot 2 g; Carbo 12 g; Fiber <1 g; T Fat 2 g; 23% Calories from Fat; Chol 6 mg; Sod 237 mg.

Batter-Bread Muffins

Mrs. Hazel T. Jones, Fairview

1 package dry yeast
2 cups warm water
1/4 cup sugar
1/3 cup vegetable oil
1 egg
3 cups (or more) self-rising flour

Dissolve yeast in water in large bowl. Stir in sugar, oil and egg. Add flour, a small amount at a time; mix well. Spoon batter into greased muffin cups. Bake immediately in preheated 425-degree oven for 10 minutes or until brown. Do not allow muffins to rise before baking. May be stored, covered, in refrigerator for 1 week. Yield: 12 servings.

Approx Per Serving: Cal 188; Prot 4 g; Carbo 28 g; Fiber 1 g; T Fat 7 g; 33% Calories from Fat; Chol 18 mg; Sod 402 mg.

Honey-Wheat Bread

Nola Vandergriff, Powell

1 1/2 cups water
1/2 cup honey
1 cup cream-style cottage cheese
1/4 cup butter
1 egg, beaten
2 packages dry yeast
2 tablespoons sugar
2 tablespoons salt
6 cups flour
1 cup whole wheat flour

Combine first 4 ingredients in saucepan. Heat mixture until very warm. Combine egg, yeast, sugar and salt in large mixer bowl, mixing well. Add cottage cheese mixture, 3 cups flour and whole wheat flour. Beat at medium speed for 2 minutes. Gradually stir in enough remaining flour to make soft dough. Turn dough onto well-floured surface. Knead for 5 minutes or until smooth and elastic. Place in well-greased bowl, turning to grease all sides; cover. Let rise in warm place for 1 hour. Punch down. Let rest for 5 minutes. Divide dough in half; shape each half into 1 loaf. Place loaf in greased 5-by-9-inch loaf pan. Cover. Let rise in warm place for 1 hour or until doubled in bulk. Bake in preheated 350-degree oven for 45 minutes. Remove from pan; let cool on wire rack. Yield: 20 servings.

Approx Per Serving: Cal 224; Prot 7 g; Carbo 42 g; Fiber 2 g; T Fat 4 g; 14% Calories from Fat; Chol 18 mg; Sod 710 mg.

White Bread

Sue Waters, Big Sandy

2 cakes yeast
1/2 cup sugar
1 quart lukewarm potato water
1/4 cup melted lard, cooled
12 1/2 cups sifted flour
1 tablespoon salt

Dissolve yeast and sugar in warm potato water (water drained from boiled potatoes). Add lard and 6 cups flour; beat until smooth. Add 6 cups flour and salt. Add about 1/2 cup flour to make dough that can be easily handled. Knead until smooth and elastic. Place in greased bowl; set aside for about 1 hour. Mold into loaves to halfway fill well-greased loaf pans. Cover with towel. Let rise for 1 hour or until doubled in bulk. Bake in preheated 375-degree oven for 45 minutes or until brown. Grease bread with lard. Let cool. Wrap well for storage. Yield: 60 servings.

Approx Per Serving: Cal 99; Prot 2 g; Carbo 19 g; Fiber 1 g; T Fat 1 g; 10% Calories from Fat; Chol 1 mg; Sod 36 mg.

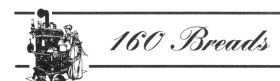

Cream Cheese Bread

Edna Wison, Lafayette

1 cup sour cream
1 1/4 cups sugar
1 teaspoon salt
1/2 cup butter
2 packages dry yeast
2 eggs, beaten
4 cups flour
16 ounces cream cheese
1 egg, beaten
2 teaspoons vanilla extract
1/2 teaspoon salt
2 cups confectioners' sugar
1/4 cup milk
1 teaspoon vanilla extract

Heat sour cream in saucepan over low heat. Stir in 1/2 cup sugar, 1 teaspoon salt and butter. Dissolve yeast in 1/2 cup warm water. Add to sour cream mixture. Add 2 eggs and flour; mix well. Refrigerate overnight. Divide dough into 4 portions. Roll each to 9-by-12 inches in size. Combine cream cheese, 3/4 cup sugar, 1 egg, 2 teaspoons vanilla and 1/2 teaspoon salt; mix well. Spread 1/4 the cream cheese mixture on each rolled-out piece. Roll up. Place 2 rolls in each greased 9-by-13-inch pan. Let rise for 15 minutes. Bake in preheated 350-degree oven for 20 to 30 minutes. Combine remaining ingredients; mix well. Drizzle over hot rolls. Yield: 16 servings.

Approx Per Serving: Cal 432; Prot 8 g; Carbo 56 g; Fiber 1 g; T Fat 20 g; 41% Calories from Fat; Chol 93 mg; Sod 365 mg.

Homemade Bread

Ella Cunningham, Clarksville

2 1/2 teaspoons salt
3 tablespoons vegetable oil
2 tablespoons honey
2 cups skim milk
1 package dry yeast
3 tablespoons lukewarm water
6 cups sifted flour

Place salt, oil and honey in bowl. Scald milk. Pour over honey mixture; let cool to lukewarm. Dissolve yeast in lukewarm water. Add to milk mixture. Stir in flour. Roll on floured surface. Knead for 10 minutes or until smooth. Cover. Allow to rise in warm place until doubled in bulk. Punch down. Let rise again for 30 minutes. Place dough into two 5-by-9-inch loaf pans. Let rise until doubled in bulk. Bake in preheated 350-degree oven for 35 to 45 minutes. Brush with melted butter. Yield: 20 servings.

Approx Per Serving: Cal 160; Prot 5 g; Carbo 29 g; Fiber 1 g; T Fat 2 g; 14% Calories from Fat; Chol <1 mg; Sod 280 mg.

Sour Cream Coffee Cake

Mrs. Ernest Smith, Whitwell

1/2 cup vegetable shortening
1 1/4 cups sugar
2 eggs, beaten
1 cup sour cream
1 teaspoon vanilla extract
2 cups flour
1 teaspoon baking powder
1 teaspoon baking soda
1/2 teaspoon salt
1/3 cup packed brown sugar
1/2 cup chopped pecans
1 tablespoon cinnamon

Preheat oven to 350 degrees. Cream shortening and sugar in mixer bowl. Add eggs, sour cream and vanilla; mix well. Sift flour, baking powder, baking soda and salt together. Add to creamed mixture; mix well on low until thick. Pour half the mixture into greased and floured tube pan. Combine remaining ingredients: mix well. Sprinkle half the mixture over batter in tube pan. Add remaining batter. Sprinkle with remaining topping. Bake for 45 to 55 minutes or until cake tests done. Yield: 16 servings.

Approx Per Serving: Cal 254; Prot 3 g; Carbo 33 g; Fiber 1 g; T Fat 13 g; 44% Calories from Fat; Chol 33 mg; Sod 156 mg.

Monkey Bread

Sweeney Belle Hay, Friendship

1 cup milk
1 package dry yeast
4 tablespoons sugar
1 teaspoon salt
1/2 cup melted butter
31/2 cups sifted flour
1/4 cup melted butter

Scald milk; cool to lukewarm. Dissolve yeast in milk in bowl. Stir in sugar, salt, 1/2 cup butter and flour; beat well. Cover. Let rise in warm place until almost doubled in bulk, about 1 hour. Punch down. Roll out on lightly floured surface to 1/4-inch thick. Cut into diamond-shaped pieces about 21/2 inches long. Dip each piece in 1/4 cup melted butter. Arrange in layers in 9-inch angel food cake pan. Let rise until almost doubled in bulk. Bake in preheated 400-degree oven for 30 minutes or until golden brown. Yield: 12 servings.

Approx Per Serving: Cal 254; Prot 4 g; Carbo 31 g; Fiber 1 g; T Fat 13 g; 44% Calories from Fat; Chol 34 mg; Sod 306 mg.

Tasty Monkey Bread

Pam Morphis, Humboldt

2 packages dry yeast
1 cup lukewarm water
2 eggs, beaten
3/4 cup sugar
1 cup vegetable oil
11/2 teaspoons salt
63/4 cups bread flour
1 cup boiling water
1 cup chopped pecans
2 cups sugar
2 tablespoons cinnamon
3/4 cup butter, melted

Dissolve dry yeast in lukewarm water; set aside. Beat eggs and 3/4 cup sugar in mixer bowl. Add oil, salt and 2 cups bread flour; mix well. Add boiling water; mix well. Add yeast; mix well. Add remaining flour; mix well. Place dough in large bowl; let rise until doubled in bulk. Divide dough into 2 parts. Roll each part into 12 balls. Sprinkle pecans on bottom of 2 greased tube pans. Combine remaining ingredients. Coat each ball with mixture. Stack in tube pans. Let dough rise for 30 minutes. Bake at 350 degrees for 30 minutes. Let cool on wire rack. Yield: 12 servings.

Approx Per Serving: Cal 781; Prot 10 g; Carbo 103 g; Fiber 3 g; T Fat 38 g; 43% Calories from Fat; Chol 66 mg; Sod 397 mg.

Hunky Monkey Bread

Mrs. Eleanor Downing, Pikeville

2 packages dry yeast
1 cup lukewarm water
1 cup vegetable shortening
3/4 cup sugar
11/2 teaspoons salt
1 cup boiling water
2 eggs, slightly beaten
6 cups unsifted flour
1/2 cup melted butter

Dissolve yeast in lukewarm water; set aside. Combine shortening, sugar and salt in bowl. Add boiling water; cool slightly. Add eggs; mix well. Add flour and yeast alternately, mixing thoroughly after each addition. Cover. Let rise until doubled in bulk. Roll out on floured surface until 1/2-inch thick. Cut with biscuit cutter. Dip each piece in butter. Place in layers in greased and lightly floured bundt pan. Cover. Let rise until doubled in bulk. Bake in preheated 300-degree oven for 1 hour or until lightly browned. Yield: 12 servings.

Approx Per Serving: Cal 511; Prot 8 g; Carbo 61 g; Fiber 2 g; T Fat 26 g; 46% Calories from Fat; Chol 56 mg; Sod 357 mg.

Wild Onion Bread

Dee Huddleston, Byrdstown

1 1/2 (3-ounce) packages onion soup mix
3/4 cup hot water
1 package dry yeast
2 tablespoons sugar
2 tablespoons warm water
1 egg
2 recipes Dry Baking Mix
1 cup Sourdough starter

Combine soup mix and hot water. Let stand until lukewarm. Dissolve yeast and sugar with warm water in large bowl. Add soup mixture with egg, 1 cup each Dry Baking Mix and Sourdough Starter; mix well. Stir in remaining Baking Mix to make stiff dough. Place on floured surface. Knead until smooth. Place in greased bowl, turning to grease top. Cover. Let rise for 2 hours. Shape into round loaf. Place in greased pan; cover. Let rise for 45 minutes. Bake in preheated 375-degree oven for 35 minutes. Yield: 24 servings.

Dry Baking Mix:

2 cups flour
1 tablespoon sugar
1 tablespoon baking
  powder

1 teaspoon salt
1/3 cup lard or shortening

Sift dry ingredients. Cut in lard until mixture resembles fine meal.

Sourdough Starter:

1 quart lukewarm water
1 package dry yeast

2 teaspoons sugar
4 cups flour

Place water in heavy bowl. Add yeast and sugar to soften. Stir in flour. Cover mixture with a clean cloth. Let rise until mixture is light and slightly aged, about 2 days. Mixture will thin as it stands; add flour if needed. As you use Starter replace with equal amounts flour and water.

Approx Per Serving: Cal 180; Prot 4 g; Carbo 27 g; Fiber 1 g; T Fat 6 g; 32% Calories from Fat; Chol 14 mg; Sod 303 mg.

Sourdough Coffee Cake

Jan Powell, Woodbury

1 cup sourdough starter
1 cup flour
1 egg
1/2 cup vegetable oil
1 teaspoon vanilla extract
1/2 cup sugar
1/2 teaspoon baking soda
1/4 teaspoon salt
1/4 cup butter
1 cup packed light brown sugar
1/2 cup pecans

Preheat oven to 350 degrees. Combine first 8 ingredients in bowl; mix well. Pour into greased and floured 9-inch pan. Cut butter into sugar in bowl with fork. Add pecans. Pour over batter. Bake for 30 minutes. Yield: 10 servings.

Approx Per Serving: Cal 371; Prot 4 g; Carbo 45 g; Fiber 1 g; T Fat 20 g; 48% Calories from Fat; Chol 34 mg; Sod 160 mg.

CHAPTER 7

Cakes

Little River

Rushing waters of the Little River brush eagerly past the rocks and trees of the Great Smoky Mountains as they swiftly make their way from Gatlinburg to Cades Cove.

Cream Cheese Frosting

Mrs. James K. Anglin, Franklin

"This frosting can be used on Watergate Cake or any other cake you like," said Mrs. James K. Anglin.

1/2 cup margarine
2 tablespoons milk
8 ounces cream cheese, softened
4 cups confectioners' sugar
1/2 teaspoon vanilla extract
1 cup chopped pecans

Melt margarine. Combine with milk and cream cheese. Beat until fluffy. Add confectioners' sugar and vanilla; beat until smooth. Fold in pecans. Spread over cake. Yield: 10 servings.

Approx Per Serving: Cal 429; Prot 3 g; Carbo 51 g; Fiber <1 g; T Fat 25 g; 52% Calories from Fat; Chol 25 mg; Sod 176 mg.

Angel Food Cake

Fay Webb, Dunlap

This recipe is from a 1905 cookbook

1 cup flour
1 1/2 cups sugar
1 cup egg whites at room temperature
1 teaspoon cream of tartar
1 teaspoon vanilla extract

Preheat oven to 325 degrees. Sift flour and sugar in bowl 3 times. Beat egg whites until foamy in bowl. Add cream of tartar. Beat until stiff peaks form. Fold in sugar mixture gradually, folding well after each addition. Add vanilla. Pour into new 10-inch tube pan. Bake for 25 to 30 minutes or until tests done. Invert on funnel to cool. Remove from pan carefully. Yield: 12 servings.

Approx Per Serving: Cal 144; Prot 3 g; Carbo 33 g; Fiber <1 g; T Fat <1 g; 1% Calories from Fat; Chol 0 mg; Sod 28 mg.

Green Apple Cake

Evelyn Chapman, Covington

3 cups flour
2 teaspoons cinnamon
1/2 teaspoon allspice
1/2 teaspoon ground cloves
1/2 teaspoon freshly grated nutmeg
1 teaspoon salt
1 teaspoon baking soda
2 teaspoons baking powder
2 cups sugar
1/2 cup strong, cool coffee
1 1/4 cups vegetable oil
4 eggs, well beaten
1 cup raisins
3 cups finely chopped sour apples

Preheat oven to 350 degrees. Sift first 8 ingredients in bowl. Combine with sugar, coffee, oil and eggs, mixing well. Add raisins and apples. Pour into 3 greased and floured 9-inch cake pans. Bake for 30 minutes. Let cool on wire rack.

Cream Cheese Icing:

8 ounces cream cheese, softened
6 tablespoons butter
1 (16-ounce) package. confectioners' sugar
1 teaspoon vanilla extract

Combine all ingredients except vanilla, in bowl. Whip until smooth and creamy. Add vanilla. Spread on layers of cooled cake. Yield: 12 servings.

Approx Per Serving: Cal 793; Prot 7 g; Carbo 111 g; Fiber 2 g; T Fat 37 g; 41% Calories from Fat; Chol 107 mg; Sod 439 mg.

Apple Pudding Cake

Marilyn Taylor, Benton

1 cup margarine
1 1/2 cups sugar
2 eggs
2 cups flour
2 teaspoons cinnamon
1 teaspoon nutmeg
1/4 teaspoon baking soda
2 teaspoons vanilla extract
3 cups diced apples

Preheat oven to 375 degrees. Cream margarine and sugar in bowl. Add eggs to mixture one at a time, mixing well after each addition. Sift flour, cinnamon, nutmeg and baking soda in separate bowl; add vanilla. Add egg mixture. Fold in apples. Pour into greased and floured 8-by-12-inch casserole. Bake for 45 minutes. Let cool on wire rack. Yield: 8 servings.

Approx Per Serving: Cal 509; Prot 5 g; Carbo 69 g; Fiber 2 g; T Fat 25 g; 43% Calories from Fat; Chol 53 mg; Sod 336 mg.

Apple Cake

Mrs. Elizabeth Proctor, Bells

2 1/3 cups dried apples, finely mashed
2 cups sugar
1 cup vegetable shortening
4 cups flour
4 teaspoons baking soda
Pinch of salt
1 teaspoon cinnamon
1 teaspoon nutmeg
1 cup ground pecans
1 (16-ounce) package raisins, ground

Preheat oven to 350 degrees. Combine all ingredients in bowl, mixing well after each addition. Pour into 4 greased 8-inch layer cake pans. Bake for about 30 minutes or until toothpick inserted in center comes out clean. Let cool on wire rack.

Buttermilk Icing:

2 cups sugar
3/4 cup buttermilk
1/4 cup butter
1 teaspoon vanilla extract

Combine all ingredients in saucepan. Bring to a boil. Boil for 10 minutes or until of spreading consistency. Spread on cool cake layers. Garnish with pecan halves. Yield: 16 servings.

Approx Per Serving: Cal 602; Prot 5 g; Carbo 105 g; Fiber 4 g; T Fat 20 g; 29% Calories from Fat; Chol 8 mg; Sod 261 mg.

Dried Apple Cake

Maudy Lee Barnes, Smithville

2 1/2 cups cooked dried apples
1 cup butter
2 cups sugar
2 teaspoons allspice
2 teaspoons cloves
2 teaspoons cinnamon
4 teaspoons baking soda
4 cups flour
1 cup pecans
1 cup raisins

Preheat oven to 350 degrees. Combine apples, butter, sugar, spices, baking soda and flour in large bowl. Add pecans and raisins; mix well. Pour into greased and floured tube pan. Bake for 45 minutes to 1 hour or until tests done. Let cool on wire rack. Cake will keep for 2 to 3 weeks in tight container. Yield: 16 servings.

Approx Per Serving: Cal 416; Prot 4 g; Carbo 64 g; Fiber 3 g; T Fat 17 g; 36% Calories from Fat; Chol 31 mg; Sod 333 mg.

Banana Cake

Florence Edwards, Finley

1 1/2 cups sugar
3/4 cup vegetable oil
2 eggs, beaten
2 cups flour
1 1/2 teaspoons baking powder
1 scant teaspoon baking soda
1 teaspoon allspice
1/2 teaspoon nutmeg
3 tablespoons buttermilk
2 cups mashed bananas
1 1/2 cups chopped pecans

Preheat oven to 350 degrees. Cream sugar and oil. Add eggs. Sift together dry ingredients. Add to creamed mixture; mix well. Add remaining ingredients; mix well. Pour into 3 greased cake pans. Bake for 30 minutes. Let cool.

Icing:

3 tablespoons sugar
3 tablespoons boiling
  water
1/2 cup butter
1 large banana, mashed
1/2 cup finely chopped
  pecans
5 cups confectioners'
  sugar

Brown sugar in heavy skillet; add boiling water and butter. Beat in banana and pecans. Combine with confectioners' sugar in bowl. Beat until of spreading consistency. Spread on layers and top. Yield: 16 servings.

Approx Per Serving: Cal 567; Prot 4 g; Carbo 82 g; Fiber 2 g; T Fat 27 g; 41% Calories from Fat; Chol 42 mg; Sod 153 mg.

Black Pepper Cake

Mrs. Hooper Finchum, New Market

1 cup black walnuts
1/2 cup vegetable shortening
2 cups packed dark brown sugar
3 eggs, well beaten
3 cups flour
1/2 teaspoon salt
1 teaspoon black pepper
1/2 teaspoon cinnamon
1/2 teaspoon each nutmeg, cloves
1 teaspoon baking powder
3/4 cup milk

Preheat oven to 350 degrees. Place walnuts in boiling water to cover for 1 minute; drain. Cream shortening and brown sugar in mixer bowl. Add eggs; mix well. Sift dry ingredients together. Add alternately with milk to creamed mixture. Add walnuts. Pour into three 9-inch layer pans. Bake for about 20 minutes. Let cool on wire rack. Frost as desired. Yield: 16 servings.

Approx Per Serving: Cal 296; Prot 6 g; Carbo 42 g; Fiber 1 g; T Fat 12 g; 37% Calories from Fat; Chol 41 mg; Sod 114 mg.

Chess Cake

Mrs. I. T. Ballou, Lafayette

2 cups sifted flour
2 teaspoons baking powder
Pinch of salt
1 cup sugar
2 1/4 cups packed light brown sugar
1 cup butter, melted
4 eggs, separated
1 teaspoon vanilla extract
1 cup chopped pecans

Preheat oven to 325 degrees. Sift flour, baking powder and salt together. Combine sugar and brown sugar with melted butter. Add egg yolks and vanilla. Combine with flour mixture and pecans; mix well. Fold in stiffly beaten egg whites. Pour into greased 9-by-13-inch baking pan. Bake for 25 to 30 minutes. Let cool; cut into squares. Yield: 16 servings.

Approx Per Serving: Cal 367; Prot 4 g; Carbo 50 g; Fiber <1 g; T Fat 18 g; 43% Calories from Fat; Chol 84 mg; Sod 185 mg.

Carolina Cake

Margaret Denison, Dickson

3 cups flour
1 teaspoon baking soda
1 teaspoon cinnamon
1 teaspoon allspice
2 cups sugar
¹/₂ cup margarine
4 large eggs, beaten
1 cup buttermilk
1 cup dark corn syrup
1 cup raisins
1 cup crushed walnuts
1 cup crushed pineapple
1 cup mashed bananas

Preheat oven to 350 degrees. Sift flour, baking soda, cinnamon and allspice together in bowl. Cream sugar and margarine in bowl. Add eggs, buttermilk and corn syrup; mix well. Add sifted flour; mix well. Fold in remaining ingredients. Pour into 4 greased layer pans. Bake until toothpick inserted in center comes out clean. Let cool on wire rack.

Icing:

2 egg whites, beaten
2 cups sugar
1 cup milk
¹/₂ cup margarine
1 cup crushed pineapple

Combine all ingredients in saucepan. Cook on low for 30 minutes. Remove from heat. Let cool for 30 minutes. Spread on cake layers. Yield: 16 servings.

Approx Per Serving: Cal 591; Prot 7 g; Carbo 104; Fiber 2 g; T Fat 18 g; 27% Calories from Fat; Chol 56 mg; Sod 260 mg.

Chocolate-Cola Cake

Mrs. Rogers Martin, Sparta

2 cups flour
2 cups sugar
1 cup margarine
3 tablespoons baking cocoa
1 cup cola
¹/₂ cup buttermilk
2 eggs, beaten
1 teaspoon baking soda
1 teaspoon vanilla extract
1¹/₂ cups miniature marshmallows

Preheat oven to 350 degrees. Combine flour and sugar in bowl. Bring margarine, cocoa and cola to a boil in saucepan. Pour over flour mixture; mix well. Combine buttermilk, eggs, baking soda, vanilla and marshmallows. Add to batter; mix well. Pour into greased 9-by-13-inch baking pan. Bake for 30 to 40 minutes or until tests done.

Cola Frosting:

¹/₂ cup margarine
3 tablespoons baking cocoa
6 tablespoons cola
1 (16-ounce) package confectioners' sugar
1 cup chopped pecans

Combine margarine, cocoa and cola in saucepan. Bring to a boil. Pour immediately over confectioners' sugar; beat well. Add pecans. Spread over hot cake. Yield: 12 servings.

Approx Per Serving: Cal 675; Prot 5 g; Carbo 98 g; Fiber 2 g; T Fat 31 g; 40% Calories from Fat; Chol 36 mg; Sod 363 mg.

Chocolate Sheath Cake

Mrs. John W. Clemmons, Lebanon

2 cups flour
2 cups sugar
1/2 cup margarine
1/2 cup vegetable shortening
4 tablespoons baking cocoa
1 cup water
1 teaspoon baking soda
1 cup buttermilk
1/2 cup margarine
4 tablespoons baking cocoa
6 tablespoons milk
1 (16-ounce) package confectioners' sugar
1 teaspoon vanilla extract
1 cup chopped pecans

Preheat oven to 400 degrees. Sift flour and sugar together in large bowl. Set aside. Combine 1/2 cup margarine, shortening, 4 tablespoons cocoa and water in saucepan. Bring to a boil. Pour over flour mixture; mix well. Dissolve baking soda in buttermilk. Combine with cocoa mixture, mixing well. Pour into greased 9-by-13-inch baking pan. Bake for 20 minutes. Combine 1/2 cup margarine, 4 tablespoons cocoa and milk in saucepan. Bring to a boil. Remove from heat. Add confectioners' sugar, vanilla and pecans; mix well. Pour over hot cake. Yield: 12 servings.

Approx Per Serving: Cal 651; Prot 5 g; Carbo 92 g; Fiber 2 g;
T Fat 32 g; 42% Calories from Fat; Chol 2 mg; Sod 274 mg.

German Chocolate Upside Down Cake

Flora Cobble, Mosheim

1 cup coconut
1 cup chopped pecans
1/2 cup butter, melted
8 ounces cream cheese, softened
1 (16-ounce) package confectioners' sugar
1 (16-ounce) package German chocolate
  cake mix

Preheat oven to 350 degrees. Grease 9-by-13-inch baking pan. Sprinkle coconut and pecans over bottom of pan. Combine melted butter, cream cheese and confectioners' sugar in bowl; beat until smooth. Pour over coconut and pecans. Prepare German chocolate cake mix according to package directions. Bake for 50 minutes to 1 hour or until tests done. Cut into squares to serve. Allow cake to remain in pan to assure moistness. Yield: 12 servings.

Approx Per Serving: Cal 635; Prot 5 g; Carbo 77 g; Fiber 1 g;
T Fat 35 g; 49% Calories from Fat; Chol 97 mg; Sod 556 mg.

Old-Fashioned Chocolate Cake

Mrs. Dee Bayne, Watertown

1 1/2 cups flour
1 cup sugar
3 teaspoons baking cocoa
1/2 teaspoon salt
1 teaspoon baking soda
1 teaspoon vanilla extract
1 tablespoon vinegar
1 cup warm water
1/2 cup melted butter

Preheat oven to 350 degrees. Sift flour, sugar, cocoa, salt and baking soda into 8-inch square cake pan. Add vanilla and vinegar to warm water. Pour over dry ingredients. Pour in butter. Mix all ingredients thoroughly with a fork. Bake until cake springs back when touched with finger. Serve plain or top with ice cream and chocolate syrup.
Yield: 8 servings.

Approx Per Serving: Cal 286; Prot 3 g; Carbo 43 g; Fiber <1 g;
T Fat 12 g; 37% Calories from Fat; Chol 31 mg; Sod 354 mg.

Peanut Butter Fudge Cake

Molly J. Copeland, Grimsley

3 (1-ounce) squares unsweetened
  chocolate, melted
1 cup peanut butter
¾ cup vegetable oil
2 teaspoons vanilla extract
3 eggs
1½ cups buttermilk
3 cups flour
¾ teaspoon baking soda
¾ teaspoon salt
2¼ cups sugar

Preheat oven to 350 degrees. Melt chocolate in small amount of water. Cream peanut butter, oil and vanilla in mixer bowl. Add eggs; beat until fluffy. Add melted chocolate; blend well. Add buttermilk; mix well. Stir together dry ingredients; add to mixture. Pour into greased tube pan. Bake for 45 minutes or until cake tests done.

Peanut Butter Fudge Frosting:

2 cups sugar
1 cup light cream
½ cup peanut butter
1 (1-ounce) square
  chocolate

Combine all ingredients in heavy saucepan. Cook over high heat for 3 minutes. Cook until mixture reaches soft-ball stage. Let cool. Beat until creamy. Add a little cream if icing gets too thick. Spread over cooled cake.
Yield: 12 servings.

Approx Per Serving: Cal 835; Prot 15 g; Carbo 106 g; Fiber 4 g; T Fat 43 g; 44% Calories from Fat; Chol 76 mg; Sod 394 mg.

Mississippi Mud Cake Deluxe

Betty Davis, Morrison

1 cup margarine
½ cup baking cocoa
2 cups sugar
4 eggs, slightly beaten
1½ cups flour
Pinch of salt
1½ cups chopped pecans
1 teaspoon vanilla extract
1½ cups miniature marshmallows

Preheat oven to 350 degrees. Melt margarine and cocoa in saucepan. Remove from heat. Stir in sugar and eggs; mix well. Add flour, salt, pecans and vanilla; mix well. Spoon batter into greased 9-by-13-by-2-inch baking pan. Bake for 35 to 40 minutes or until tests done. Sprinkle marshmallows on top of warm cake. Cover with Chocolate Frosting.

Chocolate Frosting:

1 (16-ounce) package
  confectioners' sugar
⅓ cup baking cocoa
1 cup milk
¼ cup margarine,
  softened

Combine confectioners' sugar, cocoa, milk and margarine in bowl. Beat until smooth. Spread on hot cake.
Yield: 12 servings.

Approx Per Serving: Cal 671; Prot 7 g; Carbo 95 g; Fiber 3 g; T Fat 32 g; 42% Calories from Fat; Chol 73 mg; Sod 259 mg.

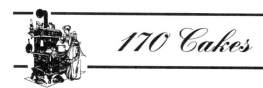

Marvelous Mississippi Mud Cake

June Jenkins, Newport

2 cups sugar
1 cup butter
3 tablespoons baking cocoa
4 eggs, slightly beaten
1 teaspoon vanilla extract
1 1/2 cups self-rising flour
1 1/2 cups coconut
1 1/2 cups pecans
1 (16-ounce) jar marshmallow creme
2 cups confectioners' sugar
1/2 cup butter
3 tablespoons baking cocoa
1/4 cup hot coffee

Preheat oven to 350 degrees. Cream sugar, 1 cup butter, 3 tablespoons cocoa, eggs and vanilla in mixer bowl; mix well. Add flour, coconut and pecans. Beat mixture on high speed for 1 to 2 minutes or until thoroughly mixed. Pour mixture into large sheet cake pan. Bake for about 30 minutes or until tests done. Spread marshmallow creme over hot cake. Cream confectioners' sugar, 1/2 cup butter, 3 tablespoons cocoa and coffee in mixer bowl until mixture is smooth. Spread over cooled cake. Yield: 16 servings.

Approx Per Serving: Cal 570; Prot 4 g; Carbo 78 g; Fiber 2 g; T Fat 29 g; 44% Calories from Fat; Chol 100 mg; Sod 363 mg.

Peter Paul Mound Cake

Opie Henson, Memphis

1 (16-ounce) package devil's food cake mix
2 cups sugar
1 cup milk
20 large marshmallows
1 1/2 cups angel flake coconut
1/2 teaspoon almond flavoring
1 teaspoon vanilla extract
2 1/2 cups sugar
1 cup evaporated milk
1/2 cup butter
1 cup marshmallow creme
1 cup semisweet chocolate chips

Prepare and bake cake mix according to package directions in a 9-by-13-inch baking pan. Let cool completely. Split cake in half lengthwise. Place 2 cups sugar and milk in saucepan. Bring to a boil. Cook mixture to soft-ball stage. Stir in marshmallows until dissolved. Add coconut, almond flavoring and vanilla; mix well. Spread between cake layers. Place 2 1/2 cups sugar, evaporated milk and butter in saucepan. Cook to soft-ball stage. Remove from heat. Add marshmallow creme and chocolate chips; mix until chocolate chips melt. Ice top and sides of cake. Yield: 16 servings.

Approx Per Serving: Cal 629; Prot 5 g; Carbo 103 g; Fiber 2 g; T Fat 23 g; 33% Calories from Fat; Chol 64 mg; Sod 356 mg.

Turtle Cake

Mrs. Roy Crabtree, South Fulton

1 (16-ounce) package German chocolate
  cake mix
1 (14-ounce) package caramels
1 cup milk
1 cup chocolate chips
1 cup chopped pecans

Preheat oven to 350 degrees. Prepare cake mix according to package directions. Pour half the mixture into greased and floured 9-by-13-inch baking pan. Bake for 10 minutes. Melt caramels with milk over low heat. Pour over cake. Sprinkle with chocolate chips and pecans. Pour remaining batter over chocolate chips. Bake for 17 to 20 minutes longer or until cake tests done. Yield: 16 servings.

Approx Per Serving: Cal 400; Prot 5 g; Carbo 54 g; Fiber 1 g; T Fat 20 g; 43% Calories from Fat; Chol 45 mg; Sod 384 mg.

Toasted Coconut Cake

Mrs. Howard Littlejohn, Stanton

1 (16-ounce) package yellow cake mix
1 (3-ounce) package vanilla instant
   pudding and pie filling mix
1¹/₃ cups water
4 eggs
¹/₄ cup vegetable oil
2 cups flaked coconut
2 cups chopped walnuts

Preheat oven to 350 degrees. Blend cake mix, pudding mix, water, eggs and oil in large mixer bowl. Beat at medium speed for 4 minutes. Stir in coconut and walnuts. Pour into 3 greased and floured 9-inch cake pans. Bake for 35 minutes. Let cool in pans for 15 minutes.

Cream Cheese Frosting:

4 tablespoons butter
2 cups flaked coconut
8 ounces cream cheese,
   softened

2 tablespoons milk
3¹/₂ cups confectioners'
   sugar
¹/₂ teaspoon vanilla extract

Melt 2 tablespoons butter in skillet. Add coconut; stir constantly over low heat until golden brown. Spread coconut on paper towel to cool. Cream 2 tablespoons butter with cream cheese. Add milk. Fold in sugar gradually. Blend in vanilla. Stir in 1³/₄ cups coconut. Spread on top of cake layers; stack. Sprinkle with remaining coconut. Yield: 10 servings.

Approx Per Serving: Cal 884; Prot 11 g; Carbo 104 g; Fiber 5 g; T Fat 50 g; 49% Calories from Fat; Chol 123 mg; Sod 589 mg.

Daffodil Cake

Odesia Beaty, Pall Mall

1¹/₄ cups flour
1³/₄ cups sugar
1³/₄ cups egg whites
1¹/₂ teaspoons cream of tartar
¹/₄ teaspoon salt
1¹/₂ teaspoons vanilla extract
5 egg yolks
2 tablespoons flour
2 tablespoons sugar
1 tablespoon grated lemon rind

Preheat oven to 375 degrees. Combine 1¹/₄ cups flour and ³/₄ cup sugar; sift 3 times. Set aside. Beat egg whites, cream of tartar and salt in large mixer bowl for 2 minutes or until soft peaks form. Gradually beat in 1 cup sugar for 3 minutes or until stiff peaks form. Gently fold ¹/₂ cup flour mixture into beaten whites. Repeat with remaining flour mixture. Add vanilla; mix well. Remove ¹/₃ the batter to a medium-sized bowl. Beat yolks, 2 tablespoons flour and 2 tablespoons sugar in bowl for 2 minutes or until mixture is pale yellow. Stir in lemon rind. Fold yolk mixture into reserved egg white batter mixture. Spoon yellow and white batters alternately into ungreased 10-inch tube pan. Run long, thin knife gently through batters to eliminate air pockets and swirl batters together. Bake in lower third of oven for 35 to 40 minutes or until golden brown and wooden pick tests clean. Invert tube pan on bottle to cool. Remove cake from pan. Serve plain or with lemon-flavored whipped cream. Yield: 12 servings.

Approx Per Serving: Cal 214; Prot 6 g; Carbo 43 g; Fiber <1 g; T Fat 2 g; 10% Calories from Fat; Chol 88 mg; Sod 96 mg.

Fruitcake for Diabetics

Mrs. Lofton Stuart, Stanton

2 cups raisins
2 cups water
1 cup unsweetened applesauce
2 eggs, beaten
2 tablespoons liquid Sweeta
³/4 cup vegetable oil
1 teaspoon baking soda
2 cups flour
1 1/4 teaspoons cinnamon
1/2 teaspoon nutmeg
1 teaspoon vanilla extract

Preheat oven to 350 degrees. Cook raisins in water in saucepan, until water is absorbed. Add applesauce, eggs, Sweeta and oil; mix well. Combine dry ingredients. Add to first mixture. Add vanilla; mix well. Pour into 5-by-9-inch greased loaf pan. Bake for 1 hour. This is like good raisin bread. Yield: 10 servings.

Approx Per Serving: Cal 360; Prot 5 g; Carbo 48 g; Fiber 3 g; T Fat 18 g; 43% Calories from Fat; Chol 42 mg; Sod 107 mg.

Japanese Fruitcake

Dot Mullins, LaVergne

1 pound pitted dates, chopped
1 quart chopped pecans
1 1/2 cups sugar
1 cup flour
4 egg yolks, well beaten
Dash of salt
2 teaspoons vanilla extract
3 teaspoons baking powder
4 egg whites, slightly beaten

Preheat oven to 325 degrees. Combine first 8 ingredients in large bowl; mix well. Add slightly beaten egg whites; mix well. Pour into well greased bundt pan. Bake for 1 hour. Yield: 16 servings.

Approx Per Serving: Cal 398; Prot 5 g; Carbo 51 g; Fiber 5 g; T Fat 22 g; 46% Calories from Fat; Chol 53 mg; Sod 79 mg.

Unbaked Fruitcake

Mrs. David Cunningham, Michie

1 1/2 cups margarine
1 pound marshmallows
1 pound graham cracker crumbs
1 pound red candied cherries, chopped
1 pound red candied pineapples, chopped
1 pound pecans, chopped
1 pound raisins
1 (16-ounce) can coconut

Melt margarine and marshmallows in saucepan over low heat until smooth, stirring constantly. Remove from heat. Add crumbs; mix well. Combine cherries, pineapple, pecans, raisins and coconut in bowl; mix well. Add to crumb mixture; mix well. Pour into tube pan, rubbed with oil and lined with waxed paper. Decorate with additional fruit and pecans. Refrigerate for 24 hours. Unmold; store in covered container. Yield: 16 servings.

Approx Per Serving: Cal 949; Prot 7 g; Carbo 131 g; Fiber 7 g; T Fat 49 g; 44% Calories from Fat; Chol 0 mg; Sod 395 mg.

Hurricane Cake

Elise Poore West, Pall Mall

2 eggs
1 cup sugar
1/2 teaspoon salt
1 cup undiluted evaporated milk
2 1/3 cups flour
2 teaspoons baking powder
3 teaspoons instant coffee
1 tablespoon boiling water
1 tablespoon butter
1 1/4 cups confectioners' sugar
1/4 cup (or more) milk

Preheat oven to 350 degrees. Beat eggs. Add sugar, salt and evaporated milk. Sift flour and baking powder together. Add to first mixture; mix well. Pour into greased 9-inch square pan. Bake until cake tests done. Let cool. Dissolve coffee in water. Add butter; stir to melt. Stir in confectioners' sugar. Add as much milk as needed to make of spreading consistency. Frost cake. Yield: 8 servings.

Approx Per Serving: Cal 383; Prot 8 g; Carbo 75; Fiber <1 g; T Fat 6 g; 13% Calories from Fat; Chol 67 mg; Sod 284 mg.

Duff's Hurricane Cake

Hortense Mountain, New Tazewell

1 1/2 cups sugar
2 cups flour
2 teaspoons baking soda
2 eggs, beaten
1/4 cup Coffee Mate
1/4 cup water
1 (16-ounce) can chopped peaches
    with juice
1 1/2 cups milk
1 cup sugar
Pinch of salt
1 cup butter
3 tablespoons cornstarch

Preheat oven to 325 degrees. Combine 1 1/2 cups sugar with next 7 ingredients in bowl; mix well. Mixture will be lumpy. Pour into 9-by-12-inch baking pan. Bake for 35 minutes or until cake tests done. Let cool. Combine milk, 1 cup sugar, salt and butter in saucepan. Bring to a boil. Cook until smooth. Mix small amount of hot mixture with cornstarch in cup, making a paste. Return to saucepan. Cook until thick, stirring constantly. Cut cake into squares. Pour topping over squares. Yield: 12 servings.

Approx Per Serving: Cal 385; Prot 5 g; Carbo 53 g; Fiber <1 g; T Fat 18 g; 42% Calories from Fat; Chol 81 mg; Sod 325 mg.

Harlequin Cake

Eunice Stinnett, Seymour

2 1/2 cups sifted cake flour
2 teaspoons baking powder
1 teaspoon salt
1 cup soft vegetable shortening
1 1/2 teaspoons vanilla extract
1 cup sugar
1 egg, unbeaten
2 egg yolks, unbeaten
2 cups milk
3/4 cup well-chilled semisweet chocolate
    pieces, finely ground
1 cup finely chopped pecans

Preheat oven to 375 degrees. Grease and line with waxed paper two 9-inch layer pans. Sift together flour, baking powder and salt. Mix shortening with vanilla and sugar in large mixer bowl at medium speed. Add egg and egg yolks. Beat until light and fluffy. Beat in flour mixture alternately with milk. Beat just until smooth. Fold in ground chocolate and pecans. Turn mixture into pans. Bake for 35 minutes or until cake tests done. Let cool in pans on wire rack for 10 minutes. Remove from pans; peel off paper. Let cool. Frost if desired. Yield:10 servings.

Approx Per Serving: Cal 554; Prot 7 g; Carbo 55 g; Fiber 2 g; T Fat 36 g; 57% Calories from Fat; Chol 70 mg; Sod 313 mg.

Honey Bun Cake

Jackie Morton, Watertown

1 (16-ounce) package yellow cake mix
8 ounces sour cream
4 eggs
³/₄ cup vegetable oil
¹/₂ cup sugar
³/₄ cup packed dark brown sugar
3 teaspoons cinnamon
2 cups confectioners' sugar
3 or 4 tablespoons milk
1 teaspoon vanilla extract

Preheat oven to 275 degrees. Combine cake mix with next 4 ingredients; mix well. Pour half the batter into greased 9-by-13-inch pan. Combine brown sugar and cinnamon in bowl. Sprinkle half the cinnamon mixture over cake. Pour in the remaining cake batter. Top with remaining cinnamon mixture. Bake at 275 degrees for 50 minutes to 1 hour or until tests done. Combine confectioners' sugar, milk, and vanilla in bowl; mix well. Pour over hot cake. Let cool and enjoy. Yield: 12 servings.

Approx Per Serving: Cal 506; Prot 5 g; Carbo 70 g; Fiber <1 g; T Fat 24 g; 42% Calories from Fat; Chol 81 mg; Sod 287 mg.

Italian Cream Cheese Cake

Mrs. George (Dorothy) Diggs, Paris

¹/₂ cup margarine, softened
1 cup vegetable shortening
2 cups sugar
5 eggs yolks
2 cups flour
1 teaspoon baking soda
1 cup buttermilk
1 teaspoon vanilla extract
1 (16-ounce) can coconut
1 cup chopped pecans
5 egg whites, stiffly beaten
¹/₄ cup margarine
8 ounces cream cheese, softened
1 (16-ounce) package confectioners' sugar
1 teaspoon vanilla extract
¹/₂ cup chopped pecans

Preheat oven to 350 degrees. Cream ¹/₂ cup margarine and shortening in bowl. Add sugar and egg yolks; beat well. Sift together flour and baking soda in bowl. Add alternately with buttermilk to first mixture. Add 1 teaspoon vanilla, coconut and 1 cup pecans. Fold in beaten egg whites. Pour into 3 greased 9-inch baking pans. Bake until cake tests done. Let cool. Combine ¹/₄ cup margarine, cream cheese and confectioners' sugar in bowl until well blended. Add 1 teaspoon vanilla and ¹/₂ cup pecans; mix well. Spread between and on top of cake layers. Yield: 12 servings.

Approx Per Serving: Cal 999; Prot 9 g; Carbo 109 g; Fiber 7 g; T Fat 61 g; 54% Calories from Fat; Chol 110 mg; Sod 405 mg.

Jam Cake

Bertha Orr, Culleoka

This recipe won fifth place in the 1985 Tennessee Dairy Recipe Contest.

1 cup butter
2 cups sugar
4 eggs
1 cup blackberry jam
1 scant teaspoon baking soda
1 cup buttermilk
3 cups flour, sifted
1 teaspoon cinnamon
1 teaspoon allspice
1 teaspoon cloves
1/2 teaspoon salt

Preheat oven to 350 degrees. Cream butter and sugar in mixer bowl until light and fluffy. Add eggs, one at a time, beating well after each addition. Add blackberry jam; beat well. Add baking soda to buttermilk. Sift dry ingredients together. Add alternately with buttermilk to jam mixture, beating vigorously after each addition. Line two 9-inch square pans with brown paper; grease and flour. Pour batter into pans. Bake for 45 minutes or until cake tests done. Let cool for a few minutes in pan. Turn out on wire rack. Let cool completely.

Filling:

1 (8-ounce) can crushed pineapple
1 1/2 cups sugar
1 tablespoon flour
2/3 cup butter
2 tablespoons water

Combine all ingredients in double boiler. Cook until thick. Spread between layers of cake.

Caramel Icing:

2 cups packed dark brown sugar
1 1/2 cups sugar
2 cups heavy cream
2 tablespoons light corn syrup
1/2 cup butter

Combine first 4 ingredients in heavy saucepan. Cook over medium heat, stirring constantly, to soft-ball stage. Remove from heat. Add butter. Stir until well blended. Let cool to lukewarm. Beat until creamy. Spread on sides and top of cake. Yield: 12 servings.

Approx Per Serving: Cal 1105; Prot 7 g; Carbo 163 g; Fiber 1 g; T Fat 50 g; 40% Calories from Fat; Chol 215 mg; Sod 582 mg.

Old-Fashioned Jam Cake

Mrs. William F. Story, Fayetteville

1 cup raisins
2 cups sugar
1 cup vegetable shortening
3 eggs
3 cups flour
1/4 teaspoon salt
1 1/2 teaspoons baking soda
1 teaspoon cinnamon
1 teaspoon nutmeg
1 teaspoon cloves
1 teaspoon allspice
2 cups buttermilk
1 1/2 cups moist jam
1 cup pecans
1 (16-ounce) package dark brown sugar
1/2 cup sugar
1 tablespoon butter
Pinch of baking soda
1/4 cup milk

Preheat oven to 350 degrees. Place raisins in hot water to cover to moisten. Cream 2 cups sugar and shortening. Add eggs, one at a time, beating well after each addition. Sift and measure flour. Resift with salt, baking soda and spices. Add dry ingredients to creamed mixture alternately with buttermilk. Stir in jam, raisins and pecans. Spread in three 9-inch layer pans with waxed paper and dusted with flour. Bake for 25 to 30 minutes or until cake tests done. Let cool. Combine brown sugar, 1/2 cup sugar, butter and baking soda in saucepan; mix well. Add milk. Cook until of spreading consistency. Let cool. Frost top and sides of cake. Yield: 16 servings.

Approx Per Serving: Cal 614; Prot 6 g; Carbo 107 g; Fiber 2 g; T Fat 20 g; 29% Calories from Fat; Chol 43 mg; Sod 189 mg.

Strawberry Jam Cake

Mrs. Ted Horner, Centerville

2 cups flour
1 cup packed light brown sugar
1/8 teaspoon salt
1/2 teaspoon cloves
1/2 teaspoon nutmeg
1 teaspoon cinnamon
1 teaspoon baking soda
1/2 cup buttermilk
3 eggs
1 cup vegetable shortening
1/2 cup chopped pecans
2 cups strawberry jam

Preheat oven to 350 degrees. Combine flour, brown sugar, salt and spices in large bowl. Dissolve baking soda in buttermilk in large mixer bowl. Add eggs and shortening. Stir dry ingredients into egg mixture until blended; beat well. Add pecans and jam; mix well. Pour into greased loaf pan. Bake until cake tests done. Let cool on wire rack. Frost if desired. Yield: 10 servings.

Approx Per Serving: Cal 581; Prot 6 g; Carbo 83 g; Fiber 1 g; T Fat 26 g; 40% Calories from Fat; Chol 64 mg; Sod 156 mg.

Nutmeg Cake

Mrs. Margie Smith, Rogersville

2 cups packed light brown sugar
2 cups sifted flour
1/2 cup butter
1 cup sour cream
1 teaspoon baking soda
1 egg
1 teaspoon nutmeg
1/2 cup pecans

Preheat oven to 350 degrees. Blend brown sugar, flour and butter with fingers in bowl until crumbly. Place half the crumbs in greased 9-by-11-inch pan. Combine sour cream and baking soda in large bowl. Add to remaining crumbs with egg and nutmeg; mix well. Pour batter over crumbs. Sprinkle with chopped pecans. Bake for 35 to 40 minutes or until tests done. Yield: 8 servings.

Approx Per Serving: Cal 497; Prot 5 g; Carbo 69 g; Fiber 1 g; T Fat 24 g; 42% Calories from Fat; Chol 70 mg; Sod 261 mg.

Mandarin Orange Cake

Mrs. Rowe B. Cox, Bruceton

1 (16-ounce) package yellow cake mix
1 (16-ounce) can mandarin oranges and juice
4 eggs
3/4 cup vegetable oil
1 (8-ounce) can crushed pineapple and juice
1 (3-ounce) package vanilla instant pudding mix
1 (9-ounce) container frozen whipped topping

Preheat oven to 350 degrees. Combine cake mix with oranges, eggs and oil in bowl; mix well. Pour into greased oblong pan. Bake until cake tests done. Let cool. Combine pineapple and pudding mix in bowl; mix well. Fold in whipped topping until smooth. Spread over cake. Refrigerate. Yield: 10 servings.

Approx Per Serving: Cal 513; Prot 5 g; Carbo 60 g; Fiber 1 g; T Fat 29 g; 50% Calories from Fat; Chol 86 mg; Sod 475 mg.

Peach Baby Cake

Ruth Lewis, White Bluff

1 cup vegetable oil
2 cups sugar
3 eggs
2 (2-ounce) jars peach baby food
2 cups self-rising flour
1 cup chopped pecans

Preheat oven to 350 degrees. Combine oil and sugar in bowl. Add eggs, one at a time, beating well after each addition. Add baby food and flour; mix well. Stir in pecans. Pour into greased and floured bundt pan. Bake for approximately 1 hour. Let cool for about 20 minutes before removing from pan. Yield: 12 servings.

Approx Per Serving: Cal 455; Prot 4 g; Carbo 52 g; Fiber 1 g; T Fat 26 g; 51% Calories from Fat; Chol 53 mg; Sod 281 mg.

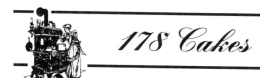

Peach Layer Cake

1 (16-ounce) can peaches, drained
1 cup sugar
2 cups self-rising flour
1/2 cup milk
1/2 cup crushed pineapple
1/4 cup butter
1 teaspoon vanilla extract
2 tablespoons sugar

Sharon Skaggs, Collinwood

Preheat oven to 350 degrees. Crush 3 peach halves in bowl. Combine with 1 cup sugar and next 5 ingredients; mix well. Pour half the batter into greased loaf pan. Layer remaining peaches over batter. Pour remaining batter over peaches. Sprinkle with 2 tablespoons sugar. Bake until cake tests done. Yield: 10 servings.

Approx Per Serving: Cal 258; Prot 3 g; Carbo 51 g; Fiber 1 g; T Fat 5 g; 18% Calories from Fat; Chol 14 mg; Sod 373 mg.

Pecan Cake

1 cup butter
2 cups sugar
6 egg yolks, beaten
1/2 cup molasses
1 teaspoon baking soda
1 cup grape juice
6 egg whites, stiffly beaten
3 cups flour
1 teaspoon cinnamon
1 teaspoon nutmeg
Salt to taste
1/2 teaspoon cloves
1 pound white raisins
1/2 pound candied pineapple
1/2 pound candied cherries
2 pounds pecans, chopped

Mrs. Preston Pruett, Sardis

Preheat oven to 275 degrees. Cream butter and sugar in bowl. Add beaten egg yolks, molasses and baking soda; mix well. Add grape juice. Fold in beaten egg whites. Stir in flour and spices. Add fruits and pecans; mix well. Pour into 3 greased small loaf pans. Bake for 3 hours. Let cool on wire rack. Yield: 24 servings.

Approx Per Serving: Cal 604; Prot 7 g; Carbo 73 g; Fiber 4 g; T Fat 35 g; 50% Calories from Fat; Chol 74 mg; Sod 134 mg.

Pig Lickin' Cake

1 (16-ounce) package butter recipe
    cake mix
4 eggs, beaten
3/4 cup vegetable oil
1 (16-ounce) can mandarin oranges
    with juice
1 (8-ounce) carton whipped topping
1 (3-ounce) package vanilla instant
    pudding mix
1 (16-ounce) can crushed pineapple
    with juice

Mrs. Joyce Buchanan, Antioch

Preheat oven to 350 degrees. Combine cake mix, eggs, oil and oranges in mixer bowl. Beat for 4 minutes. Pour into three 8-inch greased and floured cake pans. Bake for 20 to 25 minutes or until cake tests done. Let cool. Combine remaining ingredients in bowl; mix well. Frost cooled cake. Keep refrigerated. Yield:16 servings.

Approx Per Serving: Cal 333; Prot 3 g; Carbo 41 g; Fiber <1 g; T Fat 18 g; 47% Calories from Fat; Chol 53 mg; Sod 110 mg.

Piña Colada Cake

Mrs. Welton Price, Cornersville

1 (16-ounce) package yellow cake mix
  with pudding mix
1 (16-ounce) can piña colada mix
1 (10-ounce) can sweetened condensed
  milk
1 (8-ounce) carton whipped topping
1 (12-ounce) package frozen coconut

Prepare and bake cake mix according to package directions. Bake in 9-by-13-inch greased and floured pan. Combine piña colada mix and sweetened condensed milk; mix well. Punch holes through hot cake with handle of wooden spoon. Pour mixture over cake. Allow to cool completely. Spread with whipped topping. Sprinkle coconut on top. Refrigerate for 24 hours. Cut into small squares to serve. Keep refrigerated. Yield: 24 servings.

Approx Per Serving: Cal 259; Prot 3 g; Carbo 32 g; Fiber 2 g; T Fat 14 g; 48% Calories from Fat; Chol 29 mg; Sod 171 mg.

Pineapple Crunch Cake

Irene Yoder, Whiteville

1 (20-ounce) can crushed pineapple
2/3 cup vegetable shortening
1 cup sugar
2 teaspoons vanilla extract
2 eggs
2 1/2 cups sifted flour
3 teaspoons baking powder
1/2 teaspoon salt
2/3 cup packed light brown sugar
1 cup chopped pecans
6 tablespoons butter, melted

Preheat oven to 350 degrees. Drain pineapple thoroughly, reserving 1 cup syrup. Cream shortening, sugar and vanilla in bowl; mix well. Add eggs; beat well. Sift together next 3 ingredients. Add to creamed mixture alternately with reserved syrup, beating well after each addition. Spread half the batter evenly in greased 9-by-13-inch cake pan. Spoon pineapple over batter. Cover with remaining batter. Combine brown sugar, pecans and butter in bowl. Sprinkle over batter. Bake for 35 to 40 minutes or until cake tests done. Cut into squares. Serve warm with ice cream. Yield: 16 servings.

Approx Per Serving: Cal 343; Prot 3 g; Carbo 42 g; Fiber 1 g; T Fat 19 g; 48% Calories from Fat; Chol 38 mg; Sod 184 mg.

Plum Baby Food Cake

Nan Gordon, Lobelville

2 cups sugar
1 cup vegetable oil
3 eggs
2 cups self-rising flour
1/2 teaspoon cinnamon
1 teaspoon vanilla extract
2 (2-ounce) jars plum baby food

Preheat oven to 350 degrees. Cream sugar and oil in bowl. Beat in eggs. Add remaining ingredients; mix well. Pour into greased and floured bundt pan. Bake for about 1 hour or until cake tests done. Yield: 8 servings.

Approx Per Serving: Cal 583; Prot 5 g; Carbo 76 g; Fiber <1 g; T Fat 29 g; 45% Calories from Fat; Chol 80 mg; Sod 421 mg.

Fresh Apple Pound Cake

Mable Smith, Fayetteville

3 cups flour
1 teaspoon baking soda
1 teaspoon salt
1/2 teaspoon cinnamon
1/2 teaspoon nutmeg
1 1/2 cups vegetable oil
2 cups sugar
3 eggs
2 teaspoons vanilla extract
2 cups chopped peeled apples
1 cup broken pecans
1/2 cup golden raisins

Preheat oven to 325 degrees. Sift together flour, baking soda, salt and spices. Combine oil, sugar, eggs and vanilla in bowl; mix until well blended. Add dry ingredients; beat well. Stir in apples, pecans and raisins. Spoon batter into well greased and floured 10-inch bundt pan. Bake for 1 hour and 15 minutes or until done. Let cool on rack for 10 minutes before removing from pan. Prick top of cake with fork. Glaze while cake is still hot.

Apple Cider Glaze:

1/2 cup packed light
  brown sugar
2 tablespoons butter

1/2 cup apple cider
1/2 cup apple jack

  Combine all ingredients in small pan. Bring to a boil, stirring until sugar is dissolved. Spoon over hot cake. Yield: 16 servings.

Approx Per Serving: Cal 505; Prot 4 g; Carbo 57 g; Fiber 2 g; T Fat 28 g; 49% Calories from Fat; Chol 44 mg; Sod 215 mg.

Banana-Buttermilk Pound Cake

Kay Davis, Hollow Rock

1 cup buttermilk
1/2 teaspoon baking soda
3 small bananas, sliced
1 teaspoon Fruit Fresh
2 1/2 cups flour
1/2 cup self-rising flour
1/2 teaspoon baking powder
3/4 teaspoon salt
1 cup vegetable shortening
2 1/2 cups sugar
4 eggs
2 teaspoons vanilla extract
1/2 banana, mashed
2 cups confectioners' sugar
1 tablespoon lemon juice

Preheat to 350 degrees. Combine buttermilk and baking soda in cup. Add Fruit Fresh to banana slices. Sift together flours, baking powder and salt. Cream together shortening and sugar in mixer bowl. Add eggs, one at a time, beating until fluffy. Add vanilla. Add buttermilk alternately with flour mixture to creamed mixture. Beat for 2 minutes at high speed. Fold in sliced bananas. Pour into well-greased, floured bundt pan. Bake for 50 minutes. Combine remaining ingredients in bowl. Spread on warm cake. Yield: 16 servings.

Approx Per Serving: Cal 421; Prot 5 g; Carbo 69 g; Fiber 1 g; T Fat 15 g; 31% Calories from Fat; Chol 54 mg; Sod 218 mg.

Chocolate Pound Cake

Audrey Bowling, Savannah

1 cup butter
1/2 cup solid vegetable shortening
3 cups sugar
5 eggs
1/2 cup baking cocoa
3 cups self-rising flour
1 1/4 cups milk
Dash of salt
1 teaspoon vanilla extract

Measure all ingredients 1 hour before mixing. Preheat oven to 350 degrees. Cream butter, shortening and sugar in mixer bowl; mix well. Add eggs, one at a time, beating well after each addition. Add cocoa. Add flour and milk alternately, ending with flour. Add salt and vanilla; beat well. Pour batter into tube pan of which only the bottom has been greased. Bake for 1 hour and 35 minutes. Yield: 16 servings.

Approx Per Serving: Cal 428; Prot 6 g; Carbo 57 g; Fiber 1 g; T Fat 21 g; 43% Calories from Fat; Chol 100 mg; Sod 445 mg.

Pumpkin Pound Cake

Mrs. Hilda Keyees, Alcoa

3 cups sugar
3 cups flour
2 teaspoons baking powder
1/2 teaspoon baking soda
3 teaspoons pumpkin pie spices
1 cup vegetable oil
3 eggs
2 cups canned pumpkin

Preheat oven to 350 degrees. Sift and measure sugar into bowl. Add flour and dry ingredients; sift twice. Combine oil, eggs and pumpkin in bowl; blend well. Blend dry ingredients into pumpkin mixture. Pour into greased and floured tube pan. Bake for 30 minutes. Reduce temperature to 275 degrees. Bake for 30 minutes longer. Let cake cool in pan for 10 minutes. Wrap in foil. Cake freezes well. Yield: 12 servings.

Approx Per Serving: Cal 503; Prot 5 g; Carbo 78 g; Fiber 2 g; T Fat 20 g; 35% Calories from Fat; Chol 53 mg; Sod 163 mg.

Ruth's Pound Cake

Mrs. Ruth L. Lamons, Seymour

2 cups flour
2 cups sugar
1 cup solid vegetable shortening
6 eggs
2 teaspoons vanilla butternut flavoring

Preheat oven to 350 degrees. Combine all ingredients in mixer bowl. Mix on low speed for about 1 minute. Switch to medium speed; beat for 10 minutes. Pour batter into well greased and floured bundt pan. Bake for 1 hour. Yield: 16 servings.

Approx Per Serving: Cal 295; Prot 4 g; Carbo 37 g; Fiber <1 g; T Fat 15 g; 45% Calories from Fat; Chol 80 mg; Sod 24 mg.

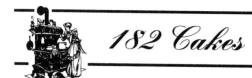

Irish Potato Cake

Joyce Clegg, Nashville

2 cups sugar
3/4 cup butter
4 eggs, separated
1 cup mashed cooked Irish potatoes
2 cups flour
1/2 cup baking cocoa
1 teaspoon nutmeg
1 teaspoon baking powder
1 teaspoon baking soda
1 teaspoon cinnamon
1 cup buttermilk
1/2 cup pecans

Preheat oven to 350 degrees. Cream sugar and butter in large mixer bowl. Add egg yolks and mashed potatoes. Sift together all dry ingredients. Add to mixture alternately with buttermilk, beating well after each addition. Add pecans. Fold in beaten egg whites. Pour into three 9-inch layer pans. Bake for 30 to 35 minutes or until test done. Top with Seven-Minute Icing.

Seven-Minute Icing:

1 cup sugar
1/2 teaspoon cream of tartar
1/4 teaspoon salt
2 unbeaten egg whites
3 tablespoons water
1 teaspoon vanilla extract

Combine all ingredients in double boiler. Beat continuously over boiling water for 7 minutes.
Yield: 16 servings.

Approx Per Serving: Cal 347; Prot 5 g; Carbo 55 g; Fiber 2 g; T Fat 13 g; 33% Calories from Fat; Chol 77 mg; Sod 355 mg.

California Prune Cake

Miss Anna Laura Rupert, Greeneville

1/2 cup vegetable shortening
1 1/2 cups sugar
3 eggs
2 1/4 cups sifted flour
1 teaspoon baking powder
1 teaspoon salt
3/4 teaspoon baking soda
1/2 teaspoon nutmeg
1/8 teaspoon cloves
2 teaspoons cinnamon
1 cup cooked prune juice
1 teaspoon vanilla extract
1 cup chopped cooked prunes
1/2 cup chopped walnuts

Preheat oven to 350 degrees. Cream shortening in bowl. Add sugar; mix well. Add eggs, one at a time, beating thoroughly after each addition. Sift together flour, baking powder, salt, baking soda and spices. Blend into creamed mixture, alternately with prune juice. Stir in vanilla, prunes and walnuts. Spread batter in greased and floured 9-by-12-inch pan. Bake for 40 to 50 minutes or until tests done in center. Frost as desired. Yield: 12 servings.

Approx Per Serving: Cal 355; Prot 5 g; Carbo 56 g; Fiber 3 g; T Fat 13 g; 33% Calories from Fat; Chol 53 mg; Sod 275 mg.

Pumpkin Cake

Mrs. Robert Pendergrass, Pikeville

3 cups sugar
1 cup vegetable shortening
3 eggs
1 (16-ounce) can pumpkin
3 cups flour
1 teaspoon baking soda
1/2 teaspoon baking powder
1/4 teaspoon salt
1 teaspoon vanilla extract
1/4 teaspoon cinnamon
1/4 teaspoon cloves
1/4 teaspoon allspice
1/4 teaspoon nutmeg
1 cup chopped pecans

Preheat oven to 350 degrees. Cream sugar and shortening in bowl. Add eggs and pumpkin; mix well. Add remaining ingredients in order listed; mix well. Pour into greased and floured tube pan. Bake for 10 minutes. Lower heat to 300 degrees. Bake for 55 minutes longer. Let cool. Remove cake from pan and frost.

Frosting:

8 ounces cream cheese, softened
1/4 cup butter
2 teaspoons vanilla extract
8 ounces confectioners' sugar
1/2 cup chopped pecans

Combine all ingredients in bowl; mix well. Spread over cake. Yield: 16 servings.

Approx Per Serving: Cal 572; Prot 6 g; Carbo 74 g; Fiber 2 g; T Fat 30 g; 45% Calories from Fat; Chol 63 mg; Sod 180 mg.

Punch Bowl Cake

Mrs. Ross Broyles, Sr., Jonesborough

1 (16-ounce) package yellow cake mix
1 (4-ounce) package vanilla instant pudding mix
1 (16-ounce) can crushed pineapple
1 (16-ounce) can cherry pie filling
1 (12-ounce) frozen package fresh coconut
1 (9-ounce) container whipped topping

Prepare and bake cake mix according to package directions in sheet pan. Prepare pudding mix according to package directions. Divide all ingredients in half. Crumble half the cake into punch bowl. Layer half of each ingredient as follows: pudding, pineapple, pie filling, coconut, whipped topping. Repeat layers with whipped topping as final topping. Garnish with maraschino cherries. Refrigerate. Yield: 25 servings.

Approx Per Serving: Cal 248; Prot 3 g; Carbo 36 g; Fiber 2 g; T Fat 11 g; 39% Calories from Fat; Chol 22 mg; Sod 237 mg.

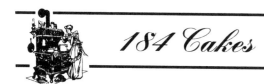

Seven-Up Cake

Mrs. Mable Stewart, Fayetteville

1 (16-ounce) package lemon supreme
   cake mix
1 (4-ounce) package pineapple instant
   pudding mix
1/2 cup vegetable oil
4 eggs
1 (10-ounce) bottle Seven-Up
1 (10-ounce) can coconut
2 eggs
1/2 cup margarine
1 1/2 cups sugar
1 (8-ounce) can crushed pineapple
2 teaspoons flour

Preheat oven to 325 degrees. Combine cake mix, pudding mix, oil, 4 eggs and Seven-Up in bowl; mix well. Pour into 2 greased layer cake pans. Bake until cake tests done. Reserve 1/3 cup coconut. Combine 2 eggs with remaining ingredients in saucepan. Cook until thick, stirring constantly. Spread over cake layers. Top with reserved coconut. Yield: 12 servings.

Approx Per Serving: Cal 606; Prot 6 g; Carbo 82 g; Fiber 3 g; T Fat 30 g; 44% Calories from Fat; Chol 106 mg; Sod 500 mg.

Snowball Cake

Pat Davis, Morrison

2 (1-ounce) envelopes unflavored gelatin
1 cup water
1 cup sugar
1 (8-ounce) can crushed pineapple
Juice of 1 lemon
2 (4-ounce) packages dessert topping mix
1 large angel food cake
2 (4-ounce) packages dessert topping mix
1 cup confectioners' sugar

Combine gelatin, water and sugar in bowl; mix until dissolved. Add pineapple and lemon juice. Chill until slightly thickened. Prepare 2 packages dessert topping mix according to package directions. Add to gelatin mixture. Crumble cake. Add to gelatin mixture; mix well. Place in shallow dish. Let set until thickened. Prepare 2 packages dessert topping mix according to package directions. Fold in confectioners' sugar. Spread over cake. Garnish with coconut. Cut into squares to serve. Yield: 12 servings.

Approx Per Serving: Cal 361; Prot 6 g; Carbo 70 g; Fiber <1 g; T Fat 7 g; 17% Calories from Fat; Chol 5 mg; Sod 435 mg.

Grand Champion Sponge Cake

Mrs. Robert Tegethoff, Mckenzie

1¹/4 cups sifted flour
1 cup sugar
¹/2 teaspoon baking powder
¹/2 teaspoon salt
6 egg whites
1 teaspoon cream of tartar
¹/2 cup sugar
6 egg yolks
¹/4 cup water
1 teaspoon vanilla extract

Preheat oven to 350 degrees. Sift together flour, 1 cup sugar, baking powder and salt in large bowl. Beat egg whites until frothy; add cream of tartar. Gradually beat in ¹/2 cup sugar. Beat until whites are stiff but not dry. Combine egg yolks, water, vanilla and sifted dry ingredients in mixer bowl. Beat at medium high speed for 4 minutes or until light and fluffy. Fold egg yolk mixture gently into beaten egg whites. Turn into ungreased 10-inch tube pan. Bake for about 45 minutes. Invert pan to cool.

Icing:

¹/4 cup butter
¹/4 cup vegetable
   shortening
3 cups sifted
   confectioners' sugar
1 (8-ounce) can crushed
   pineapple, drained

¹/8 teaspoon salt
¹/4 teaspoon vanilla
   extract
¹/2 teaspoon grated
   lemon rind

Cream butter and shortening in bowl. Gradually add sifted confectioners' sugar; beat until light and fluffy. Blend in crushed pineapple, salt, vanilla and lemon rind; mix well. Frost cake. Yield: 16 servings.

Approx Per Serving: Cal 269; Prot 3 g; Carbo 47 g; Fiber <1 g; T Fat 8 g; 27% Calories from Fat; Chol 87 mg; Sod 147 mg.

Strawberry Cake

May McMurtry, Crockett County

1 (16-ounce) package yellow cake mix
1 (4-ounce) package strawberry gelatin
1 cup strawberries
¹/4 cup vegetable oil
¹/4 cup water
4 eggs, beaten

Preheat oven to 350 degrees. Combine all ingredients in order listed in bowl; mix well. Pour into 3 greased and floured layer cake pans. Bake until cake tests done. Let cake cool.

Icing:

8 ounces cream cheese
¹/4 cup butter
1 cup confectioners'
   sugar

1 cup coconut
1 cup chopped pecans
1 cup strawberries

Melt cream cheese and butter in saucepan. Add confectioners' sugar; mix well. Remove from heat. Add coconut, pecans and strawberries; mix well. Spread over cake layers. Yield: 12 servings.

Approx Per Serving: Cal 505; Prot 7 g; Carbo 55 g; Fiber 3 g; T Fat 30 g; 52% Calories from Fat; Chol 103 mg; Sod 390 mg.

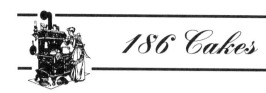

Sweet Potato Pie Cake

Martha Brumley, Mt. Juliet

1 (16-ounce) package yellow cake mix
1 cup butter
4 eggs
2 cups mashed cooked sweet potatoes
1 cup sugar
1 (8-ounce) can sweetened condensed milk
1 1/4 teaspoons nutmeg
1 1/4 teaspoons cinnamon
1 teaspoon vanilla extract
1/2 cup flour
1/2 cup packed dark brown sugar
1 cup chopped pecans

Preheat oven to 350 degrees. Reserve 1 cup cake mix. Combine remaining cake mix, 1/2 cup melted butter and 1 egg in large bowl. Press into 9-by-13-inch pan. Combine sweet potatoes, 3 eggs, 1 cup sugar, 1/4 cup melted butter, condensed milk, 1 teaspoon nutmeg, 1 teaspoon cinnamon and 1 teaspoon vanilla in bowl. Pour over crust. Combine reserved cake mix, flour, brown sugar, 1/4 teaspoon nutmeg, 1/4 teaspoon cinnamon and 1/4 cup butter; mix until crumbly. Sprinkle over pie mixture. Top with pecans. Bake for 40 minutes. Good served with a dollop of whipped topping or vanilla ice cream.
Yield: 16 servings.

Approx Per Serving: Cal 448; Prot 5 g; Carbo 58 g; Fiber 2 g; T Fat 22 g; 44% Calories from Fat; Chol 89 mg; Sod 343 mg.

Texas Tornado Cake

Mrs. Camille Still, Oliver Springs

1 1/2 cups sugar
2 cups flour
2 teaspoons baking soda
Dash of salt
2 eggs, beaten
2 cups fruit cocktail with juice
1/2 cup packed dark brown sugar
1 cup English walnuts

Preheat oven to 350 degrees. Sift together sugar, flour, baking soda and salt in bowl. Add eggs and fruit cocktail; mix well. Pour into lightly greased and floured 9-by-13-inch pan. Combine brown sugar and walnuts. Sprinkle over batter. Bake for 40 minutes.

Icing:

3/4 cup sugar
1/2 cup butter

1/2 cup evaporated milk
1 cup flaked coconut

Place sugar, butter and evaporated milk in saucepan. Boil for 2 minutes. Add coconut. Spoon icing over cake as soon as cake is removed from oven. Yield: 12 servings.

Approx Per Serving: Cal 467; Prot 6 g; Carbo 74 g; Fiber 2 g; T Fat 18 g; 33% Calories from Fat; Chol 59 mg; Sod 464 mg.

Vanilla Fluff Cake

Norine Mabery, Baxter

1 cup sifted all-purpose flour
1/2 cup sugar
1 1/2 teaspoons baking powder
1/4 teaspoon salt
4 egg whites
1/2 teaspoon cream of tartar
1/2 cup sugar
1/4 cup vegetable oil
1/4 cup water
1 teaspoon vanilla extract
4 egg yolks

Sift first 4 ingredients into mixing bowl. Beat egg whites with cream of tartar in large mixer bowl at high speed until stiff peaks form. Gradually beat in 1/2 cup sugar, at same speed; continue beating for about 2 minutes or until whites are very stiff. Make a well in dry ingredients. Add oil, water, vanilla and egg yolks; beat at medium speed for 30 seconds or until mixture is smooth. Add egg yolk mixture to egg whites, gently combining with rubber spatula until blended. Spoon carefully into ungreased 9-inch tube pan 3 1/2 to 4 inches deep. Cut through batter with knife 5 or 6 times. Bake for 1 hour or until cake tests done. Invert pan over large funnel to cool. Frost if desired.
Yield: 12 servings.

Approx Per Serving: Cal 166; Prot 3 g; Carbo 24 g; Fiber <1 g; T Fat 6 g; 34% Calories from Fat; Chol 71 mg; Sod 107 mg.

Wonderful Watergate Cake

Mrs. Dennis Stroud, Sweetwater

1 (16-ounce) package white cake mix
3 eggs, beaten
3/4 cup vegetable oil
1 1/2 cups Seven-Up
1/2 cup coconut
1/2 cup pecans
1 (4-ounce) package pistachio instant
    pudding mix
2 (4-ounce) packages dessert topping mix
1 (4-ounce) package pistachio instant
    pudding mix
1 1/2 cups cold milk
1/2 cup chopped pecans
1/2 cup coconut

Preheat oven to 375 degrees. Combine first 7 ingredients in mixer bowl. Beat on medium speed for 4 minutes. Pour in greased and floured 9-by-13-inch pan. Bake for 45 minutes or until cake tests done. Combine next 3 ingredients in mixer bowl. Beat at medium speed until blended. Add pecans and coconut. Refrigerate before spreading on cake. Keep cake refrigerated.
Yield: 12 servings.

Approx Per Serving: Cal 604; Prot 6 g; Carbo 66 g; Fiber 2 g; T Fat 36 g; 53% Calories from Fat; Chol 57 mg; Sod 579 mg.

Watergate Cake Special

Mrs. Jewel Martin, Allons

1 (16-ounce) package white cake mix
1 cup vegetable oil
3 eggs
1 (4-ounce) package pistachio instant
   pudding mix
1/2 cup chopped pecans
1 cup club soda

Preheat oven to 350 degrees. Combine all ingredients in mixer bowl. Beat for 4 minutes at medium speed of electric mixer. Pour batter into a greased and floured 10-inch tube pan. Bake for 45 to 50 minutes or until tests done. Turn out to cool.

Pistachio Frosting:

2 (2-ounce) packages
   dessert topping mix
1 1/2 cups cold milk

1 (4-ounce) package
   pistachio pudding mix

Combine dessert topping mix and milk; beat at high speed until peaks form. Add pudding mix; beat until fluffy. Spread on cake. Garnish with pecans. Yield: 16 servings.

Approx Per Serving: Cal 387; Prot 4 g; Carbo 41 g; Fiber <1 g; T Fat 24 g; 55% Calories from Fat; Chol 43 mg; Sod 427 mg.

Zucchini Cake

Mrs. Dallas Hines, Mt. Pleasant

3 eggs
1 cup vegetable oil
2 cups packed grated unpeeled zucchini
2 cups sugar
2 cups flour
1/4 teaspoon baking powder
2 teaspoons baking soda
1 teaspoon salt
3 teaspoons cinnamon
1 cup chopped pecans
3 teaspoons vanilla extract

Preheat oven to 350 degrees. Combine first 3 ingredients in bowl; mix well. Add all dry ingredients at once; mix well. Add pecans and vanilla. Pour into 5-by-9-inch greased baking pan. Bake for 1 hour. Test for doneness after 45 minutes of baking. Yield: 10 servings.

Approx Per Serving: Cal 554; Prot 6 g; Carbo 64 g; Fiber 2 g; T Fat 32 g; 51% Calories from Fat; Chol 64 mg; Sod 407 mg.

CHAPTER 8

Pies

Feeding Time

While bottle-feeding one of the family's
Jersey calves, Helen Wengard of Henry
County provides lots of gentle, loving care.
The traditional approach the Wengard family
takes to farming means they all pull together
to make the dairy operation productive.

Apple Pie

Mrs. Thomas Davis, Mt. Pleasant

1 egg, beaten
1¼ cups sugar
¼ cup butter, melted
1 teaspoon cinnamon
¼ teaspoon salt
1½ cups grated apples
1 (9-inch) unbaked pie shell

Preheat oven to 350 degrees. Combine egg, sugar, butter, cinnamon, salt and apples in bowl; mix well. Pour into pie shell. Bake for 1 hour or until firm.
Yield: 8 servings.

Approx Per Serving: Cal 323; Prot 2 g; Carbo 48 g; Fiber 1 g; T Fat 14 g; 39% Calories from Fat; Chol 42 mg; Sod 255 mg.

Two Apple Pies

Mrs. Fred Love, Five Points

2 cups sugar
2 tablespoons flour
¼ teaspoon cinnamon
2 eggs, beaten
½ margarine, melted
4 cups grated apples
2 (9-inch) unbaked pie shells

Preheat oven to 300 degrees. Combine sugar, flour and cinnamon in bowl. Add eggs and margarine; mix well. Add apples. Pour into pie shells. Bake for 1 hour.
Yield: 12 servings.

Approx Per Serving: Cal 414; Prot 3 g; Carbo 60 g; Fiber 2 g; T Fat 19 g; 41% Calories from Fat; Chol 35 mg; Sod 263 mg.

Deep-Dish Apple Pie

Mrs. Geraldine Hewitt, Selmer

2 quarts tart apples, peeled and sliced
¾ cup sugar
½ cup raisins
1 tablespoon flour
3 teaspoons cinnamon
2 cups flour
1 cup firmly packed light brown sugar
½ teaspoon salt
1 cup butter

Preheat oven to 375 degrees. Combine apples, sugar, raisins, 1 tablespoon flour and cinnamon in large bowl; mix well. Spoon into bottom of 6-by-10-inch casserole. Combine 2 cups flour, brown sugar and salt in bowl. Cut in butter until crumbly. Sprinkle over apples. Bake, uncovered, for 35 minutes. Yield: 16 servings.

Approx Per Serving: Cal 299; Prot 2 g; Carbo 47 g; Fiber 2 g; T Fat 12 g; 36% Calories from Fat; Chol 33 mg; Sod 123 mg.

Sour-Cream Apple Pie

Marilyn Noble, Petersburg

2 eggs
1 cup sour cream
1 cup sugar
2 tablespoons flour
1 teaspoon vanilla extract
¼ teaspoon salt
3 cups chopped peeled cooking apples
1 (9-inch) unbaked pie shell
3 tablespoons butter, melted
¼ cup packed light brown sugar
4 tablespoons flour

Preheat oven to 375 degrees. Beat eggs in large bowl. Add sour cream. Stir in sugar, 2 tablespoons flour, vanilla and salt; mix well. Stir in apples. Pour into pie shell. Bake for 15 minutes. Remove from oven. Combine butter, brown sugar and 4 tablespoons flour. Sprinkle over apples. Return pie to oven. Bake for 20 to 25 minutes or until filling is set. Let cool completely on wire rack.
Yield: 8 servings.

Approx Per Serving: Cal 404; Prot 5 g; Carbo 54 g; Fiber 1 g; T Fat 20 g; 43% Calories from Fat; Chol 77 mg; Sod 266 mg.

Sugarless Apple Pie

Julene Purser, Dayton

1 (12-ounce) can frozen unsweetened
   apple juice
3 tablespoons cornstarch
1 teaspoon cinnamon
1/2 teaspoon nutmeg
1/4 teaspoon salt
5 cups sliced apples
Pastry for 2-crust pie
2 tablespoons margarine

Preheat oven to 400 degrees. Combine apple juice, cornstarch, cinnamon and nutmeg in saucepan. Cook until thick, stirring constantly. Add salt; mix well. Add apples; mix well. Pour into pastry lined 9-inch pie pan. Cover with remaining pastry. Prick holes in pastry. Top with margarine. Bake until golden brown.
Yield: 8 servings.

Approx Per Serving: Cal 668; Prot 5 g; Carbo 68 g; Fiber 3 g;
T Fat 35 g; 47% Calories from Fat; Chol 0 mg; Sod 511 mg.

Dutch Apple Pie

Mrs. Hubert Treece, Corryton

2 cups all-purpose flour, sifted
1 teaspoon salt
2/3 cup vegetable shortening
1/2 cup hot water
3 peeled apples, thinly sliced
2 tablespoons flour
1 cup sugar
1 teaspoon cinnamon
1/2 teaspoon nutmeg
2 tablespoons grated orange peel
1 cup packed light brown sugar
3 tablespoons flour
1/4 cup butter
Juice of 1/2 orange
3 tablespoons light corn syrup

Preheat oven to 400 degrees. Combine flour, salt and shortening in mixer bowl. Pour hot water over electric mixer beaters. Beat to combine thoroughly. Refrigerate for at least 30 minutes. Divide pastry into 2 portions. Roll out 1 portion on floured surface. Fit into 9-inch pie plate. Chill remaining pie pastry for later use. Place apples in bowl with salted water to cover. Let stand for a few minutes; drain. Combine apples, 2 tablespoons flour, sugar, cinnamon, nutmeg and orange peel in bowl; mix well. Arrange in pie crust. Combine brown sugar, 3 tablespoons flour and butter in small bowl; mix well. Sprinkle over apple mixture. Pour orange juice over apples. Add corn syrup over all. Bake for 15 minutes. Reduce temperature to 350 degrees. Bake for 1 hour longer. Yield: 8 servings.

Approx Per Serving: Cal 568; Prot 4 g; Carbo 88 g; Fiber 2 g;
T Fat 23 g; 36% Calories from Fat; Chol 16 mg; Sod 344 mg.

Two Banana Split Pies

Delcie B. Lee, Rogersville

3 tablespoons flour
1 cup sugar
1 (20-ounce) can crushed pineapple,
   drained
1/4 cup butter, melted
2 (9-inch) graham cracker crusts
3 bananas, sliced
1 cup broken pecans
2 cups whipping cream, whipped

Combine flour and sugar in saucepan. Add pineapple; mix well. Add butter. Cook over low heat until thick, stirring constantly. Let cool. Line bottom and side of pie crusts with bananas. Sprinkle pecans over bananas. Spread whipped cream over tops. Chill until serving time.
Yield: 16 servings.

Approx Per Serving: Cal 470; Prot 3 g; Carbo 52 g; Fiber 2 g;
T Fat 29 g; 54% Calories from Fat; Chol 49 mg; Sod 273 mg

Banana Split Pie

Thadra Duke, Coffee County

This recipe won fifth place in the 1985 Tennessee Dairy Recipe Contest.

6 squares graham crackers, crushed
6 tablespoons butter, softened
1 (8-ounce) can crushed pineapple
2²/₃ cups instant dry milk
¹/₂ cup sugar
6 tablespoons butter, softened
2 teaspoons vanilla extract
2 bananas
1 cup fresh strawberries, sliced
**1 (16-ounce) can whole black cherries,
   drained**
1 (6-ounce) container whipped cream
8 tablespoons coconut

Combine cracker crumbs with 6 tablespoons butter in bowl. Press into 8-inch square dish. Drain pineapple, reserving juice. Combine reserved juice, dry milk, sugar, 6 tablespoons butter and vanilla in bowl; mix well. Spread evenly over crust. Slice bananas over filling. Top with half the strawberries and cherries. Spread whipped cream over fruit. Top with reserved pineapple and remaining fruit. Sprinkle coconut over top. Chill for several hours or overnight. Yield: 12 servings.

Approx Per Serving: Cal 310; Prot 7 g; Carbo 36 g; Fiber 1 g; T Fat 16 g; 46% Calories from Fat; Chol 45 mg; Sod 242 mg.

Original Diabetic Banana Pie

Mrs. A. H. Finchum, New Market

24 vanilla wafers
2 bananas
2 eggs, beaten
2 tablespoons cornstarch
2 cups skim milk
Pinch of salt
1 tablespoon low-calorie liquid sweetener
1 teaspoon vanilla extract

Line bottom and sides of 9-inch glass pie plate with vanilla wafers. Slice bananas over wafers. Combine eggs, cornstarch, milk, salt and sweetener in top of double boiler. Cook until thickened. Add vanilla. Pour cooked filling over wafers and sliced bananas. Garnish with coarsely crumbled vanilla wafers, banana slices and miniature marshmallows. Yield: 8 servings.

Approx Per Serving: Cal 126; Prot 5 g; Carbo 20 g; Fiber 1 g; T Fat 3 g; 23% Calories from Fat; Chol 61 mg; Sod 90 mg.

Frosted Blackberry Pie

Mrs. J. C. Burkhart, Knoxville

4 cups cornflakes
¹/₃ cup butter, melted
1 egg white
1 cup sugar
¹/₄ cup water
¹/₂ teaspoon cream of tartar
1 teaspoon vanilla extract
2 cups fresh blackberries

Crush cornflakes to make 1 cup crumbs. Combine crumbs and melted butter; mix well. Press into 9-inch pie plate. Chill. Place unbeaten egg white, sugar, water and cream of tartar in top of double boiler. Beat constantly over boiling water for 7 minutes or until thickened and soft peaks form. Remove from heat. Add vanilla; beat until cool. Arrange blackberries in pie shell. Pour frosting over fruit. Garnish with whole berries. Yield: 8 servings.

Approx Per Serving: Cal 234; Prot 2 g; Carbo 41 g; Fiber 2 g; T Fat 8 g; 29% Calories from Fat; Chol 21 mg; Sod 213 mg.

Blackberry Custard Pie

Mrs. T. J. Rogers, Morrison

1 cup sugar
2 tablespoons flour
2 egg yolks, beaten
1/2 cup buttermilk
1 teaspoon vanilla extract
2 tablespoons butter, melted
1 cup blackberries
1 (9-inch) baked pie shell
2 egg whites
1/4 cup sugar

Preheat oven to 350 degrees. Combine 1 cup sugar and flour in bowl. Combine egg yolks, buttermilk, vanilla and butter in saucepan. Add sugar-flour mixture. Cook for a few minutes. Add blackberries. Cook until thick, stirring constantly. Pour into pie shell. Beat egg whites until soft peaks form. Add 1/4 cup sugar gradually beating until stiff peaks form. Spread on custard. Bake until brown. Yield: 8 servings.

Approx Per Serving: Cal 307; Prot 4 g; Carbo 47 g; Fiber 1 g; T Fat 12 g; 35% Calories from Fat; Chol 61 mg; Sod 183 mg.

Butterscotch Pie

Mrs. Roy Myers, Crossville

1 cup sugar
3 tablespoons butter
4 tablespoons cream
1 cup milk
6 tablespoons flour
2 egg yolks, beaten
1 (9-inch) baked pie shell

Combine sugar, butter and cream in saucepan. Cook until thick and brown, stirring constantly. Remove from heat. Combine milk, flour and egg yolks. Stir small amount of hot mixture into egg yolk mixture. Add to hot mixture. Cook until thick, stirring constantly. Pour into pie shell. Yield: 8 servings.

Approx Per Serving: Cal 334; Prot 4 g; Carbo 42 g; Fiber 1 g; T Fat 17 g; 46% Calories from Fat; Chol 79 mg; Sod 186 mg.

Caramel Pie

Mrs. H. D. Rochelle, Bon Aqua

1 cup sugar
5 egg yolks
1 teaspoon flour
1 teaspoon baking powder
1 cup sugar
1 cup butter
1 teaspoon vanilla extract
1 cup milk
2 (9-inch) unbaked pie shells
4 egg whites
1 cup sugar

Preheat oven to 350 degrees. Melt 1 cup sugar in iron skillet until brown. Combine egg yolks, flour, baking powder, 1 cup sugar, butter, vanilla and milk in saucepan. Bring to boil over medium heat, stirring constantly. Add browned sugar to mixture in saucepan, stirring until thick. Pour into pie shells. Bake until set. Beat egg whites until soft peaks form. Add 1 cup sugar gradually, beating until stiff peaks form. Spread over pies. Return to oven until brown. Yield: 16 servings.

Approx Per Serving: Cal 398; Prot 4 g; Carbo 49 g; Fiber <1 g; T Fat 21 g; 48% Calories from Fat; Chol 99 mg; Sod 284 mg.

Cherry-Nut Pie

Mrs. Betty Cary, Holladay

1 cup margarine
2 cups flour
1 cup chopped pecans
3 cups confectioners' sugar
8 ounces cream cheese, softened
2 (6-ounce) containers whipped topping
1 (20-ounce) can cherry pie filling

Preheat oven to 250 degrees. Melt margarine in saucepan. Add flour and pecans; mix well. Press into bottom and sides of 9-by-13-inch baking pan. Bake for 45 minutes. Increase temperature to 300 degrees. Bake until lightly brown. Let cool. Cream confectioners' sugar and cream cheese in bowl until light and fluffy. Fold in whipped topping. Spread over cool crust. Top with cherry pie filling. Chill for several hours or overnight.
Yield: 8 servings.

Approx Per Serving: Cal 910; Prot 8 g; Carbo 102 g; Fiber 2 g; T Fat 55 g; 53% Calories from Fat; Chol 31 mg; Sod 400 mg.

Chess Pie

Mrs. Mark Thurman, Lynnville

1 1/2 cups sugar
3 eggs, beaten
1/2 cup butter, melted
1 tablespoon flour
1 tablespoon cornmeal
1 teaspoon vanilla extract
1 1/2 teaspoons vinegar or lemon juice
1 (9-inch) unbaked pie shell

Preheat oven to 300 degrees. Combine first 7 ingredients in bowl; mix well. Pour mixture into pie shell. Bake for 40 minutes. Yield: 8 servings.

Approx Per Serving: Cal 401; Prot 4 g; Carbo 50 g; Fiber <1 g; T Fat 21 g; 47% Calories from Fat; Chol 111 mg; Sod 263 mg.

Chess Pie Deluxe

Mrs. Earl H. Tignor, Luray

5 egg yolks
2 1/2 cups sugar
1 cup butter
1 tablespoon flour
1 teaspoon cornmeal
1/4 teaspoon salt
1/2 cup wine
1 teaspoon vanilla extract
1/2 cup milk
1 (9-inch) unbaked pie crust

Preheat oven to 350 degrees. Beat egg yolks. Add sugar; mix well. Melt butter. Add to egg mixture. Add flour, cornmeal, salt, wine, vanilla and milk; mix well. Pour into pie crust. Bake for 35 minutes. Yield: 8 servings.

Approx Per Serving: Cal 625; Prot 4 g; Carbo 75 g; Fiber <1 g; T Fat 35 g; 49% Calories from Fat; Chol 197 mg; Sod 436 mg.

Brown Sugar Chess Pie

Ione Lashlee, Camden

1 cup sugar
1/2 cup packed light brown sugar
2 eggs
1 tablespoon each flour, cornmeal
1/4 cup milk
1/4 cup butter, melted
1/2 teaspoon vinegar
1 tablespoon vanilla extract
1 (9-inch) pastry shell

Preheat oven to 325 degrees. Combine first 9 ingredients in bowl; mix well. Pour mixture into pastry shell. Bake for 30 minutes or until center is set. Yield: 8 servings.

Approx Per Serving: Cal 336; Prot 4 g; Carbo 47 g; Fiber <1 g; T Fat 15 g; 40% Calories from Fat; Chol 70 mg; Sod 204 mg.

Easy Chocolate Pie

Rubye Simmons, Cleveland

3 eggs
3/4 cup sugar
Dash of salt
4 tablespoons baking cocoa
2 teaspoons vanilla extract
1/2 cup coconut
1/2 cup baking mix
1 1/4 cups milk
2 tablespoons butter

Preheat oven to 350 degrees. Combine all ingredients in blender container. Blend at medium speed for 1 minute. Pour into 9-inch pie plate. Bake for 25 minutes or just until top is firm. A cake-like crust will form on top and bottom, with a luscious chocolate custard in between. Serve warm or cold with whipped topping. Yield: 8 servings.

Approx Per Serving: Cal 207; Prot 5 g; Carbo 29 g; Fiber 1 g; T Fat 9 g; 38% Calories from Fat; Chol 93 mg; Sod 164 mg.

Crusty Coconut Pie

Ouida P. Meacham, Ripley

1 cup milk
1 1/2 cups coconut
1/2 cup butter, softened
1 1/2 cups sugar
2 tablespoons cornstarch
3 eggs, well beaten
1 teaspoon lemon or vanilla extract
1 (10-inch) unbaked pie shell

Preheat oven to 350 degrees. Pour milk over coconut in bowl; set aside. Cream butter, sugar and cornstarch together. Add beaten eggs and vanilla. Beat well. Add coconut and milk mixture; mix well. Pour in pie shell. Bake for 30 minutes or until pie is brown and center is firm; don't overcook. Yield: 10 servings.

Approx Per Serving: Cal 397; Prot 4 g; Carbo 47 g; Fiber 2 g; T Fat 22 g; 49% Calories from Fat; Chol 92 mg; Sod 236 mg.

French Coconut Pie

Mrs. Leecy Sparks, Speedwell

1/2 cup butter, melted
1 1/2 cups sugar
3 eggs, slightly beaten
1 tablespoon vinegar
1 teaspoon vanilla extract
1 1/2 cups coconut
1 (9-inch) unbaked pie shell

Preheat oven to 350 degrees. Combine first 6 ingredients in bowl; mix well. Pour into pie shell. Bake for 1 hour. Yield: 8 servings.

Approx Per Serving: Cal 458; Prot 4 g; Carbo 54 g; Fiber 2 g; T Fat 26 g; 50% Calories from Fat; Chol 111 mg; Sod 266 mg.

French Coconut Pie in Homemade Pie Crust

Mrs. Ruth W. Whetsel, Whitesburg

3 eggs, beaten
1/2 cup light corn syrup
1 cup sugar
Pinch of salt
1/4 cup margarine
1 teaspoon vanilla extract
1 cup coconut
1 (9-inch) unbaked pie crust

Preheat oven to 350 degrees. Combine all ingredients in saucepan. Cook until butter melts. Pour into unbaked pie crust. Bake for 25 to 30 minutes.

Pastry for 4 Pie Crusts:

1 egg	1 tablespoon sugar
1/2 cup milk	1 teaspoon salt
4 cups flour	1 cup shortening

Beat egg in measuring cup. Add milk to equal 1/2 cup liquid. Combine dry ingredients in bowl; mix well. Add shortening and egg mixture; mix well. Divide dough into 4 portions. Roll 1 portion on floured surface. Place in 9-inch pie plate. Repeat with remaining pastry.
Yield: 8 servings.

Approx Per Serving: Cal 396; Prot 5 g; Carbo 57 g; Fiber 2 g; T Fat 18 g; 39% Calories from Fat; Chol 87 mg; Sod 188 mg.

Impossible Coconut Pie

Mrs. Jack Haney, Greeneville

"Impossible Coconut Pie can be made in a hurry," says Mrs. Haney of her favorite dessert. "It even forms its own crust."

4 eggs, beaten
1 1/3 cups sugar
1/2 cup self-rising flour
2 cups milk
1 teaspoon vanilla extract
1/4 cup butter, melted
7 ounces flaked coconut

Preheat oven to 350 degrees. Combine all ingredients in bowl. Pour into 2 greased and floured 9-inch pie pans. Bake for 25 to 30 minutes. Yield: 16 servings.

Approx Per Serving: Cal 196; Prot 3 g; Carbo 26 g; Fiber 2 g; T Fat 9 g; 41% Calories from Fat; Chol 65 mg; Sod 112 mg.

Impossible Coconut Pie-in-an-Instant

Mrs. W. W. Cruze, Seymour

4 eggs
1 3/4 cups sugar
1/2 cup sifted flour
2 cups milk
1 teaspoon vanilla extract
1/4 cup margarine, melted
7 ounces coconut

Preheat oven to 350 degrees. Grease and flour two 9-inch pans. Beat eggs well. Add sugar, flour and milk. Add vanilla and melted margarine. Stir in coconut. Divide equally into two pans. Bake for 25 minutes.
Yield: 16 servings.

Approx Per Serving: Cal 215; Prot 3 g; Carbo 31 g; Fiber 2 g; T Fat 9 g; 37% Calories from Fat; Chol 57 mg; Sod 67 mg.

Easy French Coconut Pie

Mary Cooper, Maryville

"Oldy but goody," and "so easy," says Mary Cooper.

1/2 cup butter, melted
1 1/2 cups sugar
1 teaspoon vanilla extract
1 tablespoon vinegar
3 eggs, beaten
1 (7-ounce) can flaked coconut
1 (9-inch) unbaked pie shell

Preheat oven to 325 degrees. Combine first 6 ingredients in bowl; mix well. Pour into pie shell. Bake for 1 hour. Yield: 8 servings.

Approx Per Serving: Cal 503; Prot 5 g; Carbo 59 g; Fiber 3 g; T Fat 29 g; 51% Calories from Fat; Chol 111 mg; Sod 268 mg.

Old-Fashioned Cream Pie

Gerry Houston, Silver Point

This recipe won third place in the Tennessee Dairy Recipe Contest.

1/3 cup apricot preserves
1 (9-inch) unbaked pie shell
3 tablespoons sugar
3 tablespoons flour
Pinch of salt
3 tablespoons sour cream
1 cup whipping cream
1 cup half and half
2 egg whites, stiffly beaten
Nutmeg to taste

Preheat oven to 350 degrees. Spread preserves on bottom and sides of pie shell. Combine sugar, flour, salt and sour cream in bowl. Add whipping cream and half and half. Fold in egg whites. Pour into pie shell. Sprinkle with nutmeg. Bake for 40 minutes or until knife inserted in center comes out clean. Refrigerate until cold. Garnish with fresh apricot slices and fresh peppermint leaves. Yield: 8 servings.

Approx Per Serving: Cal 337; Prot 4 g; Carbo 29 g; Fiber 1 g; T Fat 24 g; 62% Calories from Fat; Chol 54 mg; Sod 167 mg.

Anna's Egg Custard Pie

Anna Laura Rupert, Greeneville

3 eggs
1/2 cup sugar
1/2 teaspoon salt
1/2 teaspoon nutmeg
1 teaspoon vanilla extract
2 cups milk
1 (9-inch) unbaked pie shell

Preheat oven to 450 degrees. Beat eggs in bowl until light. Add next 5 ingredients. Pour into pie shell. Place on cookie sheet. Bake for 10 minutes. Reduce heat to 300 degrees. Bake for 30 minutes longer or until set. Yield: 8 servings.

Approx Per Serving: Cal 232; Prot 6 g; Carbo 26 g; Fiber <1 g; T Fat 12 g; 45% Calories from Fat; Chol 88 mg; Sod 309 mg.

Etta's Egg Custard Pie

Etta Slater, Rogersville

4 eggs, beaten
1/2 cup sugar
1/4 teaspoon salt
1 teaspoon vanilla extract
2 1/2 cups milk, scalded
1 (9-inch) unbaked pie shell
Nutmeg to taste

Preheat oven to 400 degrees. Beat eggs in bowl. Add sugar; beat well. Add salt and vanilla; mix well. Add scalded milk. Pour into pie shell. Sprinkle with nutmeg. Bake for 20 to 25 minutes. Yield: 8 servings.

Approx Per Serving: Cal 251; Prot 7 g; Carbo 27 g; Fiber <1 g; T Fat 13 g; 46% Calories from Fat; Chol 116 mg; Sod 257 mg.

Old-Fashioned Egg Custard Pie

Mrs. Dennie Barber, Stantonville

2¹/₂ cups milk
3 eggs
1 cup sugar
¹/₄ teaspoon salt
1 teaspoon vanilla extract
1 (9-inch) unbaked pie shell
Dash of nutmeg

Preheat oven to 350 degrees. Heat milk in saucepan over low heat until begins to boil or foams to top. Set aside to cool. Combine eggs, sugar, salt and vanilla with mixer. Add warm milk; mix well. Pour into pie shell. Sprinkle with nutmeg. Bake for 45 minutes or until soft. Serve while hot or cold.

Pie Crust:

1 cup shortening	1 egg
3 cups flour	1 tablespoon lemon juice
¹/₄ teaspoon salt	³/₄ cup water

Cut shortening into flour until mixture is crumbly. Add remaining ingredients; mix well. Refrigerate overnight. Makes 5 single pie crusts. Yield: 8 servings.

Approx Per Serving: Cal 253; Prot 6 g; Carbo 36 g; Fiber <1 g; T Fat 10 g; 34% Calories from Fat; Chol 95 mg; Sod 143 mg.

Betty's Old-Fashioned Egg Custard Pie

Betty McClaran, Smyrna

3 eggs
²/₃ cup sugar
Dash of salt
2 tablespoons melted butter
2 cups milk
1 teaspoon vanilla extract
1 (9-inch) unbaked pie shell
Nutmeg to taste

Preheat oven to 450 degrees. Beat eggs well. Blend with sugar and salt. Beat mixture until well blended. Add melted butter, milk and vanilla; mix well. Pour into pie shell. Sprinkle with nutmeg. Bake until top and crust begin to brown. Reduce heat to 300 degrees. Bake until tester comes out clean. Yield: 8 servings.

Approx Per Serving: Cal 274; Prot 6 g; Carbo 30 g; Fiber <1 g; T Fat 15 g; 48% Calories from Fat; Chol 96 mg; Sod 205 mg.

Hawaiian Pie

Mrs. Roy Owens, Alamo

¹/₂ cup margarine
¹/₂ cup sugar
1¹/₂ cups crushed graham crackers
3 bananas, sliced
¹/₃ cup lemon juice
1 (10-ounce) can sweetened condensed milk
1 (8-ounce) can crushed pineapple, drained
1 envelope dessert topping mix
¹/₂ cup chopped pecans
1 cup coconut

Preheat oven to 325 degrees. Combine margarine, sugar and crumbs in bowl. Press in bottom of 9-inch pie pan. Bake for 8 minutes. Let cool. Line pie shell with banana slices. Sprinkle small amount of lemon juice over bananas. Combine condensed milk and ¹/₃ cup lemon juice. Spread over bananas. Spread pineapple over above mixture. Prepare dessert topping mix according to package directions. Fold pecans and coconut into whipped topping. Spread over pie. Chill until firm. Yield: 8 servings.

Approx Per Serving: Cal 546; Prot 7 g; Carbo 72 g; Fiber 3 g; T Fat 28 g; 44% Calories from Fat; Chol 14 mg; Sod 331 mg.

Holy Smoke Pie

Mrs. LeRoy Lakin, Knoxville

¹/₂ cup margarine, softened
1 cup flour
¹/₂ cup chopped pecans
1 cup confectioners' sugar
8 ounces cream cheese
1 (9-ounce) container whipped topping
1 (6-ounce) package chocolate instant
    pudding mix
2²/₃ cups cold milk

Preheat oven to 350 degrees. Cut margarine into flour. Add pecans; mix until crumbly. Pat into 9-by-13-inch baking dish. Bake for 15 minutes. Let cool. Combine confectioners' sugar and cream cheese in bowl. Fold in 1 cup whipped topping. Spread over cooled crust. Combine pudding mix with milk in bowl. Spread over cheese mixture. Spread remaining whipped topping on top of pie. Sprinkle additional chopped pecans on top.
Yield: 12 servings.

Approx Per Serving: Cal 395; Prot 5 g; Carbo 39 g; Fiber 1 g;
T Fat 25 g; 56% Calories from Fat; Chol 28 mg; Sod 380 mg.

Japanese Fruit Pie

Mrs. Mary Louise Coleman, Charleston

¹/₂ cup butter
1 cup sugar
2 eggs
1 tablespoon vinegar
¹/₂ cup raisins
¹/₂ cup chopped pecans
¹/₂ cup coconut
1 (9-inch) unbaked pie shell

Preheat oven to 350 degrees. Melt butter; cool. Add sugar; mix well. Add eggs; beat well. Add vinegar, mixing well. Stir in raisins, pecans and coconut. Pour into pie shell. Bake for 40 minutes or until lightly brown.
Yield: 8 servings.

Approx Per Serving: Cal 438; Prot 4 g; Carbo 47 g; Fiber 2 g;
T Fat 27 g; 54% Calories from Fat; Chol 84 mg; Sod 258 mg.

Ah-So Fruit Pie

Mrs. Jack Haney, Greeneville

2 eggs, beaten
¹/₂ cup melted butter
1 cup raisins
1 cup coconut
¹/₂ cup chopped pecans
1 teaspoon vinegar
1 cup sugar
1 (9-inch) unbaked pie shell

Preheat oven to 300 degrees. Combine first 7 ingredients in bowl. Blend well. Pour into pie shell. Bake for 50 minutes to 1 hour. Yield: 8 servings.

Approx Per Serving: Cal 490; Prot 5 g; Carbo 57 g; Fiber 3 g;
T Fat 29g; 51% Calories from Fat; Chol 84 mg; Sod 260 mg.

Gelatin and Fruit Pie

Connie Bates, Trenton

1 (3-ounce) package nutra-sweet gelatin
1 1/2 cups water
3 tablespoons cornstarch
6 packets artificial sweetener
1 (16-ounce) can favorite fruit, drained
1 (9-inch) baked pastry shell

Combine gelatin, water and cornstarch. Microwave for 3 minutes or until mixture thickens. Quick cool by setting bowl in sink of ice water. Add sweetener and fruit. Pour mixture into pie shell. Yield: 8 servings.

Approx Per Serving: Cal 201; Prot 8 g; Carbo 25 g; Fiber <1 g; T Fat 8 g; 35% Calories from Fat; Chol 0 mg; Sod 358 mg.

Frozen Lemon Icebox Pie

Sue McGill, Rockford

This pie is quick, light and very, very good!

1 cup frozen lemon juice, thawed
2 (3-ounce) packages lemon sugar-free gelatin
1/2 gallon frozen vanilla low-fat yogurt
1 cup whipped topping
10 packets Equal sweetener
24 plain graham cracker squares

Bring lemon juice and gelatin to a boil in small saucepan, stirring until dissolved. Blend yogurt, whipped topping and Equal on low speed in large mixer bowl. Slowly add gelatin-juice mixture to yogurt mixture, blending well. Line 13-inch dish with graham cracker squares. Pour yogurt mixture on top, spreading evenly. Top with more graham cracker squares. Cover with plastic wrap. Freeze. Cut pie into squares; wrap each square in plastic wrap. Serve as sandwich. It's quick, light and very, very good! Yield: 12 servings.

Approx Per Serving: Cal 271; Prot 15 g; Carbo 44 g; Fiber <1 g; T Fat 5 g; 16% Calories from Fat; Chol 7 mg; Sod 476 mg.

Lemon Meringue Pie

Dixie Nell Lehman, McEwen

1 cup sugar
1/2 cup flour
2 cups boiling water
2 egg yolks, beaten
Juice of 3 lemons
2 tablespoons butter
1/8 teaspoon salt
1 (9-inch) baked pie shell
2 egg whites
1/4 teaspoon cream of tartar
1/4 cup sugar

Preheat oven to 350 degrees. Combine 1 cup sugar and flour in saucepan. Slowly add boiling water. Cook over high heat until mixture boils; reduce heat. Cook until thick, stirring constantly. Remove from heat. Add eggs gradually, beating continuously. Return to heat. Cook for 2 minutes. Remove from heat. Add lemon juice, butter and salt. Mix well. Pour into pie shell. Beat egg whites with cream of tartar until soft peaks form. Add 1/4 cup sugar. Beat until stiff peaks form. Pour on pie; seal edges. Bake until brown. Yield: 8 servings.

Approx Per Serving: Cal 317; Prot 4 g; Carbo 50 g; Fiber 1 g; T Fat 12 g; 34% Calories from Fat; Chol 61 mg; Sod 201 mg.

Sugar-Free Lemon Pie

Lillian Milburn, Manchester

1 (5-ounce) package sugar-free lemon
  gelatin
1 cup boiling water
1 (8-ounce) container sugar-free lemon
  yogurt
1 (9-inch) pie baked pie shell

Dissolve gelatin in boiling water. Add yogurt; stir until smooth. Refrigerate for 15 to 30 minutes or until slightly set. Pour into pie shell. Refrigerate until set. Yield: 8 servings.

Approx Per Serving: Cal 135; Prot 3 g; Carbo 13 g; Fiber <1 g; T Fat 8 g; 52% Calories from Fat; Chol 1 mg; Sod 165 mg.

Ice Cream Tropical Pie

Mae Jackson, Sparta

1 cup cornflake crumbs
2 tablespoons sugar
1/3 cup melted butter
1 cup milk or half-and-half
1 (3-ounce) package vanilla instant
  pudding mix
1 pint vanilla ice cream, slightly softened
1 1/2 cups crushed pineapple
1/2 cup pineapple juice
1 tablespoon cornstarch

Blend crumbs, sugar and butter in bowl until well mixed. Press into 9-inch pie plate. Chill. Pour milk into mixing bowl. Add pudding mix and ice cream. Beat slowly for 1 or 2 minutes or until well blended. Pour into crust. Refrigerate. Drain pineapple reserving 1/2 cup juice. Add juice to cornstarch gradually in saucepan, stirring to keep mixture smooth. Cook over low heat, stirring constantly, until mixture is thickened and clear. Add pineapple; mix well. Let cool. Spoon over pie. Chill for at least 1 hour before serving. Yield: 8 servings.

Approx Per Serving: Cal 296; Prot 3 g; Carbo 45 g; Fiber 1 g; T Fat 13 g; 37% Calories from Fat; Chol 39 mg; Sod 394 mg.

Oatmeal Pie

Mrs. Archie Robertson, Martin

3 eggs, beaten
1 cup sugar
3/4 cup dark corn syrup
1/2 cup milk
1/8 teaspoon salt
1 teaspoon vanilla extract
6 tablespoons butter
3/4 cup uncooked quick-cooking oats
1/4 cup chopped pecans
1 (9-inch) unbaked pie shell

Preheat oven to 300 degrees. Combine eggs, sugar, syrup, milk, salt, vanilla and melted butter in saucepan. Heat until warm. Add oats and pecans. Pour into pie shell. Bake for 45 minutes or until firm. Yield: 8 servings.

Approx Per Serving: Cal 470; Prot 6 g; Carbo 66 g; Fiber 1 g; T Fat 22 g; 41% Calories from Fat; Chol 105 mg; Sod 322 mg.

Parfait Pie

Mrs. Rosemary Cates, Alamo

2 eggs
1 cup sugar
1 1/2 cups pineapple juice
1 (3-ounce) package orange gelatin
1 (14-ounce) can evaporated milk, chilled
2 (9-inch) graham cracker crumb crusts

Combine eggs, sugar and pineapple juice in saucepan. Cook until mixture thickens, about as thick as soft custard, stirring constantly. Add gelatin. Let cool. Whip evaporated milk until thick. Add pineapple mixture to whipped milk. Pour into pie crusts. Sprinkle graham cracker or vanilla wafer crumbs on top. Refrigerate for about 2 hours before serving. Yield: 16 servings.

Approx Per Serving: Cal 325; Prot 5 g; Carbo 40 g; Fiber 1 g; T Fat 13 g; 34% Calories from Fat; Chol 34 mg; Sod 280 mg.

Pecan Pie

Ollie Mae Sesler, Charlotte

3 eggs
1 cup sugar
1/2 cup dark corn syrup
1/4 cup melted butter
Dash of salt
1 teaspoon vanilla extract
1 cup chopped pecans
1 (9-inch) unbaked pie shell

Preheat oven to 350 degrees. Combine first 7 ingredients in bowl. Pour into pie shell. Bake until center is almost set. Pie becomes firm when cool. Yield: 8 servings.

Approx Per Serving: Cal 451; Prot 5 g; Carbo 54 g; Fiber 1 g; T Fat 26 g; 49% Calories from Fat; Chol 95 mg; Sod 229 mg.

Crustless Pecan Pie

Linda Huling, Ten Mile

3 egg whites
1 cup sugar
1 cup vinegar
1 teaspoon baking powder
1 teaspoon vanilla extract
1 cup pecans
20 Ritz crackers, crushed

Preheat oven to 350 degrees. Beat egg whites until very stiff. Gradually add sugar. Fold in remaining ingredients. Pour in well greased 9-inch pie plate. Bake for 25 minutes. Yield: 8 servings.

Approx Per Serving: Cal 148; Prot 3 g; Carbo 9 g; Fiber 1 g; T Fat 12 g; 69% Calories from Fat; Chol 0 mg; Sod 126 mg.

Honey-Pecan Pie

May McMurtry, Humboldt

1/4 cup butter
1/2 cup packed dark brown sugar
3 eggs
3/4 cup honey
1 teaspoon vanilla extract
Pinch of salt
1 cup pecans
1 (8-inch) unbaked pie shell

Preheat oven to 450 degrees. Melt butter in saucepan. Add brown sugar; stir to melt. Remove from heat. Beat in eggs, 1 at a time. Add honey, vanilla, salt and pecans. Pour into pie shell. Bake for 10 minutes. Reduce heat to 350 degrees. Bake for 30 minutes longer or until custard is set. Yield: 6 servings.

Approx Per Serving: Cal 564; Prot 7 g; Carbo 66 g; Fiber 2 g; T Fat 33 g; 50% Calories from Fat; Chol 127 mg; Sod 262 mg.

Butter Pecan Pie

Linda Marshall, Russellville

¹/₂ cup sugar
¹/₂ cup packed dark brown sugar
2 tablespoons cornstarch
2 egg yolks, beaten
1 cup 2% milk
¹/₂ cup evaporated milk
¹/₂ cup chopped pecans
1 tablespoon butter
1 teaspoon vanilla extract
¹/₂ teaspoon maple flavoring
1 (9-inch) baked pie shell
2 tablespoons sugar
1 tablespoon cornstarch
¹/₂ cup water
2 egg whites
¹/₈ teaspoon salt
4 tablespoons sugar
¹/₂ teaspoon vanilla extract

Preheat oven to 350 degrees. Combine ¹/₂ cup sugar, brown sugar and 2 tablespoons cornstarch in saucepan. Beat egg yolks, milk and evaporated milk in bowl. Add to sugar mixture. Cook until thickened, stirring constantly. Add pecans, butter and flavorings. Pour into pie shell. Combine 2 tablespoons sugar with 1 tablespoon cornstarch and water in small pan. Cook over medium heat, stirring constantly, until mixture is thick and clear. Beat egg whites with salt and 4 tablespoons sugar until soft peaks form. Beat in vanilla. Spread over filling. Bake for about 20 minutes or until browned.
Yield: 8 servings.

Pie Crusts:

2 cups sifted flour	**1 egg, beaten**
1 teaspoon salt	**2 teaspoons vinegar**
¹/₂ cup shortening	**¹/₄ to ¹/₃ cold water**

Preheat oven to 400 degrees. Sift flour and salt. Cut in shortening until mixture is crumbly. Combine egg, vinegar and water. Add to flour mixture. Form into ball. Roll out immediately on floured surface or chill for later use or freeze. Bake for 15 minutes or until browned.
Yield: Two 9-inch crusts.

Approx Per Serving: Cal 370; Prot 6 g; Carbo 51 g; Fiber 1 g; T Fat 16 g; 39% Calories from Fat; Chol 77 mg; Sod 238 mg.

Southern Pecan Pie

Jane W. Bruhin, Knoxville

¹/₃ cup shortening
1 cup sifted flour
¹/₂ teaspoon salt
3 to 4 tablespoons ice water
1 cup pecan halves or pieces
3 eggs
1 cup light corn syrup
1 tablespoon melted butter
¹/₂ teaspoon vanilla extract
1 tablespoon flour
1 cup sugar

Preheat oven to 350 degrees. Cut shortening into flour and salt. Add ice water to mixture, 1 tablespoon at a time, until moist enough to hold together well. Roll out on floured surface. Fit into 9-inch pie pan. Flute edges. Arrange pecans in pie shell. Beat eggs until well mixed but not foamy. Add corn syrup, melted butter and vanilla to eggs. Combine 1 tablespoon flour and sugar; add to egg mixture. Pour over pecans in pie shell. Let stand until pecans rise to top. Bake for 45 minutes or until center is set. During the last few minutes of baking, cover pie with aluminum foil so pecans will not become too brown.
Yield: 8 servings.

Approx Per Serving: Cal 474; Prot 5 g; Carbo 71 g; Fiber 1 g; T Fat 21 g; 39% Calories from Fat; Chol 83 mg; Sod 222 mg.

Peach Custard Pie

Mrs. Louise Small, Lexington

¹/₂ pound dried peaches
7 packets Sweet 'n' Low
3 tablespoons flour
7 packets Sweet 'n' Low
1 egg
1¹/₂ cups milk
1 tablespoon butter
1 teaspoon vanilla extract
1 (9-inch) baked pie crust
1 package D-Zerta whipped topping mix

Cook peaches until tender. Add 7 packets Sweet 'n' Low; mix well. Set aside to cool. Combine flour, 7 packets Sweet 'n' Low and egg in top of double boiler; mix well. Beat for few minutes. Add milk gradually; cook until thickened. Add butter and vanilla. Place cooked peaches in pie crust. Top with custard. Prepare D-Zerta whipped topping mix according to package directions. Spread topping over custard. Yield: 8 servings.

Approx Per Serving: Cal 291; Prot 6 g; Carbo 38 g; Fiber 3 g; T Fat 14 g; 42% Calories from Fat; Chol 39 mg; Sod 189 mg.

Peaches 'n' Cream Pie

Bettye Ammons, Hohenwald

8 ounces cream cheese, softened
2 tablespoons sugar
2 tablespoons milk
2 cups whipped topping
1 (9-inch) baked pie shell, cooled
2 peeled medium peaches, pitted and diced
1 (3-ounce) package vanilla instant pudding mix
1 cup cold milk
¹/₄ teaspoon almond extract
1¹/₂ cups whipped topping

Beat cream cheese until smooth. Blend in sugar and 2 tablespoons milk. Fold in 2 cups whipped topping. Spread on crust. Top with diced peaches, pressing down lightly. Chill. Prepare pudding mix with 1 cup milk according to package directions. Add almond extract. Let set for 5 minutes. Fold in 1¹/₂ cups whipped topping. Spoon over cream cheese mixture. Freeze for 1 hour or refrigerate for 3 hours before serving. Garnish with whipped topping and peach slices. Yield: 8 servings.

Approx Per Serving: Cal 403; Prot 5 g; Carbo 36 g; Fiber 1 g; T Fat 27 g; 60% Calories from Fat; Chol 36 mg; Sod 384 mg.

Frozen Pineapple Pie

Doris Lindsey, Collinwood

¹/₂ cup butter
1 cup confectioners' sugar
2 eggs, beaten
24 vanilla wafers, crushed
1 cup whipping cream
1 (8-ounce) can crushed pineapple
1 (10-ounce) bottle maraschino cherries, drained

Cream butter and sugar together slowly. Add eggs. Line 8-inch square pan with vanilla wafer crumbs. Pour mixture over crumbs. Whip cream. Add pineapple and cherries. Spread over first mixture. Freeze overnight. Yield: 6 servings.

Approx Per Serving: Cal 530; Prot 4 g; Carbo 54 g; Fiber 1 g; T Fat 34 g; 57% Calories from Fat; Chol 176 mg; Sod 243 mg.

Pinto Bean Pie

1/2 cup pinto beans, cooked and drained
1/2 cup coconut
1 3/4 cups sugar
2 eggs
1 teaspoon vanilla extract
1 (9-inch) unbaked pie shell

Mrs. Alonzo H. Breeding, Crossville

Preheat oven to 350 degrees. Place first 5 ingredients in mixing bowl; beat well. Pour into pie shell. Bake for 45 minutes. Yield: 8 servings.

Approx Per Serving: Cal 367; Prot 6 g; Carbo 63 g; Fiber 3 g; T Fat 11 g; 26% Calories from Fat; Chol 53 mg; Sod 141 mg.

Nutty Pinto Bean Pie

1 cup cooked unseasoned pinto beans, mashed
4 eggs
3 cups sugar
1 cup butter, melted
1 (4-ounce) can coconut
1 cup chopped pecans
1 teaspoon vanilla extract
3 (9-inch) pie shells

Mrs. John Cox, Maynardville

Preheat oven to 300 degrees. Combine first 7 ingredients in order listed in bowl; mix well. Pour into 3 pie shells. Bake for 1 hour. Yield: 24 servings.

Approx Per Serving: Cal 359; Prot 4 g; Carbo 40 g; Fiber 2 g; T Fat 21 g; 52% Calories from Fat; Chol 56 mg; Sod 212 mg.

Iced Pinto Bean Pie

3 eggs
1 1/2 cups sugar
1 cup milk
1 teaspoon vanilla extract
1/4 cup melted butter
1/2 cup flour
1/4 teaspoon salt
1 teaspoon baking powder
2 cups well-cooked pinto beans, mashed
1 (9-inch) unbaked pie crust

Mattie Hankins, Pikeville

Preheat oven to 350 degrees. Beat eggs well. Add next 8 ingredients; mix well. Pour into pie crust. Bake until brown and tests done. Top with white icing or cocoa, if desired. Yield: 8 servings.

Approx Per Serving: Cal 449; Prot 9 g; Carbo 67 g; Fiber 5 g; T Fat 17 g; 33% Calories from Fat; Chol 99 mg; Sod 328 mg.

Pumpkin Pie

Mrs. Irene A. Greene, Sparta

1 1/2 cups cooked pumpkin
1 cup packed light brown sugar
1/2 teaspoon cinnamon
1/8 teaspoon allspice
1/8 teaspoon nutmegt
2 tablespoons honey
3 eggs
1 (10-ounce) can sweetened condensed
  milk
1 (9-inch) unbaked pie shell

Preheat oven to 425 degrees. Combine pumpkin, brown sugar, spices and honey in bowl; mix well. Add eggs and condensed milk; mix thoroughly. Pour mixture into pie shell. Bake for 40 to 45 minutes or until knife inserted in center comes out clean. Yield: 8 servings.

Approx Per Serving: Cal 371; Prot 7 g; Carbo 59 g; Fiber 1 g; T Fat 13 g; 30% Calories from Fat; Chol 91 mg; Sod 200 mg.

Coconut-Pumpkin Pie

Mildred Cunningham, Michie

3 eggs, beaten
1 1/2 cups sugar
1 tablespoon vinegar
1 tablespoon vanilla extract
1 teaspoon orange flavoring
1/2 cup butter
1 (8-ounce) can coconut
1 (16-ounce) can pumpkin pie filling
1 (9-inch) unbaked pie shell

Preheat oven to 350 degrees. Combine first 8 ingredients in bowl; mix well. Pour into pie shell. Bake for 20 minutes. Reduce heat to 300 degrees. Bake for 1 hour longer. Yield: 8 servings.

Approx Per Serving: Cal 584; Prot 5 g; Carbo 76 g; Fiber 4 g; T Fat 30 g; 46% Calories from Fat; Chol 111 mg; Sod 387 mg.

David's Pumpkin Pie

Jane Ann Lane, Jackson

1 teaspoon flour
2 eggs, slightly beaten
16 ounces mashed cooked pumpkin
1/2 cup Sprinkle Sweet
1/4 cup sugar
1/2 teaspoon salt
1 teaspoon cinnamon
1/2 teaspoon ginger
1/4 teaspoon cloves
12 ounces evaporated skim milk
2 (8-inch) unbaked pie shells

Preheat oven to 425 degrees. Combine first 10 ingredients in order listed in bowl. Pour into pie shells. Bake for 15 minutes. Reduce heat to 350 degrees. Bake for 35 minutes or until inserted knife comes out clean. Yield: 12 servings.

Approx Per Serving: Cal 204; Prot 5 g; Carbo 23 g; Fiber 1 g; T Fat 10 g; 45% Calories from Fat; Chol 36 mg; Sod 277 mg.

Uncooked Pumpkin Pie

Mrs. Clayton Glenn, Woodbury

1 envelope dessert topping mix
1/2 cup milk
1 teaspoon vanilla extract
2/3 cup milk
1 to 1 1/2 cups canned pumpkin
1 (3-ounce) package butterscotch instant
   pudding mix
1/4 teaspoon cinnamon
1/4 teaspoon nutmeg
1/4 teaspoon ginger
1 (9-inch) baked pie shell

Beat dessert topping mix, 1/2 cup milk and vanilla together until thick. Add 2/3 cup milk with next 5 ingredients. Continue to beat at low speed until well blended. Pour into baked pie shell. Chill until serving time.
Yield: 8 servings.

Approx Per Serving: Cal 256; Prot 4 g; Carbo 32 g; Fiber 2 g; T Fat 13 g; 46% Calories from Fat; Chol 5 mg; Sod 308 mg.

Raisin Pie

Mrs. Earl Dewey Garrett, Lewisburg

1/2 cup sugar
1/2 cup packed light brown sugar
2 tablespoons flour
Pinch of salt
1 cup milk
1/2 cup butter
3 egg yolks, beaten
1 cup raisins
1/2 teaspoon vanilla extract
1 (8-inch) baked pie shell
3 egg whites
1/3 cup sugar

Preheat oven to 450 degrees. Combine 1/2 cup sugar with next 8 ingredients in large saucepan. Cook slowly until mixture thickens. Pour into pie shell. Beat egg whites with 1/3 cup sugar until stiff peaks form. Spread on top of pie. Bake until light brown. Yield: 6 servings.

Approx Per Serving: Cal 595; Prot 8 g; Carbo 81 g; Fiber 2 g; T Fat 29 g; 42% Calories from Fat; Chol 153 mg; Sod 361 mg.

Rosy Rhubarb Pie

Paula Barnhardt, Waynesboro

10 stalks fresh rhubarb
Few drops of red food coloring
1 cup packed dark brown sugar
1/4 teaspoon ground nutmeg
1/4 teaspoon cloves
1/4 teaspoon cinnamon
Cornstarch
1 (9-inch) baked pie shell

Wash and remove stems and leaves from rhubarb stalks. Slice into 1-inch slices. Heat 1 cup water in small saucepan. Simmer stalks for 10 minutes. Add few drops of food coloring, brown sugar and spices. Add enough water to make 2 cups sauce. Cook rhubarb until tender. Thicken with cornstarch. Cook until mixture is clear. Pour into pie shell. Chill until set. Serve with spoonful whipped topping on top. Yield: 8 servings.

Approx Per Serving: Cal 223; Prot 2 g; Carbo 37 g; Fiber 3 g; T Fat 8 g; 31% Calories from Fat; Chol 0 mg; Sod 134 mg.

Squash Pie

Mrs. Geraldine Blankenship, Smithville

2 cups young tender squash, cooked
1 cup sugar
3 tablespoons flour
1/2 cup milk
1/4 teaspoon salt
1 teaspoon vanilla extract
3 egg yolks, well beaten
1 (9-inch) unbaked pie shell
3 egg whites
1/2 teaspoon vanilla extract
1/4 teaspoon cream of tartar
6 tablespoons sugar

Preheat oven to 450 degrees. Run squash through colander. Place in saucepan. Add 1 cup sugar, flour, milk, salt, 1 teaspoon vanilla and egg yolks. Cook until thick. Pour into pie shell. Bake until crust is brown. Reduce heat to 350 degrees. Beat egg whites with 1/2 teaspoon vanilla and cream of tartar until soft peaks form. Gradually add 6 tablespoons sugar, beating until stiff and glossy and sugar is dissolved. Spread meringue over filling, sealing meringue to edge of pastry. Bake for 12 to 15 minutes or until peaks of meringue are golden brown.
Yield: 8 servings.

Approx Per Serving: Cal 319; Prot 5 g; Carbo 40 g; Fiber 1 g; T Fat 10 g; 28% Calories from Fat; Chol 81 mg; Sod 200 mg.

Delicate Squash Pie

Mrs. B. M. Hickenbottom, Morrison

2 cups yellow crookneck squash
3 eggs, slightly beaten
2 cups sugar
1/2 (scant) teaspoon salt
1 teaspoon cinnamon
1/4 teaspoon nutmeg
1 1/2 cups evaporated milk
1 (9-inch) unbaked pie shell

Preheat oven to 450 degrees. Cook squash in small amount water; drain well. Blend in blender until smooth; set aside. Combine eggs with next 5 ingredients. Add squash; mix well. Pour into pie shell. Bake for 10 minutes. Reduce heat to 350 degrees. Bake for 40 to 45 minutes or until knife inserted in center comes out clean. This is better than pumpkin pie because it has a delicate taste.
Yield: 8 servings.

Approx Per Serving: Cal 410; Prot 7 g; Carbo 67 g; Fiber 1 g; T Fat 13 g; 29% Calories from Fat; Chol 93 mg; Sod 330 mg.

Kelly's Squash Pie

Kelly Holt, College Grove

1/4 cup butter, melted
1 1/2 cups sugar
2 eggs
2 cups grated raw yellow squash
2 tablespoons flour
3 teaspoons lemon flavoring
2 teaspoons coconut flavoring
1 (9-inch) unbaked pie shell

Preheat oven to 350 degrees. Cream butter with sugar in bowl. Add eggs. Stir in next 4 ingredients. Pour into pie shell. Bake for 30 to 35 minutes or until golden brown.
Yield: 8 servings.

Approx Per Serving: Cal 362; Prot 4 g; Carbo 53 g; Fiber 1 g; T Fat 15 g; 37% Calories from Fat; Chol 69 mg; Sod 198 mg.

Strawberry Pie

Sheila Cox, Lexington

4 packets Equal or Sweet 'n' Low
1 1/2 cups water
4 teaspoons cornstarch
1 (3-ounce) package strawberry sugar-free
   gelatin
2 cups strawberries
1 (9-inch) graham cracker crust

Combine sweetener, water, cornstarch and gelatin in medium saucepan. Cook until mixture thickens and becomes clear. Let cool. Add strawberries. Pour into graham cracker crust. Yield: 8 servings.

Approx Per Serving: Cal 223; Prot 3 g; Carbo 31 g; Fiber 2 g; T Fat 10 g; 41% Calories from Fat; Chol 0 mg; Sod 261 mg.

Creamy Strawberry Pie

Nelle Byrd, Counce

8 ounces cream cheese, softened
1/4 cup sugar
1/2 teaspoon vanilla extract
Dash of nutmeg
1 cup sliced strawberries
1 (9-inch) graham cracker crust
1 cup whipped topping
1/4 cup confectioners' sugar

Combine cream cheese, sugar, vanilla, nutmeg and strawberries in bowl; mix well. Pour into crust. Combine topping and confectioners' sugar. Spread over pie. Chill. Yield: 8 servings.

Approx Per Serving: Cal 374; Prot 4 g; Carbo 41 g; Fiber 2 g; T Fat 23 g; 53% Calories from Fat; Chol 31 mg; Sod 318 mg.

Strawberry De-Lite Pie

Mrs. Faye Russell, Campbell County

This recipe won fourth place in the 1985 Tennessee June Dairy Month Recipe Contest.

1 cup graham cracker crumbs
2 tablespoons sugar
2 tablespoons butter, melted
1/2 cup 2% milk
2 cups low-fat small curd cottage cheese
1/2 cup instant nonfat dry milk powder
4 eggs
1/4 cup self-rising flour
1/8 teaspoon salt
1 tablespoon lemon juice
1 teaspoon vanilla extract
1 teaspoon almond extract
1/2 cup sugar
4 cups fresh strawberries
5 tablespoons low-calorie sweetener

Preheat oven to 300 degrees. Combine crumbs, 2 tablespoons sugar and butter in bowl; mix well. Press evenly into bottom of 9-inch springform pan. Combine next 9 ingredients with 1/2 cup sugar in 5-cup container of electric blender. Process for 1 minute or until smooth. Pour into crust. Bake for 1 hour. Turn off heat. Leave in oven for 1 hour. Set aside to cool. Wash and cap strawberries. Add sweetener. Slice and arrange berries on top of pie. Chill. Yield: 10 servings.

Approx Per Serving: Cal 240; Prot 12 g; Carbo 33 g; Fiber 2 g; T Fat 7 g; 26% Calories from Fat; Chol 96 mg; Sod 397 mg.

Old-Fashioned Strawberry Pie

Edith Morelock, Greeneville

1 recipe pie crust
2 quarts fresh strawberries
2 cups sugar
3 tablespoons cornstarch
1 cup water
2 tablespoons butter

Preheat oven to 350 degrees. Line iron skillet with half the pie crust. Wash and clean strawberries. Combine sugar and cornstarch. Stir into berries. Pour mixture into skillet. Bring water to a boil. Pour over berries. Place remaining crust over top. Dot with butter. Bake until golden brown. Yield: 8 servings.

Approx Per Serving: Cal 392; Prot 2 g; Carbo 73 g; Fiber 4 g; T Fat 11 g; 25% Calories from Fat; Chol 8 mg; Sod 154 mg.

Fresh Strawberry Pie

Mrs. Paul Bailey, Greenback

"If I were to give a recipe for the thing my family asks for most these days, it would have to be Fresh Strawberry Pie," says Mrs. Paul (Ruth) Bailey of Greenback.

2 cups sugar
6 tablespoons cornstarch
1 (3-ounce) package strawberry gelatin
2 cups boiling water
1 quart ripe strawberries
2 (9-inch) baked pie shells, cooled

Combine sugar, cornstarch and gelatin in bowl. Add slowly, stirring constantly, to boiling water in saucepan. Cook until slightly thickened. Let cool. Cap and wash strawberries; drain. Add strawberries to cooled gelatin mixture. Pour into pie shells. Refrigerate for 2 hours or until set. Serve with whipped cream or whipped topping. Yield: 12 servings.

Approx Per Serving: Cal 344; Prot 3 g; Carbo 61 g; Fiber 2 g; T Fat 11 g; 27% Calories from Fat; Chol 0 mg; Sod 182 mg.

Frosty Strawberry Creme Pie

Wilma Hostetler, Guthrie, Kentucky

1 cup flour
1/2 cup butter
1/4 cup packed light brown sugar
1/2 cup coconut
1 cup strawberries
1 unbeaten egg white
1/2 cup sugar
3 teaspoons lemon juice
1 cup whipped topping

Preheat oven to 350 degrees. Combine first 4 ingredients until crumbly. Press into 9-inch pie pan. Bake for 15 minutes. Combine strawberries, egg white, sugar and lemon juice. Beat at high speed until thick and creamy. Gently fold in whipped topping. Spoon into pie crust. Freeze for 4 to 6 hours before serving. Yield: 8 servings.

Approx Per Serving: Cal 287; Prot 3 g; Carbo 36 g; Fiber 1 g; T Fat 16 g; 48% Calories from Fat; Chol 31 mg; Sod 130 mg.

Fresh Strawberry Tarts

Mary Phillips, Dixon Springs

2 egg yolks, slightly beaten
2 cups milk
1 (3-ounce) package vanilla pudding mix
6 ounces cream cheese
2 egg whites
1/4 cup sugar
8 (3-inch) tart shells, baked and cooled
1 1/2 cups fresh strawberries
1 cup sugar

Combine egg yolks and milk in bowl. Cook pudding mix according to package directions, using egg-milk mixture as liquid. Remove from heat. Cut cream cheese into pieces; add to hot pudding. Beat until cheese is melted. Let mixture cool for 10 minutes. Beat egg whites until soft peaks form. Gradually add sugar, beating until stiff peaks form. Fold egg whites into pudding. Spoon into tart shells. Chill. Spoon sugared strawberries over tarts. Yield: 8 servings.

Approx Per Serving: Cal 399; Prot 7 g; Carbo 56 g; Fiber 3 g; T Fat 18 g; 39% Calories from Fat; Chol 85 mg; Sod 254 mg.

Mom's Apple Cobbler

Lucille Conner, Lafayette

1/2 cup butter
2 cups sugar
2 cups water
1/2 cup vegetable shortening
1 1/2 cups sifted self-rising flour
1/3 cup milk
1 teaspoon cinnamon
2 cups finely chopped apples

Preheat oven to 350 degrees. Melt butter in 9-by-13-inch baking dish. Heat sugar and water in saucepan until sugar melts. Cut shortening into flour until particles are like fine crumbs. Add milk. Stir with fork only until dough leaves side of bowl. Turn out onto lightly floured board; knead just until smooth. Roll out into large rectangle 1/4-inch thick. Sprinkle cinnamon over apples. Sprinkle apples evenly over dough. Roll dough up like jelly roll. Dampen edge of dough with water; seal. Slice dough into about 16 slices, 1/2-inch thick. Place in pan with melted butter. Pour sugar syrup carefully around rolls. Crust will absorb liquid. Bake for 55 minutes to 1 hour. Yield: 8 servings.

Approx Per Serving: Cal 509; Prot 3 g; Carbo 71 g; Fiber 1 g; T Fat 25 g; 43% Calories from Fat; Chol 32 mg; Sod 396 mg.

Blackberry Pinwheel Cobbler

Sandy Buckner, Cumberland Furnace

2 cups water
1 1/2 cups sugar
1/2 cup butter
2 cups self-rising flour
1/2 cup milk
3/4 cup sugar
4 cups blackberries
2 tablespoons butter

Preheat oven to 350 degrees. Bring water and 1 1/2 cups sugar to a boil in saucepan. Set aside to cool. Cut butter into flour in large bowl until mixture resembles coarse meal. Add milk; mix until soft dough is formed. Turn dough onto floured surface. Knead 4 to 5 times. Roll dough into 1/8-inch thick 9-by-12-inch rectangle. Spread 3/4 cup sugar onto dough; top with blackberries. Dot with 2 tablespoons butter. Roll up in jelly-roll-fashion. Cut into 12-inch slices. Place slices in 9-by-13-inch baking pan. Pour syrup over slices. Bake for 35 to 40 minutes. Yield: 12 servings

Approx Per Serving: Cal 334; Prot 2 g; Carbo 59 g; Fiber 2 g; T Fat 10 g; 27% Calories from Fat; Chol 27 mg; Sod 367 mg.

Iva's Peach Cobbler

Mrs. Kenneth O'Dell, Sparta

6 to 8 large ripe peaches, peeled and
    sliced
2 1/2 tablespoons cornstarch
3/4 cup sugar
1 cup flour
2 egg yolks
1/4 cup melted butter
1 teaspoon baking powder
1 cup sugar
2 egg whites, stiffly beaten

Preheat oven to 375 degrees. Combine peaches, cornstarch and 3/4 cup sugar in bowl; mix well. Pour into greased 9-by-13-inch baking pan. Combine next 4 ingredients with 1 cup sugar; mix well. Gently fold egg whites into batter. Spread over peaches. Bake for 45 minutes or until fruit is bubbling around edges and top is golden brown. Yield: 12 servings.

Approx Per Serving: Cal 235; Prot 3 g; Carbo 47 g; Fiber 1 g; T Fat 5 g; 18% Calories from Fat; Chol 46 mg; Sod 78 mg.

Strawberry Cobbler

Betty Denton, Dayton

1 1/4 cups flour
1 1/4 teaspoons baking powder
1/2 teaspoon salt
4 tablespoons butter
3/4 cup sugar
1 teaspoon vanilla extract
1 egg
1/2 cup milk
3 cups halved strawberries
1/4 cup butter
1/4 cup sugar
1/4 cup flour

Preheat oven to 350 degrees. Combine 1 1/4 cups flour, baking powder and salt. Cream 4 tablespoons butter, 3/4 cup sugar and vanilla. Beat in egg until blended. Add flour mixture and milk; beat only until smooth. Spread over bottom of buttered 8-inch square baking dish. Sprinkle strawberries on top. Combine 1/4 cup butter, 1/4 cup sugar and 1/4 cup flour. Beat until smooth. Drop by teaspoonfuls over strawberries. Bake for 45 minutes. Great with whipping cream or ice cream. Yield: 8 servings.

Approx Per Serving: Cal 336; Prot 4 g; Carbo 51 g; Fiber 3 g; T Fat 13 g; 35% Calories from Fat; Chol 60 mg; Sod 319 mg.

Delicious Strawberry Cobbler

Mrs. Mary Gray, McEwen

1 quart sweetened strawberries
3/4 cup sugar
3 tablespoons cornstarch
3 tablespoons butter
3/4 cup sugar
1 cup flour
1 teaspoon baking powder
1/4 cup vegetable oil
1/2 cup milk
1 teaspoon vanilla extract
1 egg

Preheat oven to 350 degrees. Drain strawberries, reserving juice. Add water to juice to equal 1 cup liquid. Combine 3/4 cup sugar and cornstarch in saucepan. Gradually add juice. Bring to a boil. Stir until thick. Add butter; mix well. Let cool. Add strawberries. Pour into 9-by-13-inch baking pan. Combine 3/4 cup sugar with remaining ingredients; mix well. Beat for 4 minutes. Pour mixture over fruit. Bake for 35 to 40 minutes or until done. Let cool. Yield: 12 servings.

Approx Per Serving: Cal 287; Prot 2 g; Carbo 53 g; Fiber 2 g; T Fat 8 g; 25% Calories from Fat; Chol 27 mg; Sod 68 mg.

CHAPTER 9

Candy & Cookies

Puffs of Cotton

As spring unfolds across the ridges of East Tennessee, layers of billowy, cotton-like fog nestle into the valleys and hollows.

Apple Squares

Mrs. Paul Anderson, Dyersburg

1 cup sugar
1/2 cup butter
1 egg
1 cup self-rising flour
1/2 teaspoon baking soda
1/2 teaspoon cinnamon
1/2 teaspoon nutmeg
1 cup chopped Golden Delicious apples
1/2 cup chopped pecans

Preheat oven to 350 degrees. Cream sugar and butter in large mixer bowl. Add egg; mix well. Combine flour, baking soda, cinnamon and nutmeg in medium bowl. Add to creamed mixture; mix well. Fold in apples and pecans. Pour into buttered 8-inch square cake pan. Bake for 35 minutes. Let cool; cut into squares.
Yield: 16 servings.

Approx Per Serving: Cal 161; Prot 2 g; Carbo 20 g; Fiber <1 g; T Fat 9 g; 47% Calories from Fat; Chol 29 mg; Sod 188 mg.

Chess Bars

Barbara Terry, Oneida

1/2 cup butter, melted
4 eggs
1 (2-layer) package yellow butter cake mix
1 (1-pound) package confectioners' sugar
8 ounces cream cheese, softened

Preheat oven to 325 degrees. Combine butter, 1 egg and cake mix in large bowl; mix well. Press in bottom of 9-by-13-inch baking pan. Combine 3 eggs, confectioners' sugar and cream cheese in large mixer bowl; mix until smooth. Pour over cake mixture. Bake for 40 to 45 minutes or until tests done. Let cool; cut into bars.
Yield: 36 servings.

Approx Per Serving: Cal 265; Prot 4 g; Carbo 45 g; Fiber 0 g; T Fat 8 g; 27% Calories from Fat; Chol 37 mg; Sod 52 mg.

Chocolate-Pecan Bars

Helen Freels, Hendersonville

1/2 cup butter, softened
1 1/2 cups packed dark brown sugar
2 cups flour
1 cup chopped pecans
2/3 cup butter, melted
1 cup semisweet chocolate chips

Preheat oven to 350 degrees. Cream 1/2 cup butter in mixer bowl. Add 1 cup brown sugar, beating at medium speed. Add flour gradually, mixing well. Press mixture into ungreased 9-by-13-inch baking pan; sprinkle with pecans. Combine 2/3 cup melted butter and 1/2 cup brown sugar in saucepan. Bring to a boil over medium heat, stirring constantly. Boil for 30 seconds, stirring constantly. Remove from heat; pour over crust. Bake for 18 minutes. Remove from oven. Sprinkle immediately with chocolate chips. Let cool; cut into squares. Yield: 48 servings.

Approx Per Serving: Cal 113; Prot <1 g; Carbo 12 g; Fiber <1 g; T Fat 7 g; 55% Calories from Fat; Chol 12 mg; Sod 48 mg.

Chewy Cocoa-Oatmeal Squares

Mrs. Hillard Fox, Pleasant View

1 cup butter
2 cups packed dark brown sugar
2 eggs
1 teaspoon vanilla extract
2 cups flour
1/3 cup unsweetened baking cocoa
1 teaspoon baking soda
1/2 teaspoon salt
2 cups uncooked oats
1/2 cup chopped walnuts
1 cup semisweet chocolate chips

Preheat oven to 400 degrees. Cream butter and sugar in large mixer bowl until fluffy. Beat in eggs and vanilla. Stir in flour, cocoa, baking soda and salt. Add oats; mix well. Spread into buttered 10-by-15-inch baking pan. Sprinkle with walnuts and chocolate pieces. Bake for 10 minutes or until tests done. Let cool in pan. Cut into 2-by-3 1/2-inch bars. Yield: 24 servings.

Approx Per Serving: Cal 247; Prot 4 g; Carbo 33 g; Fiber 2 g; T Fat 12 g; 43% Calories from Fat; Chol 38 mg; Sod 170 mg.

Coconut Jam Bars

Mrs. Don Finchum, Strawberry Plains

1 (2-layer) package yellow cake mix
1/3 cup butter, softened
4 eggs
1 (12-ounce) jar red raspberry preserves
1 cup sugar
2 tablespoons butter, softened
2 tablespoons flour
1/4 teaspoon baking powder
1/4 teaspoon salt
1 1/2 cups flaked coconut

Preheat oven to 350 degrees. Combine cake mix, 1/3 cup butter and 1 egg in large mixer bowl. Mix at low speed until crumbly. Press into greased 10-by-15-inch baking pan. Bake for 10 to 20 minutes or until tests done; crust will be soft. Let cool slightly. Spread preserves gently over crust. Mix sugar and 2 tablespoons butter in medium mixer bowl. Add 3 eggs; beat for 1 minute at medium speed. Stir in flour, baking powder and salt until blended. Fold in coconut. Spread mixture gently over preserves to cover. Return to oven; bake for 15 to 20 minutes or until light golden brown. Let cool completely; cut into bars. Yield: 48 servings.

Approx Per Serving: Cal 113; Prot 1 g; Carbo 18 g; Fiber <1 g; T Fat 4 g; 33% Calories from Fat; Chol 23 mg; Sod 109 mg.

Fruit and Nut Squares

Mrs. Wallace Cantrell, Smithville

1 cup flour
1 teaspoon baking soda
1/2 teaspoon cinnamon
1 cup water
1/2 cup chopped prunes
1/2 cup chopped raisins
1/2 cup chopped dates
1/2 cup chopped nuts
1/2 cup margarine
2 eggs, beaten
1 teaspoon vanilla extract

Preheat oven to 350 degrees. Sift together flour, baking soda and cinnamon into medium bowl. Bring water to a boil in 3-quart saucepan. Add prunes, raisins, dates and nuts. Simmer for 4 minutes. Remove from heat; add margarine. Let cool slightly. Stir in eggs, vanilla and flour mixture. Pour into greased and floured 9-inch square baking pan. Bake for 30 minutes. Let cool. Cut into squares. Yield: 36 servings.

Approx Per Serving: Cal 82; Prot 1 g; Carbo 11 g; Fiber <1 g; T Fat 4 g; 42% Calories from Fat; Chol 12 mg; Sod 57 mg.

Gooey Bars

Mrs. Jack Harris, Lenoir City

1 (2-layer) package yellow cake mix
1/2 cup melted butter
3 eggs
8 ounces cream cheese
1 (1-pound) package confectioners' sugar

Preheat oven to 325 degrees. Combine cake mix, butter and 1 egg in large bowl; mix well. Press into 9-by-13-inch baking pan. Reserve 2 tablespoons confectioners' sugar. Combine cream cheese, 2 eggs and remaining confectioners' sugar in large mixer bowl. Beat for 5 minutes. Spread over dough mixture. Bake for 30 minutes. Sprinkle lightly with reserved confectioners' sugar. Let cool overnight. Cut into bars. Freezes well.
Yield: 36 servings.

Approx Per Serving: Cal 161; Prot 2 g; Carbo 24 g; Fiber <1 g; T Fat 7 g; 38% Calories from Fat; Chol 32 mg; Sod 143 mg.

Hello Dolly Cookies

Mrs. J. R. Lawson, Maryville

1/2 cup butter
1 cup graham cracker crumbs
1 cup shredded coconut
1 cup chocolate chips
1 cup broken pecans
1 (14-ounce) can sweetened condensed milk

Preheat oven to 350 degrees. Melt butter in 9-inch square baking pan in oven. Sprinkle crumbs over melted butter; stir and spread evenly in pan. Sprinkle coconut over crumbs. Sprinkle chocolate chips over coconut. Sprinkle pecans over chocolate chips. Pour condensed milk over top; do not stir. Bake for 30 minutes. Let cool. Cut into squares. Yield: 36 servings.

Approx Per Serving: Cal 130; Prot 2 g; Carbo 13 g; Fiber <1 g; T Fat 8 g; 56% Calories from Fat; Chol 11 mg; Sod 68 mg.

Iced Lemon-Butter Bars

Bettie Hackett, Carthage

1 1/3 cups flour
1 cup sugar
1/2 cup butter, softened
2 eggs
2 tablespoons flour
1 teaspoon grated lemon peel
2 tablespoons lemon juice
2 tablespoons confectioners' sugar

Preheat oven to 350 degrees. Combine 1 1/3 cups flour, 1/4 cup sugar and butter in large bowl; blend until dough forms ball. Pat into ungreased 9-inch square baking pan. Bake for 15 minutes. Combine eggs, remaining sugar, 2 tablespoons flour, lemon peel and lemon juice in medium bowl; blend well. Pour into partially baked crust. Bake for 18 to 20 minutes or until filling is set. Sift confectioners' sugar over top. Let cool in pan on wire rack. Cut into bars. Yield: 16 servings.

Approx Per Serving: Cal 154; Prot 2 g; Carbo 22 g; Fiber <1 g; T Fat 6 g; 37% Calories from Fat; Chol 42 mg; Sod 67 mg.

Big Mac's Peach Squares

Sandra E. Pratt, Brownsville

2 cups flour
1/2 cup confectioners' sugar
1/8 teaspoon salt
1 cup butter, softened
4 eggs, slightly beaten
2 ripe peaches, puréed
2 cups sugar
1/2 cup cornstarch
2 tablespoons confectioners' sugar

Preheat oven to 350 degrees. Combine flour, 1/2 cup confectioners' sugar and salt in large bowl. Cut in butter until well blended. Press dough evenly into 10-by-15-inch baking pan. Bake for 15 to 20 minutes or until tests done. Combine eggs, peaches, sugar and cornstarch in large bowl; mix well. Pour over hot crust. Bake for 25 minutes. Let cool. Cut into 2-by-3-inch bars. Dust with 2 tablespoons confectioners' sugar. Yield: 25 servings.

Approx Per Serving: Cal 200; Prot 2 g; Carbo 30 g; Fiber <1 g; T Fat 8 g; 37% Calories from Fat; Chol 54 mg; Sod 96 mg.

All-Time Favorite Cookies

Alice Smith, Cottage Grove

2 cups raisins
1 cup water
1 3/4 cups sugar
1 cup vegetable shortening
2 eggs
1 teaspoon vanilla extract
3 1/2 cups flour
1 teaspoon baking powder
1 teaspoon baking soda
1/2 teaspoon ground cinnamon
1/2 teaspoon ground nutmeg
1/2 teaspoon salt
1 cup chopped nuts

Preheat oven to 350 degrees. Combine raisins and water in saucepan; boil for 2 minutes. Let cool; do not drain. Add sugar gradually to shortening in large mixer bowl, beating well after each addition. Add eggs; beat well. Stir in raisins with liquid and vanilla. Combine flour, baking powder, baking soda, cinnamon, nutmeg and salt in large bowl. Add gradually to raisin mixture. Stir in nuts. Drop by teaspoonfuls onto cookie sheet. Bake for 10 minutes or until brown. Yield: 72 servings.

Approx Per Serving: Cal 93; Prot 1 g; Carbo 13 g; Fiber <1 g; T Fat 4 g; 39% Calories from Fat; Chol 6 mg; Sod 33 mg.

Banana Sesame Cookies

Ginger Ware, Waynesboro

1 cup sesame seeds
2 cups whole wheat flour
1 teaspoon sea salt
1 teaspoon low sodium baking powder
1/2 teaspoon nutmeg
3/4 cup butter, softened
1 cup honey
1 egg
1 cup mashed bananas
1 teaspoon vanilla extract

Preheat oven to 350 degrees. Toast sesame seeds lightly for 5 to 7 minutes. Sift together flour, salt, baking powder and nutmeg into large bowl. Cream butter and honey in large mixer bowl until fluffy. Add egg; beat well. Add bananas; mix well. Add dry ingredients, a third at a time, mixing well after each addition. Add vanilla and sesame seeds; mix well. Drop by teaspoonfuls onto lightly buttered cookie sheet. Bake for 8 to 20 minutes or until golden brown. Yield: 36 servings.

Approx Per Serving: Cal 117; Prot 2 g; Carbo 15 g; Fiber 1 g; T Fat 6 g; 46% Calories from Fat; Chol 16 mg; Sod 103 mg.

Brown Sugar Drop Cookies

Mrs. Ruth Henley, Limestone

1 cup vegetable shortening
2 cups packed dark brown sugar
2 eggs
3½ cups self-rising flour
1 teaspoon baking soda
½ cup buttermilk
1 cup chopped black walnuts

Combine shortening, brown sugar and eggs in large bowl; mix well. Sift together flour and baking soda in large bowl. Add dry ingredients and buttermilk alternately to sugar mixture. Add walnuts; mix well. Chill for 1 hour or overnight. Preheat oven to 400 degrees. Drop by rounded teaspoonfuls onto greased baking sheet. Bake for 8 to 10 minutes or until test done. May substitute sour milk for buttermilk if desired. Yield: 72 servings.

Approx Per Serving: Cal 79; Prot 1 g; Carbo 10 g; Fiber <1 g; T Fat 4 g; 45% Calories from Fat; Chol 6 mg; Sod 94 mg.

Cherry Winks

Jane Stapleton, Dandridge

5 cups cornflakes
2¼ cups flour
1 teaspoon baking powder
½ teaspoon baking soda
½ teaspoon salt
¾ cup margarine, softened
1 cup sugar
2 eggs
1 teaspoon vanilla extract
1 cup chopped nuts
1 cup finely chopped pitted dates
⅓ cup finely chopped maraschino cherries
15 maraschino cherries, cut into quarters

Preheat oven to 375 degrees. Crush cornflakes into coarse crumbs. Sift together flour, baking powder, baking soda and salt into large bowl. Combine margarine and sugar in large mixer bowl; beat until light and fluffy. Add eggs and vanilla; beat well. Add dry ingredients; mix until combined. Stir in nuts, dates and finely chopped cherries. Shape level tablespoonfuls of dough into balls; roll in cornflakes. Place on greased baking sheets. Top each cookie with cherry quarter. Bake for 12 minutes or until lightly browned. Remove immediately from baking sheets. Let cool on wire racks. Yield: 60 servings.

Approx Per Serving: Cal 86; Prot 1 g; Carbo 12 g; Fiber <1 g; T Fat 4 g; 40% Calories from Fat; Chol 7 mg; Sod 81 mg.

Chocolate Chip-Eggnog Balls

Peggy Sue Smith, Jamestown

6 ounces cream cheese, softened
4 cups sifted confectioners' sugar
1 tablespoon heavy cream
1 teaspoon brandy extract
½ teaspoon salt
¼ teaspoon cinnamon
⅛ teaspoon nutmeg
½ cup semisweet chocolate chips
1¼ cups finely chopped pecans

Combine cream cheese, confectioners' sugar, cream, brandy extract, salt, cinnamon and nutmeg in large mixer bowl; beat until creamy. Stir in chocolate chips. Drop by rounded teaspoonfuls onto cookie sheets. Chill for 5 minutes. Roll into balls. Coat completely with pecans. Yield: 40 servings.

Approx Per Serving: Cal 90; Prot <1 g; Carbo 12 g; Fiber <1 g; T Fat 5 g; 46% Calories from Fat; Chol 5 mg; Sod 40 mg.

Chocolate Muffins

Lib Worrell, Newbern

4 squares unsweetened baking chocolate
1 cup margarine
¹/₄ teaspoon butter flavoring
1¹/₂ cups broken pecans
1³/₄ cups sugar
1 cup flour
2 eggs
1 teaspoon vanilla extract

Preheat oven to 325 degrees. Melt chocolate and margarine in heavy saucepan. Add butter flavoring and pecans. Stir to coat pecans; remove from heat. Combine sugar, flour, eggs and vanilla. Mix until blended; do not beat. Add chocolate-nut mixture; mix carefully without beating. Pour into greased muffin cups. Bake for 30 to 35 minutes or until test done. Yield: 18 servings.

Approx Per Serving: Cal 299; Prot 3 g; Carbo 28 g; Fiber 2 g; T Fat 21 g; 60% Calories from Fat; Chol 24 mg; Sod 127 mg.

Chocolate-Oatmeal Cookies

Mrs. Sharon Skaggs, Collinwood

2 cups sugar
²/₃ cup milk
¹/₃ cup baking cocoa
2 tablespoons light corn syrup
¹/₄ teaspoon salt
2 tablespoons butter
1 teaspoon vanilla extract
1 cup marshmallow creme
¹/₂ cup chopped nuts
1 cup peanut butter
3 cups oatmeal

Combine sugar, milk, cocoa and corn syrup in saucepan. Cook until mixture reaches 234 degrees on candy thermometer or small amount dropped into very cold water forms soft ball which flattens when removed. Remove from heat. Add butter, vanilla and marshmallow creme; mix until melted. Add nuts and peanut butter. Add oatmeal. Place pan in small amount of cold water in sink. Stir until mixture is almost stiff but still soft. Drop by teaspoonfuls onto greased waxed paper or cooking foil.
Yield: 96 servings.

Approx Per Serving: Cal 61; Prot 1 g; Carbo 10 g; Fiber <1 g; T Fat 2 g; 32% Calories from Fat; Chol <1 mg; Sod 25 mg.

Forgotten Cookies

Earlene Leath, Westmoreland

2 egg whites
²/₃ cup sugar
¹/₄ teaspoon salt
1 teaspoon vanilla extract
1 cup chopped nuts
1 cup chocolate chips

Preheat oven to 350 degrees. Beat egg whites in large mixer bowl until stiff. Fold in remaining ingredients. Place by spoonfuls onto well-greased or foil-lined baking pan. Place in oven; turn heat off immediately. Let cookies remain in oven overnight; do not open oven door.
Yield: 60 servings.

Approx Per Serving: Cal 36; Prot <1 g; Carbo 4 g; Fiber <1 g; T Fat 2 g; 51% Calories from Fat; Chol 0 mg; Sod 11 mg.

Gingersnaps

Judy Harper, Iron City

¾ cup vegetable shortening
1 cup sugar
1 egg
¼ cup molasses
2 cups flour
1 tablespoon ground ginger
2 teaspoons baking soda
1 teaspoon ground cinnamon
½ teaspoon salt
½ cup sugar

Preheat oven to 350 degrees. Cream shortening and 1 cup sugar in large mixer bowl until light and fluffy. Add egg and molasses; mix well. Combine flour, ginger, baking soda, cinnamon and salt in large bowl; mix well. Add a fourth of dry mixture at a time to creamed mixture, mixing until smooth after each addition. Shape dough into 1-inch balls; roll each ball in ½ cup sugar. Place 2 inches apart on ungreased cookie sheets. Bake for 12 minutes. Tops will crack. Yield: 54 servings.

Approx Per Serving: Cal 69; Prot <1 g; Carbo 10 g; Fiber <1 g; T Fat 3 g; 38% Calories from Fat; Chol 4 mg; Sod 52 mg.

Molasses Crinkle

Mrs. Oscar Gernt, Allardt

¾ cup vegetable shortening
1 cup packed dark brown sugar
1 egg
¼ cup dark molasses
½ teaspoon salt
2¼ cups flour
2 teaspoons baking soda
½ teaspoon cloves
1 teaspoon cinnamon
1 teaspoon ginger
¼ cup sugar

Combine shortening, brown sugar, egg, molasses and salt in large bowl; mix well. Combine salt, flour, baking soda, cloves, cinnamon and ginger in large bowl; add to mixture, mixing well. Chill dough for a few hours or overnight. Preheat oven to 400 degrees. Shape into walnut-sized balls. Dip tops of balls in sugar. Place 3 inches apart on greased cookie sheet. Sprinkle each with 3 drops of water. Bake for 12 to 15 minutes or until done.
Yield: 36 servings.

Approx Per Serving: Cal 98; Prot <1 g; Carbo 14 g; Fiber <1 g; T Fat 4 g; 41% Calories from Fat; Chol 6 mg; Sod 80 mg.

Orange Slice Cookies

Berniece Wood, Smyrna

½ cup vegetable shortening
½ cup butter
1 cup packed light brown sugar
1 teaspoon vanilla extract
2 eggs
2 cups quick-cooking oats
1 cup chopped orange slice candy
2 cups self-rising flour
1 cup coconut

Preheat oven to 400 degrees. Cream shortening, butter, brown sugar and vanilla in large mixer bowl. Add eggs; mix well. Mix together 1 cup oats and candy in bowl; add to mixture. Add remaining oats, flour and coconut; mix well. Drop by teaspoonfuls onto ungreased baking sheet. Bake for 8 to 10 minutes or until lightly brown; do not overcook. Yield: 72 servings.

Approx Per Serving: Cal 122; Prot <1 g; Carbo 22 g; Fiber <1 g; T Fat 3 g; 25% Calories from Fat; Chol 9 mg; Sod 72 mg.

Easy Orange Slice Cookies

Minnie Knowles, Sparta

1 (10-ounce) package vanilla wafers
1 pound orange slice candy
1 cup chopped pecans
1 (14-ounce) can sweetened condensed
  milk
1 cup coconut

Place wafers in blender container; blend. Cut candy into small pieces. Combine wafer crumbs, candy and pecans in large bowl. Stir in milk. Add coconut; mix well. Shape into roll. Roll up in cooking foil; chill. Slice and serve. Yield: 48 servings.

Approx Per Serving: Cal 110; Prot 1 g; Carbo 18 g; Fiber <1 g; T Fat 4 g; 31% Calories from Fat; Chol 6 mg; Sod 36 mg.

Peanut Butter Logs

Annie Laurie James, Humboldt

This dessert maintains its freshness well.

1 cup margarine, melted
1/2 cup crunchy peanut butter
2 cups quick oats
1 tablespoon vanilla extract
1 (1-pound) package confectioners' sugar
3/4 cup raisins
1 cup flaked coconut
1/2 cup chopped pecans
1 cup chocolate chips
2 ounces paraffin, shaved into thin strips

Combine margarine, peanut butter, oats, vanilla, confectioners' sugar, raisins, coconut and pecans in large bowl; mix well. Shape into 1-by-3-inch logs. Melt chocolate chips and paraffin together in saucepan; mix well. Dip logs into glaze. Drop into small bowl of water and ice cubes. Glaze will harden instantly. Lift out; place on paper towel. Yield: 36 servings.

Approx Per Serving: Cal 187; Prot 2 g; Carbo 23 g; Fiber 2 g; T Fat 10 g; 48% Calories from Fat; Chol 0 mg; Sod 79 mg.

Peanut Butter Treats

Margaret Waggoner, Greeneville

1 cup light corn syrup
1/2 cup light brown sugar
1/2 cup sugar
1 cup peanut butter
1/2 cup coconut
1/2 cup broken pecans
5 cups Special K cereal

Combine syrup and sugars in saucepan. Bring to a rapid boil; remove from heat. Add peanut butter, coconut and pecans. Add cereal; mix to combine. Roll mixture into small balls with buttered hands. Drop on waxed paper or cookie sheet. Balls may be wrapped individually. Yield: 50 servings.

Approx Per Serving: Cal 84; Prot 2 g; Carbo 12 g; Fiber <1 g; T Fat 4 g; 37% Calories from Fat; Chol <1 mg; Sod 60 mg.

Old-Fashioned Tea Cakes

Mrs. Frances Goff, Ripley; Marie Lowery, Covington

1³/₄ cups sugar
1 cup vegetable shortening
2 eggs
3 cups flour
¹/₂ cup milk
1 teaspoon vanilla extract
2 teaspoons baking powder
¹/₂ teaspoon salt

Preheat oven to 350 degrees. Cream sugar and shortening together in large mixer bowl. Add eggs; beat until creamy. Add 2 cups flour to mixture with ¹/₄ cup milk. Add remaining flour and milk; beat well. Add vanilla; beat well. Place mixture on floured board; roll to ¹/₄-inch thickness. Cut with cookie cutter. Place on cookie sheet. Bake for 12 to 15 minutes or until golden brown.
Yield: 36 servings.

Approx Per Serving: Cal 132; Prot 2 g; Carbo 18 g; Fiber <1 g; T Fat 6 g; 42% Calories from Fat; Chol 12 mg; Sod 53 mg.

Coconut-Chocolate Balls

Lena Hightower, Westmoreland

This recipe won first place at the Macon County Fair.

¹/₂ cup margarine
1 (7-ounce) can flaked coconut
1 (14-ounce) can sweetened condensed
 milk
2 (1-pound) packages confectioners' sugar
1 cup chopped nuts
1 teaspoon vanilla extract
2 (12-ounce) packages chocolate chips
¹/₂ block of paraffin

Combine margarine, coconut, condensed milk, confectioners' sugar, nuts and vanilla; mix well. Shape into balls. Chill for 1 hour. Melt chocolate chips and paraffin in top of double boiler; mix well. Dip chilled balls into chocolate mixture. Place on waxed paper to harden.
Yield: 84 servings.

Approx Per Serving: Cal 125; Prot <1 g; Carbo 20 g; Fiber <1 g; T Fat 6 g; 38% Calories from Fat; Chol 2 mg; Sod 20 mg.

Creamy Dreamy Fudge

Gladys P. Easley, Springville

1 pound butter
1 pound Velveeta cheese
4 pounds confectioners' sugar
1 cup baking cocoa
1 teaspoon vanilla extract
1 cup chopped nuts

Melt butter and cheese together in saucepan; mix well. Sift confectioners' sugar and cocoa into cheese mixture. Add vanilla and nuts; mix well. Pour into well buttered pan. Let cool. Cut into pieces. Yield: 96 servings.

Approx Per Serving: Cal 135; Prot 1 g; Carbo 20 g; Fiber <1 g; T Fat 6 g; 40% Calories from Fat; Chol 15 mg; Sod 107 mg.

C H A P T E R   10

Desserts

Frank and Jesse
Take a Rest

Taking a break from their logging
chores, Frank and Jesse, a magnificent
team of Belgian horses, wait for a sign
that it's time to go back to work. Their
owner, Benton Countian Bud French,
says there are still many folks around
who appreciate the traditional style of
logging he and his team use to cut and
haul timber out of the woods.

Apple Crisp

Judy Cheek, New Tazewell

2 cups quick oats
1 cup flour
1 cup non-fat powdered milk
1 cup packed light brown sugar
1/2 teaspoon each salt, cinnamon
1/2 teaspoon almond flavoring
1 cup butter, softened
4 cups diced fresh apples

Preheat oven to 350 degrees. Combine first 8 ingredients in bowl. Blend with a pastry blender or fork. Press 2/3 of the mixture into 9-by-13-inch glass baking pan. Top with diced apples. Cover with remainder of oatmeal mixture. Bake for 1 hour. Serve warm with ice cream. Yield: 12 servings.

Approx Per Serving: Cal 327; Prot 5 g; Carbo 41 g; Fiber 2 g; T Fat 17 g; 44% Calories from Fat; Chol 43 mg; Sod 283 mg.

Apple Dumplings

Mrs. James F. Rogers, Jr., Rock Island

3/4 cup vegetable shortening
2 cups flour
1/2 cup milk
6 peeled medium apples, cored
2 cups sugar
2 cups water
1 teaspoon cinnamon
1/2 teaspoon nutmeg
1/2 cup butter

Preheat oven to 350 degrees. Cut shortening into flour until crumbly. Stir in milk to form dough. Divide into 6 parts. Roll out into squares. Wrap 1 apple in each square. Place in baking dish. Combine remaining ingredients in saucepan. Boil for 1 minute. Let cool slightly. Pour over apples. Bake until crust is brown. Yield: 6 servings.

Approx Per Serving: Cal 857; Prot 5 g; Carbo 118 g; Fiber 4 g; T Fat 42 g; 44% Calories from Fat; Chol 44 mg; Sod 168 mg.

Easy Apple Dumplings

Betty Groce, Fayetteville

2 Granny Smith apples, peeled and cored
1 (8-count) can crescent rolls
1/8 teaspoon cinnamon
1/2 cup margarine
1 cup sugar
1 cup orange juice
1 teaspoon vanilla extract

Preheat oven to 350 degrees. Cut apples into fourths. Separate rolls. Wrap 1 apple piece in each roll. Place in 8-inch square baking dish. Sprinkle with cinnamon. Mix margarine, sugar and orange juice in saucepan. Bring to a boil; remove from heat. Stir in vanilla. Pour over rolls. Bake for 30 minutes. Spoon liquid over rolls. Yield: 6 servings.

Approx Per Serving: Cal 421; Prot 3 g; Carbo 61 g; Fiber 1 g; T Fat 19 g; 41% Calories from Fat; Chol 3 mg; Sod 513 mg.

Cinnamon Apples

Julia Webster, Friendship

1 1/2 cups water
2 tablespoons butter
1 cup sugar
1 (4-ounce) package red cinnamon candy bits
6 apples, peeled and quartered

Mix water, butter, sugar and candy in saucepan. Cook over medium heat until candy has melted; continue cooking for 10 minutes. Add apples, stirring to coat. Cook, uncovered, for 15 to 20 minutes or until apples are tender, stirring occasionally. Syrup thickens slightly. Yield: 12 servings.

Approx Per Serving: Cal 156; Prot 3 g; Carbo 26 g; Fiber <1 g; T Fat 4 g; 25% Calories from Fat; Chol 111 mg; Sod 53 mg.

Apple Ring Fritters

Barbara Norman, Englewood

1 cup flour, sifted
1 1/2 teaspoons baking powder
1/2 teaspoon salt
2 tablespoons sugar
3/4 cup milk
1 egg
4 apples
Vegetable oil for frying
1/2 cup sugar
1 teaspoon cinnamon

Sift flour, baking powder, salt and 2 tablespoons sugar in bowl. Add milk and egg; beat well. Peel and core apples; slice into rings 1/4-inch thick. Dip rings into batter. Drop in skillet containing 1/2 inch hot oil. Fry until golden brown on both sides. Drain on paper towels. Combine 1/2 cup sugar and cinnamon. Sprinkle on fritters.
Yield: 20 rings.

Nutritional information does not include oil for frying.
Approx Per Serving: Cal 57; Prot 1 g; Carbo 12 g; Fiber <1 g; T Fat 1 g; 10% Calories from Fat; Chol 12 mg; Sod 86 mg.

Banana-Butter Crackle

Anita Shelby, Pulaski

3 cups diced bananas
1/2 cup sugar
1/2 teaspoon nutmeg
1 cup packed light brown sugar
1 1/4 cups sifted flour
1 cup rolled oats
1/2 teaspoon salt
1/2 cup butter
1/3 cup vegetable shortening

Preheat oven to 375 degrees. Combine bananas, sugar and nutmeg. Place mixture in bottom of greased 6-by-10-inch baking pan. Combine brown sugar, sifted flour, oats and salt in bowl. Cut in butter and shortening as for pastry. Sprinkle over bananas. Bake for 40 minutes or until crisp and browned. Serve warm with cream.
Yield: 6 servings.

Approx Per Serving: Cal 69; Prot 6 g; Carbo 108 g; Fiber 5 g; T Fat 29 g; 36% Calories from Fat; Chol 41 mg; Sod 348 mg.

Banana Split De"Lite"

Debbie Snodgrass, Jonesborough

16 squares graham crackers,
  finely crushed
1 (6-ounce) package vanilla instant
  pudding mix
4 bananas
1 (8-ounce) container whipped topping
2 cups strawberries
2 (16-ounce) cans no sugar, crushed
  pineapple, drained
1 (7-ounce) package coconut

Spread graham cracker crumbs on bottom of 9-by-13-inch dish. Prepare pudding according to package directions. Pour mixture over graham crackers. Chill. Slice bananas over pudding. Top with whipped topping. Layer strawberries and pineapple over top. Sprinkle coconut over top.
Yield: 12 servings.

Approx Per Serving: Cal 341; Prot 4 g; Carbo 55 g; Fiber 4 g; T Fat 13 g; 34% Calories from Fat; Chol 8 mg; Sod 269 mg.

Butter Pecan Delight

Rheta Wilkins, Cookeville

3/4 cup butter, melted
90 Ritz crackers, crushed
1 (3-ounce) package French vanilla instant
   pudding mix
1 pint whipping cream, whipped
1 quart butter pecan ice cream, softened

Mix butter with Ritz crackers in bowl. Press crumb mixture into two 9-inch pie plates, reserving 1/2 cup for topping. Blend dry pudding mix with prepared whipped cream. Add softened ice cream. Pour mixture into crumb crusts. Garnish with remaining crumbs, maraschino cherries and pecan halves. Keep frozen until served. Yield: 16 servings.

Approx Per Serving: Cal 350; Prot 3 g; Carbo 24 g; Fiber <1 g; T Fat 28 g; 70% Calories from Fat; Chol 79 mg; Sod 345 mg.

Broken Glass Cake

Effie LeSueur Bacon, Johnson City

1 (3-ounce) package orange gelatin
1 (3-ounce) package strawberry gelatin
1 (3-ounce) package lime gelatin
1 envelope unflavored gelatin
1/4 cup cold water
1 cup warm pineapple juice
1 (9-ounce) container whipped topping
16 graham crackers, crushed
2 tablespoons butter, melted

Combine each flavored gelatin package in 1 1/4 cups water in 3 separate bowls. Chill until firm. Dissolve unflavored gelatin with 1/4 cup cold water. Add pineapple juice. Set aside until thick. Add gelatin mixture to whipped topping in bowl. Cut flavored gelatin into 1/2-inch cubes. Fold into whipped topping mixture. Combine crumbs and butter. Line 9-by-13-inch baking dish with graham cracker crumbs. Pour whipped topping mixture into baking dish. Sprinkle few crumbs over top. Chill. Yield: 12 servings.

Approx Per Serving: Cal 219; Prot 3 g; Carbo 34 g; Fiber <1 g; T Fat 8 g; 33% Calories from Fat; Chol 5 mg; Sod 137 mg.

Chocolate Pizza

Mrs. Jerry Jones, Normandy

1 (12-ounce) package real semisweet
   chocolate chips
14 ounces white almond bark
2 cups miniature marshmallows
1 cup crisp rice cereal
1 cup chopped pecans
1 (6-ounce) jar red maraschino cherries,
   drained and halved
3 tablespoons green maraschino cherries,
   drained and quartered
1/3 cup angel flake coconut
2 ounces white almond bark
1 teaspoon vegetable oil

Melt chocolate chips with 14 ounces almond bark, stirring until smooth in large saucepan over low heat. Remove from heat. Stir in marshmallows, cereal and pecans. Pour into greased 12-inch pizza pan. Top with cherries. Sprinkle with coconut. Melt remaining 2 ounces almond bark with oil over low heat stirring constantly. Drizzle over coconut. Chill until firm. Store at room temperature. Yield: 10 servings.

Approx Per Serving: Cal 565; Prot 3 g; Carbo 73 g; Fiber 3 g; T Fat 32 g; 49% Calories from Fat; Chol 0 mg; Sod 43 mg.

Fruit Potpie

Mrs. Byrd C. Buck, Gainesboro

1 cup coconut
1 cup raisins
1/2 cup sugar
1/2 cup pecans
1 cup crushed pineapple
1 (16-ounce) can fruit cocktail
1 (16-ounce) package yellow cake mix
1/2 cup margarine
1/2 cup water

Preheat oven to 350 degrees. Combine first 6 ingredients in bowl; mix well. Pour into 9-by-13-inch baking pan. Spread cake mix over top of fruit mixture. Melt margarine with water. Pour evenly over top of cake mix. Bake for 30 minutes or until done. Yield: 12 servings.

Approx Per Serving: Cal 410; Prot 3 g; Carbo 64 g; Fiber 3 g; T Fat 18 g; 37% Calories from Fat; Chol 1 mg; Sod 343 mg.

Lemon Dessert

Mrs. Scott Wyatt, Deer Lodge

1 cup flour
1/2 cup butter, melted
1 cup pecans
1 (9-ounce) container whipped topping
1 cup confectioners' sugar
8 ounces cream cheese, softened
2 (3-ounce) packages lemon instant
   pudding mix
3 cups milk

Preheat oven to 400 degrees. Combine flour, butter and pecans in bowl; mix well. Press into 9-inch square baking dish. Bake for 15 to 20 minutes. Let cool. Combine 1 cup whipped topping, confectioners' sugar and cream cheese in bowl. Spread over cooled crust. Combine pudding mix and milk in bowl. Spread over cream cheese mixture. Top with remaining whipped topping. Garnish with additional pecans. Yield: 8 servings.

Approx Per Serving: Cal 653; Prot 8 g; Carbo 62 g; Fiber 1 g; T Fat 43 g; 58% Calories from Fat; Chol 75 mg; Sod 537 mg.

Mint Refrigerated Dessert

Lois Coop, Crockett County

32 chocolate sandwich cookies with cream
   filling, crushed
1 pint whipping cream, whipped
2 cups miniature marshmallows
1 cup after-dinner mints

Press half the crushed cookies in bottom of 9-by-13-inch pan. Combine whipped cream, marshmallows and mints. Spread mixture over layer of crushed cookies. Sprinkle remaining crumbs on top. Refrigerate for 2 days before serving. May be kept frozen until needed.
Yield: 10 servings.

Approx Per Serving: Cal 437; Prot 3 g; Carbo 52 g; Fiber 1 g; T Fat 25 g; 51% Calories from Fat; Chol 65 mg; Sod 223 mg.

Old New Orleans Fruit Dessert

Sherry Sanders, Franklin

2 oranges, sectioned and cut
2 bananas. sliced
2 cups strawberries, halved
1 cup grapes, sliced
2 peaches, peeled and sliced
1 small pineapple, cut into chunks
1 cup apricot preserves
2 tablespoons sugar
1/3 cup bourbon

Combine fruit in large bowl. Heat preserves in saucepan until warm. Add sugar; stir to dissolve. Remove from heat. Stir in bourbon. Pour mixture over fruit; mix well. Refrigerate for several hours before serving. Yield: 8 servings.

Approx Per Serving: Cal 228; Prot 2 g; Carbo 54 g; Fiber 4 g; T Fat 1 g; 3% Calories from Fat; Chol 0 mg; Sod 18 mg.

Orange Delight

Mrs. Ray Peterson, Limestone

1 cup sugar
2 eggs, well beaten
1 1/2 cups crushed pineapple
1 (6-ounce) package orange gelatin
1 (13-ounce) can evaporated milk
1/2 cup butter
1 cup chopped pecans
1 cup coconut
1 cup graham cracker crumbs

Combine sugar, eggs and pineapple in saucepan. Bring to a boil. Remove from heat. Add gelatin; mix well. Chill for 1 hour. Place evaporated milk in freezer for 1 hour. Remove. Beat until soft peaks form. Blend into gelatin mixture. Place in serving dish. Combine remaining ingredients in bowl; mix well. Sprinkle over gelatin mixture. Refrigerate overnight before serving. Yield: 10 servings.

Approx Per Serving: Cal 482; Prot 7 g; Carbo 61 g; Fiber 2 g; T Fat 25 g; 45% Calories from Fat; Chol 78 mg; Sod 264 mg.

Strawberry Delight

Hazel Storey, Dickson

1 medium angel food cake
1 (14-ounce) can sweetened condensed
   milk
Juice of 3 lemons
1 quart sweetened strawberries
1 cup whipping cream, whipped
Dash of salt
1 teaspoon vanilla extract

Crumble cake into bite-sized pieces. Combine condensed milk, lemon juice and strawberries in bowl. Fold whipped cream into mixture. Add salt and vanilla; mix well. Layer cake and berry mixture in 9-by-13-inch serving dish. Chill. Yield: 12 servings.

Approx Per Serving: Cal 381; Prot 7 g; Carbo 68 g; Fiber 2 g: T Fat 11 g; 25% Calories from Fat; Chol 38 mg; Sod 447 mg.

Strawberry Whip

Mrs. Marvin Hayes, Samburg

1 pint whipping cream, whipped
2 quarts sliced strawberries
1 package miniature marshmallows
1 package graham cracker crumbs
Confectioners' sugar to taste

Reserve small amount of whipped cream to top each serving. Combine remaining whipped cream, strawberries, marshmallows and cracker crumbs; mix well. Add confectioners' sugar to taste. Chill. Spoon into parfait glasses. Garnish with whipped cream and strawberry.

Nutritional information for this recipe is not available.

Desserts 229

Strawberries and Cream Dessert

Vicki Ward, Decatur

1 (14-ounce) can sweetened condensed
  milk
1 1/2 cups cold water
1 (3-ounce) package vanilla instant
  pudding mix
2 cups whipping cream, whipped
1 (12-ounce) loaf pound cake, cubed
1 quart fresh strawberries
1/2 cup strawberry preserves

Combine condensed milk and water in large bowl. Add pudding mix; beat well. Chill for 5 minutes. Fold in whipped cream. Spoon 2 cups pudding mixture into 4-quart glass serving bowl. Top with half of each: cake cubes, strawberries, preserves and remaining pudding. Repeat layers, ending with pudding. Garnish with strawberries and almonds. Chill. Refrigerate leftovers. Yield: 12 servings.

Approx Per Serving: Cal 426; Prot 5 g; Carbo 52 g; Fiber 2 g; T Fat 23 g; 48% Calories from Fat; Chol 128 mg; Sod 277 mg.

Layered Cream Cheese and Strawberries

Barbara Yarberry, Sweetwater

1 1/4 cups round, buttery crackers, crushed
1/4 cup butter, melted
8 ounces cream cheese, softened
2 tablespoons sugar
2 tablespoons milk
1 1/2 cups strawberries, halved
1 (4-ounce) package vanilla or lemon
  instant pudding mix
1 1/2 cups milk
1 3/4 cups whipped topping, thawed

Combine crackers and butter. Press into bottom of 8-inch square pan. Chill. Beat cream cheese with sugar and 2 tablespoons milk in bowl until smooth. Spread evenly in crumb-lined pan. Arrange strawberries on cream cheese mixture. Prepare pudding mix with 1 1/2 cups milk according to package directions. Fold in 1/2 cup whipped topping. Spoon over strawberries. Chill for 2 hours or until set. Garnish with remaining whipped topping and strawberries. Cut into squares. Yield: 9 servings.

Approx Per Serving: Cal 321; Prot 4 g; Carbo 28 g; Fiber 1 g; T Fat 22 g; 60% Calories from Fat; Chol 48 mg; Sod 418 mg.

Strawberries and Cream Shortcake

Peggy Ottinger, Parrottsville

2 cups flour
1/4 cup sugar
1 tablespoon baking powder
1 teaspoon grated orange rind
1/4 teaspoon salt
2/3 cup vegetable shortening
2/3 cup milk
1 egg, beaten
1 teaspoon vanilla extract
1 (14-ounce) can sweetened condensed
  milk
1/2 cup cold water
1 (3-ounce) package vanilla instant
  pudding mix
1 (4-ounce) container frozen non-dairy
  whipped topping, thawed
1 quart fresh strawberries, sliced

Preheat oven to 450 degrees. Combine flour, sugar, baking powder, orange rind and salt in medium bowl. Cut in shortening until mixture is crumbly. Combine milk, egg and vanilla in medium bowl. Add to dry ingredients, stirring just until moistened. Spread into 2 greased 9-inch round layer cake pans. Bake for 10 minutes or until golden brown. Remove from pans. Cool on wire rack completely. Combine condensed milk and water in large bowl. Beat in pudding mix. Chill for 5 minutes. Fold in whipped topping. Chill for 30 minutes. Place 1 shortcake layer on serving plate. Top with half each pudding mixture and strawberries. Repeat layer. Store covered in refrigerator. Yield: 12 servings.

Approx Per Serving: Cal 385; Prot 6 g; Carbo 51 g; Fiber 2 g; T Fat 18 g; 41% Calories from Fat; Chol 31 mg; Sod 286 mg.

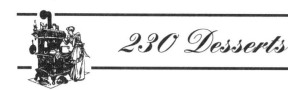

Deluxe Strawberry Pizza

Mrs. Ann Gardner, Dyer County

1/2 cup butter, melted
1 cup flour
1/4 cup confectioners' sugar
4 ounces cream cheese, softened
4 ounces strawberry cream cheese
1/4 cup lemon juice
1 (14-ounce) can sweetened condensed
   milk
1 (12-ounce) container yogurt
1 quart fresh or frozen strawberries, sliced
2 tablespoons cornstarch
1 (3-ounce) package strawberry gelatin
1 pint whipping cream, whipped
1/2 cup grated Cheddar cheese
1/4 cup grated Parmesan cheese

Preheat oven to 350 degrees. Melt butter in small saucepan. Add flour and confectioners' sugar. Place in 9-by-13-inch baking dish. Bake for 10 minutes. Blend next 5 ingredients in medium mixer bowl; mix well. Pour mixture over cooled crust. Combine next 3 ingredients in medium saucepan. Cook over medium heat until clear. Let cool. Pour over second layer. Spread whipped cream over third layer. Chill. Sprinkle cheeses over whipped cream just before serving. Yield: 12 servings.

Approx Per Serving: Cal 521; Prot 9 g; Carbo 42 g; Fiber 2 g; T Fat 36 g; 62% Calories from Fat; Chol 119 mg; Sod 268 mg.

Strawberry Supreme

Marion Williams, Shelbyville

1 (3-ounce) package strawberry gelatin
1 cup boiling water
1 (10-ounce) package quick thaw
   strawberries
1 (3-ounce) package strawberry gelatin
1 cup boiling water
1 1/2 cups vanilla ice cream

Dissolve 1 package gelatin in 1 cup boiling water. Add strawberries. Stir until slightly thickened. Pour into 5-cup mold. Chill until set but not firm. Dissolve gelatin in 1 cup boiling water. Add ice cream, stirring until melted. Spoon into mold. Chill for 4 hours. Yield: 8 servings.

Approx Per Serving: Cal 224; Prot 4 g; Carbo 48 g; Fiber 1 g; T Fat 3 g; 11% Calories from Fat; Chol 11 mg; Sod 129 mg.

Strawberry Trifle

Martha Davis, Shelbyville

This was the second-place winner in the 1985 Tennessee Dairy Recipe Contest.

1 (16-ounce) package butter cake mix
2/3 cup sugar
3 1/2 tablespoons cornstarch
1/2 teaspoon salt
2 1/2 cups milk
3 egg yolks, slightly beaten
1 teaspoon vanilla extract
2 cups plain yogurt
4 cups strawberries sweetened to taste,
   crushed
1 pint heavy whipping cream, whipped and
   sweetened to taste

Prepare and bake cake mix according to package directions. Combine sugar, cornstarch and salt in double boiler. Stir in milk. Cook, stirring, over boiling water until thickened. Cover. Cook for 15 minutes. Stir small amount of hot mixture into egg yolks. Add to remaining mixture. Cook, stirring, for 2 minutes over hot but not boiling water. Cool. Add vanilla. Fold in yogurt. Layer half the crumbled cake in 9-by-13-inch pan. Cover with half the pudding mixture and 2 cups strawberries. Cover berries with half the whipped cream. Repeat layers, ending with whipped cream. Garnish with fresh strawberries. Yield: 12 servings.

Approx Per Serving: Cal 544; Prot 8 g; Carbo 58 g; Fiber 1 g; T Fat 32 g; 52% Calories from Fat; Chol 184 mg; Sod 420 mg.

Cheesecake

Mrs. Sammie Spears, Manchester

2 cups graham crackers, crushed
1/2 teaspoon cinnamon
1/2 cup butter, melted
1/4 cup chopped pecans
3 eggs, beaten
1 cup sugar
16 ounces cream cheese, softened
3 cups sour cream
2 teaspoons vanilla extract
1/4 teaspoon salt
1/2 teaspoon almond extract

Preheat oven to 350 degrees. Combine cracker crumbs, cinnamon, butter and pecans in bowl; mix well. Reserve 2 tablespoons mixture for topping. Press remaining mixture into springform pan. Combine remaining ingredients in bowl; mix well. Pour over crumb mixture. Sprinkle with reserved topping. Bake for 1 hour or until done. Let cool completely before removing from pan.
Yield: 12 servings.

Approx Per Serving: Cal 465; Prot 7 g; Carbo 28 g; Fiber <1 g; T Fat 37 g; 70% Calories from Fat; Chol 141 mg; Sod 341 mg.

Chocolate-Amaretto Cheesecake

Violet Dyke, Speedwell

6 chocolate wafers, finely crushed
1 1/2 cups light cream cheese
1 cup sugar
1 cup 1% low-fat cottage cheese
1/4 cup plus 2 tablespoons unsweetened
   baking cocoa
1/4 cup flour
1/4 cup Amaretto
1 teaspoon salt
1 egg
2 tablespoons semisweet chocolate
   mini-morsels

Preheat oven to 300 degrees. Sprinkle chocolate wafer crumbs in bottom of 7-inch springform pan. Set aside. Position knife blade in food processor bowl. Add cream cheese and next 6 ingredients, processing until smooth. Add egg; process just until blended. Fold in chocolate morsels. Slowly pour mixture over crumbs in pan. Bake for 1 hour to 1 hour and 10 minutes or until cheesecake is set. Let cool in pan on wire rack. Cover. Chill for at least 8 hours. Remove sides from pan; transfer cheesecake to serving platter. Garnish with chocolate curls.
Yield: 12 servings.

Approx Per Serving: Cal 207; Prot 7 g; Carbo 28 g; Fiber 1 g; T Fat 7 g; 30% Calories from Fat; Chol 35 mg; Sod 366 mg.

Pineapple Cheesecake

Carole A. Covington, Only

1 3/4 cups crushed graham crackers
1/4 cup sugar
1/2 cup butter, melted
12 ounces cream cheese, softened
2 eggs
1/2 teaspoon vanilla extract
1/2 cup sugar
1 (20-ounce) can crushed pineapple,
   drained
1 cup sour cream
3 tablespoons sugar
1 teaspoon vanilla extract

Preheat oven to 350 degrees. Combine crumbs, 1/4 cup sugar and melted butter in bowl; mix well. Press into greased 8-inch square baking pan. Bake for 5 minutes. Reduce oven temperature to 325 degrees. Beat cream cheese in bowl. Add eggs, 1/2 teaspoon vanilla and 1/2 cup sugar; mix well. Fold in pineapple. Pour over crust. Bake for 35 minutes. Combine sour cream, 3 tablespoons sugar and 1 teaspoon vanilla. Pour over hot cake. Let cool. Refrigerate. Yield: 8 servings.

Approx Per Serving: Cal 569; Prot 8 g; Carbo 56 g; Fiber 1 g; T Fat 36 g; 56% Calories from Fat; Chol 144 mg; Sod 433 mg.

Strawberry Cheesecake

Colleen Winningham, Allardt

³/₄ cup ground pecans
³/₄ cup graham cracker crumbs
3 tablespoons butter, melted
32 ounces cream cheese, softened
4 eggs
1¹/₄ cups sugar
1 tablespoon fresh lemon juice
2 teaspoons vanilla extract
2 cups sour cream
¹/₄ cup sugar
1 teaspoon vanilla extract

Preheat oven to 350 degrees. Combine pecans, crumbs and butter in bowl; mix well. Press mixture into bottom of 10-inch springform pan. Set aside. Beat cream cheese in mixer bowl until smooth. Add eggs, 1¹/₄ cups sugar, lemon juice and 2 teaspoons vanilla; mix thoroughly. Spoon over crust. Bake for 50 minutes or until filling is almost set. Remove from oven. Let stand for 15 minutes. Combine sour cream, ¹/₄ cup sugar and 1 teaspoon vanilla; mix well. Spread over cake. Return to 350-degree oven for 5 minutes. Let cool to room temperature. Refrigerate for 24 hours.

Strawberry Glaze:

¹/₄ cup water
2 tablespoons cornstarch
1 (12-ounce) jar
   strawberry jelly
Red food coloring

3 tablespoons orange-
   flavored liqueur
1 quart whole fresh
   strawberries, washed
   and hulled

Prepare glaze several hours before cake is to be served. Combine water and cornstarch in saucepan. Add jelly. Cook over medium high heat, stirring constantly, until thickened. Remove from heat. Stir in food coloring and liqueur. Let cool to room temperature. Loosen and remove sides of pan just before serving. Arrange strawberries on top of cake with pointed ends up. Spoon glaze over berries, allowing to drip down side of cake.
Yield: 12 servings.

Approx Per Serving: Cal 675; Prot 10 g; Carbo 62 g; Fiber 2 g; T Fat 44 g; 57% Calories from Fat; Chol 179 mg; Sod 350 mg.

Butter Pecan Ice Cream

Amy H. Willhite, Sparta

¹/₂ cup chopped pecans
2 tablespoons melted butter
3 eggs
2¹/₂ cups sugar
1 (14-ounce) can sweetened condensed
   milk
1 (4-ounce) package butter pecan instant
   pudding mix
6 cups milk

Sauté pecans in butter until golden brown. Set aside to cool. Beat eggs at medium speed until frothy. Gradually add sugar until thick. Stir in condensed milk and pudding mix. Add pecans and enough milk to reach freezer full line. Freeze according to freezer directions. Let ripen at least 1 hour. Yield: 1 gallon.

Approx Per Serving: Cal 334; Prot 6 g; Carbo 56 g; Fiber <1 g; T Fat 10 g; 27% Calories from Fat; Chol 64 mg; Sod 205 mg.

Chocolate Ice Cream

Hallie Modrall, Shelbyville

1 (7-ounce) jar marshmallow creme
2 (14-ounce) cans sweetened condensed
   milk
1 (16-ounce) can chocolate syrup
1 teaspoon vanilla extract
Milk to make 1 gallon

Melt marshmallow creme in top of double boiler. Add condensed milk, chocolate syrup and vanilla; mix well. Pour into freezer container. Add enough milk to fill freezer container ³/₄ full. Freeze according to freezer directions for about 30 minutes. Yield: 1 gallon.

Nutritional information for this recipe is not available.

Crunchy Peanut Butter Ice Cream

Peggy C. Deakins, Gray

4 eggs, beaten
1¹/₂ cups sugar
2 (14-ounce) cans sweetened condensed
   milk
8 ounces crunchy peanut butter
1 teaspoon vanilla extract
Whole milk

Combine first 5 ingredients; mix well. Pour into 4-quart ice cream freezer can. Fill can to full line with whole milk. Freeze according to freezer directions. Remove dasher from can. Replace lid. Cover freezer with newspaper and/or cloth. Allow to ripen for about 1 hour. Yield: 1 gallon.

Nutritional information for this recipe is not available.

Peach Ice Cream

Linda Lee, Lebanon

6 cups mashed peaches
1 cup sugar
3 eggs
1¹/₂ cups sugar
2 tablespoons flour
¹/₂ teaspoon salt
1 quart milk
1 cup whipping cream
1 tablespoon vanilla extract

Combine peaches and 1 cup sugar. Set aside. Beat eggs in mixer bowl at medium speed until frothy. Combine 1¹/₂ cups sugar, flour and salt; mix well. Gradually add sugar mixture to eggs, beating until thick. Add milk; mix well. Pour egg mixture into saucepan. Cook over low heat, stirring constantly, until mixture thickens and coats metal spoon. Remove from heat. Place pan in cold water; stir gently until cool. Stir in whipping cream and vanilla. Stir in peaches. Pour mixture into 1-gallon freezer container. Freeze according to freezer directions. Yield: 1 gallon.

Approx Per Serving: Cal 285; Prot 4 g; Carbo 50 g; Fiber 2 g; T Fat 9 g; 26% Calories from Fat; Chol 68 mg; Sod 114 mg.

Homemade Vanilla Ice Cream

Wanda Burns, Bulls Gap

2 cups packed light brown sugar
1 cup sugar
1 tablespoon flour
1 tablespoon vanilla extract
3 eggs
1 (13-ounce) can evaporated milk
Milk to fill freezer

Combine first 6 ingredients in bowl; mix well. Pour into ice cream freezer container. Fill with whole milk. Freeze according to freezer directions. Yield: 1 gallon.

Nutritional information for this recipe is not available.

Strawberry Ice Cream

Mrs. J. Clifford Smith, Fayetteville

1 quart fresh strawberries, mashed
1³/₄ cups sugar
Juice of 1 lemon
2 cups whipping cream
2 cups light cream
¹/₈ teaspoon salt

Sprinkle strawberries with half the sugar and lemon juice. Cover. Set aside. Combine creams with salt and remaining sugar in freezer can. Freeze according to freezer directions until mixture becomes partially frozen. Stir in strawberry mixture. Continue to freeze. Yield: 1 quart.

Approx Per Serving: Cal 1144; Prot 6 g; Carbo 105 g; Fiber 4 g; T Fat 82 g; 62% Calories from Fat; Chol 296 mg; Sod 155 mg.

Pineapple-Mint Sherbet

Mrs. Glynn T. Edmonds, Humboldt

3 cups sugar
3 cups water
1 cup spearmint leaves, crushed
Juice of 2 lemons
Juice of 3 oranges
1 cup crushed pineapple
3 ripe bananas, mashed
Green food coloring
2 egg whites, beaten stiff

Cook sugar and water in saucepan until sugar is dissolved and syrup boils. Add mint leaves. Set aside for 1 hour. Strain mint leaves. Add lemon juice, orange juice, pineapple, bananas and food coloring. Gently fold egg whites into fruit mixture. Pour into hand freezer; begin cranking. Sherbet is frozen when handle gets hard to turn. Yield: 3 quarts.

Approx Per Serving: Cal 250; Prot 1 g; Carbo 64 g; Fiber 1 g; T Fat <1 g; 1% Calories from Fat; Chol 0 mg; Sod 10 mg.

Perfect Boiled Custard

Molly Phillips, Dixon Springs

1 (4-ounce) package vanilla instant
    pudding mix
¹/₂ cup sugar
1 tablespoon vanilla extract
5 cups milk

Prepare pudding mix according to package directions. Add sugar. Stir in vanilla. Add milk to make 2 quarts. Chill. Delicious for the holiday season! Yield: 10 servings.

Approx Per Serving: Cal 228; Prot 7 g; Carbo 34 g; Fiber <1 g; T Fat 7 g; 28% Calories from Fat; Chol 29 mg; Sod 278 mg.

Ozark Apple Pudding

Bettye Rose, Jackson

This recipe was a favorite of Harry Truman.

2 eggs
1 cup sugar
1 teaspoon vanilla extract
¹/₃ cup flour
1 tablespoon baking powder
¹/₈ teaspoon salt
2 cups chopped peeled apples
¹/₂ cup chopped pecans

Preheat oven to 325 degrees. Beat eggs, sugar and vanilla in bowl. Sift together flour, baking powder and salt. Blend into creamed mixture. Fold in apples and pecans. Turn into greased and floured 9-inch square baking pan. Bake for 30 to 35 minutes. Serve warm. Top with vanilla ice cream or whipped cream. Yield: 10 servings.

Approx Per Serving: Cal 163; Prot 2 g; Carbo 28 g; Fiber 1 g; T Fat 5 g; 27% Calories from Fat; Chol 42 mg; Sod 138 mg.

Apple Pudding

Mrs. Louise Colvett, Alamo

2 cups chopped apples
1 cup sugar
1 egg
1 cup self-rising flour
1/4 teaspoon baking powder
1/4 teaspoon each allspice, cinnamon
1/2 cup packed light brown sugar
1/4 cup water

Preheat oven to 300 degrees. Combine apples, sugar and egg. Set aside. Sift together flour, baking powder, allspice and cinnamon. Add to apple mixture; blend well. Place mixture in greased and floured 9-inch square baking dish. Bake until done. Combine brown sugar and water. Spread over pudding when taken from oven. Yield: 10 servings.

Approx Per Serving: Cal 178; Prot 2 g; Carbo 42 g; Fiber 1 g; T Fat 1 g; 3% Calories from Fat; Chol 21 mg; Sod 177 mg.

Banana Pudding

Mrs. H. P. Rochelle, Bon Aqua

1 (3-ounce) package vanilla instant
   pudding mix
1 cup sour cream
1 (9-ounce) container whipped topping
12 graham crackers
2 bananas
2 tablespoons graham cracker crumbs

Prepare pudding mix according to package directions. Combine with sour cream and whipped topping. Place layer of graham crackers in serving dish. Pour half the pudding mixture over crackers. Add sliced bananas, then layer of graham crackers. Pour remaining pudding mixture over all. Sprinkle with graham cracker crumbs. Refrigerate. Yield: 6 servings.

Approx Per Serving: Cal 428; Prot 6 g; Carbo 52 g; Fiber 1 g; T Fat 23 g; 48% Calories from Fat; Chol 27 mg; Sod 402 mg.

Wafer Banana Pudding

Mrs. Ray Brooks, Middlesboro, Kentucky

5 cups milk
3 (3-ounce) packages vanilla instant
   pudding mix
1 cup sour cream
1 (9-ounce) container whipped cream
24 vanilla wafers
4 bananas

Pour milk into deep bowl. Add pudding mix; blend until thick. Add sour cream and half the whipped cream; blend until thick. Layer vanilla wafers in 9-by-13-inch glass serving dish. Slice bananas over wafers. Pour pudding mixture over all. Top with remaining whipped cream. Chill before serving. Yield: 12 servings.

Approx Per Serving: Cal 318; Prot 5 g; Carbo 45 g; Fiber 1 g; T Fat 14 g; 39% Calories from Fat; Chol 27 mg; Sod 397 mg.

Jiffy Banana Pudding

Mrs. Rose Horner, Powell

2 (9-ounce) packages vanilla instant
   pudding mix
3 cups milk
1 (9-ounce) container whipped topping
1 cup sour cream
24 vanilla wafers
6 to 8 large bananas

Combine first 4 ingredients. Layer vanilla wafers, bananas and pudding in 9-by-13-inch dish. Garnish with crumbled wafers. Yield: 10 servings.

Approx Per Serving: Cal 508; Prot 5 g; Carbo 92 g; Fiber 2 g; T Fat 16 g; 27% Calories from Fat; Chol 26 mg; Sod 820 mg.

Farina Pudding Dessert

Mrs. Margarete McClanahan, Memphis

This recipe won second place in 1986 Tennessee June Dairy Month Recipe Contest. Farina, by the way, is a powdery substance used in making puddings or as a breakfast cereal.

3³/₄ cups milk
¹/₂ teaspoon salt
¹/₂ cup sugar
²/₃ cup farina
3 eggs
1 teaspoon vanilla extract
2 tablespoons butter
1 tablespoon sugar
¹/₂ pint whipping cream, whipped

Heat milk until scalded. Add salt and ¹/₂ cup sugar. Stir until sugar is dissolved. Add farina, stirring constantly. Cook over low heat for 5 minutes. Lightly beat eggs in bowl. Add 4 tablespoons farina mixture to beaten eggs; stir. Add to farina. Cook for a few more minutes over low heat, stirring constantly to keep from sticking. Add vanilla and butter; mix well. Pour into 1-quart mold rinsed in cold water. Cover with waxed paper. Refrigerate for several hours. Unmold and slice. Add 1 tablespoon sugar to whipped cream. Top with whipped cream. Garnish with strawberries, raspberries or peaches. Yield: 8 servings.

Approx Per Serving: Cal 334; Prot 8 g; Carbo 32 g; Fiber 1 g; T Fat 20 g; 52% Calories from Fat; Chol 144 mg; Sod 296 mg.

Molasses Pudding

Mrs. Mattie Vassar, Rockvale

1 teaspoon baking soda
¹/₂ cup buttermilk
1 cup molasses
¹/₂ cup vegetable oil
Dash of salt
1 cup sugar
2 eggs, beaten
¹/₂ teaspoon cinnamon or ginger

Preheat oven to 350 degrees. Dissolve baking soda in buttermilk. Heat molasses. Add all ingredients, stirring constantly. Pour in 1-quart baking pan. Bake for 45 minutes or until done. Yield: 6 servings.

Approx Per Serving: Cal 468; Prot 3 g; Carbo 72 g; Fiber 0 g; T Fat 20 g; 38% Calories from Fat; Chol 71 mg; Sod 200 mg.

Mother's Bread Pudding

Mrs. Albert Shipley, Greeneville

4 biscuits, crumbled
2 cups milk
²/₃ cup sugar
2 egg yolks, slightly beaten
Pinch of salt
1 teaspoon vanilla extract
1¹/₂ cups apple or blackberry jelly
2 egg whites
4 tablespoons sugar
Pinch of salt

Preheat oven to 350 degrees. Combine biscuits and milk in bowl. Add ²/₃ cup sugar, egg yolks, salt and vanilla; mix well. Pour into 2-quart baking dish. Bake until firm. Spread thick layer of jelly over pudding. Beat egg whites with 4 tablespoons sugar until stiff peaks form. Spread over pudding. Bake until light brown. Let cool.
Yield: 6 servings.

Approx Per Serving: Cal 456; Prot 6 g; Carbo 94 g; Fiber 1 g; T Fat 8 g; 15% Calories from Fat; Chol 82 mg; Sod 197 mg.

Easy Pineapple Bread Pudding

Aurora Aumiller, Sharps Chapel

1 cup butter
2 cups sugar
4 eggs
1/4 cup milk
4 cups bread cubes
1 (20-ounce) can crushed pineapple with
  juice

Preheat oven to 350 degrees. Cream butter and sugar. Beat in eggs with mixer. Fold in milk and bread. Add pineapple and juice. Bake for 1 hour in greased casserole dish. Yield: 6 servings.

Approx Per Serving: Cal 712; Prot 7 g; Carbo 96 g; Fiber 1 g; T Fat 35 g; 43% Calories from Fat; Chol 226 mg; Sod 462 mg

Pineapple-Coconut Pudding

Mrs. Jean Jackson, West Point

1 (20-ounce) can crushed pineapple
3/4 cup orange juice
1 (3-ounce) package vanilla instant
  pudding mix
1/2 cup sour cream
1 cup whipping cream, whipped
3/4 cup toasted coconut
1 1/2 cups coarsely crushed vanilla wafers
1/4 cup toasted coconut

Drain pineapple, reserving juice. Set pineapple aside. Combine pineapple liquid and orange juice to make 1 1/3 cups. Combine juice mixture, pudding mix and sour cream in bowl. Beat with rotary beater or electric mixer for 2 minutes or until mixture is smooth. Chill for 5 minutes. Stir 1 cup whipped cream, pineapple and 3/4 cup coconut into pudding. Spoon 1/3 of pudding mixture into 2-quart serving dish. Top with half the wafers. Repeat, ending with pudding. Garnish with remaining whipped cream and coconut. Chill for 1 to 2 hours. Yield: 12 servings.

Approx Per Serving: Cal 240; Prot 2 g; Carbo 31 g; Fiber 1 g; T Fat 13 g; 48% Calories from Fat; Chol 38 mg; Sod 168 mg.

Strawberry Pudding

Frances Hurst, Newport

1/2 cup sugar
1/3 cup flour
Dash of salt
4 egg yolks
2 cups milk
1/2 teaspoon vanilla extract
35 to 45 vanilla wafers
1 1/2 pints strawberries, sliced

Combine sugar, flour and salt in top of double boiler. Stir in egg yolks and milk; blend well. Cook, uncovered, over boiling water, stirring constantly until thickened. Reduce heat. Cook, stirring occasionally, for 5 minutes. Remove from heat. Add vanilla; mix well. Spread small amount on bottom of 1 1/2-quart casserole. Cover with layer of vanilla wafers. Top with layer of sliced strawberries. Pour 1/3 of custard over strawberries. Continue to layer wafers, strawberries and custard to make 3 layers of each, ending with custard. Garnish with crushed vanilla wafers and strawberries. Yield: 8 servings.

Approx Per Serving: Cal 249; Prot 5 g; Carbo 40 g; Fiber 2 g; T Fat 8 g; 29% Calories from Fat; Chol 127 mg; Sod 104 mg.

Tennessee Pudding

Mrs. J. E. Mitchell, Lebanon

1 cup butter
2 cups sugar
4 eggs, blended well
1/2 cup buttermilk
1 teaspoon baking soda
3 1/2 cups flour
1 cup chopped pecans
1 cup chopped dates
1 cup angel flake coconut
2 1/2 cups sugar
1 1/2 cups orange juice

Preheat oven to 300 degrees. Cream butter and 2 cups sugar in bowl. Add eggs, buttermilk, baking soda and flour; mix well. Add pecans, dates and coconut. Pour into tube pan. Bake for 1 hour and 30 minutes. Punch holes in top while still hot. Combine sugar and orange juice in saucepan. Heat until sugar dissolves. Pour sauce over all. Let cool in pan. Yield: 8 servings.

Approx Per Serving: Cal 1105; Prot 12 g; Carbo 182 g; Fiber 6 g; T Fat 40 g; 31% Calories from Fat; Chol 169 mg; Sod 390 mg.

Easy Chocolate Syrup

Ruby Nell Shelton, Ramer

2 1/2 cups light corn syrup
2 tablespoons cornstarch
4 tablespoons baking cocoa
2 cups hot water
2 tablespoons butter
1 teaspoon vanilla extract

Combine first 4 ingredients in saucepan in order listed. Stir over medium heat until dissolved. Boil for 4 minutes or until mixture drops from spoon like thin gravy. Remove from heat. Add butter and vanilla; mix well. Let cool. Store in refrigerator. Stir before using. May be used for beverages or as topping for ice cream. Yield: 4 cups.

Approx Per Serving: Cal 657; Prot 1 g; Carbo 163 g; Fiber 2 g; T Fat 6 g; 8% Calories from Fat; Chol 16 mg; Sod 308 mg.

Sweetened Condensed Milk

Mrs. Abe Miller, Knoxville

1/4 cup margarine
1/2 cup boiling water
1/2 cup sugar
1 1/2 cups powdered milk

Combine margarine and boiling water in blender container. Add slowly sugar and powdered milk; blend well. Refrigerate for 2 to 3 hours or until set. Recipe makes same amount as 1 can sweetened condensed milk.
Yield: 14 ounces.

Approx Per Serving: Cal 89; Prot 3 g; Carbo 11 g; Fiber 0 g; T Fat 3 g; 35% Calories from Fat; Chol 1 mg; Sod 78 mg.

CHAPTER 11

Holiday Recipes

Cedar Grove Missionary Baptist Church

Cedar Grove Missionary Baptist Church paints a portrait of tranquility as it sits peacefully among the trees atop a hill in Union County's Hickory Valley.

New Year's

Black-Eyed Pea Dip

Jean Jenkins, Somerville

2 (16-ounce) cans black-eyed peas, drained
1/2 cup chopped onion
1 pound processed cheese with jalapeños
1 teaspoon garlic powder
1/4 cup butter, melted

Mash peas in food processor. Combine with remaining ingredients in 2-quart microwave-safe bowl. Microwave on High for 2 to 3 minutes, stirring twice, until cheese melts. Yield: 36 (1 tablespoon) servings.

Approx Per Serving: Cal 78; Prot 4 g; Carbo 4 g; Fiber 2 g; T Fat 5 g; 61% Calories from Fat; Chol 15 mg; Sod 268 mg.

Hot Sausage Balls

Mrs. Hubert Walters, Jonesborough

1 pound hot sausage
1 cup baking mix
1 cup grated sharp Cheddar cheese

Preheat oven to 350 degrees. Combine all ingredients in bowl. Shape into walnut-sized balls. Place on baking pan. Bake for 30 minutes. Yield: 24 servings.

Approx Per Serving: Cal 72; Prot 3 g; Carbo 3 g; Fiber <1 g; T Fat 5 g; 64% Calories from Fat; Chol 12 mg; Sod 204 mg.

Swiss Cheese Quiche

Norene Boyett, Gibson County

1 (10-ounce) package frozen chopped broccoli
2 cups ham cubes
2 cups shredded Swiss cheese
1/2 cup shredded Cheddar cheese
1 (10-inch) unbaked pastry shell
3 tablespoons chopped green onions
2 cups milk
3 eggs, slightly beaten
1 tablespoon butter, melted
1/8 teaspoon each salt, pepper

Preheat oven to 450 degrees. Layer half the broccoli, ham and cheeses in pastry shell. Repeat layers. Sprinkle onion over top; set aside. Gradually stir milk into beaten eggs; add melted butter and seasonings. Pour into pastry shell. Bake for 10 minutes. Reduce heat to 325 degrees; bake for 30 to 40 minutes longer. Remove from oven. Let stand a few minutes before serving. Yield: 6 servings.

Approx Per Serving: Cal 539; Prot 34 g; Carbo 24 g; Fiber 2 g; T Fat 34 g; 57% Calories from Fat; Chol 191 mg; Sod 1098 mg.

Day-Ahead Party Salad

Mrs. Lance Davison, Finley

1 large head lettuce, torn into small pieces
1 medium onion, chopped
1 head cauliflower, broken into florets
3/4 pound bacon, crisp-fried and crumbled
3/4 cup reduced-calorie mayonnaise
1/4 cup Parmesan cheese

Layer lettuce, onion, cauliflower and bacon in large salad bowl. Spread mayonnaise over layers to touch side of bowl. Sprinkle cheese over mayonnaise. Cover. Chill for 24 hours. Mix well just before serving. Yield: 10 servings.

Approx Per Serving: Cal 136; Prot 6 g; Carbo 8 g; Fiber 2 g; T Fat 10 g; 62% Calories from Fat; Chol 15 mg; Sod 321 mg.

Black-Eyed Pea Corn Bread

Carol Bruce, Brownsville

This is good potluck dish that's especially appropriate for New Year's Day.

1 pound sausage
1 cup yellow or white cornmeal
1/2 cup flour
1 teaspoon salt
1/2 teaspoon baking soda
1 cup buttermilk
1/2 cup vegetable oil
2 eggs, slightly beaten
3/4 cup cream-style corn
1 onion, chopped
2 jalapeño peppers, chopped
1 (16-ounce) can black-eyed peas, drained
1/2 pound Cheddar cheese, grated

Preheat oven to 400 degrees. Brown sausage, stirring until crumbly; drain. Combine dry ingredients in bowl. Add buttermilk, oil, eggs and corn; mix well. Add remaining ingredients; mix well. Pour into lightly greased 9-by-13-inch pan. Bake for 40 to 50 minutes or until brown.
Yield: 12 servings.

Approx Per Serving: Cal 349; Prot 14 g; Carbo 24 g; Fiber 4 g; T Fat 23 g; 58% Calories from Fat; Chol 71 mg; Sod 750 mg.

Fiesta Corn Bake

Dorothy Taylor, Cumberland Gap

1 (17-ounce) can whole kernel corn
1 (17-ounce) can cream-style corn
2 eggs, beaten
1 cup sour cream
1 cup shredded Cheddar cheese
1/2 cup self-rising cornmeal
1/4 cup each red, yellow and green pepper, finely chopped

Preheat oven to 350 degrees. Combine all ingredients in bowl; mix well. Pour into greased 9-by-13-inch baking dish. Bake for 45 minutes or until golden brown and slightly puffed in center. Yield: 12 servings.

Approx Per Serving: Cal 167; Prot 6 g; Carbo 19 g; Fiber 1 g; T Fat 8 g; 43% Calories from Fat; Chol 54 mg; Sod 372 mg.

Spicy-Hot Black-Eyed Peas

Mrs. Fred Jones, Knoxville

1/2 cup chopped onion
1/2 cup chopped green pepper
1 (16-ounce) can black-eyed peas, undrained
1 (16-ounce) can unsalted stewed tomatoes, undrained
1 teaspoon dry mustard
1/2 teaspoon chili powder
1/8 teaspoon red pepper
1/2 teaspoon pepper
1 tablespoon low-sodium soy sauce
1 teaspoon liquid smoke
1 tablespoon minced fresh parsley

Coat large nonstick skillet with cooking spray. Place skillet over medium heat until hot. Add onion and green pepper. Sauté until tender-crisp. Add black-eyed peas and next 7 ingredients. Bring to a boil. Reduce heat. Simmer for 20 minutes, stirring often. Transfer to serving dish. Sprinkle with parsley. Yield: 5 servings.

Approx Per Serving: Cal 106; Prot 6 g; Carbo 20 g; Fiber 6 g; T Fat 1 g; 6% Calories from Fat; Chol 0 mg; Sod 298 mg.

Sweet Potato Chips

Peggy Huffstetler, Lebanon

³/₄ cup honey-roasted peanuts
2 peeled large sweet potatoes, sliced
   ¹/₈ inch thick
¹/₂ cup unsalted butter, melted

Preheat oven to 475 degrees. Line 2 large baking sheets with aluminum foil. Lightly butter foil. Process peanuts in blender until finely chopped but not powdered; transfer to bowl. Dip potato slices in melted butter to coat both sides. Arrange slices on prepared pans in rows that are close together but not overlapping. Sprinkle top of each potato slice generously with peanuts. Bake chips for 15 to 20 minutes or until tops are lightly browned and potatoes are just tender. Watch carefully that they do not burn. Transfer chips to paper towels to drain. Let cool for 5 minutes. Sprinkle with salt. Yield: 48 servings.

Approx Per Serving: Cal 40; Prot 1 g; Carbo 3 g; Fiber <1 g; T Fat 3 g; 68% Calories from Fat; Chol 5 mg; Sod 12 mg.

Chocolate Bundt Cake

Larrie Wiseman, Camden

1 (16-ounce) package yellow butter cake
   mix
1 (3-ounce) package chocolate instant
   pudding mix
3 eggs
³/₄ cup vegetable oil
1 (6-ounce) package chocolate chips
1 cup sour cream

Preheat oven to 350 degrees. Combine cake mix, pudding mix, eggs, ³/₄ cup water and oil in bowl; mix well. Fold in chocolate chips and sour cream. Pour into greased bundt pan. Bake for 1 hour. Remove to wire rack to cool. Yield: 12 servings.

Approx Per Serving: Cal 437; Prot 5 g; Carbo 47 g; Fiber 1 g; T Fat 27 g; 54% Calories from Fat; Chol 62 mg; Sod 129 mg.

Strawberry Bread

Jean Schiavone, Gallatin

3 cups flour
2 cups sugar
1 tablespoon ground cinnamon
1 teaspoon baking soda
1 teaspoon salt
3 eggs, well beaten
1¹/₄ cups vegetable oil
2 (10-ounce) packages frozen sliced
   strawberries, thawed

Preheat oven to 350 degrees. Lightly grease 2 loaf pans; line bottoms with aluminum foil. Combine first 5 ingredients in large bowl. Make well in center. Pour eggs and oil in well. Stir until dry ingredients just become moist. Pour strawberries and juice into container. Dip out strawberries with slotted spoon; stir gently into mixture. Add juice gradually, stirring until batter is thick. Do not get batter too thin. Pour into prepared pans. Bake for 1 hour. Let cool in pans for 15 minutes. Loosen sides of cakes with knife. Let cool on wire rack. Yield: 16 servings.

Approx Per Serving: Cal 360; Prot 4 g; Carbo 47 g; Fiber 2 g; T Fat 18 g; 45% Calories from Fat; Chol 40 mg; Sod 198 mg.

Washington's Birthday

Cherry-Cran Salad

Nancy P. Wortham, Indian Mound

1 (20-ounce) can pitted tart red cherries
1 (3-ounce) package cherry gelatin
1 (8-ounce) can jellied cranberry sauce
1 (3-ounce) package lemon gelatin
1 cup boiling water
1 (3-ounce) package cream cheese, softened
1/3 cup mayonnaise
1 (8-ounce) can crushed pineapple, undrained
1/2 cup whipping cream
1 cup miniature marshmallows
2 tablespoons chopped pecans

Drain cherries, reserving syrup. Add water to syrup to make 1 cup liquid. Bring liquid to a boil. Remove from heat. Add cherry-flavored gelatin; stir to dissolve. Break up cranberry sauce with fork; stir into cherry gelatin, blending until smooth. Stir in cherries. Turn into 9-inch square serving dish. Chill until almost set. Dissolve lemon gelatin in boiling water. Beat cream cheese with mayonnaise. Gradually add lemon gelatin. Stir in undrained pineapple. Chill until partially set. Whip cream; fold into lemon mixture with marshmallows. Spread on cherry layer. Sprinkle with pecans. Cover. Chill until firm. Yield: 12 servings.

Approx Per Serving: Cal 270; Prot 3 g; Carbo 41 g; Fiber 1 g; T Fat 12 g; 39% Calories from Fat; Chol 25 mg; Sod 106 mg.

Cherry-Nut Pound Cake

Barbara Crowe, Henderson

1 1/2 cups vegetable shortening
3 cups sugar
6 eggs
1/2 teaspoon vanilla extract
1/2 teaspoon almond extract
3 3/4 cups flour
3/4 cup milk
1 (5-ounce) bottle maraschino cherries, drained and chopped

Cream shortening and sugar in bowl. Beat for 10 to 15 minutes until mixture is creamy. Add eggs, one at a time, beating well after each addition. Add vanilla and almond flavorings; blend well. Add flour and milk alternately, mixing well after each addition. Fold in cherries. Pour into large greased tube pan. Place in cold oven. Set oven at 275 degrees. Bake for 2 hours and 10 minutes. Let cool thoroughly. Frost.

Frosting:

1/4 cup butter, softened
8 ounces cream cheese, softened
1 (16-ounce) package confectioners' sugar
1 teaspoon vanilla extract
1 teaspoon almond extract
1 cup coconut
1 cup chopped walnuts
1 (5-ounce) bottle maraschino cherries, drained and chopped

Blend butter and cream cheese in bowl until smooth. Gradually add confectioners' sugar, beating until smooth. Add flavorings; mix well. Fold in coconut, walnuts and cherries. Spread mixture over cake. Yield: 12 servings.

Approx Per Serving: Cal 976; Prot 11 g; Carbo 130 g; Fiber 2 g; T Fat 48 g; 43% Calories from Fat; Chol 139 mg; Sod 138 mg.

Cherry-Almond Clouds

Lorene Porter, Evensville

¹/₂ teaspoon almond extract
1 (20-ounce) can cherry pie filling
4 egg whites, at room temperature
³/₄ teaspoon baking powder
1¹/₄ cups sugar
¹/₂ teaspoon almond extract
15 Saltine crackers, coarsely crushed
¹/₃ cup whole blanched almonds, chopped
¹/₂ cup heavy cream, whipped

Preheat oven to 300 degrees. Add ¹/₂ teaspoon almond flavoring to cherry pie filling in bowl. Cover and chill. Beat egg whites and baking powder until soft peaks form. Gradually sprinkle in sugar, 2 tablespoons at a time, beating after each addition until stiff and glossy. Fold in ¹/₂ teaspoon almond extract, crushed crackers and almonds. Cover large cookie sheet with brown paper. Spoon mixture onto paper in 8 mounds. Spread each mound into 4¹/₂-inch circle, pulling up sides with back of spoon. Bake for about 30 minutes or until done. Remove to rack to cool. Spoon cherry filling into meringue shells to serve. Garnish with whipped cream. Yield: 8 servings.

Approx Per Serving: Cal 325; Prot 4 g; Carbo 57 g; Fiber 1 g; T Fat 10 g; 27% Calories from Fat; Chol 20 mg; Sod 175 mg.

Chocolate-Covered Cherry Cookies

Mrs. James H. Young, Elmwood

¹/₂ cup butter
1 cup sugar
1 egg
1¹/₂ teaspoons vanilla extract
1¹/₂ cups flour
¹/₂ cup baking cocoa
¹/₄ teaspoon salt
¹/₄ teaspoon baking powder
¹/₄ teaspoon baking soda
Frosting
48 maraschino cherries, blotted dry, reserve cherry juice

Preheat oven to 350 degrees. Cream together butter and sugar in mixer bowl until fluffy. Beat in egg and vanilla. Combine dry ingredients. Gradually add to creamed mixture; batter will be very firm. Shape into forty-eight 1-inch round balls. Place on ungreased cookie sheets. Push one cherry half deep into each ball. Spoon Frosting over each cherry. Bake for 10 to 12 minutes. Let cool on wire racks.

Frosting:

1 (6-ounce) package semisweet chocolate chips
¹/₂ cup sweetened condensed milk

1 to 3 tablespoons maraschino cherry juice

Melt chocolate chips in condensed milk over low heat in saucepan, stirring constantly. Remove from heat. Add cherry juice; stir until smooth. Yield: 48 (1-inch) servings.

Approx Per Serving: Cal 85; Prot 1 g; Carbo 13 g; Fiber 1 g; T Fat 4 g; 36% Calories from Fat; Chol 11 mg; Sod 43 mg.

Black Forest Cherry Pie

Mrs. Paul A Baker, Seymour

4 (1-ounce) bars unsweetened baking
  chocolate
1 (14-ounce) can sweetened condensed
  milk
1 teaspoon almond extract
1 1/2 cups whipping cream, whipped
1 (9-inch) baked pastry shell
1 (20-ounce) can cherry pie filling, chilled
Toasted almonds

Melt chocolate with condensed milk in heavy saucepan over medium low heat. Remove from heat. Stir in extract. Pour into large bowl; cool thoroughly. Beat until smooth. Fold in whipped cream. Pour into pastry shell. Chill for 4 hours or until set. Top with chilled pie filling. Garnish with toasted almonds. Yield: 8 servings.

Approx Per Serving: Cal 590; Prot 8 g; Carbo 63 g; Fiber 3 g; T Fat 37 g; 54% Calories from Fat; Chol 78 mg; Sod 241 mg.

Cherry Pie

Marie Delffs, Shelbyville

1 (16-ounce) can sour cherries
1 cup plus 2 tablespoons sugar
3 tablespoons flour
1 1/2 tablespoons butter
1/8 teaspoon almond extract
Few drops of red food coloring

Drain cherries, reserving juice. Add water to measure 3/4 cup if needed. Combine sugar and flour in saucepan, stirring to blend. Gradually add juice, stirring to blend well. Add butter, almond extract and enough food coloring to make bright red color. Cook over medium-high heat, stirring constantly, until thickened. Remove from heat. Add drained cherries; set aside to cool.

Pastry:

3 cups sifted flour
1 1/2 teaspoons salt
1 cup vegetable
  shortening, at room
  temperature

1/2 cup boiling water

Preheat oven to 375 degrees. Combine flour, salt and shortening in large mixer bowl. Mix at medium speed for about 1 minute. Add boiling water. Continue mixing on medium speed until ball is formed. Divide dough into 2 portions. Roll half the dough onto waxed paper. Line 9-inch pie pan with pastry. Trim off edge. Pour cherry mixture into pie shell. Roll remainder of pastry to 1/4-inch thickness; cut into thin strips. Place on top of cherries in crisscross, lattice design; trim edges. Bake for 30 to 35 minutes or until golden brown. For special occasions, serve with ice cream. Yield: 8 servings.

Approx Per Serving: Cal 581; Prot 5 g; Carbo 78 g; Fiber 2 g; T Fat 28 g; 43% Calories from Fat; Chol 6 mg; Sod 427 mg.

Streusel-Topped Cherry Pie

Angela Dawn Bolden, Lynnville

2 (20-ounce) cans cherry pie filling
1 unbaked deep-dish pie shell
1/2 cup flour
1/3 cup firmly packed light brown sugar
1/4 cup butter
1/4 cup chopped pecans

Preheat oven to 400 degrees. Spoon pie filling into pastry shell. Combine flour and brown sugar in bowl. Cut in butter until mixture is crumbly. Stir in pecans. Crumble over pie filling. Bake for 40 minutes or until top is golden and filling is bubbly. Let cool on wire rack. Yield: 8 servings.

Approx Per Serving: Cal 424; Prot 4 g; Carbo 65 g; Fiber 2 g; T Fat 18 g; 37% Calories from Fat; Chol 16 mg; Sod 287 mg.

Orange-Cherry Cobbler

Delores Vann, Cumberland Gap

2 1/2 cups cherry pie filling
1/4 cup water
1 tablespoon lemon juice
1 (8-count) package refrigerated orange
  Danish rolls

Preheat oven to 400 degrees. Combine pie filling, water and lemon juice in saucepan. Heat to boiling. Pour into round cake pan. Top with rolls, cut side up. Bake for 15 to 20 minutes or until brown. Spread tops with icing. Serve warm with ice cream or whipped topping. Yield: 8 servings.

Approx Per Serving: Cal 268; Prot 3 g; Carbo 49 g; Fiber 1 g; T Fat 8 g; 25% Calories from Fat; Chol 0 mg; Sod 373 mg.

St. Patrick's Day

St. Patrick's Pops

Terry L. Cotts, Philadelphia

2 cups boiling water
1 (3-ounce) package lime gelatin
1 cup sugar
1 envelope lime soft drink mix
2 cups cold water

Pour boiling water into bowl. Dissolve gelatin, sugar and soft drink mix in boiling water. Add cold water; stir. Pour into ice-cube trays. Insert wooden stick into each section. Freeze until firm. Yield: 24 servings.

Approx Per Serving: Cal 46; Prot <1 g; Carbo 12 g; Fiber 0 g; T Fat 0 g; 0% Calories from Fat; Chol 0 mg; Sod 12 mg.

Sparkling Jade Punch

Vic Nanney, Greeneville

1 package lemon-lime Kool-Aid
1/3 cup sugar
3 cups water
1 (6-ounce) can frozen concentrated
  lemonade
1 cup pineapple juice
1 (11-ounce) bottle ginger ale

Combine first 5 ingredients in bowl. Add ginger ale at serving time. Add few drops of green food coloring. Yield: 10 servings.

Approx Per Serving: Cal 81; Prot <1 g; Carbo 21 g; Fiber <1 g; T Fat <1 g; 1% Calories from Fat; Chol 0 mg; Sod 11 mg.

Fourth of July

Patio Lemonade

Flora Mae Davis, St. Petersburg, Florida

1 1/4 cups sugar
1/2 cup boiling water
1 1/2 cups fresh lemon juice
4 1/2 cups cold water
6 to 8 lemon slices

Combine sugar and boiling water in heat-resistant pitcher. Stir to dissolve sugar. Stir in lemon juice. Chill. Add cold water. Pour over ice cubes in tall glasses. Garnish with lemon slice. A sugar substitute in amount equal to sugar may be used to cut Calories. Yield: 6 servings.

Approx Per Serving: Cal 180; Prot <1 g; Carbo 48 g; Fiber <1 g; T Fat <1 g; 1% Calories from Fat; Chol 0 mg; Sod 1 mg.

Frozen Rainbow Salad

Mrs. C. E. DePriest, Giles County

1 cup sour cream
1/8 teaspoon salt
2 tablespoons lemon juice
1 (15-ounce) can crushed pineapple, drained
5 bananas, mashed
1 (8-ounce) container small curd cottage cheese
2 tablespoons cream
2 tablespoons sugar
1 cup orange sections
1 cup chopped pecans
1 (16-ounce) jar maraschino cherries, drained and chopped
2 cups heavy cream, whipped

Combine sour cream, salt and lemon juice in bowl. Add pineapple, bananas, cottage cheese with 2 tablespoons cream, sugar, orange sections, pecans and cherries; mix well. Fold in whipped cream. Pour into 1 1/2-quart serving dish. Freeze without stirring. Cut into squares.

Topping:

1 cup pineapple juice
1 egg, slightly beaten
2 tablespoons flour
1/2 tablespoon butter
1/2 cup sugar
1 cup cream, whipped
1/4 cup shredded American cheese
3 tablespoons Parmesan cheese

Cook pineapple juice, egg, flour, butter and sugar in saucepan until sauce is thick, stirring constantly. Let cool. Fold sauce into whipped cream. Frost salad squares with Topping. Sprinkle with cheeses. Yield: 8 servings.

Approx Per Serving: Cal 817; Prot 12 g; Carbo 72 g; Fiber 4 g; T Fat 57 g; 60% Calories from Fat; Chol 181 mg; Sod 361 mg.

Broccoli Salad

Helen Medling, Greenfield

1 bunch fresh broccoli, cut up
1 cup sunflower seeds
1/2 cup raisins
1 cup light mayonnaise
2 tablespoons cider vinegar
2 tablespoons sugar
1 cup bacon bits

Combine broccoli, sunflower seeds and raisins in bowl. Combine mayonnaise, vinegar and sugar. Pour over salad. Chill overnight. Add bacon bits when salad is to be served. Yield: 6 servings.

Approx Per Serving: Cal 387; Prot 16 g; Carbo 35 g; Fiber 4 g; T Fat 23 g; 50% Calories from Fat; Chol 10 mg; Sod 572 mg.

Summer Garden Pea Salad

Louise C. Haws, Fall Branch

1 quart fresh garden peas, cooked and
   drained
1 small onion, chopped
1 green pepper, chopped
3 stalks celery, chopped
1 pint fresh green beans, cooked and
   drained
1 (2-ounce) jar pimento, drained
1/2 cup sugar
1/2 cup white vinegar
1/2 cup vegetable oil
2 tablespoons water
1 teaspoon salt

Heat fresh peas for 3 to 4 minutes; drain. Add onion, green pepper, celery, green beans and pimento; mix well. Combine remaining ingredients; mix well. Pour over salad. Marinate salad for several hours in refrigerator. Yield: 8 servings.

Approx Per Serving: Cal 248; Prot 5 g; Carbo 28 g; Fiber 5 g; T Fat 14 g; 49% Calories from Fat; Chol 0 mg; Sod 286 mg.

Barbecued Spareribs

Mrs. J. T. Bradford, Hermitage

3 pounds spareribs, cut into serving pieces
1 medium onion
2 tablespoons butter or bacon drippings
2 tablespoons vinegar
2 tablespoons brown sugar
1/4 cup lemon juice
1 cup tomato catsup
3 tablespoons Worcestershire sauce
1 tablespoon mustard
1 cup water
1/2 cup chopped celery
Salt and pepper to taste

Preheat oven to 350 degrees. Brown spareribs on all sides. Set aside in baking pan. Brown onion in butter. Add remaining ingredients. Cook slowly for 15 minutes or until flavors are blended. Pour mixture over browned spareribs; cover. Bake for 1 1/2 hours or until done. Yield: 10 servings.

Approx Per Serving: Cal 270; Prot 16 g; Carbo 11 g; Fiber 1 g; T Fat 18 g; 60% Calories from Fat; Chol 69 mg; Sod 438 mg.

Pepper Relish

Mrs. Carl Driver, Fountain Run, Kentucky

12 sweet green peppers
12 sweet red peppers
12 small onions
3 cups vinegar
1 1/2 cups sugar
4 teaspoons salt
2 teaspoons celery seed

Remove seeds from peppers. Place peppers and peeled onions through food chopper. Add boiling water to cover. Let stand for 10 minutes. Drain; discard liquid. Bring pepper mixture and remaining ingredients to a boil in saucepan. Boil slowly for 15 minutes. Ladle into hot sterilized jars leaving 1/2-inch headspace. Seal at once. Peppers cut with knife look prettier. Yield: 6 pints.

Approx Per Serving: Cal 173; Prot 2 g; Carbo 44 g; Fiber 4 g; T Fat <1 g; 2% Calories from Fat; Chol 0 mg; Sod 717 mg.

New Potatoes with Lemon Horseradish

Janice Duncan, Gallatin

1 1/2 pounds (about 12) new potatoes
1/4 cup butter
1/2 teaspoon salt
1/8 teaspoon pepper
1 teaspoon horseradish
2 teaspoons lemon juice
6 thin lemon slices
2 tablespoons chopped fresh parsley

Preheat oven to 350 degrees. Wash potatoes; peel 1/2-inch strip around center of each. Melt butter in 2-quart casserole in oven for 6 to 8 minutes. Stir in salt, pepper, horseradish and lemon juice. Add potatoes; stir until well coated. Cover. Bake for 55 minutes or until potatoes are fork-tender. Garnish with lemon slices. Sprinkle with parsley. Spoon butter sauce over potatoes to serve. Yield: 6 servings.

Approx Per Serving: Cal 176; Prot 2 g; Carbo 26 g; Fiber 2 g; T Fat 8 g; 39% Calories from Fat; Chol 21 mg; Sod 263 mg.

Vegetables-on-the-Grill

Carol A. Bryant, Trezevant

Dry Italian dressing mix
Parsley
Salt and pepper to taste
Fresh vegetables to taste: whole cherry tomatoes or regular tomatoes cut in chunks, mushrooms, sliced zucchini, sliced yellow squash, onions sliced or cut into chunks, small red potatoes or other potatoes cut into chunks, green pepper sliced into strips
Butter to taste

Sprinkle dry Italian dressing mix, parsley, salt and pepper over vegetables to taste in grill-safe container. Top with butter. Cover container. Place on grill. Bake for 20 minutes or until done. Fresh corn on the cob is good grilled the same way.

Nutritional information for this recipe is not available.

Farm Apple Cake

Mrs. Paula G. Terhune, Arlington

1/4 cup vegetable shortening
1 cup sugar
1 egg
4 cups chopped apples
1 cup flour
1 teaspoon baking soda
1/8 teaspoon salt
1 teaspoon cinnamon
1/2 teaspoon nutmeg
1/4 teaspoon ground cloves

Preheat oven to 325 degrees. Cream shortening and sugar in bowl. Add egg and apples; mix well. Sift together remaining ingredients. Add to apple mixture; mix well. Spread in greased 9-inch square pan. Bake for 45 minutes or until toothpick inserted into center comes out clean. Cut into squares. Sprinkle with confectioners' sugar while cake is warm. Yield: 8 servings.

Approx Per Serving: Cal 256; Prot 2 g; Carbo 46 g; Fiber 2 g; T Fat 7 g; 25% Calories from Fat; Chol 27 mg; Sod 144 mg.

Lemon Pound Cake

Edna Delaney, McMinnville

¹/₂ cup butter
1 cup vegetable shortening
2²/₃ cups sugar
3 cups sifted flour
¹/₄ teaspoon salt
1 cup milk
2¹/₂ tablespoons lemon juice
1 teaspoon baking powder
5 eggs

Preheat oven to 325 degrees. Cream butter, shortening and sugar in mixer bowl. Add flour and salt alternately with milk. Beat at medium speed. Add lemon juice and baking powder. Add eggs, 1 at a time, beating after each only until blended. Pour into greased and floured tube pan. Bake for 1 hour. Immediately run knife around side and tube. Let cool on wire rack for 5 minutes. Yield: 16 serving.

Approx Per Serving: Cal 412; Prot 5 g; Carbo 52 g; Fiber 1 g; T Fat 21 g; 45% Calories from Fat; Chol 84 mg; Sod 140 mg.

Strawberry Cake

Amye Thomas, Stanton

1 (16-ounce) package white cake mix
¹/₂ cup water
4 eggs
1 (3-ounce) package strawberry gelatin
1 tablespoon flour
¹/₂ cup mashed strawberries
³/₄ cup vegetable oil

Preheat oven to 350 degrees. Combine all ingredients in bowl. Pour into greased 9-by-13-inch cake pan. Bake until toothpick inserted comes out clean. Do not overbrown. Let cake cool for 15 minutes in pan. Turn out on rack. Let cool completely. Place sheet cake on covered cookie sheet. Frost with Frosting/Glaze.

Frosting:
¹/₂ cup strawberries, mashed
¹/₂ cup butter, softened
1 (16-ounce) package sifted confectioners' sugar

Combine all ingredients; mix well. Frost cake. This is thin frosting. Chill cake. Yield: 16 servings.

Approx Per Serving: Cal 417; Prot 3 g; Carbo 57 g; Fiber 1 g; T Fat 20 g; 43% Calories from Fat; Chol 69 mg; Sod 277 mg.

Strawberries Topped with Custard

Bernice Vest, Limestone

¹/₂ cup sugar
2¹/₂ tablespoons cornstarch
¹/₄ teaspoon salt
1¹/₂ cups milk
4 eggs, beaten
¹/₂ cup sour cream
1¹/₂ teaspoons vanilla extract
1 quart fresh strawberries, halved

Combine sugar, cornstarch and salt in saucepan. Gradually stir in milk. Cook, stirring, over medium heat until mixture boils. Boil for 1 minute, stirring constantly. Remove from heat. Blend small amount of milk mixture into eggs. Blend egg mixture into milk mixture in saucepan. Add sour cream and vanilla. Beat with wire whisk until well blended. Cool immediately by placing in bowl of cold water for several minutes. Cover. Chill thoroughly. Spoon custard sauce over strawberries. Yield: 6 servings.

Approx Per Serving: Cal 234; Prot 7 g; Carbo 31 g; Fiber 3 g; T Fat 10 g; 37% Calories from Fat; Chol 158 mg; Sod 172 mg.

Homemade Banana Ice Cream

Jeanna Nelson, Huntingdon

1 (10-ounce) can condensed milk
2¹/₂ cups sugar
2 teaspoons vanilla extract
1 pint whipping cream
4 bananas, mashed
Milk

Combine first 5 ingredients in bowl. Add milk to blend well. Pour into freezer container. Add enough milk to bring level to fill line. Freeze according to freezer directions. Yield: 6 servings.

Nutritional information for this recipe is not available.

Chocolate Ice Cream

Wilma Raper, Bon Aqua

1 (8-ounce) container whipped topping
1 (16-ounce) can chocolate syrup
1 (14-ounce) can sweetened condensed
   milk
Milk

Combine ingredients; mix well. Pour into freezer container. Add enough milk to bring level to fill line. Freeze according to freezer directions.

Nutritional information for this recipe is not available.

Homemade Butter Pecan Ice Cream

Dollye Elam, Tullahoma

3 tablespoons melted butter
³/₄ cup chopped pecans
¹/₈ teaspoon salt
1 tablespoon sugar
¹/₂ cup packed light brown sugar
¹/₄ cup sugar
2 tablespoons cornstarch
2 eggs, beaten
¹/₃ cup maple-flavored syrup
2¹/₂ cups milk
1 cup whipping cream
2 teaspoons vanilla extract
2 quarts milk

Preheat oven to 350 degrees. Combine butter, pecans, salt and 1 tablespoon sugar on baking sheet. Spread into single layer. Roast for 15 minutes. Stir; roast for 15 minutes longer. Let cool. Combine brown sugar, ¹/₄ cup sugar, cornstarch, eggs and syrup in top of double boiler. Gradually add 2¹/₂ cups milk, stirring constantly. Cook over boiling water until mixture thickens. Remove from heat. Chill for 2 hours or overnight. Stir in toasted pecans, cream and vanilla. Place in freezer container. Add 2 quarts milk. Freeze according to freezer directions. Allow to ripen in ice cream freezer for 1 hour or firm up for 1 hour in refrigerator freezer before serving. Yield: 1 gallon.

Approx Per Serving: Cal 272; Prot 7 g; Carbo 24 g; Fiber <1 g; T Fat 17 g; 56% Calories from Fat; Chol 75 mg; Sod 137 mg.

Fresh Lemon Ice Cream

Frances McAnally, Mt. Pleasant

2 cups whipping cream or half-and-half
1 cup sugar
2 teaspoons grated lemon peel
¹/₃ cup fresh lemon juice

Combine cream and sugar in large bowl; mix until sugar is thoroughly dissolved. Add lemon peel and juice; mix well. Pour into 8-inch square pan or into sherbet dishes. Freeze for several hours until firm. Garnish with lemon cartwheel twists. Yield: About 1¹/₂ pints.

Approx Per Serving: Cal 813; Prot 3 g; Carbo 73 g; Fiber <1 g; T Fat 59 g; 63% Calories from Fat; Chol 217 mg; Sod 61 mg.

Fresh Peach Ice Cream

Charlotte White, Lenoir City

1 quart milk
1 (10-ounce) package marshmallows
1¹/₂ cups sugar
1 (14-ounce) can sweetened condensed
   milk
2 cups half-and-half
3 cups mashed fresh peaches

Combine milk and marshmallows in Dutch oven. Cook over medium heat, stirring constantly, until marshmallows are melted. Remove from heat. Add sugar and remaining ingredients; mix well. Chill. Pour mixture into 1-gallon freezer container. Freeze according to freezer directions. Pack freezer with additional ice and salt. Let stand for 1¹/₂ hours to 2 hours to ripen before serving. Yield: 1 gallon.

Approx Per Serving: Cal 313; Prot 6 g; Carbo 58 g; Fiber 1 g; T Fat 8 g; 22% Calories from Fat; Chol 28 mg; Sod 82 mg.

Homemade Ice Cream

Orvaline Mann, Trezevant

1 (3-ounce) package French vanilla instant
   pudding mix
2 cups milk
1 (14-ounce) can sweetened condensed
   milk
1 (13-ounce) can evaporated milk
1 cup sugar
Milk

Combine pudding mix with 2 cups milk in bowl; mix well. Add condensed milk, evaporated milk and sugar; mix well. Pour into freezer container. Add enough milk to bring level to fill line. Freeze according to freezer directons.

Nutritional information for this recipe is not available.

Mother's Ice Cream

Bonnie Glass, Covington

2¹/₂ cups sugar
2 tablespoons flour or cornstarch
4 eggs, well beaten
Dash of salt
Milk
2 tablespoons vanilla extract

Combine sugar, flour, eggs and salt in saucepan. Gradually add enough milk to make 1 gallon. Cook in top of double boiler until mixture coats a spoon. Let cool. Add vanilla. Freeze with ice and rock salt. Editor's Note: Mrs. Glass combines mixture in ice cream freezer container, places in deep pan of boiling water and stirs mixture constantly as it cooks.

Nutritional information for this recipe is not available.

Six ''Three's'' Ice Cream

Dot Phillips, Iron City

Juice of 3 lemons
Juice of 3 oranges
3 cups sugar
3 bananas
3 cups half-and-half
3 cups milk

Combine lemon and orange juices and sugar in bowl. Allow mixture to sit for 30 minutes. Add remaining ingredients; mix well. Pour mixture into freezer container. Freeze according to freezer directions. Yield: 1 quart.

Approx Per Serving: Cal 1043; Prot 13 g; Carbo 195 g; Fiber 2 g; T Fat 28 g; 23% Calories from Fat; Chol 92 mg; Sod 166 mg.

Tutti-Fruitti Ice Cream

Annie R. Martin, Madisonville

1 (14-ounce) can sweetened condensed
  milk
1/4 cup lemon juice
1/2 cup sugar
3 ripe bananas, mashed
1 (8-ounce) can crushed pineapple,
  undrained
1 (11-ounce) can mandarin oranges,
  drained and chopped
1 (6-ounce) jar maraschino cherries,
  drained and chopped
3 cups milk
1 cup water

Combine first 7 ingredients in bowl; blend well. Add milk and water; mix well. Pour mixture into 1-gallon freezer can. Freeze according to freezer directions. Let stand for 1 hour to ripen. Yield: 2 quarts.

Approx Per Serving: Cal 375; Prot 8 g; Carbo 73 g; Fiber 1 g; T Fat 8 g; 18% Calories from Fat; Chol 29 mg; Sod 111 mg.

Old-Fashioned Vanilla Ice Cream

Faye Turner, Mt. Juliet

2 cups heavy cream
2 cups milk
4 eggs, lightly beaten
1/2 cup sweetened condensed milk
1 1/2 cups sugar
1/4 teaspoon salt
1 teaspoon vanilla extract
6 cups heavy cream

Heat 2 cups cream with milk in top of double boiler. Combine eggs with condensed milk, sugar and salt in bowl. Blend in small amount of hot cream mixture. Gradually add to remaining cream mixture. Cook, stirring constantly, for 5 minutes or until mixture just coats spoon. Let cool. Stir in vanilla and 6 cups cream. Freeze according to freezer directions. Yield: 1 gallon.

Approx Per Serving: Cal 551; Prot 6 g; Carbo 29 g; Fiber 0 g; T Fat 47 g; 75% Calories from Fat; Chol 223 mg; Sod 121 mg.

Orange Sherbet

Villa Bradford, Fayetteville

1 (2-liter) bottle Orange Crush
1 (14-ounce) can sweetened condensed
  milk
1 (8-ounce) can crushed pineapple, drained
1 (16-ounce) mandarin oranges, drained

Combine all ingredients in bowl; mix well. Pour into freezer container. Freeze according to freezer directions. Note: Pineapple and mandarin oranges can be omitted for a smooth orange sherbet. Yield: 1 quart

Approx Per Serving: Cal 646; Prot 9 g; Carbo 139 g; Fiber <1 g; T Fat 9 g; 12% Calories from Fat; Chol 33 mg; Sod 191 mg.

Apricot Nectar Cake

Elizabeth Wilburn, Manchester

1 (16-ounce) package lemon cake mix
1/2 cup sugar
3/4 cup vegetable oil
1 cup apricot nectar
4 eggs
1 (16-ounce) can creamy deluxe butter
    pecan frosting

Preheat oven to 350 degrees. Lightly grease and flour bundt pan. Blend lemon cake mix, sugar, oil, apricot nectar and eggs, one at a time, on low speed for 1 minute; on medium speed for 2 minutes. Pour batter into bundt pan. Bake for 45 to 50 minutes or until toothpick inserted in center comes out clean. Do not over bake. Let cool for 10 minutes before removing from pan. Heat frosting in small saucepan over medium heat, stirring constantly, until of spreading consistency. Drizzle over warm cake.
Yield: 16 servings.

Approx Per Serving: Cal 379; Prot 3 g; Carbo 52 g; Fiber <1 g; T Fat 19 g; 44% Calories from Fat; Chol 53 mg; Sod 220 mg.

Hummingbird Cake

Mrs. Kermit Cates, Bradford

3 cups flour
2 cups sugar
1 teaspoon salt
1 teaspoon baking soda
1 teaspoon ground cinnamon
3 eggs, beaten
1 1/2 cups vegetable oil
1 (8-ounce) can crushed pineapple,
    undrained
1 1/2 teaspoons vanilla extract
1 cup chopped pecans
2 cups chopped bananas
Cream Cheese Frosting
1 cup chopped pecans

Preheat oven to 350 degrees. Combine dry ingredients in large mixing bowl. Add eggs and oil, stirring until dry ingredients are moistened. Do not beat. Stir in pineapple, vanilla, 1 cup pecans and bananas. Spoon batter into 3 greased and floured 9-inch pans. Bake for 25 to 30 minutes or until cake tests done. Let cool in pan for 10 minutes. Remove from pans. Let cool completely. Spread Frosting between layers and on top and side of cake. Sprinkle with 1 cup pecans.

Cream Cheese Frosting:

16 ounces cream cheese, softened	2 (16-ounce) packages confectioners' sugar
1 cup butter, softened	2 teaspoons vanilla extract

Combine cream cheese and butter in bowl. Cream until smooth. Add confectioners' sugar, beating until light and fluffy. Stir in vanilla. Spread Frosting on cake.
Yield: 16 servings.

Approx Per Serving: Cal 943; Prot 7 g; Carbo 114 g; Fiber 2 g; T Fat 53 g; 50% Calories from Fat; Chol 102 mg; Sod 399 mg.

Quick and Easy Chocolate Pie

Mrs. Bill Walters, Pulaski

1 cup sugar
1/3 cup soft butter
3 tablespoons flour
1 (5-ounce) can evaporated milk
1 (10-ounce) can chocolate syrup
3 egg yolks
1 teaspoon vanilla extract
1 (9-inch) unbaked pie shell
3 egg whites
1/8 teaspoon salt
1/4 cup sugar

Preheat oven to 350 degrees. Combine 1 cup sugar, butter, flour, evaporated milk, chocolate syrup, egg yolks and vanilla in bowl; mix well. Pour into pie shell. Bake for 30 minutes or until set. Beat egg whites with salt until soft peaks form. Add 1/4 cup sugar. Beat until stiff. Spread over pie. Bake about 10 minutes or until golden brown. Let cool on wire rack. Yield: 8 servings.

Approx Per Serving: Cal 448; Prot 6 g; Carbo 67 g; Fiber 1 g; T Fat 19 g; 37% Calories from Fat; Chol 105 mg; Sod 310 mg.

Halloween

Ghoul-Aid

Mrs. Ronald Terhune, Arlington

1 envelope unsweetened grape Kool-Aid
1 envelope unsweetened orange Kool-Aid
2 cups sugar
3 quarts cold water
1 quart ginger ale
Confectioners' sugar

Combine Kool-Aid, sugar and water in large container. Chill. Just before serving, add ginger ale. Sprinkle with confectioners' sugar to make brew "Smoke."
Yield: 16 servings.

Approx Per Serving: Cal 117; Prot 0 g; Carbo 30 g; Fiber 0 g; T Fat 0 g; 0% Calories from Fat; Chol 0 mg; Sod 15 mg.

Witch's Brew

Mrs. Judy Fox, Celina

What you will need:
  1 old, black, rusty pot
  1 broken broom stick
  1 magic black hat
  1 magic witch's brew chant
What you will do:
  1 quart pickled pumpkin juice
  4 cups crushed bat bones
  2 quarts fresh devil's cave water or dragon tears

Pour slowly into pot. Stir slowly with broken broom stick. Add 1 bag cat claws. Let stand in pot until cold and chilly. Note: Person stirring ingredients must wear magic black hat and chant the following: *"Ooga, boo; up, brew!"*

Here's how you really make the Witch's Brew:

1 package orange Kool Aid	4 cups sugar
	2 quarts water

Combine Kool-Aid (the pickled pumpkin juice), sugar (crushed bat bones), and water (cave water or dragon's tears) in large container; mix well. Add 1 bag ice (cat claws).

Nutritional information for this recipe is not available.

Goblin Pops

Diane Summerlin, Friendship

1 (10-ounce) package miniature
  marshmallows
1/2 cup butter
6 cups Rice Krispies cereal
1 cup plain M&Ms

Place marshmallows and butter in 3-quart microwave dish. Microwave for 1 to 2 minutes, stirring once halfway through cooking time. Beat until well blended. Add cereal; mix well. Add M&Ms. Fill fourteen 5-ounce plastic cups with mixture. Press down lightly. Insert 14 wooden sticks. Let cool completely. Remove from drink cups to serve. Yield: 14 pops.

Approx Per Serving: Cal 235; Prot 2 g; Carbo 36 g; Fiber 1 g; T Fat 10 g; 36% Calories from Fat; Chol 18 mg; Sod 235 mg.

Mabel's Popcorn Balls

Nancy Gordon, Knoxville

3 quarts popped corn
1/2 teaspoon salt
1 tablespoon butter
1 cup molasses
1/2 cup sugar

Place popped corn in large container; sprinkle with salt. Melt butter. Add molasses and sugar. Cook together until brittle when tested in cold water. Pour mixture gradually over popped corn, mixing with large spoon until moist. Shape into balls with slightly greased hands, handling as little as possible. Yield: 12 (1-cup) servings.

Approx Per Serving: Cal 144; Prot 1 g; Carbo 33 g; Fiber 1 g; T Fat 1 g; 8% Calories from Fat; Chol 3 mg; Sod 109 mg.

Marshmallow Pop-on-a-Stick

Connie Galloway, Lexington

1 (14-ounce) package caramels
1/2 cup butter
1 (14-ounce) can sweetened condensed
  milk
40 wooden Popsicle sticks
1 (16-ounce) package marshmallows
1 (8-ounce) box crisp rice cereal

Place caramels, butter and condensed milk in saucepan. Cook over medium heat, stirring constantly with wooden spoon, until melted and mixture is smooth. Pour into large bowl; set aside. Place wooden stick into 1 marshmallow. Holding stick carefully, dip marshmallow into caramel mixture until marshmallow is well coated. Roll marshmallow pop in cereal until well coated. Place on waxed paper until cool. Repeat until marshmallows are used.
Yield: 40 servings.

Approx Per Serving: Cal 148; Prot 2 g; Carbo 27 g; Fiber <1 g; T Fat 4 g; 24% Calories from Fat; Chol 10 mg; Sod 134 mg.

Halloween Pumpkin Cake

Mary L. Mastin, Taft

1 cup butter
2 cups sugar
4 eggs
1 teaspoon vanilla extract
3 cups flour
1/2 cup baking cocoa
2 teaspoons baking powder
1 teaspoon baking soda
1 teaspoon salt
1 1/2 teaspoons cinnamon
1/4 teaspoon nutmeg
2 cups pumpkin
1 cup chopped walnuts

Preheat oven to 350 degrees. Beat butter and sugar until fluffy in mixer bowl. Beat in eggs and vanilla. Sift dry ingredients together. Stir into creamed mixture alternately with pumpkin. Add walnuts. Divide batter evenly between 2 greased and floured 1 1/2-quart ovenproof glass bowls with round bottoms. Bake for 1 hour or until centers test done. Turn upside down on wire rack. Let cool completely.

Frosting:

1 cup butter
1 (16-ounce) package
  confectioners' sugar
1/4 cup frozen orange
  juice concentrate

Yellow and red food
  coloring
1 (7-ounce) package
  Marzipan, softened
Green food coloring

Beat butter, confectioners' sugar and orange juice concentrate in bowl. Add yellow and red food colorings to make orange frosting. Place 1 cake on top of the other to make pumpkin shape, placing 3/4 cup frosting on bottom cake to hold 2 pieces together. Trim peak of cake, if needed. Frost cake, making ridges with spatula edge to resemble pumpkin. Soften Marzipan in hands. Reserve small piece for jack-o-lantern "teeth." Knead few drops of green food coloring into remainder. Form into pumpkin handle. Roll out for jack-o-lantern eyes, nose and mouth. Form teeth. Press into frosting face.
Yield: 16 servings.

Approx Per Serving: Cal 676; Prot 6 g; Carbo 78 g; Fiber 3 g; T Fat 40 g; 51% Calories from Fat; Chol 115 mg; Sod 597 mg

Crispy Halloween Cookies

Clemma McGee, Fayetteville

1 cup butter, softened
1 cup sugar
2/3 cup packed light brown sugar
2 eggs
1/2 cup creamy peanut butter
1 teaspoon vanilla extract
1 3/4 cups flour
1 teaspoon baking powder
1 teaspoon baking soda
4 cups Triples cereal
1 cup semisweet mini-size baking M&Ms
Dash of salt

Preheat oven 350 degrees. Beat butter, sugar and brown sugar in bowl. Add eggs, peanut butter and vanilla; mix well. Sift flour, baking powder and baking soda. Add to creamed mixture. Stir in cereal and M&Ms, using yellow, orange and black M&Ms for Halloween cookies. Drop by rounded teaspoonfuls onto ungreased cookie sheets. Bake for 7 to 9 minutes or until golden brown.
Yield: 72 cookies.

Approx Per Serving: Cal 86; Prot 1 g; Carbo 11 g; Fiber <1 g; T Fat 5 g; 45% Calories from Fat; Chol 13 mg; Sod 64 mg.

Jack-O-Lantern Cookies

Martha Jean Burris, Unionville

1/2 cup butter, softened
3/4 cup sugar
3/4 teaspoon vanilla extract
1 egg
2 cups flour
1/2 teaspoon baking soda
1/2 teaspoon salt
Candy corn and sugar for faces

Preheat oven to 350 degrees. Cream butter and 3/4 cup sugar until light and fluffy in bowl. Add vanilla and egg; mix well. Combine flour, baking soda and salt. Add to creamed mixture, blending well; mixture will be very stiff. Divide dough into 3 parts. Roll each part on lightly floured waxed paper to 1/8-inch thickness. Cut out cookies with round or jack-o-lantern cutter. Place on lightly greased cookie sheets. Make face on the unbaked cookies with candy corn. Use larger pieces of corn to make mouths and smaller triangle pieces to make eyes. Sprinkle sugar lightly on top. Bake for 10 minutes or until lightly browned. As cookies bake, candy melts to form the jack-o-lantern "face" with transparent eyes and mouth. Yield: 24 cookies.

Approx Per Serving: Cal 99; Prot 1 g; Carbo 14 g; Fiber <1 g; T Fat 4 g; 37% Calories from Fat; Chol 19 mg; Sod 103 mg.

Monster Cookies

Linda Parker, Mt. Pleasant

1/2 cup butter, softened
1 cup sugar
1 cup plus 2 tablespoons firmly packed
  dark brown sugar
3 eggs
2 cups peanut butter
3/4 teaspoon light corn syrup
1/4 teaspoon vanilla extract
4 1/2 cups uncooked regular oats
2 teaspoons baking soda
1/4 teaspoon salt
1 cup candy-coated milk chocolate pieces
1 (6-ounce) package semisweet chocolate
  morsels

Preheat oven to 350 degrees. Cream butter in mixer bowl. Gradually add sugar and brown sugar, beating at medium speed. Add eggs, peanut butter, syrup and vanilla; mix well. Add oats, baking soda and salt; mix well. Stir in remaining ingredients. Dough will be stiff. Pack dough in 1/4-cup measure. Drop 4 inches apart on lightly greased cookie sheets. Lightly press each cookie into 3 1/2-inch circle with fingertips. Bake for 12 to 15 minutes; centers will be slightly soft. Let cool slightly on cookie sheets. Let cool completely on wire racks. Yield: 30 cookies.

Approx Per Serving: Cal 291; Prot 7 g; Carbo 33 g; Fiber 3 g; T Fat 16 g; 47% Calories from Fat; Chol 30 mg; Sod 202 mg.

Not-So-Spooky Spiders

Pam Wright, Jamestown

1 cup semisweet chocolate morsels
1/2 cup Rice Krispies cereal
1/4 cup sweetened shredded coconut
1/2 cup thin chow mein noodles
Nerds candy for eyes

Line baking sheet with waxed paper. Melt chocolate in small heavy saucepan over low heat, stirring occasionally. Stir in cereal and coconut. Drop by teaspoonfuls onto waxed paper, forming spider-body shapes. Stick 4 noodles into each side of "Body" for spider legs. Add eyes on top of spider. Refrigerate for 15 minutes or let stand at room temperature for about 1 hour. Store in covered container.

Nutritional information for this recipe is not available.

Witches' Brooms

Charlotte Petty, Charlotte

1 cup sugar
1 cup light corn syrup
1 cup smooth peanut butter
5 cups shredded wheat cereal, crushed
1 cup plain M&Ms
32 (8-inch) pretzel rods

Grease 2 large baking sheets; set aside. Combine sugar and syrup in small saucepan. Bring to a boil. Boil for 1 minute. Remove from heat. Stir in peanut butter. Place cereal and candies in large buttered roasting pan. Pour peanut butter mixture over all, tossing to coat well. Drop mixture by rounded tablespoonfuls onto prepared baking sheets, spacing about 2 inches apart and staggering rows 2 inches apart. Form each mound into broom shape. Place pretzel rod into top of each "broom" to form a handle. Refrigerate for 35 minutes or until set. Store in single layers in covered container. Yield: 32 servings.

Approx Per Serving: Cal 207; Prot 4 g; Carbo 36 g; Fiber 2 g; T Fat 6 g; 25% Calories from Fat; Chol 0 mg; Sod 301 mg.

Thanksgiving

Cranberry Punch

Tomah Smith, Washburn

1 (6-ounce) can frozen orange juice
1 (6-ounce) can frozen lemonade
3 cups pineapple juice
1 1/2 quarts cranberry juice
1 cup sugar

Add water to orange juice and lemonade according to directions on can; mix well. Add remaining ingredients; mix well. Add ice cubes. Yield: 16 servings

Approx Per Serving: Cal 148; Prot <1 g; Carbo 37 g; Fiber <1 g; T Fat <1 g; 1% Calories from Fat; Chol 0 mg; Sod 3 mg.

Cranberry Relish

Mrs. Eunice Palmer, Morris Chapel

3 cups fresh cranberries
2 tablespoons grated orange rind
Juice of 1 orange
2 teaspoons prepared horseradish
1 1/2 cups sugar
2 seedless oranges, chopped

Wash cranberries; chop. Combine orange rind, orange juice, horseradish and sugar in saucepan. Cook over medium heat, stirring constantly, until sugar is melted. Add cranberries. Simmer for 25 minutes. Remove from heat. Stir in oranges. Pour in bowl. Let cool. Cover. Refrigerate for at least 24 hours before serving. Yield: 4 cups.

Approx Per Serving: Cal 368; Prot 1 g; Carbo 94 g; Fiber 4 g; T Fat <1 g; 1% Calories from Fat; Chol 0 mg; Sod 4 mg.

Creamy Pumpkin Soup

Marian Moore, Knoxville

¹/₄ cup butter
1 cup chopped onion
¹/₂ cup thinly sliced celery
1 clove of garlic, crushed
¹/₂ teaspoon salt
¹/₄ teaspoon ground white pepper
3 cups chicken broth
1³/₄ cups solid-pack pumpkin
1 cup half-and-half

Melt butter in large saucepan. Sauté onion, celery and garlic until soft. Add salt and pepper. Cook for 1 minute. Add broth. Simmer, uncovered, for 15 minutes. Stir in pumpkin and half-and-half. Cook for 5 minutes. Pour into blender container. Cover. Blend until creamy. Serve warm. Garnish with sour cream, chives, salsa, shredded cheese, green onions, bacon bits or tortilla strips. Yield: 6 servings

Approx Per Serving: Cal 177; Prot 5 g; Carbo 11 g; Fiber 3 g; T Fat 13 g; 65% Calories from Fat; Chol 36 mg; Sod 673 mg.

Turkey Casserole

Mrs. Edna E. Teamer, Covington

2 cups chopped cooked turkey
1 cup chopped celery
¹/₂ cup chopped onion
1 (10-ounce) can cream of chicken soup
1 cup mayonnaise
¹/₂ cup butter
1 cup chopped almonds
Salt and pepper to taste
1 (6-ounce) package potato chips

Preheat oven to 350 degrees. Combine first 8 ingredients in bowl; mix well. Pour in 9-by-13-inch casserole. Crumble potato chips over top. Bake for 30 minutes. Can be prepared and frozen to use later. Yield: 12 servings.

Approx Per Serving: Cal 406; Prot 11 g; Carbo 13 g; Fiber 2 g; T Fat 35 g; 97% Calories from Fat; Chol 51 mg; Sod 493 mg.

Fried Turkey

Lorene Williams, Cleveland

1 turkey breast
Salt and pepper to taste
Flour
1 cup vegetable oil

Slice turkey breast about ³/₈-inch thick. Add salt and pepper. Roll turkey slices in flour. Fry in hot oil. If turkey begins to harden on edges, add a little water and simmer.

Nutritional information for this recipe is not available.

Asparagus Casserole

Earlene Creasy, Westmoreland

2 (20-ounce) cans asparagus
3 tablespoons butter
5 tablespoons flour
¹/₂ teaspoon salt
¹/₄ teaspoon paprika
1¹/₂ cups milk
1 (4-ounce) package Velveeta cheese
3 hard-cooked eggs, sliced
¹/₂ cup Ritz cracker crumbs
2 tablespoons butter

Preheat oven to 350 degrees. Drain asparagus, reserving liquid. Place asparagus in greased 9-by-13-inch baking dish. Melt 3 tablespoons butter in saucepan. Add flour, salt, paprika, liquid from asparagus and enough milk to make 2 cups liquid. Cook until thick. Add cheese and eggs. Pour over asparagus. Cover with cracker crumbs and 2 tablespoons butter. Bake until brown. Yield: 12 servings.

Approx Per Serving: Cal 156; Prot 7 g; Carbo 8 g; Fiber 1 g; T Fat 11 g; 62% Calories from Fat; Chol 79 mg; Sod 658 mg.

Sweet Potato Casserole

Mrs. Hilliard Kincaid, Minor Hill

2 cups mashed cooked sweet potatoes
1¼ cups sugar
2 eggs, beaten
6 tablespoons margarine, melted
1 cup milk
½ teaspoon nutmeg
½ teaspoon cinnamon

Preheat oven to 300 degrees. Combine all ingredients in bowl. Pour into greased casserole. Bake for 20 minutes.

Topping:
½ cup packed light
  brown sugar
6 tablespoons
  margarine, melted
¾ cup crushed
  cornflakes
½ cup pecans

Preheat oven to 300 degrees. Combine all ingredients in bowl; mix well. Spread on top of baked potatoes. Bake for 10 minutes. Yield: 10 servings.

Approx Per Serving: Cal 386; Prot 4 g; Carbo 51 g; Fiber 2 g; T Fat 20 g; 45% Calories from Fat; Chol 46 mg; Sod 251 mg.

Crispy Sweet Potato Balls

Ophelia Plemons, Rockwood

2 (16-ounce) cans sweet potatoes
4 tablespoons butter, melted
2 tablespoons dark brown sugar
1 teaspoon salt
¼ teaspoon nutmeg
⅛ teaspoon pepper
1 teaspoon lemon juice

Mash sweet potatoes in large bowl. Add remaining ingredients; beat until fluffy. Shape into 8 balls.

Coating Mixture:
¾ cup coarse bread
  crumbs
2 tablespoons dark
  brown sugar
⅛ teaspoon cinnamon
⅛ teaspoon nutmeg
⅛ teaspoon salt
2 tablespoons melted
  butter

Preheat oven to 325 degrees. Combine all ingredients in pie pan. Roll potato balls in mixture to coat well. Place in shallow baking pan. Bake for 40 minutes or until coating is brown and crisp. Yield: 8 potato balls.

Approx Per Serving: Cal 234; Prot 3 g; Carbo 35 g; Fiber 2 g; T Fat 9 g; 35% Calories from Fat; Chol 23 mg; Sod 530 mg.

Cornmeal-Pumpkin Muffins

Peggy Huffstetler, Lebanon

2 cups self-rising cornmeal mix
½ teaspoon cinnamon
½ teaspoon ground nutmeg
1 egg, beaten
½ cup canned pumpkin
½ cup milk
¼ cup honey
¼ cup vegetable oil

Preheat oven to 400 degrees. Combine cornmeal mix, cinnamon and nutmeg in bowl. Combine remaining ingredients. Add all at once to dry ingredients, stirring just until dry ingredients are moistened. Fill greased muffin cups ⅔ full. Bake for 18 to 20 minutes. Yield: 12 muffins.

Approx Per Serving: Cal 177; Prot 3 g; Carbo 28 g; Fiber <1 g; T Fat 6 g; 30% Calories from Fat; Chol 19 mg; Sod 348 mg.

Pumpkin Bread with Spread

Mildred Rogers, Livingston

2 cups sugar
3/4 cup vegetable oil
4 eggs
1 (16-ounce) can pumpkin
3 1/3 cups flour
2 teaspoons baking soda
1/2 teaspoon baking powder
1 teaspoon salt
2 teaspoons pumpkin pie spice
1 teaspoon ground cinnamon
1 teaspoon ground nutmeg
2/3 cup water
2 teaspoons vanilla extract
1 cup chopped pecans

Preheat oven to 350 degrees. Combine sugar and oil in bowl, stirring well. Add eggs, one at a time, mixing well after each addition. Stir in pumpkin. Combine next 7 ingredients in bowl. Add to pumpkin mixture alternately with water, beginning and ending with flour mixture. Stir in vanilla and pecans. Spoon batter into 2 lightly greased and floured 5-by-9-inch loaf pans. Bake for 1 hour and 10 minutes. Let cool in pans for 10 minutes. Remove from pans. Let cool on wire racks. Yield: 16 servings.

Cream Cheese and Peach Preserves Spread:

1/4 cup peach preserves
1/4 teaspoon ground ginger
8 ounces cream cheese, softened

Combine preserves and ginger. Spoon over block of cheese. Serve with bread.

Approx Per Serving: Cal 422; Prot 6 g; Carbo 52 g; Fiber 2 g; T Fat 22 g; 46% Calories from Fat; Chol 69 mg; Sod 308 mg.

Pumpkin Cheesecake

Charlene K. McGaha, Sevierville

2 1/2 cups graham cracker crumbs
1/2 cup melted butter
2 tablespoons sugar
1/2 teaspoon cinnamon
1 envelope unflavored gelatin
3/4 cup pineapple juice
1 (16-ounce) can pumpkin
1 cup packed light brown sugar
3 eggs, beaten
1 teaspoon cinnamon
1/2 teaspoon ginger
16 ounces cream cheese, softened
1 tablespoon vanilla extract
1 cup whipping cream
1 (20-ounce) can crushed pineapple, drained
1/2 cup miniature marshmallows

Preheat oven to 350 degrees. Combine graham cracker crumbs, butter, sugar and 1/2 teaspoon cinnamon in bowl; mix well. Press mixture over bottom and 1 1/2 inches up side of springform pan. Bake for 10 minutes. Let cool on wire rack. Soften gelatin in pineapple juice in saucepan. Add pumpkin, brown sugar, eggs, 1 teaspoon cinnamon and ginger; mix well. Simmer, covered, for 30 minutes, stirring occasionally. Beat cream cheese with vanilla in mixer bowl until fluffy. Add to warm pumpkin mixture, stirring just until blended. Pour into prepared springform pan. Chill, covered, for 8 hours. Whip cream in mixer bowl until stiff. Gently fold in pineapple and marshmallows. Spoon over cheesecake. Chill until serving time; remove side of pan. Yield: 16 servings.

Approx Per Serving: Cal 386; Prot 6 g; Carbo 38 g; Fiber 2 g; T Fat 24 g; 55% Calories from Fat; Chol 107 mg; Sod 281 mg.

Pecan-Pumpkin Cake

Mrs. Dorothy Bryant, Indian Mound

2 cups crushed vanilla wafers
1 cup chopped pecans
3/4 cup butter, softened
1 (18-ounce) package spice cake mix
1 (16-ounce) can solid-packed pumpkin
1/4 cup butter, softened
4 eggs

Preheat oven to 350 degrees. Combine wafer crumbs, pecans and 3/4 cup butter in large mixer bowl. Beat at medium speed for 1 to 2 minutes or until crumbly, scraping bowl often. Press mixture evenly on bottom of 3 greased and floured 9-inch round cake pans. Combine cake mix, pumpkin, 1/4 cup butter and eggs in same bowl. Beat at medium speed for 2 to 3 minutes or until well mixed, scraping bowl often. Spread 1 3/4 cups batter over crumbs in each pan. Bake for 20 to 25 minutes or until wooden pick inserted in center comes out clean. Let cool for 5 minutes. Remove from pans. Let cool completely.

Filling:

3 cups confectioners' sugar
2/3 cup butter, softened
4 ounces cream cheese, softened
2 teaspoons vanilla extract
1/4 cup caramel topping
2 cups pecan halves

Combine confectioners' sugar, butter, cream cheese and vanilla in small mixer bowl. Beat at medium speed for 2 to 3 minutes or until light and fluffy, scraping bowl often. Place cake, crumb side down, on serving plate. Spread 1/2 cup filling between each layer. Frost side only with remaining filling. Spread caramel topping over top of cake, drizzling some over frosted sides. Arrange pecan halves in rings on top of cake. Store in refrigerator.
Yield: 16 servings.

Approx Per Serving: Cal 652; Prot 6 g; Carbo 67 g; Fiber 2 g; T Fat 42 g; 56% Calories from Fat; Chol 119 mg; Sod 493 mg.

Oatmeal-Pumpkin Cookies

Renee Long, Rockwood

1/2 cup corn oil margarine, softened
1/2 cup sugar
1/2 cup firmly packed light brown sugar
1 egg
1 cup canned pumpkin
1/2 teaspoon lemon extract
1/2 teaspoon vanilla extract
1 1/2 cups flour
1 teaspoon cinnamon
1/2 teaspoon baking soda
1 1/2 cups quick-cooking oats
1/3 cup chopped walnuts

Preheat oven to 375 degrees. Cream margarine in bowl; mix well. Add sugar and brown sugar, beating for 5 minutes or until light and fluffy. Add egg; beat well. Add pumpkin and flavorings; beat until well-blended. Sift flour, cinnamon and baking soda together in bowl. Stir in oats. Gradually add to creamed mixture, mixing well. Stir in walnuts. Cover. Chill for 30 minutes. Drop dough by tablespoonfuls onto cookie sheets coated with cooking spray. Bake for 15 minutes or until lightly browned. Transfer to wire racks to cool. Yield: 48 cookies.

Approx Per Serving: Cal 65; Prot 1 g; Carbo 9 g; Fiber 1 g; T Fat 3 g; 37% Calories from Fat; Chol 4 mg; Sod 34 mg.

Frozen Pumpkin Pie

Thanna Owen, Hornbeak

1 tablespoon cornstarch
3/4 cup sugar
1/2 teaspoon cinnamon
1/4 teaspoon ginger
2 egg yolks, slightly beaten
1 cup milk
3/4 cup cooked pumpkin
1/2 cup whipping cream
2 egg whites, stiffly beaten
1/2 cup whipping cream
1 (9-inch) baked deep-dish pie crust

Combine cornstarch, sugar, cinnamon and ginger in top of double boiler. Stir in egg yolks and milk. Cook over hot water until thickened, stirring constantly. Remove from heat. Stir into pumpkin in bowl. Freeze until firm. Remove from freezer; thaw slightly. Beat with mixer until smooth but not melted. Repeat freezing and beating steps for smoother mixture. Beat 1/2 cup whipping cream until stiff. Stir stiff egg whites and both beaten and unbeaten whipping cream into pumpkin mixture. Pour into baked pie shell. Garnish with walnuts and pecans. Freeze. Serve frozen. Store in airtight container in freezer to preserve freshness. Yield: 8 servings.

Approx Per Serving: Cal 345; Prot 5 g; Carbo 34 g; Fiber 1 g; T Fat 22 g; 56% Calories from Fat; Chol 98 mg; Sod 193 mg.

Baked Pumpkin Pudding

Gladys Chaney, Trezevant

1/4 cup butter, melted
2 cups sugar
5 eggs
1/2 cup flour
1/2 cup milk
2 cups mashed cooked pumpkin
1 teaspoon cinnamon
1/2 teaspoon each nutmeg, ginger
1/2 teaspoon each mace, cloves
2 teaspoon vanilla extract
1 cup pecan halves

Preheat oven to 350 degrees. Combine butter and sugar in bowl; mix well. Add eggs; mix well. Stir in flour and milk. Add pumpkin, spices and vanilla; mix until smooth. Pour batter into well-greased 2-quart casserole. Bake for 55 minutes or until firm. Top with pecan halves. Yield: 10 servings.

Approx Per Serving: Cal 345; Prot 5 g; Carbo 50 g; Fiber 2 g; T Fat 15 g; 38% Calories from Fat; Chol 120 mg; Sod 86 mg.

Pumpkin Chiffon Refrigerator Dessert

Celia Billingsly, Oneida

1 3/4 cups graham cracker crumbs
1 cup sugar
1/2 cup butter
8 ounces cream cheese, softened
2 eggs
2 (4-ounce) packages vanilla instant pudding mix
3/4 cup milk
2 cups mashed cooked pumpkin
Dash of ground cinnamon
1 (12-ounce) carton whipped topping
1/2 cup chopped pecans

Preheat oven to 350 degrees. Combine graham cracker crumbs, 1/4 cup sugar and butter. Press into 9-by-13-inch baking dish. Combine cream cheese, eggs and 3/4 cup sugar; beat until fluffy. Spread over crust. Bake for 20 minutes. Let cool. Combine pudding mix and milk in mixer bowl. Beat for 2 minutes at medium speed. Add pumpkin and cinnamon; mix well. Stir in 1 cup whipped topping. Spread pudding mixture over cream cheese layer. Spread remaining whipped topping over pudding layer. Sprinkle with pecans. Store in refrigerator. Yield: 15 servings.

Approx Per Serving: Cal 396; Prot 4 g; Carbo 47 g; Fiber 1 g; T Fat 22 g; 50% Calories from Fat; Chol 63 mg; Sod 430 mg.

Christmas

Christmas Punch

Mrs. Bob Reynolds, Athens

3 cups cranberry juice
3 cups pineapple juice
1/3 cup packed light brown sugar
3 sticks cinnamon, broken
2 teaspoons whole cloves
2 teaspoons allspice

Combine juices and 1 1/2 cups water in bottom part of percolator. Place remaining ingredients in percolator basket. Perk for 5 to 10 minutes. Yield: 10 servings.

Approx Per Serving: Cal 108; Prot <1 g; Carbo 27 g; Fiber <1 g; T Fat <1 g; 1% Calories from Fat; Chol 0 mg; Sod 5 mg.

Spiced Coffee Eggnog Punch

Mauline Singleton, Adamsville

2 cups very strong coffee
1 1/2 sticks cinnamon, broken
6 whole cloves
6 whole allspice
2 (32-ounce) containers eggnog
1 tablespoon vanilla extract
1 cup whipping cream, whipped
1 quart vanilla ice cream, softened
Ground nutmeg

Combine coffee, cinnamon, cloves and allspice in saucepan. Simmer for 15 minutes. Strain and chill. Combine eggnog, vanilla and coffee mixture in large bowl; chill. Fold in whipped cream. Spoon ice cream into punch bowl. Pour eggnog mixture into bowl; stir. Sprinkle with nutmeg. Yield: 20 (1/2 cup) servings.

Approx Per Serving: Cal 218; Prot 5 g; Carbo 19 g; Fiber <1 g; T Fat 14 g; 57% Calories from Fat; Chol 81 mg; Sod 75 mg.

Hot Mulled Cider

E. Mae Guffey, Athens

1 medium orange, cut into 5 slices
2 quarts apple cider
1/2 cup firmly packed light brown sugar
1 teaspoon whole allspice
16 cloves
10 cinnamon sticks

Cut 2 orange slices into fourths. Combine remaining orange slices, cider, brown sugar, allspice, cloves and 2 cinnamon sticks in 3-quart saucepan. Bring to a boil. Reduce heat. Simmer for 15 minutes. Pour into serving mugs. Garnish each with orange fourth and cinnamon stick. Yield: 8 servings.

Approx Per Serving: Cal 166; Prot <1 g; Carbo 42 g; Fiber 1 g; T Fat <1 g; 2% Calories from Fat; Chol 0 mg; Sod 12 mg.

Brandy-Cranberry Sauce

Mrs. Eunice Palmer, Savannah

1 1/2 cups whole cranberry sauce
1/3 cup brandy
3 tablespoons light brown sugar
1 teaspoon crystallized ginger
2 tablespoons cornstarch
1/4 cup water

Combine first 4 ingredients in bowl. Mix cornstarch and water until smooth in saucepan. Add cranberry mixture. Cook until thickened and clear, stirring constantly. Serve warm over puddings or hot over ice cream. Yield: 2 cups.

Approx Per Serving: Cal 489; Prot <1 g; Carbo 103 g; Fiber 4 g; T Fat <1 g; 1% Calories from Fat; Chol 0 mg; Sod 67 mg.

Cranberry-Orange Relish

Hassie Wyatt, Deer Lodge

1 (3-ounce) package raspberry gelatin
1 cup boiling water
1/2 cup pineapple juice
1 1/2 tablespoons lemon juice
1 (8-ounce) can crushed pineapple, drained
1 (14-ounce) jar orange-cranberry relish
1 cup unpeeled sliced apples
3 cups chopped pecans
1/2 cup celery

Dissolve gelatin in boiling water. Combine pineapple juice, lemon juice and gelatin in bowl. Chill until slightly thickened. Fold in pineapple, relish, apples, pecans and celery. Rinse salad mold in cold water. Fill with salad mixture. Chill until firm. Yield: 8 servings.

Approx Per Serving: Cal 460; Prot 5 g; Carbo 49 g; Fiber 5 g; T Fat 30 g; 56% Calories from Fat; Chol 0 mg; Sod 50 mg.

Red Cucumber Cinnamon Rings

Mrs. Ray Sutton, Southside

2 cups dehydrated lime
8 1/2 quarts cold water
2 gallons large cucumber rings, peeled
1 cup cider vinegar
1 small bottle red food coloring
1 tablespoon alum
2 cups cider vinegar
2 cups water
10 cups sugar
8 sticks cinnamon
1 (10-ounce) package red hot candies

Combine lime and 8 1/2 quarts water in large container. Place cucumber rings in lime water. Let stand for 24 hours. Drain rings. Wash in cool water. Pour cold water over rings in large container. Soak for 3 hours; drain. Combine 1 cup vinegar, red coloring and alum in large saucepan. Add water to cover. Simmer for 2 hours; drain. Combine 2 cups vinegar, 2 cups water, sugar, cinnamon sticks and red hot candies in saucepan. Bring to a boil. Pour over rings; cover. Let stand overnight. Drain and reheat syrup for 3 mornings. Heat rings and liquid to boiling on third morning. Pour into hot sterilized jars leaving 1/2-inch headspace. Seal. Yield: 6 quarts.

Approx Per Serving: Cal 1618; Prot 7 g; Carbo 411 g; Fiber 9 g; T Fat 1 g; 1% Calories from Fat; Chol 0 mg; Sod 32 mg.

Christmas Layered Salad

Mrs. Zeke Butler, Erwin

1 (3-ounce) package lime gelatin
1 cup boiling water
1/2 cup cold water
1 (8-ounce) can crushed pineapple, drained
1 (3-ounce) package lemon gelatin
6 ounces cream cheese, softened
1 cup boiling water
1 cup cold water
1 (3-ounce) package strawberry gelatin
1 cup boiling water
1 (10-ounce) package frozen strawberries
  and juice, thawed

Bottom Layer: Dissolve lime gelatin in 1 cup boiling water. Add 1/2 cup cold water. Add pineapple. Pour into 9-inch glass dish. Chill until partially set. **Middle Layer:** Blend lemon gelatin and cream cheese in mixer bowl; mix well. Add 1 cup boiling water. Blend until smooth. Add 1 cup cold water; mix well. Spread over Bottom Layer. Chill until partially set. **Top Layer:** Dissolve strawberry gelatin in 1 cup boiling water. Stir in strawberries and juice. Pour over Middle Layer. Chill until set. Yield: 8 servings.

Approx Per Serving: Cal 223; Prot 4 g; Carbo 37 g; Fiber 1 g; T Fat 6 g; 29% Calories from Fat; Chol 23 mg; Sod 145 mg.

Christmas Breakfast Casserole

Donna Troutt, Camden

1 (6-ounce) package instant long grain and wild rice mix
1 pound sausage
1 pound ground beef
1 onion, chopped
1 (8-ounce) can sliced mushrooms, drained
1 (8-ounce) can water chestnuts, drained and sliced
3 tablespoons soy sauce
1 (3-ounce) package sliced almonds

Cook rice mix according to package directions. Set aside. Cook sausage, ground beef and onion in skillet until brown; drain. Add rice, mushrooms, water chestnuts and soy sauce; stir well. Spoon into ungreased casserole; cover. Refrigerate overnight. Preheat oven to 325 degrees. Remove from refrigerator; allow to set at room temperature for 30 minutes. Sprinkle almonds on top. Bake, uncovered, for 50 minutes. Yield: 8 servings.

Approx Per Serving: Cal 427; Prot 24 g; Carbo 28 g; Fiber 3 g; T Fat 25 g; 52% Calories from Fat; Chol 64 mg; Sod 1311 mg.

Christmas Ham with Apricot Glaze

Linda Witt, Quebeck

1 (10 to 12-pound) ham
3 bay leaves
6 juniper berries
1½ cups white wine
½ cup apricot nectar
½ cup catsup
¼ cup vinegar
1 teaspoon onion pepper
1 teaspoon lemon pepper
1 teaspoon dry mustard powder
1 teaspoon Worcestershire sauce
3 drops of Tabasco sauce
2 tablespoons brown sugar

Preheat oven to 400 degrees. Line large baking dish with foil; spray foil with nonstick cooking spray. Trim excess fat from ham. Place ham on foil, skin-side up. Heat bay leaves, juniper berries and wine in saucepan. Pour over ham. Cover ham with heavy-duty foil; seal around edges of pan. Bake for 1 hour. Combine remaining ingredients for glaze in saucepan. Bring to a boil. Simmer for 10 minutes. Baste ham with half the glaze. Bake ham for 1 hour longer, basting 2 or 3 times more. Place ham on serving tray. Strain gravy, removing excess grease; mix with remaining half of glaze. Heat to serve with ham. Yield: 14 servings.

Approx Per Serving: Cal 644; Prot 98 g; Carbo 6 g; Fiber <1 g; T Fat 22 g; 31% Calories from Fat; Chol 214 mg; Sod 5322 mg.

Cranberry-Glazed Ham

Mrs. Becky Knox, Graysville

1 (8 to 10-pound) fully cooked smoked ham
½ cup chopped onion
4 teaspoons curry powder
¾ cup margarine
1 (16-ounce) can whole cranberry sauce
2 tablespoons light corn syrup

Preheat oven to 325 degrees. Score ham. Place on rack in roasting pan. Bake, uncovered, for 2 hours. Cook onion and curry powder in margarine in saucepan until onion is tender but not brown. Stir in cranberry sauce and corn syrup; heat. Brush ham with glaze. Bake ham for 20 minutes longer. Keep glaze warm. Serve with ham. Yield: 16 servings.

Approx Per Serving: Cal 572; Prot 71 g; Carbo 14 g; Fiber 1 g; T Fat 24 g; 39% Calories from Fat; Chol 156 mg; Sod 3871 mg.

Christmas Smokies

Denise Gavin, Smyrna

3/4 cup mustard
1 (10-ounce) jar red currant jelly
1 pound small smoked sausages

Combine mustard and currant jelly in saucepan. Cook over medium heat until dissolved. Simmer until mixed. Place sausages in heated mixture. Simmer until hot. Serve hot with toothpicks. Yield: 48 servings.

Approx Per Serving: Cal 34; Prot 1 g; Carbo 4 g; Fiber <1 g; T Fat 2 g; 39% Calories from Fat; Chol 3 mg; Sod 93 mg.

Holiday Cheese Potatoes

Mrs. Taft Droke, Adamsville

1 (26-ounce) package frozen hashed brown potatoes
1/2 pound sharp Cheddar cheese, grated
1 (10-ounce) can cream of chicken soup
2 cups sour cream
1 cup chopped onion
1/2 cup butter, melted
1 teaspoon salt
Pepper to taste

Combine all ingredients together in order listed. Place mixture in 9-by-13-inch baking dish.

Topping:

2 cups cornflakes, crushed   1/4 cup butter, melted

Preheat oven to 350 degrees. Combine topping ingredients in bowl. Spread over potato mixture. Bake for 1 hour or until bubbly. Yield: 10 servings.

Approx Per Serving: Cal 426; Prot 10 g; Carbo 23 g; Fiber 1 g; T Fat 33 g; 69% Calories from Fat; Chol 84 mg; Sod 826 mg.

Christmas Crunchies

Linda Young, Monroe

1/2 cup butter, softened
1/2 cup sugar
1/2 cup firmly packed dark brown sugar
1 egg
1/2 teaspoon vanilla extract
1 cup flour
1/4 teaspoon baking powder
1/2 teaspoon baking soda
1/4 teaspoon salt
1 cup uncooked regular oats
1 cup cornflakes
1/2 cup shredded coconut
1/2 cup coarsely chopped pecans

Preheat oven to 350 degrees. Cream butter in bowl. Add sugar and brown sugar, beating well. Add egg; beat well. Stir in vanilla. Combine flour, baking powder, baking soda and salt in small mixing bowl. Add to creamed mixture, beating well. Stir in oats, cornflakes, coconut and pecans. Shape dough into 1-inch balls. Place 2 inches apart on lightly greased cookie sheets. Bake for 10 to 12 minutes. Remove to wire racks to cool. Yield: 42 servings.

Approx Per Serving: Cal 74; Prot 1 g; Carbo 9 g; Fiber 1 g; T Fat 4 g; 45% Calories from Fat; Chol 11 mg; Sod 58 mg.

Holiday Divinity

Libby Doubler, Murfreesboro

3 cups sugar
³/₄ cup light corn syrup
³/₄ cup water
¹/₄ teaspoon salt
2 egg whites
1 (3-ounce) package flavored gelatin
1 teaspoon vanilla extract
¹/₂ cup flaked coconut
¹/₂ cup finely chopped pecans

Place sugar, corn syrup, water and salt in 2-quart saucepan. Cover with tight lid. Bring to a boil. Remove lid. Cook to 250 degrees on candy thermometer without stirring. Remove from heat; set aside. Beat egg whites in mixer bowl until soft peaks form. Add gelatin; beat to blend. Pour hot syrup slowly over beaten egg whites, beating constantly on high speed with electric mixer until soft peaks form and hold. Stir in vanilla, coconut and pecans. Drop from teaspoon onto waxed paper. Yield: 70 candies.

Approx Per Serving: Cal 56; Prot <1 g; Carbo 13 g; Fiber <1 g; T Fat 1 g; 12% Calories from Fat; Chol 0 mg; Sod 17 mg.

Graham Cracker Christmas Cookies

Mrs. Katheryn F. Dickens, Gordonsville

¹/₂ cup butter
2 cups sugar
¹/₂ cup evaporated milk
2 cups miniature marshmallows
2 cups graham cracker bits
1 cup coconut
1 cup pecans
¹/₂ cup chopped red candied cherries

Combine butter, sugar and evaporated milk in saucepan. Bring to a boil. Boil for 5 minutes, stirring constantly. Remove from heat. Stir in marshmallows; continue to stir until melted. Add remaining ingredients; stir well. Drop by teaspoonfuls onto waxed paper. If mixture becomes too thick, add 1 teaspoon evaporated milk to thin. Repeat as necessary. Yield: 12 servings.

Approx Per Serving: Cal 446; Prot 3 g; Carbo 69 g; Fiber 2 g; T Fat 19 g; 38% Calories from Fat; Chol 24 mg; Sod 216 mg.

Holiday Crescents

Mrs. Gail Webb, Smithville

¹/₃ cup evaporated milk
³/₄ teaspoon vanilla extract
³/₄ cup butter, softened
2¹/₄ cups flour
³/₄ cup confectioners' sugar
1¹/₂ cups finely chopped pecans
1 cup confectioners' sugar

Preheat oven to 350 degrees. Combine evaporated milk and vanilla in mixer bowl. Beat in butter, 1 tablespoon at a time. Combine flour and ³/₄ cup confectioners' sugar in bowl. Add flour mixture, ¹/₄ cup at a time; mix well after each addition. Add pecans. Pinch off teaspoon dough; roll into 2-inch strip. Bend strip to form half moon. Repeat with remaining dough. Place on ungreased baking sheet on top rack. Bake for 12 minutes. Do not brown. Roll in 1 cup confectioners' sugar while warm, handling carefully as warm crescents break easily. Yield: 60 servings.

Approx Per Serving: Cal 73; Prot 1 g; Carbo 8 g; Fiber <1 g; T Fat 4 g; 54% Calories from Fat; Chol 7 mg; Sod 25 mg.

Berlon's Christmas Fruitcake

Brenda Leslie, Westport

6 eggs
2 cups sugar
1 cup buttermilk
3 cups self-rising flour
2 tablespoons baking powder
1 cup margarine
1 cup raisins
1 cup blackberry jam
1 cup chopped pecans
1/2 teaspoon allspice
1 teaspoon nutmeg
1 teaspoon ginger
1 teaspoon cinnamon
1/4 pound candy cherries

Preheat oven to 350 degrees. Beat eggs. Add sugar; beat until smooth. Add buttermilk and flour, 1 cup at a time, mixing well after each addition. Add remaining ingredients; beat well. Pour into three 8-inch cake pans. Bake for 30 to 35 minutes or until brown. Let cool on wire rack.

Icing:

8 egg yolks
2 cups margarine
2 cups sugar
2 cups raisins
2 cups pecans

Cook egg yolks, margarine and sugar in double boiler over medium heat until thick, stirring constantly. Add remaining ingredients. Ice cake. Decorate top with cherries. Yield: 10 servings.

Approx Per Serving: Cal 1476; Prot 18 g; Carbo 166 g; Fiber 7 g; T Fat 87 g; 52% Calories from Fat; Chol 298 mg; Sod 1406 mg.

Snow Cake

Doris Burks, Fayetteville

1 1/2 cups sifted flour
1 3/4 cups sugar
1/2 teaspoon salt
4 eggs, unbeaten
1 teaspoon vanilla extract
1 1/2 cups chopped walnuts
1 cup melted margarine
1 (4-cup) package miniature marshmallows

Preheat oven to 350 degrees. Sift flour, sugar and salt into bowl. Add eggs and vanilla; mix well. Stir in walnuts. Fold in melted margarine. Turn into greased and floured 9-by-13-inch pan. Bake for 35 to 40 minutes or until golden. Remove from oven. Sprinkle marshmallows on top, arranging to completely cover warm top, leaving surface slightly "bumpy." Suggestion: Thread 3 large and 11 small marshmallows on very fine wire in shape of snowmen. Place in different positions on top of cake with other small Christmas decorations. Cake keeps well in the pan for 5 to 7 days. May be easily removed from pan and placed on bed of crumpled green tissue paper or other Christmas greenery for party. Yield: 12 servings.

Approx Per Serving: Cal 471; Prot 6 g; Carbo 56 g; Fiber 1 g; T Fat 26 g; 49% Calories from Fat; Chol 71 mg; Sod 298 mg.

Children's Recipes

A Captive Audience

Young Matthew Layman carefully cuddles his kitten while jabbering excitedly as if to tell it about his morning farm adventures. Matthew represents a new generation of potential farmers on the heritage-rich Layman farm in McMinn County.

Instant Hot Chocolate Mix

Caroline Vaughn, Smyrna

1 (8-quart) package powdered milk
1 (4-ounce) jar powdered non-dairy
   creamer
1 (16-ounce) package
   confectioners' sugar
1 (16-ounce) package instant
   chocolate mix

Combine all ingredients in bowl; mix well. Add 4 heaping teaspoons chocolate mix to 1 cup boiling water; mix well. Serve hot. Store in airtight container.

Orange Julius

Elizabeth Bowen, Bells

1 (6-ounce) can frozen orange juice
1 cup water
1 cup milk
1/4 cup sugar
10 ice cubes
1 teaspoon vanilla extract

Combine all ingredients in blender container. Blend for 30 seconds. Serve cold. Yield: 4 servings.

Kool Punch

Mrs. Earl D. Watkins, Maryville

1 (46-ounce) can unsweetened
   pineapple juice
1 cup lemon juice
2 quarts water
2 packages lemon-lime Kool-Aid
3 cups sugar
1 quart water

Combine pineapple juice, lemon juice, 2 quarts water and Kool-Aid in bowl; mix well. Set aside. Combine sugar and 1 quart water in saucepan. Bring to a boil. Remove from heat. Let cool. Add to first mixture; mix well. Yield: 1 quart.

Sunny Day Salad

Bobbie King, Friendship

4 peach halves
16 pineapple chunks
1 maraschino cherry, cut into
   quarters
8 raisins

Place peach halves, rounded-side up, on lettuce salad plates. Cut pineapple chunks in half lengthwise, forming 32 pieces. Arrange 8 pineapple pieces around each peach half. Place 1 maraschino cherry quarter and 2 raisins on peach to make "happy face." Chill until serving time. Yield: 4 salads.

Raggedy Ann Salad

Angie Hurley, Dayton

Angie Hurley,12, sent along an original drawing to show how her Raggedy Ann Salad should look.

1 peach half
Small celery sticks
1/2 hard-cooked egg
Raisins
Cherry or cinnamon candy
Grated American cheese
Lettuce leaf

Place peach half, rounded side up, on plate. Arrange celery sticks for arms and legs. Place egg for head. Arrange raisins as eyes, nose, buttons and shoes. Place cherry candy for mouth. Sprinkle grated cheese for hair. Add ruffled lettuce leaf for skirt. Yield: 1 Raggedy Ann Salad.

School House Soup

Jewel Collins, Jackson

1/4 cup dry ice
1 small carrot, grated
2 tablespoons finely chopped onion
2 cups chicken broth
1 teaspoon parsley flakes
Salt and pepper to taste
2 cups diced cooked chicken
3/4 cup milk

Simmer rice and vegetables in chicken broth; have 2 cups broth remaining when rice is tender. Add seasonings, chicken and milk. Bring to boiling point; do not boil. Serve hot.

Delicious Drumsticks

Ben Painter, Rockwood, Kristin Lamb, Bedford

1/2 cup flour
1 teaspoon salt
1/2 teaspoon paprika
1/4 teaspoon pepper
6 chicken drumsticks
1/4 cup butter or margarine, melted
and cooled

With help from an adult, preheat oven to 425 degrees. Mix flour, salt, paprika and pepper in bowl. Dip chicken drumsticks in butter. Roll in flour mixture to coat. Arrange in ungreased 8-inch square pan. Again, get an adult to assist you in baking drumsticks, uncovered, for about 50 minutes or until done.

Egg Burritos

Nicky Cole, Rockwood

This recipe won second place in the Junior-Senior Category 1987 Tennessee Egg Cooking Contest.

10 eggs
1/2 cup diced onion
1/2 cup diced green pepper
2 (8-ounce) jars taco sauce
2 cups Monterey Jack cheese,
shredded
10 (8-inch) floured tortillas
1 medium avocado, peeled and
cubed

Combine eggs, onion and green pepper in 2-quart bowl with 1 jar taco sauce; beat. Microwave on HIGH for 6 minutes, stirring after 3 minutes. Add 2/3 cup cheese. Cook on HIGH for 4 to 6 minutes or until eggs are slightly set, stirring after 2 minutes. On each tortilla, spread 1/3 cup egg mixture down center; roll tortilla around filling. Place rolls, seam-side down, in 8-by-12-inch baking dish. Cover with remaining taco sauce and cheese. Cook, covered, on HIGH for 4 to 5 minutes or until cheese melts. Turn dish 1/4 turn every 2 minutes. Top with avocado. Serve immediately. Yield: 10 servings.

Party Pizzaettes

Suzanne Lamb, Shelbyville

1 (10-count) can refrigerated
biscuits
1 small can pizza sauce
1 cup shredded mozzarella cheese
Toppings: pepperoni, sausage,
ground beef, mushrooms or
deviled ham

With help from an adult, preheat oven to 450 degrees. Roll each biscuit into 4-inch circle. Place on greased baking sheet. Spread small amount of pizza sauce on each biscuit. Top with cheese and favorite topping. Have an adult help you bake pizzaettes for 10 minutes.

Child's Banana Bread

Carolee Smith, Bradford

4 ripe bananas
1 egg
1 cup sugar
1 1/2 cups self-rising flour
1/4 cup melted butter or margarine
1/2 cup chopped pecans

With help from an adult, preheat oven to 325 degrees. Grease 5-by-9-inch loaf pan. On large dinner plate, mash bananas with fork. Combine egg and sugar in bowl; mix well. Add remaining ingredients; blend well. Pour into prepared pan. With help from an adult bake for 1 hour.

Friendship Coffee Cake

Jennifer Bates, Gallatin

Pecan pieces
1 (24-count) package frozen dinner rolls
1 (4-ounce) package butterscotch pudding mix
1 cup packed dark brown sugar
1/2 cup butter
1/4 teaspoon cinnamon

With help from an adult, preheat oven to 350 degrees. Grease bundt pan. Sprinkle pecans in bottom. Place frozen rolls in pan. Top with more pecans. Sprinkle dry pudding mix over all. Place brown sugar, butter and cinnamon in Microwave. Heat until butter is melted. Pour mixture over rolls. Add more pecans. Cover. Let rise overnight. With help from adult, bake for 30 minutes. Invert onto serving plate.

Kid's Doughnuts

Shane Robinson, Sparta

1 (16-ounce) package confectioners' sugar
4 cups vegetable oil
1 (10-count) can biscuits

Place 1 cup confectioners' sugar in small mixing bowl; set aside. With help from adult, place 2 cups vegetable oil in frypan. Heat to 350 degrees. Open canned biscuits; make hole in center of each biscuit. Being sure you have help from an adult, drop each biscuit into hot oil. Fry until golden brown. Remove from oil with fork. Immediately drop in bowl of confectioners' sugar. Shake until well coated.

Peanut-Apple Sandwich

Mary Ann Green, Maryville

1/2 apple, peeled and grated
1/4 cup peanut butter
2 slices bread

Combine apple and peanut butter in bowl; mix well. Spread mixture on 1 slice of bread; cover with another slice. Yield: 1 sandwich.

Broiler Banana Splits

Dorothy Peavyhouse, Jamestown

2 medium bananas
Lemon juice
1/4 cup butter or margarine
1/2 cup packed light brown sugar
2 tablespoons light cream
1/2 cup cornflakes, crushed
Vanilla ice cream

Peel bananas. Split in half lengthwise, then in half crosswise. Place in shallow pan. Brush with lemon juice. Melt butter in saucepan. Stir in sugar and cream. Cook until bubbly. Remove from heat. Add cornflakes. Spoon mixture over bananas. Broil 5 inches from heat for about 2 minutes or until bubbly. Spoon into dishes. Top with scoops of ice cream. Yield: 4 servings.

Easy Treat

June Triplett, Birchwood

Peanut butter
Hi-Ho crackers
Large marshmallows

With help from an adult, preheat oven to 350 degrees. Spread peanut butter on crackers. Top with marshmallow. Bake for 4 to 5 minutes or until marshmallows are lightly browned.

Chocolate Wafers

Peggy Huffstetler, Lebanon

6 ounces semisweet chocolate
18 to 24 waffle-style potato chips

Melt chocolate in top of double boiler over medium heat. Remove from heat. Dip potato chips, 1 at a time, into chocolate, turning to coat completely. Place on tray lined with waxed paper. Refrigerate for about 10 minutes or until chocolate is hard.

Mini Jelly Rolls

Esther Beachy, Belvidere

1 slice bread
Peanut butter
Jelly

Cut crust from piece of bread. Roll bread with a rolling pin. Spread with peanut butter and jelly. Roll up bread. Cut into 1/2-inch pieces.

Peanut Butter Balls

Mrs. Lance Davidson, Finley

1 cup dry milk
1 cup oatmeal
1/2 cup peanut butter
1/2 cup honey

Combine all ingredients in bowl; mix well. Roll small amounts of dough into balls. No baking necessary. **Variations:** Use graham cracker crumbs instead of oatmeal; add chopped nuts or raisins as children prefer; use crunchy peanut butter; roll finished balls in coconut.

Yum Yums

Donna Strasser, Nashville

1/2 cup butter or margarine
1 1/2 cups graham cracker crumbs
1 (12-ounce) package chocolate
  chips
1 (6-ounce) package butterscotch
  chips
1 (10-ounce) can sweetened
  condensed milk

With help from an adult, preheat oven to 350 degrees. With help from an adult, melt butter. Add crumbs. Press into bottom of 9-by-13-inch pan. Alternate chocolate and butterscotch chips over crumbs. Pour milk evenly over all. With adult help, bake for 15 minutes or until brown.

Index

286 Index

MAIL ORDER FORM

WHAT'S COOKIN'?

Name _____

Address _____

City/State/Zip _____

Number of Copies _____ x

Cost **$14.95** per book _____

(includes TN sales tax,
shipping and handling)

Total _____

Before ordering your recipe books, you may want to check with your local Farmers Co-op. Many of the Co-ops are stocking the books in their stores.

Make check payable to: **Tennessee Farmers Cooperative Communications Department**
P. O. Box 3003
LaVergne, Tennessee 37086

- -

MAIL ORDER FORM

WHAT'S COOKIN'?

Name _____

Address _____

City/State/Zip _____

Number of Copies _____ x

Cost **$14.95** per book _____

(includes TN sales tax,
shipping and handling)

Total _____

Before ordering your recipe books, you may want to check with your local Farmers Co-op. Many of the Co-ops are stocking the books in their stores.

Make check payable to: **Tennessee Farmers Cooperative Communications Department**
P. O. Box 3003
LaVergne, Tennessee 37086

Tennessee Farmers' Cooperative Cookbook